A COAT OF
MANY COLORS

A COAT OF MANY COLORS
Jewish Subcommunities in the United States

EDITED AND COMPILED BY

ABRAHAM D. LAVENDER

GREENWOOD PRESS *Contributions in Family Studies*
WESTPORT, CONNECTICUT, *Number 1*
LONDON, ENGLAND

Library of Congress Cataloging in Publication Data

Main entry under title:

A Coat of many colors.

    (Contributions in family studies; no. 1)
    Includes index.
    1. Jews in the United States—Social conditions
—Addresses, essays, lectures. 2. Jews in the South-
ern States—Social conditions—Addresses, essays,
lectures. 3. Women, Jewish—United States—Ad-
dresses, essays, lectures. 4. Sephardim—United
States—Addresses, essays, lectures. 5. United States
—Social conditions—1960- —Addresses, essays, lec-
tures. I. Lavender, Abraham D. II. Series.
E184.J5C58   301.45'19'24073   77-71865
ISBN 0-8371-9539-X

Library of Congress Catalog Card Number: 77-71865
ISBN: 0-8371-9539-X
ISSN: 0147-1023

First published in 1977

Greenwood Press, Inc.
51 Riverside Avenue, Westport, Connecticut 06880

Printed in the United States of America

dedicated to

DAVID

November 8, 1955-July 21, 1976

CONTENTS

ACKNOWLEDGMENTS

No book—at least not this one— is a product of one person. The completion of this book has been much easier because of the help and encouragement I received along the way. To the staff of the department of sociology at the University of Maryland—and particularly to Gladys Graham and Dorothy Bowers—goes much appreciation for much cooperation. To the staff of the Hillel Foundation at the University of Maryland—and particularly to Rabbi Meyer Greenberg, Rabbi Bob Saks, and Rabbi Moishe Silverman—also goes appreciation for cooperation and encouragement. To Leslie Smolin, Sandy Bernstein, and John Blanchfield go appreciation for their assistance over many months.

This book was motivated and furthered largely by the sounding board provided by my teaching of courses in sociology of the American Jewish community and sociology of world Jewish communities at the University of Maryland, and appreciation is expressed to Bob Shoenberg, dean of undergraduate studies, Ken Kammeyer, chairperson of the department of sociology, and Joe Lengermann, former acting chairperson of the department of sociology, for their support and encouragement in making this sounding board possible. And to my students in these classes since 1973 go many thanks for the give and take and for support in a more general sense. To the late Rabbi David Gruber, who instilled in me a pride in my Jewishness, again goes a special appreciation for helping me be where I am. And finally, a special thanks to a special person—Susan Elizabeth Clark.

Grateful acknowledgment is made to the following authors and publishers for permission to reprint selections: "Jews in Small Towns: As They See Themselves" by Susan Rebecca Brown and "Jews in Small Towns: Problems and Potentials" by Eugen Schoenfeld, reprinted by permission of the publishers from *Jewish Heritage*, Winter 1974. © 1974 by B'nai B'rith Adult Jewish Education; "Small-Town Jews and Their Neighbors in the United States" by Peter Rose, first published in *The Jewish Journal of Sociology*, volume 3, no. 1, December 1961, pp. 174-191, reprinted by permission of the editor and Peter Rose; "Small-Town Jews' Integration into Their Communities," first published in *Rural Sociology*, volume 35, June 1970, pp. 175-190, reprinted by permission of the editor and Eugen Schoenfeld; "Southern Jews: The Two Communities" by Theodore Lowi, first published in *The Jewish Journal of Sociology,* volume 6, July 1964, pp. 103-117, reprinted by permission of the editor and Theodore Lowi; "Is Miami Beach Jewish?" by Harold Mehling, first published in *The Most of Everything* by Harold Mehling, © 1960 by Harcourt, Brace, and World, Inc., reprinted by permission of the publisher; "The Invisible Jewish Poor" by Ann G. Wolfe, "Comment: The Invisible Jewish Poor" by Saul Kaplan, "Comment: The Invisible Jewish Poor" by James P. Rice, and "Reply: The Invisible Jewish Poor" by Ann G. Wolfe, first published in *Journal of Jewish Communal Service,* spring and summer 1972, reprinted by permission of the editor; "Jewish Poverty Hurts in South Beach" by Elinor Horwitz, first published in *National Jewish Monthly,* January 1972, reprinted by permission of Elinor Horwitz; "Left Behind, Left Alone" by Mark Effron, first published in *National Jewish Monthly,* volume 88, April 1974, reprinted by permission of Mark Effron; "Chassidic Community Behavior" by Israel Rubin, first published in *Anthropological Quarterly,* July 1964, reprinted with permission of the publisher; "Hasidim of Brooklyn" by Stephen Isaacs, first published in *Washington Post,* February 17, 1974, reprinted by permission of publisher; "New Square: Bridge Over the River Time" by Harry Steinberg, first published in *The Times of Israel,* March, 1974, reprinted by permission of Harry Steinberg and the Julian Bach Literary Agency, Inc., © 1974 by *The Times of Israel;* "The Rebbe: In His Torah There Is Room for All Jews" by Irving Spiegel, first published in *National Jewish Monthly,* March 1976, reprinted by permission of Irving Spiegel; "Explorations and Responses: Black Judaism in New York" by Albert Ehrman, first published in *Journal of Ecumenical Studies,* volume 8, no. 1, Winter 1971, pp. 103-114, reprinted by permission of the *Journal of Ecumenical Studies,* Temple University; "A Black Rabbi Looks to Israel" by Frank Ross, © 1973 by the New York Times Company, reprinted by permission; "Blacks and Conversion to Judaism" by Harold Goldfarb, © 1970, the *Jewish Exponent* of Philadelphia, reprinted with permission; "Black and Jewish—And Unaccepted" by Robert T. Coleman, first published in *Sh'ma,* 4/70, March 22, 1974, reprinted by permission of the editor, Eugene B. Borowitz; "Women's Lib and Jewish Tradition" by Eugene J. Lipman, reprinted by permission of the publishers from *Jewish Heritage* magazine, winter 1971/72, © 1972 by B'nai B'rith Adult Jewish Education; "Can a Woman Be a Jew?" by Ruth F. Brin, first published October 25, 1968, reprinted with permission of *Reconstructionist,* published by the Jewish Reconstructionist Foundation, 15 West 86 Street, New York, N.Y. 10024; "Feminism: Is It Good for the Jews?" by Blu Greenberg, © 1976 *Hadassah Magazine,* reprinted with permission of the publisher and Blu Greenberg; "Sephardic Culture in America" by Marc D. Angel, reprinted with permission from *Jewish Life,* a publication of the Union of Orthodox Jewish Congregations of America; "Washington's Moroccan Jews—A Community of Artisans" by John J. Schulter, first published in *Washington Post,* July 26, 1970, reprinted by permission of John J. Schulter, author, and editor of *InTowner*, Washington, D.C.; "Cuban Jewish Community in South Florida" by Seymour B. Liebman, reprinted with permission of the American Jewish Committee and the Jewish Publication Society of America; "The Sephardic Revival in the United States" by Abraham D. Lavender, first published in *The Journal of Ethnic Studies*, volume 3, fall 1975, pp. 21-31, © 1975, reprinted by permission of the publisher; "Contemporary Studies of Sephardi Jews in the United States" by Victor D. Sanua, presented at the Sixth World Congress of Jewish Studies, Jerusalem, August 1973, reprinted with permission of Victor D. Sanua; "Shalom—with a Southern Accent: An Examination of Jews in the South" by Abraham D. Lavender, first published as "Shalom, Y'all: Accent on Southern Jewry" in *Contemporary Jewry: A Journal of Social Inquiry*, volume 4, fall/winter 1977, reprinted by permission of the Association for the Sociological Study of Jewry; "Jewish College Women: Future Leaders of the Jewish Community?" by Abraham D. Lavender, first published in *The Journal of Ethnic Studies*, volume 5, summer 1977, © 1977, reprinted by permission of the publisher. Appreciation is also expressed to Dr. Jerome A. Wolfe, a native southerner and professor at the University of Miami, for "The Future of Jews in the South."

Every reasonable effort has been made to trace the owners of copyright materials in this book, but in some instances this has proven impossible. The publishers will be glad to receive information leading to more complete acknowledgments in subsequent printings of the book, and in the meantime extend their apologies for any omissions.

INTRODUCTION

The American Jewish community is generally characterized as a white, middle-class group, primarily of German or East European background, concentrated in the northeast part of the United States or at least in urban areas of the country, acculturated into the American society, and led by males. As a generalization of the total American Jewish community—and it usually is analyzed as a single group—this characterization is accurate. The American Jewish community is over 99 percent white,[1] with an average income well above the average.[2] Approximately 98 percent of America's Jews have European backgrounds,[3] with at least 80 percent having East European backgrounds.[4] Nearly two-thirds of America's Jews live in the northeastern United States, with almost half living in the New York City metropolitan area.[5] With the North Central and West claiming much of the remainder, only 8 percent of America's Jews live in the twelve southern states. Even most of those Jews who live outside the New York City metropolitan area live in urban areas, with between 1 percent and 5 percent living in rural or small-town areas. In fact, 78 percent live in ten population centers.[6] Close to three-fourths of America's Jews identify themselves as Reform or Conservative.[7] Both of these movements are basically modern and reached their blossoming in the United States because they made available an Americanized version of traditional Judaism. Even many of those individual Jews (about 15 percent) who follow Orthodoxy have largely acculturated to American society in a nonreligious sense, and even official Orthodoxy has not totally escaped some Americanization.[8] Not only are most policy makers and leaders within the Jewish community male, but restrictions remain prohibiting women from fully participating in all religious observances.

Despite this general homogeneity, the American Jewish community is facing major challenges in its attitude toward Jewish women. One of the biggest issues in recent years has been the attitude of the Jewish community toward the Jewish poor, and black Jews are challenging their general nonacceptance by the Jewish community. Hasidic Jews are attempting to counteract the modernization and alienation of Jewish youth, while small-town Jews and some southern Jews are facing the potential loss of their youth through assimilation and intermarriage in a pervasive gentile and provincial environment. Sephardic Jews are questioning the predominance of Ashkenazic definitions of Jewishness.

There is not a great deal of factual material on the American Jewish community, and particularly on the issues raised in this book. Because America's Jews are a small group—less than 3 percent of the total U.S. population—they are often overlooked in large national surveys. Only studies specifically designed to collect data from or about Jews are likely to provide information about this group, but there is also a paucity of specifically Jewish studies. Sklare has noted that there is a bulk of literature on American Jews but that this literature is "centered on the study of the Jewish past" without much attention to the current community.[9] Rose observed that most of the writing about American Jews has been by Jews and has been primarily concerned with contributing to "continuing deliberations with fellow Jews about themselves and their problems." He concluded that it is "little wonder the general public remains in the dark and that the non-Jew learns so little" about Jews.[10]

There are exceptions, as Rose pointed out, among them work by Seymour Martin Lipset, Nathan Glazer, Sidney Goldstein, Seymour Leventman, and Marshall Sklare. These few researchers have been unable thus far to correct the situations described above, but they, along with other researchers of recent years, have begun to correct these situations and to provide more accurate knowledge of the American Jewish community. Sklare and Greenblum's *Jewish Identity on the Suburban Frontier* was published in 1967,[11] and Goldstein and Goldscheider's *Jewish Americans* was published in 1968.[12] The first National Jewish Population Study was completed in 1972,[13] and Dashefsky and Shapiro's *Ethnic Identification Among American Jews* was published in 1974.[14] The Association for the Sociological Study of Jewry was founded and began publishing a journal, *Jewish Sociology and Social Research,* in the mid-1970s.[15] As the assimilationist bias of American society and American sociologists has yielded somewhat in recent years, perhaps in part as a result of the increasing emphasis on black pride brought about by the civil-rights movement, America's Jews—along with a number of other ethnic groups—have increasingly begun to question whether they should be required to reject their differentness in order to be accepted as Americans.

With the increasing attention that is being given to the American Jewish community, it is also being rediscovered by Jews and discovered by non-Jews that not all Jews are alike and that the American Jewish community is diversified—sometimes disastrously and sometimes creatively—on many of the same issues that divide the larger American society. Perhaps this new micro-approach is a luxury, made possible by the increasing number of scholars and orientations of interests represented. Perhaps it is a long overdue necessity, made possible by two factors: the increased concern with the overall Jewish community that has resulted from partial rejection of the assimilationist goal and the fact that those same forces that have affected the larger society have also affected the Jewish community. For example, poverty was "rediscovered" in the United States in the 1960s.[16] By the 1970s it was also rediscovered in the Jewish community. As women in the larger society increasingly have questioned their role in that society, women in the Jewish community have increasingly questioned their role as Jewish women. As Eastern religions (such as Zen Buddhism) have appealed to American youth alienated from American values, so has Hasidism (and other groups) appealed to Jewish youth alienated from the American version of Judaism.[17] As many small towns have lamented the loss of their youth to urban areas, so have small Jewish communities lamented not only the loss of their youth but also the potential loss of their existence as a community.

This is not to say that the idea of a homogeneous American Jewish community has been denied by all, Jews or non-Jews. Despite the increasing attention from scholars as well as the demand for recognition made by different minorities within the American Jewish community, traditional generalizations of the archetypal American Jew have persisted. It is still assumed, for example, that Jews in the United States are professionally and economically successful, and Jews are usually as surprised as non-Jews to discover the extent of Jewish poverty. Jewishness in the United States is still usually interpreted as being synonymous with Yiddishkeit, and it is assumed—by Jews probably more than non-Jews—that all Jews know certain "Jewish" (Yiddish) words, eat certain "Jewish" (German or East European) foods, and have a "Jewish" (German or East European derived) name. As Angel notes, however, the "Jewish" foods eaten by Sephardic Jews are not the same "Jewish" foods eaten by Ashkenazic Jews. He also notes that Sephardic Jews have often not been readily accepted by Ashkenazic Jews because they (Sephardic Jews) do not have "Jewish" names, and that politicians who speak in Jewish neighborhoods often use Yiddish even when the Jewish neighborhood is Sephardic.[18] And what small-town Jew, particularly one from the South, when describing his background, has not heard the expression, often expressed in an amused if not unbelieving manner, "What is a Jew doing there?" As Edelman quotes, "Everybody thinks Jews in the hinterlands are 'second-class' citizens who know nothing about Israel, Soviet Jewry, or what's going on in the world."[19] And as Evans says, "In the South especially, Jews languished as the provincials, the Jews of the periphery . . . overlooked, and ridiculed, out on the rim where it didn't count."[20] In those few cases where southern Jewry has been noticed, the attention has mostly been given to Jews in the cities.[21] Most black Jews are not readily accepted as Jews, as Goldfarb states, on the "presumption [that] the historical Jewish community since time immemorial has consisted of whites."[22]

This book is about seven subcommunities within the American Jewish community—groups that are not part of the Jewish mainstream and hence are likely to be lost in studies of the total American Jewish community: small-town, southern, poor, Hasidic, black, Sephardic, and female Jews. These seven groups are neglected in studies of the American Jewish community just as Jews are neglected in studies of American society—not necessarily because of prejudice but because of lack of power, lack of visibility, or lack of sensitivity on the part of the larger community, or simply lack of large numbers. (It should be pointed out that Hasidic Jews do receive considerable attention perhaps largely because of their exotic character, and Jewish women have begun to receive considerable attention—although there is still little empirical research—in the last few years.)

And yet, if it is inaccurate to apply gentile criteria of "American" to all Americans because Gentiles comprise most of the population, is it not also inaccurate to apply Ashkenazic criteria of "Jewishness" to all Jews because Ashkenazim comprise most of the American Jewish population? The question may not be one only of inaccuracy but also one of injustice. If it is unjust to treat black Americans and female Americans as second-class citizens, is it not also unjust to treat black Jews and female Jews as second-class Jews? If it is inhumane to neglect the poor in the larger world society, is it not also inhumane to neglect the Jewish poor? This is not to say that gaining accurate knowledge of a group leads to amelioration of an injustice directed toward the group. Often, however, the first step in such amelioration is accurately portraying the situation of the group both to increase awareness of the group's situation and to provide information on which ameliorative actions are needed.

The American Jewish community has begun to come of age; it has begun to have the researchers and interests to analyze itself as a group separate from the total American society and to permit objective generalizations of its overall characteristics. It has tremendous interest in itself, expressed in such divergent ways as the popularity of Jewish novels and the unprecedented demand for Jewish studies in colleges and universities.[23] It is now time for it to begin to heed its own subcommittees, both to give a more detailed picture of the total American Jewish community and to obtain more accurate information on those subcommunities that have been neglected. Perhaps in the process Jews will rediscover that there are many ways of expressing one's Jewishness, and non-Jews will discover that not all Jews are alike.

This book presents separate sections on each of the seven groups. A brief review of some literature available on the specific group is presented in the introduction to each section. The selections in each section—varying from empirical studies to self-evaluations by spokespersons for the group—then discuss in more detail the background of the group, its characteristics, its interaction with the larger American Jewish community and with the American society, its problems in maintaining its status, and its probable future. (See the appendix for group definitions.) First, a brief overview on each group.

SMALL-TOWN JEWS

It is fitting that the first Jewish settlement in the United States—in 1654 by twenty-three Sephardic Jewish refugees from the Inquisition in Portuguese Brazil —was in New York City (New Amsterdam until 1664), for New York City has become not only the center of American Jewish life but also the largest single Jewish community in the world.

The American Jewish community grew slowly in the decades following this first settlement; by 1700, there were only 200 to 300 Jews in the colonies.[24] As the growth continued slowly in the following decades, Jewish settlers dispersed throughout the colonies. This dispersion was primarily to other East Coast cities, however, so that by the 1770s an estimated 50 to 60 percent of America's Jews lived in Newport, New York City, Philadelphia, Charleston, and Savannah. While it is impossible to compute the percentage of the remainder who lived in small towns from those who lived in rural areas, it is evident that the American Jew was essentially an urban dweller—primarily in commercial and shipping centers—at an early date.[25] The "typical Jew of this period . . . was a small shopkeeper, or a merchant or merchant shipper who engaged in retailing, wholesaling, commission sales, importing and exporting."[26] Until 1812, Richmond, Virginia, had the only sizable Jewish community not located in a seaport.[27]

Primarily as a result of Jewish migration from Germany, the American Jewish community grew from 3,000 in 1820 to 250,000 in 1880.[28] It was not until this period, approximately two hundred years after the beginning of the American Jewish community, that we can document the beginning of numerous Jewish settlements in rural areas and small towns. The migration of German Jews coincided with the westward movement in the United States,[29] and the German Jewish immigrants—many with experience as merchants—were part of this movement, "peddling and keeping store, stopping, when they caught their breath, to build religious and spiritual foundations in every town and village where they could gather a quorum of ten adult males."[30] Glanz has stated that there was a vast multiplication of Jewish communities in the few decades before the Civil War, and by the time of the war, there were approximately 160 Jewish communities in the United States with some kind of Jewish institution. Many of these communities were on water arteries, and "in such locations an urban element like the Jews, coming from the Atlantic with already established mercantile connections, had a special chance to establish permanent residence."[31] Some German Jewish immigrants also moved to small towns in the southern United States, mainly as peddlers or merchants. Despite these westward and southward movements, however, the American Jewish community remained predominantly urban throughout this period.

With the beginning of the mass migration of Jews from Eastern Europe— 2,326,458 Jewish immigrants came from 1881 through 1924—the American Jewish community was to become even less rural and small town. There were some efforts by already established Jews to settle these East European immigrants in small towns, and even agricultural colonies, on the belief that it was "not for the best that the refugees settle in the large cities, and live in crowded tenement houses."[32] But few of these immigrants settled in small towns and even fewer on farms or in rural areas (and even when Jewish immigrants settled on farms, their children usually moved).[33] Most of them remained in large cities—particularly New York City—where they were better able to find jobs and where the transition to American society was less severe. By 1927, the five boroughs of New York City alone had 42 percent of the American Jewish population; less than 6 percent of America's Jews lived in communities with fewer than 2,000 Jews, and only one-fourth of 1 percent lived in communities with fewer than 100 Jews.[34]

With the decline in rural and small-town populations in the United States in recent decades, the American Jewish population has also continued to become even less rural and small town. Even though there has been a population movement out of large cities since World War II,[35] this movement has been into suburbs or into small towns near metropolitan areas and not into small towns in rural areas. Some of these small Jewish communities in or near metropolitan areas face the same problems as do small Jewish communities in more isolated areas,[36] but generally the problems are more severe for those small Jewish communities which are further removed from contacts with larger Jewish communities.

No precise definition of "small-town Jews" applies to all cases. Generally the term refers to Jews who live in a small town, but it has also been used to refer to Jewish communities that are small regardless of the population of the larger community in which the Jewish community is located. In addition, the numerical definition of small varies for different researchers. Hence, the number of small-town Jews depends on the definition utilized. According to the *American Jewish Yearbook* figures for 1976 (1974 data), less than 1 percent of America's Jews live in communities with Jewish populations of fewer than 150.[37] Within the ranges of definition generally utilized, no more than 5 percent and perhaps as few as 1 percent of America's Jews live in small towns.

Small-town Jews face serious problems in maintaining their identity in a pervasive gentile (secular)—if not Christian—environment. Despite the fact that they usually have a higher rate of synagogue affiliation than urban Jews, they still face specific problems such as providing Jewish activities for themselves and their children, providing Jewish education for their children, and obtaining objects needed for religious rituals and observances.

SOUTHERN JEWS

It is also fitting that the first Jewish settlement in the United States was in New York City, for that was also to become representative of the regional distribution of America's Jews.

At least a handful of Jews had resided in Charleston, South Carolina, since 1695, but the first Jewish settlement in the South was in 1733 in Georgia.[38]

Georgia was the only place in the United States where there was an attempt to form a Jewish—both Ashkenazic and Sephardic—colony of considerable size.[39] Southern Jewish communities grew in the following decades, so that by 1770 perhaps as much as one-fourth of America's Jewish population lived in the southern states,[40] with Charleston and Savannah being two of the five major Jewish communities in the United States.[41] The second synagogue in the United States was established in Charleston in 1749, and by 1800 this synagogue had the largest membership (107) of any other in the United States.[42] During the first decade of the 1800s, Charleston "was considered the most cultured and wealthiest Jewish community in America."[43] In 1824 the first Reform synagogue in the United States was begun in Charleston.[44]

In the middle decades of the nineteenth century, an increasing number of small Jewish communities appeared in the South, primarily in connection with the preparation and marketing of cotton.[45] Despite the movement of some German Jewish immigrants into the South, the region's share of the American Jewish community declined during the 1800s—particularly with the beginning of the East European migration in the 1880s.

There were some efforts to settle East European Jews in the South; for example, the Industrial Removal Office sent almost 400 East European Jewish immigrants to Birmingham, Alabama, from 1901 to 1915.[46] These efforts were very small, however, and as the East European Jews continued to settle in the North, the southern Jewish community—while increasing slightly in absolute numbers—continued to decline in its percentage of the total American Jewish population.[47] By 1929, for instance, only 5 percent of America's Jews lived in the twelve southern states, even though these twelve states had 26 percent of the total United States population. The 210,646 Jews in the South in 1929 represented only two-thirds of 1 percent of the southern population. By 1937, southern Jews represented an even smaller percentage of America's Jewish population, as well as a smaller percentage of all southerners.[48]

Since 1939, eight of the twelve southern states have had a decrease in the percentage of their residents who are Jewish, and three states have had only slight increases. Only Florida had a major increase in the percentage of its residents who are Jewish—from 1.3 percent in 1937 to 3.7 percent in 1974. By 1974, 531,090 Jews lived in the South; 42.4 percent of these were in Miami. The sixty-five-mile coastal area stretching from Miami through Fort Lauderdale to Palm Beach alone accounts for over half (53.3 percent) of southern Jews. Even with this increase, however, southern Jews still represent only 9.3 percent of America's Jews and only 0.9 percent of all southerners.[49]

Some of the statements made about small-town Jews also apply to southern Jews. Despite a movement of southern Jews from small towns to urban areas, southern Jews (with the exception of the Miami-Palm Beach area) are more likely than nonsouthern Jews to reside in small towns and hence face to a larger extent the same problems faced by small-town Jews elsewhere. Small-town Jews in the

South also face more problems than small-town Jews outside the South because of their settlement patterns. In the Midwest, for instance, German Jews tended to settle in small towns where German Christians had already settled, thus making their differentness less obvious.[50] In the South, on the other hand, small-town Jews were likely to settle in a community that—despite its possible philo-Semitic admiration for "the Old Testament and Hebrew prophets"—was strongly nativist, with strong regional beliefs and strong fundamentalist Christian beliefs.[51] The overlap between small-town Jewry and southern Jewry is limited, of course, for most of southern Jewry also is urban.[52] However, urban southern Jews are also more likely than urban nonsouthern Jews to live in a society in which to be different is to be more obvious and less accepted. And all southern Jews, whether small-town or urban, have been vitally affected by one factor that has not affected their nonsouthern cousins in the same manner: the controversy regarding racial integration. In fact, it is the manner of responding to this issue that has often split southern Jewish communities themselves as well as increasing the Jewish community's feeling of marginality in the larger southern society. Southern Jews generally have been found to be more liberal than southern Gentiles but more conservative than northern Jews on most issues—but the more closely related the issue is to the racial controversy, the more southern Jews are pressured to imitate southern Gentiles.[53] Southern Jews are caught, however, between southern Gentiles and blacks. Levy, for example, has noted (for the United States) Jewish fears of becoming "scapegoats for increasingly assertive blacks" and black fears that "Jews would assert their 'whiteness' to maintain their influence and power."[54]

The split in some southern Jewish communities has not revolved around the racial controversy alone, however. The "old Jewish families," more integrated into the secular community and usually of "old money" background, often regard the Jewish newcomers as too "pushy," too nouveau riche, and too willing to stand out.[55] This issue is not as salient for the Miami community and some of the other larger communities because they are less affected on a daily basis by concern about the prejudices of non-Jewish neighbors. This difference can be illustrated politically in Palm Beach County—"predominantly WASP and classically Southern conservative until the condo boom began" in the middle and late 1960s—where condominium dwellers, mostly "Democratic, Jewish, educated, and aware . . . have brought their political memories, know-how, and activism with them to their new homes in the sun."[56] Nevertheless, some students of southern Jewry suggest that the amount of anti-Semitism in the South has been—and may still be—underestimated, and may indeed—as suspected by the "old families"—surface to lash out at any time.[57]

POOR JEWS

When those twenty-three Jewish refugees arrived in New York City in 1654, they were denied admittance to the colony. Later they were admitted only on the condition that they not be a financial burden on the colony, that they "take care of their own."[58] This condition of acceptance was not a burden, for Judaism —unlike social Darwinism and Puritanism, which were to shape American attitudes toward the less fortunate—had a strong commitment to communal responsibility for the poor.[59] Jewish ethics are permeated with laws to protect the poor and to ensure that private property rights—while sanctioned—do not take precedence over personal rights.[60]

There were some impoverished members of the Jewish community during the early decades, and "a sizable portion of the Jewish community's budget, at least in New York, went for 'pious works' and charities" to take care of these people.[61] There are, however, few indications that there was any significant amount of poverty among these early Jewish refugees or those Jewish settlers who were to come in the following decades.[62] Indeed, some of these early Jewish settlers established some of the earliest fortunes in the United States.[63] With the arrival, and rapid rise into the middle class,[64] of the German Jews in the first part of the 1800s, the American Jewish community was to become well established financially.

The mass migration of Jews from Eastern Europe changed this status, however. Most of the East European immigrants came with little material belongings, and they were characterized by "as many workers, and as many impoverished workers, as any other ethnic group."[65] The impoverishment was real and widespread, as illustrated, for instance, by Gold's *Jews Without Money.*[66] The American Jewish community—comprised by this time primarily of assimilationist-oriented middle-class German Jews—discouraged large-scale migration of these poor and unacculturated Jews because of the threat they posed to the status of these earlier Jewish settlers.[67]

Despite such opposition to large-scale migration, however, the established American Jewish community early devoted itself to helping these Jewish immigrants.[68] Also, these new immigrants were "from a people who had suffered under worse oppressions before, and they remained optimistic and hopeful" despite their economic condition.[69] It was among the new immigrants themselves, for example— many of whom had only the basic necessities—that the first communal institutions were "charitable societies to care for the needy."[70] It was the philanthropic area in which the American Jewish community made its earliest and most successful effort at cooperation.[71] With the help of the larger American Jewish community, with the sense of solidity within the East European communities, and with a strong commitment to long hours of work and to the importance of education for the children, it was not long before this segment of American Jewry had also risen to the middle and upper-middle class. Sklare, comparing the German Jews' mobility to that of the East Eurpean Jews, has suggested that the social mobility of the East European Jew "may be in fact a more spectacular achievement, having been accomplished against greater odds."[72] Currently American Jews "are disproportionately concentrated in the upper ranks of the class structure."[73]

Not all American Jews have become middle class or better, however. Particularly in New York City, a considerable number remain in manual-labor occupations.[74] The image of the American Jewish community as one that has "made it" economically has been so pervasive, however, that very little attention has been given to the Jewish working class and even less attention has been given to the Jewish poor since the first few decades of the 1900s. In fact, there had been little attention given to the poor in America until Harrington's *The Other America* in 1962 led to the "rediscovery" of poverty in the United States.[75]

Finally, in 1971 Jewish poverty was also "rediscovered." Wolfe discussed "The Invisible Jewish Poor" in which she concluded that there were 700,000 to 800,000 Jewish poor in the United States, representing about 13 percent of the total American Jewish population.[76] Elderly Jews and Hasidic Jews were particularly affected. The result was a heated controversy in the American Jewish community, in which Wolfe's figures were criticized for being too high. On the other hand, her findings also encouraged an even more serious questioning of Jewish priorities.[77] The internal policies of the American Jewish community have been reexamined, as well as the "Jewish acquiescence" in the policies of government-sponsored antipoverty programs that generally have excluded Jews from participation.[78] Many of these antipoverty programs, for instance, required that a community have a high rate of unemployment, a high crime rate, and a high rate of broken families. Elderly Jews are not counted in unemployment figures because they are above the age for official employment, and they do not have a high crime rate or a high rate of broken families. Hasidic Jews often have a high unemployment rate, but they do not have a high crime rate or a high rate of broken families. Since the vast majority of poor Jews come from these two groups, these three criteria have effectively prevented many poor Jewish communities that were not located in non-Jewish areas from qualifying for federal antipoverty funds. Whatever the conclusion on the actual number of Jewish poor, however, there was little doubt that the Jewish poor had been underestimated in size and overlooked. The result has been an increase in the amount of funding and attention given to the Jewish poor by both the Jewish community and governmental antipoverty programs. At the same time, organizations and individuals have cautioned against forces that might cause one minority group to be turned against another in the fight for limited funds.[79]

The problems of the Jewish poor remain, however. In addition to the direct problems that result from poverty, most of the Jewish elderly poor are also trapped in neighborhoods with high crime rates and little physical security. Living in neighborhoods from which most other Jewish residents have long since moved, they have few (if any) Jewish institutions with which to affiliate and few Jewish activities in which to participate. Many refuse to move to strange neighborhoods, and many will not apply for available funds they need because of a strong sense of self-reliance.[80] In addition to the problems that result from poverty, the Hasidic poor also suffer more because of the demands that Jewish ritual makes—the need to buy kosher food, for example.[81]

HASIDIC JEWS

Unlike the other groups discussed so far, Hasidic Jews are a new segment within the American Jewish community. The ultra-Orthodox Hasidic movement—

"Hasid" is the Hebrew word for pious—originated in Poland and the Ukraine in the 1700s.[82] Victimized by anti-Semitism, Polish and Ukrainian Jews lived in a downtrodden state. With neither the "means nor the opportunity to study with the great rabbis of their age" they were also opposed to the "arid legalism of the rabbinical schools," which were unable to approach them on an understandable level.[83] Also disillusioned by the failure of the pseudomessiah Sabbatai Zevi from which they had expected messianic redemption, they were in a state of religious despair. Under these conditions, they easily followed the leadership of the Baal Shem Tov (Master of the Good Name) who taught the simple life and the ideal that sincerity is more important than scholarship. In addition to helping meet the religious and social stresses of life and providing a way of opposing the Jewish establishment, it has been suggested that Hasidism helped integrate mysticism—which was important to large numbers of Jews—into intellectual respectability.[84]

Despite strong opposition from the mithnagdim—"those of the rabbinical school who held that God is best served through knowledge of his law"[85]—and later opposition from supporters of the Jewish enlightenment (Haskalah), Hasidism rapidly flourished in Eastern Europe. At its height, it was followed by about half of the Jews of Eastern Europe.[86]

The very nature of their emphasis on tradition and simplicity, however, discouraged Hasidic Jews from migrating to the United States. The traditionalists, and especially the Hasids, "feared to come because of the weinig yiddishkeit [little Jewishness] prevailing in America."[87] Thus, those East European Jews with a Hasidic background who came to the United States were likely to be the least traditional and did not establish a Hasidic life-style in the United States.

It was not until during and after World War II that Hasidic Jews—as the remaining Hasidic refugees from nazism—established themselves as communities in the United States,[88] mainly in New York City. While there are a number of sects or movements—a group that follows a specific rebbe or Hasidic leader—in the United States as there were in Europe, the two largest in the United States are the Satmar Hasidism and the Lubavitcher Hasidism. The Satmar, primarily from Hungary, are centered in the Williamsburg section of Brooklyn, and the Lubavitcher, primarily from Poland, are centered in the Crown Heights area in Brooklyn. In 1962 some Satmar attempted to establish a colony in Mount Olive Township in New Jersey but were denied zoning permission. In 1974, as a result of a desire to relieve the crowding of the Satmar area of Williamsburg, to escape from some of the threats of the secular world, and to allow better housing for some Satmar, a colony was begun in Monroe, Orange County, New York.[89] The Satmar are more traditional and introverted than the Lubavitcher, whereas the Lubavitcher are more "committed to coming to grips with the modern world"[90] and have an outreach program previously limited to college campuses and synagogues to "convert Jews to Judaism." The Lubavitcher have recently extended this program into the larger American Jewish community, undertaking "a massive program to carry that old-time religion to the American Jew."[91] In July 1974, for example, seventy-five two-member teams of Lubavitcher rabbinic students left to visit 750 Jewish communities in the United States to stress the role of traditional Judaism.[92] In addition to the Satmar and the Lubavitcher sects, another group that has received considerable attention is comprised of the followers of the Skverer rebbe, originally from the community of Skvera in the Ukraine. In 1956 they purchased a farm in Rockland County, New York, and later (1961) incorporated it as the village of New Square as they moved there from Williamsburg.[93]

It is estimated that the total number of Hasidism in the United States is about 100,000 (including roughly 50,000 Satmar and 35,000 Lubavitcher), but the figure is difficult to establish with accuracy.[94] The dropout rate is low, but the birthrate is unusually high, and the Lubavitcher movement reports about 200 conversions a year in the New York City area.[95]

The biggest problem faced by the Hasidic Jews is their attempt to maintain a traditional way of life in the midst of a modern secular society. They have been extremely successful in maintaining their traditional life-style within their communities, but this success has brought them into sometimes bitter conflict with the larger society.[96] The "Maccabee" safety partol, for example, was founded in the mid-1960s to protect elderly poor Orthodox and Hasidic Jews, but the group was viewed as antiblack and some resentment remains yet.[97]

Another major problem—arising from the limited availability of jobs that do not interfere with their religious observance, lack of advanced secular education, and the tendency to have large families—is poverty and its related problems. The unemployment rate for Satmar Hasidism, for example, normally ranges around 6 percent but reached about 20 percent in the 1974 recession.[98]

BLACK JEWS

There are records of individual black Jews in the United States before the 1900s,[99] but it was not until the 1900s that all-black Jewish congregations appeared.[100] Polner states that the first may have been in Portsmouth, Virginia, in 1905, but this one, like many others that followed, likely had a mixture of Jewish, pagan, and Christian dimensions.[101] A number of all-black congregations that identified themselves as Jewish had appeared in several American cities by the 1920s, but it was in New York City, where Negro leaders came into close contact with white Jews, that the most congregations were established. Many of these early black Jews in New York City were West Indians.[102] The earliest major individual associated with the movement was Arnold Ford who around 1924 organized Beth B'nai Abraham congregation in New York City, which he served as rabbi.[103] Ford disappeared in the early 1930s, but before disappearing he had ordained Rabbi Wentworth A. Matthew who served as rabbi of New York's largest black Jewish congregation, The Commandment Keepers Ethiopian Hebrew Congregation,[104] until his death in the early 1970s.

The number of black Jews in the United States is difficult to ascertain with accuracy. The estimated number in New York City ranges from a little over 3,000[105] to 16,000.[106] Waitzkin noted that Matthew claimed 3,000 followers in

Harlem alone, with black Jewish congregations in Brooklyn, Philadelphia, Pittsburgh, Youngstown, Ohio, Chicago, St. Thomas (Virgin Islands), and Jamaica also looking to Matthew as their leader.[107] The estimated number nationally ranges from 12,000 (excluding quasi-Jewish black cults) to 100,000.[108]

The major problem facing black Jews is the question of their authenticity as Jews.[109] There are several somewhat overlapping hypotheses to explain their origins. They claim that the biblical Hebrews were black and that the current black Jews are their descendants who had their Jewish identity and culture taken from them during slavery. Brotz has suggested that this idea may have arisen from the close affinities between Negroes and Jews that fundamentalist black Protestantism stressed in the South.[110]

Another suggestion is that black Jews are descendants of slaves who belonged to Jewish slaveowners in the West Indies, Latin America, or the southern United States. Waitzkin has argued against this suggestion because black Judaism has a nationalistic flavor—the belief that the first Jews were black and thus the belief that black Jews are the "chosen people" and the only authentic Jews—that it would not have if it was simply adopted from white Jewish slaveowners and because "the ritual of the early Jews resembled orthodox Jewish ritual very little."[111] It must also be noted that Judaism, because it does not claim to be the only true religion, has not been a proselytizing religion in recent centuries.

Brotz has suggested two origins of black Jews: that blacks identified with the cultural heritage of the Old Testament Hebrews in order to develop a positive identity with which to counteract white racism and that blacks were influenced by Booker T. Washington's admiration for the pride and faith Jews had in themselves despite the suffering they had endured.[112] Waitzkin has suggested that residential contacts in northern cities during the first few decades of the 1900s between poor East European Jewish immigrants and poor black migrants from the South "was most likely an important factor in the rise of black Judaism."[113]

Some black Jews have undergone formal conversion "in order to 'normalize' [their] status in Jewish law,"[114] but most—claiming that they are already Jews—have vigorously refused to convert formally.[115] As a result of the controversy over their authenticity as Jews, a number of conflicts have occurred, such as the expulsion of three black Jewish students from an Orthodox yeshiva in New York City in 1971 and the denial of Israeli citizenship under the Law of Return to a group of black Jews from the United States in 1973.[116] Black Jews tend to have a slightly higher socioeconomic status than other blacks, but most of the black Jewish congregations are in poor neighborhoods, and the members face the problems that result from living in such areas. In addition, as Safier found in a recent doctoral dissertation, black Jews are in a state of incongruity as a result of their dual minority status—rating "their ascribed membership group ('Black Americans') negatively and their voluntary membership group ('Jewish American') positively."[117]

Some attempts have been made to confront the problems black Jews face. For example, the Committee on Black Jews of the Synagogue Council of America "has focused on a number of problems confronting the black Jewish community in the areas of housing, Jewish education, employment and other important social services."[118] The National Conference on Black Jews, sponsored by the Synagogue Council of America, was attended by 120 religious and community leaders, including black Jews, in May 1973.

JEWISH WOMEN

Jewish women differ from the other groups of the American Jewish community discussed in this book in that they are not a distinct subcommunity within the Jewish community. They are sometimes recipients of unequal treatment and are outside the mainstream community in terms of power, however. Hence, we are concerned with the factors that have led to the position that women occupy and the role that they fulfill within the American Jewish community.

A number of writers have concluded that, other than in the area of religious observance, the Jewish woman has traditionally enjoyed more equality with the Jewish man than the non-Jewish woman has enjoyed with the non-Jewish man. Adler noted, for instance, that Jewish women for centuries have had "rights which other women lacked until a century ago. A Jewish woman could not be married without her consent. Her ketubah (marriage document) was a legally binding contract which assured that her husband was responsible for her support (a necessity in a world in which it was difficult for a woman to support herself), and that if divorced, she was entitled to a monetary settlement. Her husband was not permitted to abstain from sex for long periods of time without regard to her needs and her feelings."[119] Epstein, in discussing the period from 900 C.E. to 1500 C.E., noted that women occupied a significant place in the life of the community and extended their influence into social, economic, and other areas.[120] Patai, in comparing the Jewish woman to the Moslem woman, concluded that "one can state in general terms that everywhere in the Middle East the position of the Jewish woman, while strongly influenced by that of the Muslim woman of the immediate environment, was on the whole better."[121] Chouraqui has reached the same conclusion from his research on Jewish communities in North Africa.[122]

While the rights given to Jewish women by religious authorities have not kept pace with the increased rights toward equality that women have gained in the secular world, Zuckoff has noted that the traditional socioeconomic status of Jewish women continued even into the early twentieth-century shtetl culture of Eastern Europe. She noted, for instance, that "the shtetl socio-economic patterm differed considerably from classical patriarchy . . . women were not seen as sex objects; their beauty was not their primary attraction. What was admired in a woman was her ability to manage well, to be strong and realistic."[123] Zborowski and Herzog, from their study of the shtetl, also noted that it was not uncommon for the Jewish woman to earn the family's livelihood.[124]

It was this background of "more-equal" socioeconomic status from which the mass migration of East European Jews came to the United States in the 1880-1924 period, and the women brought with them this conception of their position in the community and home. While data on the situation for American Jewish women who were here before the mass migration are scarce, Brav suggests that the American Jewish woman in this earlier period also exemplified the traditional Jewish position. Discussing the role of Jewish women in the 1860s, he concluded that she was "far more than a mere marital companion, a breeder of progeny, and a slave to household chores. Her domestic status, in the eyes of the Jewish press of the day, was an elevated one. . . . She left the portals of her menage to play an ever increasingly significant role in synagogue worship and congregational activity, in Jewish community social and cultural programs, and in the organization and execution of valuable philanthropic and patriotic enterprises."[125]

As the socioeconomic status of American Jews increased, however, the situation for Jewish women changed. As Jewish men in the United States succeeded economically and assimilated into the American culture, the woman's function as a provider and partner was no longer needed. Jewish men looked at non-Jewish women and at the wives of Jews who had assimilated, saw them as "passive, unassertive, and fearful, existing just for the family (i.e., men),"[126] and encouraged their wives to be the same as a mark of assimilation and social prestige. The Jewish woman thus became a housewife and a dependent.[127] Simultaneously, the prestige of being "only" a housewife decreased, and the importance of women as the preservers of Jewish identity decreased.[128]

Despite their traditional status of relative equality in the community, family, and economic areas, Jewish women have been and continue to be treated as unequal in religious terms. Traditional Judaism still prohibits women from performing, or fully participating in, a number of religious functions. The religious situation has improved in the United States, however. The Reform movement early removed all official restrictions to women's participation, and the Reconstructionist movement—from its founding in 1922—has had no barriers against women. The Conservative movement has also begun to ease some restrictions, but the Orthodox movement remains steadfastly tied to the traditional position.[129] Even to the extent that women have gained some equality within some branches of Judaism, however, they still are vastly underrepresented in the Jewish organizational leadership.[130]

The problems that Jewish women face in the United States can thus be viewed as both religious and cultural. They have gained more religious rights than they previously had, but they are still restricted from enjoying full equality. Culturally they are better off than non-Jewish women, but they have less status within the Jewish community than Jewish women have traditionally had.[131]

Jewish women are beginning to question this status. A large proportion of leaders in the women's liberation movement in the United States have been Jewish women,[132] but in the last few years an increasing number of Jewish women have begun to work both as Jews and as women to change the status of women within the Jewish community. Jewish women were perhaps particularly beset by conflicting roles: the important wife and mother within a strong family unit on one hand and the member of a liberal and highly educated group on the other hand.[133]

In 1971 Ezrat Nashim was founded to push for equality for women in Judaism, and in 1972 it began to actively challenge sex restrictions in Judaism.[134] In 1973 almost 500 Jewish women attended the first national Jewish women's conference,[135] and in 1974 the Jewish Feminist Organization was founded, mostly by college-educated Jewish women in their twenties and thirties, to coordinate the efforts of various groups and individuals.[136] The college campus has been a major area of innovation, such as in religious services.[137]

There are other evidences of change within the Jewish community. In 1972 the Reform movement confirmed the first female rabbi in the United States (and the second in history according to some accounts),[138] and the Reconstructionist Rabbinical College had a female graduate at its 1974 graduation.[139] With the ordination of the third female rabbi in the United States in 1975, and others since then, the precedent has been laid for the Reform and Reconstructionist movements.[140] The Conservative movement voted in 1973 to allow individual congregations to count women in a minyan.[141] The Conservative seminary has delayed on plans to allow females to be rabbis, but the president of the 1,100-member Rabbinical Assembly (organization of Conservative rabbis) called in 1974 for allowing female rabbis who have been ordained by the Reform or Reconstructionist movements to become members of the assembly.[142] In 1975 the new president followed the previous line by predicting that "women will be serving in the denomination's pulpits in the foreseeable future."[143] The Orthodox movement has not changed its position, even though some "modern" Orthodox are reexamining the traditional role of women[144] and at least a few leaders are sensitive to the issues.[145] In fact, indicative of the more general Orthodox position, the Orthodox movement not only condemned the Conservative minyan change as an "act of desperation" but strongly opposed the equal-rights amendment to the Constitution as a threat to Orthodox policies.[146] While most of the debate over positions has dealt with the rabbinate, there are other positions of importance, and along this line, the Reform movement graduated the first official female cantor or "hazzan" at its 1975 graduation ceremonies.[147]

SEPHARDIC JEWS

This introduction to subcommunities within the American Jewish community ends, as it began, with those first twenty-three Jewish settlers in New York City in 1654. These settlers were Sephardic Jews, descendants of Jews expelled from Spain or Portugal who had gone to Western Europe or the Americas, and themselves refugees from the Portugese Inquisition in Brazil.[148] In January 1655 they presented, in the name of "the Jewish nation," a petition—which was at first rebuffed—for permission to settle in New Amsterdam.[149] They persisted, however, in their demand for religious rights and set a precedent for other religious minorities as well as for later Jewish immigrants.[150]

With this early beginning, Sephardim were to form the majority of American Jewry for several decades, but by 1720 they were outnumbered by Ashkenazim.[151]

Even in this earlier period there were relatively many Ashkenazim; even in specific communities where they outnumbered the Sephardim, however, these Ashkenazim often assimilated into the Sephardic culture.[152] Because of the high social status of the Sephardim and the positions of leadership they filled in the American Jewish community, the American Jewish community was to remain basically Sephardic in culture until the beginning of the 1800s.

With the virtual cessation of Sephardic migration, a high rate of intermarriage and conversion from Judaism among the colonial Sephardim, and the continued increase in migration of German Jews in the first decades of the 1800s, however, the American Jewish community increasingly became Ashkenazic in culture as in numbers.[153] With the addition of over two million Ashkenazic Jews from Eastern Europe in the 1880-1924 period, the Sephardim were to diminish further in relative size and influence. Birmingham has suggested that most of the descendants of the early Sephardic settlers are Christian now,[154] and Angel has stated that descendants of these early Sephardim "have dwindled in number and influence, so that today very few congregations of this tradition still enjoy a vibrant existence."[155]

There have been two additional Sephardic migrations to the United States. In the early years of the 1900s, and particularly from 1908 through 1924, approximately 20,000 to 25,000 Sephardic Jews from the Levant (mainly Turkey, Greece, and Syria) came to the United States. Mostly descendants of Jews expelled from Spain who had gone to the Ottoman Empire, they were pushed to leave the Ottoman Empire "because of political upheavals and rising nationalism"[156] as well as pulled by the attraction of economic and social mobility in the United States.[157] Then, in the decade or two following the independence of Israel, and in the surge of nationalism following World War II, most Jews from Arabic and Islamic countries, including North Africa, were pressured to leave their respective countries.[158] Most of these Jews went to Israel,[159] but some also migrated to the United States.[160] In addition, a sizable number of Cuban Jewish refugees (about a fourth of them Sephardic) came to the United States in the 1950s and 1960s.[161]

The number of Sephardic Jews in the United States today is generally estimated to be 100,000 (although estimates vary to as high as 300,000),[162] with almost all being representative of the two migrations since 1900. Most live in New York City, but sizable communities are found in Washington, D.C., Atlanta, Georgia, Portland, Oregon, Seattle, Washington, Los Angeles, California, and Miami, Florida, as well as in other cities.

The major problem the American Sephardim face is continuation of their culture within the larger Ashkenazic Jewish community, and recognition as a separate but valid segment of the American Jewish community by the larger Jewish community. Fragmentation within the Sephardic community—based largely on national origin—has also stymied attempts to organize a viable Sephardic community. Sephardic Jews in the United States also have a particular concern with helping improve the condition of Sephardic Jews in Israel and in Arabic countries.

Some progress has been made in the last few years toward alleviating some of these problems. To preserve the Sephardic traditions and to train new rabbis, teachers, and cantors in the Sephardic tradition, a Sephardic studies program was established at Yeshiva University in 1964.[163] The American Society of Sephardic Studies, "an organization of academicians and scholars devoted to the promulgation of Sephardic culture, literature, religious life and mores," held its first annual conference in 1968.[164] In 1973, 500 delegates of Sephardic background met in New York City for the first convention of the World Institute of Sephardic Studies in an attempt to develop ways of encouraging the renewal of cultural and charitable activities among Sephardic Jews.[165] Other organizations have also been formed, among them the American Association of Jewish Refugees from Arab Lands, composed of individuals who have left Arab countries, particularly Libya, Egypt, Syria, and Iraq, since 1948.[166]

NOTES

1. Bruce Felton, "Black Jews in New York," *The Times of Israel* 1 (February 1974): 53.

2. Kenneth L. Woodward, "The American Jew Today," *Newsweek* 77 (March 1, 1971): 63.

3. Daniel J. Elazar, "American Political Theory and the Political Notions of American Jews: Convergences and Contradictions," *Jewish Journal of Sociology* 9 (June 1967): 6.

4. Marc D. Angel, "The Sephardim of the United States: An Exploratory Study," in Morris Fine and Milton Himmelfarb, eds., *American Jewish Yearbook* (New York: American Jewish Committee, 1973), pp. 77-138.

5. Alvin Chenkin, "Jewish Population in the United States, 1972," in Fine and Himmelfarb, *American Jewish Yearbook*, pp. 307-315.

6. Marshall Sklare, *America's Jews* (New York: Random House, 1971), p. 44.

7. Charles S. Liebman, *The Ambivalent American Jew* (Philadelphia: The Jewish Publication Society of America, 1973), p. 61.

8. Gilbert S. Rosenthal, *Four Paths to One God* (New York: Bloch Publishing Company, 1973).

9. Sklare, *America's Jews*, p. xi. Also see Abraham D. Lavender and John M. Forsyth, "The Sociological Study of Minority Groups as Reflected by Leading Sociological Journals," *Ethnicity* 3 (December 1976): 388-398. This article documents the neglect of not only Jews, but also other ethnic groups in the United States.

10. Peter I. Rose, Foreword to Sklare, *America's Jews*, p. ix.

11. Marshall Sklare and Joseph Greenblum, *Jewish Identity on the Suburban Frontier: A Study of Group Survival in the Open Society* (New York: Basic Books, 1967).

12. Sidney Goldstein and Calvin Goldscheider, *Jewish Americans: Three Generations in a Jewish Community* (Englewood Cliffs, N.J.: Prentice-Hall, 1968), p. 14.

13. The National Jewish Population Study was sponsored by the Council of Jewish Federations and Welfare Funds and was conducted under the direction of Fred Massarik. The NJPS, the first comprehensive national study made of the Jewish population of the United States, was conducted between late 1970 and early 1972 and was designed to achieve a representative sample of Jews throughout the United States. The study has not been published but a series of reports have been.

14. Arnold Dashefsky and Howard Shapiro, *Ethnic Identification Among American Jews* (Lexington, Mass.: Lexington Books, 1974).

15. The Association for the Sociological Study of Jewry was formally established in August 1971. The first issue of the *Newsletter of the Association for the Sociological Study of Jewry* was published in the summer of 1974 under the editorship of Joshua Fishman and David Glanz. In 1976 the newsletter was expanded and changed into a journal, *Jewish Sociology and Social Research*, under the editorship of Murray Binderman. In 1977, under the editorship of Murray Binderman, the journal changed to *Contemporary Jewry: A Journal of Social Inquiry* and be-

came a part of the *Transaction* series. For a review of the changing status of the sociological study of Jewry, see Abraham D. Lavender, "Contemporary Jewish Studies: A Review of the Field," *Jewish Sociology and Social Research,* forthcoming.

16. Michael Harrington, *The Other America* (New York: The Macmillan Company, 1962).

17. Efraim Shmueli, "The Appeal of Hasidism for American Jewry Today," *Jewish Journal of Sociology* 11 (June 1969): 27.

18. See Marc D. Angel, "Sephardic Culture in America," *Jewish Life* 38 (March-April 1971): pp. 7-11, and his "Ruminations About Sephardic Identity," *Midstream* 18 (March 1972): 64-67. Also see William Greenberg, "Sephardim—As Others See Us," *American Sephardi* 2 (1968): 64-67, and Leon A. Ligier, "The Chicago and Los Angeles Sephardic Communities in Transition," *American Sephardi* 2 (1968): 80-82.

19. Lily Edelman, "Editor's Note: Small-Town Jewry Makes Itself Heard," *Jewish Heritage* 15 (Winter 1974): 3.

20. Eli Evans, *The Provincials: A Personal History of Jews in the South* (New York: Atheneum, 1973), p. vii.

21. Alfred O. Hero, Jr., *The Southerner and World Affairs* (Baton Rouge: Louisiana State University Press, 1965), p. 213.

22. Harold Goldfarb, "Blacks and Conversion to Judaism," *Jewish Digest* 17 (March 1972): p. 32.

23. For a statement on the popularity of Jewish studies, see Arnold J. Band, "Jewish Studies in American Liberal-Arts Colleges and Universities," in Morris Fine and Milton Himmelfarb, eds., *American Jewish Yearbook* (New York: American Jewish Committee, 1966), pp. 3-30. Also see William Greenberg, "Sephardim—As Others See Us," *American Sephardi* 2 (1968): winter 1973 issue of *Conservative Judaism.*

24. Priscilla Fishman, ed., *The Jews of the United States* (New York: Quadrangle/New York Times Book Company, 1973), p. 7.

25. Jacob Rader Marcus, *The Colonial American Jew* (Detroit: Wayne State University Press, 1970), 4: 392.

26. Fishman, *The Jews of the United States,* p. 8.

27. Rudolf Glanz, "The Spread of Jewish Communities Through America Before the Civil War," *Yivo Annual of Jewish Social Science* 15 (1974): 38.

28. Ira Rosenwaike, "The Jewish Population of the United States as Estimated from the Census of 1820," *American Jewish Historical Quarterly* 53 (1963): 138-152.

29. Jacob Rader Marcus, ed., "Trail Blazers of the Trans-Mississippi West," *American Jewish Archives* 8 (October 1956): 58.

30. Jacob Rader Marcus, "Tercentenary 1654-1954," *American Jewish Archives* 6 (June 1954): 76.

31. Glanz, "The Spread of Jewish Communities," p. 26.

32. Jacob Rader Marcus, ed., "A Colony in Kansas—1882," *American Jewish Archives* 17 (November 1965): 115.

33. Joseph Brandes in association with Martin Douglas, *Immigrants to Freedom* (Philadelphia: The Jewish Publication Society of America, 1971), p. 12.

34. American Jewish Yearbook, "The Jews of the United States," in Harry Schneiderman, ed., *American Jewish Yearbook* (New York: American Jewish Committee, 1938-1939), pp. 538-543.

35. Daniel J. Elazar, "The Geography of American Jewish Communal Life," *Congress Bi-Weekly* 40 (January 26, 1973); 10. Also see Conrad Taeuber and Irene B. Taeuber, *The Changing Population of the United States* (New York: John Wiley and Sons, 1958), p. 140, and U.S. Bureau of the Census, Census of Population, 1970, 1, *Characteristics of the Population,* Part A, Number of Inhabitants, Section 1, p. 34.

36. Elazar, "The Geography of American Jewish Communal Life," p. 11.

37. Alvin Chenkin, "Jewish Population in the United States, 1974," in Morris Fine and

Milton Himmelfarb, eds., *American Jewish Yearbook* (New York: American Jewish Committee, 1976), pp. 229-238.

38. Leonard Dinnerstein, Introduction to Leonard Dinnerstein and Mary Dale Palsson, eds., *Jews in the South* (Baton Rouge: Louisiana State University Press, 1973), p. 3.

39. Janice O. Rothschild, "Southern and Jewish," *Hadassah Magazine* 55 (November 1973): 20. This is a review of *Jews in the South* by Dinnerstein and Palsson.

40. Marcus, *The Colonial American Jew*, 4: 393.

41. Nathan Glazer et al., "Social Characteristics of American Jews," in *The Characteristics of American Jews* (New York: Jewish Education Committee Press, 1965), p. 11.

42. Ira Rosenwaike, "An Estimate and Analysis of the Jewish Population of the United States in 1790," *Publications of the American Jewish Historical Society* 50 (1960): 34.

43. Fishman, *The Jews of the United States*, p. 22.

44. Rosenthal, *Four Paths to One God*, p. 28.

45. Glanz, "The Spread of Jewish Communities," p. 34.

46. Steven Hertzberg, review of *A Century of Jewish Life in Dixie: The Birmingham Experience* by Mark H. Elovitz, *American Jewish Historical Quarterly* 65 (September 1975): p. 91.

47. Dinnerstein and Palsson, *Jews in the South*, p. 22.

48. H.S. Linfield, "The Jewish Population of the United States," in Harry Schneiderman, ed., *American Jewish Yearbook* (New York: American Jewish Committee, 1942-1943), pp. 419-421.

49. Chenkin, "Jewish Population in the United States, 1974," pp. 229-238.

50. See Dinnerstein, Introduction, pp. 8-13, and Marcus, "Trailer Blazers," pp. 58-130 for a discussion of this topic.

51. Dinnerstein, Introduction, p. 17.

52. Chenkin, "Jewish Population in the United States, 1974," pp. 229-238.

53. Hero, *The Southerner and World Affairs*, p. 230.

54. Eugene Levy, " 'Is the Jew a White Man?' Press Reaction to the Leo Frank Case, 1913-1915," *Phylon* 35 (June 1974): p. 212.

55. Theodore Lowi, "Southern Jews: The Two Communities," *Jewish Journal of Sociology* 6 (July 1964): pp. 103-117. Also see Morris N. Kertzer, *Today's American Jew* (New York: McGraw-Hill Book Company, 1967), p. 266.

56. Myra MacPherson, " 'Condo' Vote Helps Jackson in Florida," *Washington Post*, March 8, 1976.

57. Hero, *The Southerner and World Affairs*, p. 223, and Arnold Shankman, review of *Send These to Me: Jews and Other Immigrants in Urban America* by John Higham, *The Journal of Ethnic Studies* 3 (Winter 1976): p. 122. Also see Levy, " 'Is the Jew a White Man?' " pp. 212-222, and Melvin I. Urofsky, "Jews in the South," *Midstream* 20 (March 1974): 82. The latter is a review of *Jews in the South* by Dinnerstein and Palsson and *The Provincials* by Evans.

58. Fishman, *The Jews of the United States*, p. 5.

59. Commission on Urban Affairs, *The Jewish Poor and the War Against Poverty* (New York: American Jewish Congress, 1971), p. 3.

60. Richard G. Hirsch, *There Shall Be No Poor* (New York: Union of American Hebrew Congregations, 1965). Also see Edward Day, "The Treatment of Inferiors in Israel," *American Journal of Sociology* 9 (November 1903): 373-385.

61. Fishman, *The Jews of the United States*, p. 12.

62. E. Digby Baltzell, "The Development of a Jewish Upper Class in Philadelphia: 1782-1940," in Marshall Sklare, ed., *The Jews: Social Patterns of an American Group* (Glencoe, Ill.: The Free Press, 1958), p. 274. Fishman also notes that as a group the Jews in New York appeared to be slightly better off economically than their neighbors.

63. Stephen Birmingham, *The Grandees* (New York: Harper and Row, 1971).

64. Sklare, *America's Jews*, p. 7.

65. Nathan Glazer, "The American Jew and the Attainment of Middle-Class Rank: Some Trends and Explanations," in Sklare, *The Jews,* p. 144.

66. Michael Gold, *Jews Without Money* (New York: International Publishers, 1930). Also see Ande Manners, *Poor Cousins* (Greenwich, Conn.: Fawcett, 1972).

67. Sklare, *America's Jews,* p. 9.

68. Ibid.

69. Moses Rischin, "The Lower East Side," in Kenneth T. Jackson and Stanley K. Schultz, eds., *Cities in American History* (New York: Alfred A. Knopf, 1972), p. 197.

70. Commission on Urban Affairs, *The Jewish Poor,* p. 4.

71. Sklare, *America's Jews,* p. 106.

72. Ibid., p. 10.

73. Goldstein and Goldscheider, *Jewish Americans,* p. 63.

74. Ibid.

75. Harrington, *The Other America.*

76. Ann G. Wolfe, "The Invisible Jewish Poor," *Journal of Jewish Communal Service* 48 (Spring 1972): 6.

77. Barbara Welner, "A View of Jewish Priorities," *American Zionist* 62 (December 1971): 33, and Benjamin R. Sprafkin, "The Jewish Poor: Who Are They? Are We Helping Them Enough?" *Journal of Jewish Communal Service* 49 (Spring 1973): 206-209.

78. Welner, "A View of Jewish Priorities."

79. "Officials Sworn in Ceremony Here," *New York Times,* January 6, 1975, p. 30.

80. Paul Cowan, "Her Crowd," *New York Times,* December 4, 1972, p. 39; and Lillian Barney, "Drive to Aid Poor L.I. Jews," *New York Times,* May 6, 1973, p. 145.

81. Stephen Isaacs, "Hasidim of Brooklyn," *Washington Post,* February 17, 1974, and Jack Simcha Cohen, "Jewish Poverty: Measurement Problems," *Journal of Jewish Communal Service* 49 (Spring 1973): 210-223.

82. S.M. Dubnow, "Hasidism," in Isodore Singer, ed., *The Jewish Encyclopedia* (New York: Funk & Wagnalls Company, 1925), pp. 251-256.

83. Herbert Bloom, "Hasidism," in Louis Shores, ed., *Collier's Encyclopedia* (New York: Crowell-Collier Educational Corporation, 1971), p. 677.

84. Werner Cahnman, review of *Jewish Society Through the Ages,* ed. H.H. Ben-Sasson and S. Ettinger, *American Jewish Historical Quarterly* 62 (September 1974): 220-222.

85. Bloom, "Hasidism."

86. Ibid.

87. Bernard D. Weinryb, "Jewish Immigration and Accommodation to America," in Sklare, *The Jews,* p. 16.

88. Sklare, *America's Jews,* p. 24.

89. George Dugan, "Jewish Sect to Go to Orange County," *New York Times,* July 21, 1974, p. 40; and Michal Knight, "Brooklyn Hasidim Believed Planning Large Colony at Upstate Resort Site," *New York Times,* September 16, 1974, pp. 37, 71.

90. Evelyn Lauter, "Chaim Potok Talks About Hasidism and U.S. Jewry," *National Jewish Monthly* 82 (June 1968): 20.

91. Ray Schultz, "The Call of the Ghetto," *New York Times,* November 10, 1974, sec. 6, p. 34.

92. "150 Rabbinic Students Here Begin Jewish-Identity Tour," *New York Times,* July 8, 1974, p. 9.

93. James Feron, "New Square: Its Hasidim Do Not Live by Bread Alone," *New York Times,* July 18, 1975, p. 33.

94. Harry Steinberg, "In Williamsburg the Lines Are Drawn," *The Times of Israel* 1 (April 1974): 51; and Fishman, *The Jews of the United States,* p. 157. Also see Knight, "Brooklyn Hasidim," p. 37, and Emanuel Perlmutter, "Hasidic Sect Hurt by Unemployment," *New York Times,* December 26, 1974, p. 41, for estimate of Satmar total. For estimate of Lubavitcher

total, see Gerald F. Lieberman, "Brooklyn Hasidim Fighting Districting," *New York Times,* June 16, 1974, p. 86.

95. Schultz, "The Call of the Ghetto," p. 120.

96. See, for example, Wolfgang Saxon, "Jews and Police Clash in Brooklyn," *New York Times,* June 3, 1973, p. 21, as well as follow-up articles to this particular incident on June 4, p. 8, June 5, p. 19, and June 12, p. 13.

97. Grace Lichtenstein, " 'Transitional' Crown Heights Now in Midst of Comeback," *New York Times,* August 1, 1974, p. 31.

98. Perlmutter, "Hasidic Sect Hurt," p. 41.

99. See, for example, "Old Billy," *American Jewish Archives* 15 (April 1963): 3-5.

100. Howard M. Brotz. *The Black Jews of Harlem* (New York: Schocken Books, 1964), p. 9. Brotz states that organized congregations did not occur until about 1915, but Polner states that the first may have been as early as 1905.

101. Murray Polner, "Being Black and Jewish," *National Jewish Monthly* 87 (October 1972): 41.

102. Howard Waitzkin, "Black Judaism in New York," *Harvard Journal of Negro Affairs* 1 (1967): 14.

103. Albert Ehrman, "Explorations and Responses: Black Judaism in New York," *Journal of Ecumenical Studies* 8 (Winter 1971): 105.

104. Ibid., p. 106.

105. Felton, "Black Jews in New York," p. 53.

106. Albert Ehrman, "Tracing the Beginnings of Black Judaism," *Jewish Digest* 18 (October 1972): 51.

107. Waitzkin, "Black Judaism in New York," p. 20.

108. Polner, "Being Black and Jewish," p. 40.

109. See Robert T. Coleman, "Black and Jewish—and Unaccepted," *Sh'ma* 4 (March 22, 1974): 74-76. Coleman notes that individual black Jews who have formally converted also face nonacceptance in many cases.

110. Brotz, *The Black Jews of Harlem,* p. 7.

111. Waitzkin, "Black Judaism in New York," p. 14.

112. Brotz, *The Black Jews of Harlem,* p. 8.

113. Waitzkin, "Black Judaism in New York," p. 17.

114. Synagogue Council of America, press release, June 4, 1973, p. 3. For an article on an individual black who converted to Judaism, see Larry Lewis, "Black American Soldier in the Israeli Army," *Sepia* 24 (October 1975): 18-24.

115. Ehrman, "Explorations and Responses," p. 114.

116. For comments on the first incident mentioned, see Polner, "Being Black and Jewish," p. 39; for comments on the second incident, see the *Washington Post,* August 11, 1973.

117. Arno Safier, "Dual Minority Status, Group Identification and Membership Conflict: A Study of Black Jews" (Ph.D. diss., New York University, 1971).

118. Synagogue Council of America, Annual Report of the Committee on Black Jews, 1973. The address is 432 Park Avenue South, New York, N.Y. 10016.

119. Rachel Adler, "The Jew Who Wasn't There: Halacha and the Jewish Woman," *Response* 18 (Summer 1973): 81.

120. I. Epstein, "The Jewish Woman in the Responsa," *Response* 18 (Summer 1973): 30.

121. Raphael Patai, *The Tents of Jacob* (Englewood Cliffs, N.J.: Prentice-Hall, 1971), p. 179.

122. André N. Chouraqui, *Between East and West: A History of the Jews of North Africa* (New York: Atheneum, 1973), p. 206.

123. Aviva Cantor Zuckoff, "The Oppression of the Jewish Woman," *Response* 18 (Summer 1973): 51

124. Mark Zborowski and Elizabeth Herzog, *Life Is with People* (New York: Schocken Books, 1962), p. 131.

125. Stanley R. Brav, "The Jewish Woman, 1861-1865," *American Jewish Archives* 17 (April 1965): 74.

126. Zuckoff, "The Oppression of the Jewish Woman," p. 52.

127. Charlotte Baum, "What Made Yetta Work? The Economic Role of Eastern European Jewish Women in the Family," *Response* 18 (Summer 1973): 38.

128. Zuckoff, "The Oppression of the Jewish Woman," p. 53.

129. Rosenthal, *Four Paths to One God*, p. 76.

130. Trude Weiss-Rosmarin, "Female Consciousness-Raising," *Jewish Spectator* 38 (September 1973): 6.

131. By "better off" is meant higher socioeconomic status and fuller participation in the total society. In Goldstein and Goldscheider, *Jewish Americans*, pp. 65, 78, for example, it is noted that Jewish females have a median of 12.7 years of school completed, whereas total females have a median of 10.1 years. Considering occupations of employed persons, Jewish females had 17.9 percent in the professional category, and 12.7 percent in the managerial and proprietoral categories, whereas the comparable percentages for total females were 10.5 and 2.4. While these figures for Jewish females are from one community, other studies indicate that they are accurate for the United States as a whole.

132. Blu Greenberg and Irving Greenberg, "Equality in Judaism," *Hadassah Magazine* 56 (December 1973): 14. Aviva Cantor, in "Do Women Have It Tough?" *The Jewish Floridian,* December 24, 1976, p. 11B, also notes the large number of Jewish women in the women's liberation movement. She lists Susan Brownmiller, Dr. Phyllis Chesler, Andrea Dworkin, Shulamith Firestone, Betty Friedan, Robin Morgan, and Barbara Seaman, as well as Germaine Greer and Gloria Steinem as "part-Jewish."

133. George E. Johnson, "Halakha and Women's Liberation," *Midstream* 20 (January 1974): 60.

134. Greenberg and Greenberg, "Equality in Judaism," p. 36. Also see Leah Laiman, "Feminism and Judaism," *The Times of Israel* 1 (January 1974): 62. "Ezrat Nashim" literally translates as "women's aid" but generally refers to the women's section in an Orthodox Synogogue. The choice of these words is a pun. For a discussion of how Ezrat Nashim has responded to the issues, see Alan Silverstein, "The Evolution of Ezrat Nashim." *Conservative Judaism* 30 (Fall 1975): 41-51.

135. "450 Women Attend National Jewish Women's Conference," *Network* March 7, 1973, p. 2.

136. Eleanor Blau, "Feminists Decry the Role of Women in Jewish Life," *New York Times,* April 21, 1975, p. 32, and "150 Jewish Feminists Ponder a Conflict," ibid., November 3, 1975, p. 76.

137. Irving Spiegel, "Equality Sought by Jewish Coeds," *New York Times,* April 20, 1975, p. 33.

138. Eleanor Blau, "First Woman Rabbi in U.S. Ordained," *New York Times,* June 4, 1972, p. 76. Also see Leah Laiman, "The Rabbi Is a Lady," *The Times of Israel* 1 (January 1974): 64-65. Also see "Rabbi Sally, The First Woman Rabbi, 1972," *American Jewish Archives* 26 (November 1974): 236-238 for a discussion of Rabbi Regina Jonas who was ordained in Germany in the 1930s. She finished her studies at the Berlin Academy for the Science of Judaism. Her dissertation, "Can a Woman Become a Jew?" was accepted by the faculty, but the professor of Talmud, who was the licensing authority, refused to ordain her. She was ordained by an individual rabbi, however, and practiced "primarily in homes for the aged." She was sent to the Theresienstadt concentration camp by the Nazis in 1940. The question of whether Regina Jonas was the first rabbi, and hence whether Sally Priesand was the first or second, stems from the circumstances of Regina Jonas's ordination. In 1975 Rabbi Jacqueline Tabick was ordained in London, the "first [or second?] woman rabbi outside the United States" (*New York Times,* July 1, 1975, p. 37).

139. George Dugan, "Female Rabbinical Students Ask Increased 'Femininity' in Judaism," *New York Times,* May 7, 1972, p. 37.

140. Dena Kleiman, "She Is Young, Vivacious, Attractive—and Also a Rabbi," *New York Times,* May 26, 1974, p. 106; and Irving Spiegel, "First Woman Cantor, An Alto, Invested Here," *New York Times,* June 9, 1975, p. 35.

141. Irving Spiegel, "Conservative Jews Vote for Women in Minyan," *New York Times,* September 11, 1973, p. 1.

142. Irving Spiegel, "Conservative Seminary Is Urged to Train Women as Rabbis," *New York Times,* May 7, 1974, p. 23.

143. Irving Spiegel, "Conservative Rabbi Sees Women in the Pulpit Soon," *New York Times,* April 21, 1975, p. 32.

144. Eleanor Blau, "Population Shifts Beset Jewish Community Here," *New York Times,* August 21, 1975, p. 1.

145. Sheila F. Segal, "Feminists for Judaism," *Midstream* 21 (August-September 1975): 64.

146. Irving Spiegel, "Orthodox Rabbis Call Easing of Minyan Rules 'Desperation,' " *New York Times,* September 12, 1973, p. 50.

147. Spiegel, "First Woman Cantor," p. 35.

148. Fishman, *The Jews of the United States,* p. 5.

149. José Faur, "Early Zionist Ideals Among Sephardim in the Nineteenth Century," *Judaism* 25 (Winter 1976): 54.

150. Ruth Birnbaum, "The Uniqueness of the Early Sephardic Community in America," *Judaism* 25 (Winter 1976): 48.

151. Sklare, *America's Jews,* p. 6.

152. Angel, "The Sephardim of the United States," p. 82.

153. Birnbaum, "The Uniqueness of the Early Sephardic Community in America," p. 53.

154. Birmingham, *The Grandees,* p. 19.

155. Angel, "The Sephardim of the United States," p. 79.

156. Victor D. Sanua, "A Study of the Adjustment of Sephardi Jews in the New York Metropolitan Area," *Jewish Journal of Sociology* 9 (June 1967): 25.

157. Angel, "The Sephardim of the United States," p. 84.

158. Joseph A. Hasson, "Jews in Arab Countries," *American Sephardi* 3 (September 1969): 94-102. Hasson notes, for example, that the Jewish community of Egypt numbered about 80,000 twenty years previously, but only about 2,500 in mid-1968. Libya had 40,000 Jews before World War II but about 5,000 by mid-1967. Presently, the number is less than 100. In Syria there were about 40,000 Jews in the 1940s but now only about 4,000. Iraq had 130,000 Jews at the end of the 1940s. By 1967 there were 3,000, with no accurate figures available since that time. Also see appropriate volumes of *American Jewish Yearbook.*

159. Hasson, "Jews in Arab Countries," p. 94. Also see Daniel J. Elazar, "Israel's Sephardim: The Myth of the 'Two Cultures,' " *American Sephardi* 1 (June 1967): 34-38, and Alan D. Corré, "The 60 Percent Minority," *The Sephardic World* 1 (Winter 1973): 18-20.

160. The numbers of those who came to the United States are difficult to establish exactly because many first went to Europe or Israel and later to the United States.

161. Hyman J. Campeas, "Questions to the Editor," *American Sephardi* 1 (December 1966): 17. Also see Seymour B. Liebman, "Cuban Jewish Community in South Florida," in Fine and Himmelfarb, *American Jewish Yearbook* (1969), pp. 238-246.

162. "Sephardic Heritage and Language Feared on Wane," *New York Times,* August 26, 1973, p. 35.

163. "Sephardic Studies Program," *American Sephardi* 4 (Autumn 1970): 119.

164. "The American Society of Sephardic Studies," *American Sephardi* 2 (1968): 13-15.

165. "Organization Set Up by Sephardic Jews to Promote Culture," *New York Times,* February 26, 1973, p. 22.

166. "Association Formed," *Yeshiva University's Sephardic Bulletin* (December 1973): 3.

1

SMALL-TOWN JEWS

Little attention has been given to small-town Jews—for they are few in numbers, isolated, and hence invisible to the larger community.[1] A few impressionistic articles about Jewish life in small towns were published in the 1940s and 1950s. *Commentary*, for instance, had several articles on American Jewish communities, including Shafter's "The Fleshpots of Maine" in 1949[2] and Levinger's "The Disappearing Small-Town Jew" in 1952.[3] Levinger concluded that village Jews were disappearing: "Their only chance for survival lies in the growth of their town, in its transformation into a suburb by the spread of a metropolitan area. . . . But then the town is no longer a village, and its Jews are no longer village Jews. . . . It seems that we shall soon have to write off most of the 150,000 village Jews from the roster of American Jewry."[4] Laser's "The Only Jewish Family in Town" appeared in 1959.[5] She wrote that she and her family were the first Jews many of the towns-people had known and that they were assumed to be experts on—and representatives of—Judaism. She noted that while the townspeople did not know Jewish customs and rituals and consequently made many faux pas, they were well meaning and respectful. Burston, somewhat whimsically, has suggested that small-town Gentiles are so open and "really anxious to learn" about Jews that it is difficult for a Jew to lose his Jewishness even if he came to the small town for that purpose.[6]

While these articles presented informal observations of small-town Jews, the first empirically based study was published in 1953. Shosteck's *Small-Town Jewry Tell Their Story* was based on a survey of United States and Canadian small-town Jewish communities that he had conducted for the B'nai B'rith Vocational Service.[7] He reported that the major advantages of small towns over big cities were perceived as being "(a) easier to make a living; (b) friendlier and more intimate social relations; and (c) more leisurely and quieter life," whereas the major disadvantages were perceived as being "(a) a lack of or limited social life; (b) inadequacy of Jewish religious facilities and leadership; (c) limited cultural and recreational facilities; and (d) fears of intermarriage and loss of Jewishness on part of children."[8] Shosteck noted, however, that the advantages were perceived as outweighing the disadvantages. Greenblum and Sklare also used the B'nai B'rith data for their article "The Attitude of the Small-Town Jew Toward His Community."[9] In 1957 *The Eternal Stranger* by Kaplan was published (it was based on his doctoral dissertation).[10] Studying three small-town Jewish communities in Louisiana, Kaplan disagreed with Shosteck's conclusion about the advantages of the small town. He stated that the Jews in these small towns "live out their lives, on the surface at least, as other people do, but they are never quite normal, never quite at ease, never completely secure. . . . They are, at best, divided beings, each 'a Hamlet forever soliloquizing—to be or not to be a Jew,' " and concluded that they were in danger of disappearing through assimilation.[11]

A major empirical study specifically oriented to analyzing small-town Jewry was Rose's 1959 doctoral dissertation, "Strangers in Their Midst: A Sociological Study of the Small-Town Jew and His Neighbors."[12] Schoenfeld's doctoral dissertation, "Small-Town Jewry: A Study in Identity and Integration," made another major empirical contribution in 1967.[13] The findings from these dissertations have been published in the form of several articles, and Rose's study—with a follow-up—was published as *Strangers in Their Midst*, in 1977.[14] In "Jewish Identity and Voting Patterns Among Small-Town Jews" Schoenfeld noted that those small-town Jews who perceived their identity in religious terms felt that what the townspeople thought of them was more important than what their fellow Jews thought of them and that they valued the "synagogue as a symbol of respectability."[15] He found that they were political conservatives seemingly as a consequence of "status concern and a desire for mobility."[16]

While Schoenfeld's study—based on twelve small communities in southern Illinois in 1967—concluded that Jews are "integrated" into small-town society, Rose's studies—based on twenty small communities in upstate New York—concluded that Jews are "strangers" in small-town society. All studies were methodologically good. The different conclusions may be due to differences in time, but one would not expect such large changes in these time periods. The differences could be due to location. Perhaps small Jewish communities close to large Jewish areas such as New York City really are different from Jewish communities in middle America. These questions point out once again the need for a comprehensive study.

Gordon's study of the 174 Jewish inhabitants of "Middletown" was published in 1964.[17] While this Jewish community would not be considered a small-town community by all researchers because it is located in a city of 70,000 inhabitants, the study provides valuable information on the interaction between a small Jewish community and the larger non-Jewish community. Elazar's "The Geography of American Jewish Communal Life," a knowledgeable review although not an empirical study, was published in 1973.[18] He noted that unless small-town Jews are "involved with a great metropolitan federation, they are able to maintain only the minimum in the way of Jewish institutions locally. Scattered widely among many small towns, they are tied together at most by a common fund raising system for overseas needs."[19]

An indication of more attention being given to small-town Jewry was the conclave, "The Jew in the Small Town," held in November 1973 in College Park, Maryland. Sponsored by B'nai B'rith, it was attended by 150 small-town delegates and resource persons. The winter 1974 issue of *Jewish Heritage* was devoted to results of the conclave.[20]

The selections in this section describe small-town Jews. First is an article by Brown from the special issue of *Jewish Heritage* that presents the situation as seen by the small-town Jew.[21] This is followed by Rose's article suggesting that small-town Jews are "strangers"[22] and by Schoenfeld's article suggesting that small-town Jews are "integrated."[23] Finally, Schoenfeld's article from the special issue of *Jewish Heritage* presents the "problems and potentials" for small-town Jews.[24]

NOTES

1. Leon H. Ginsberg, "Twice a Minority," *Jewish Heritage* 15 (Winter 1974): 9.

2. Toby Shafter, "The Fleshpots of Maine," *Commentary* 7 (January 1949): 60-67.

3. Lee J. Levinger, "The Disappearing Small-Town Jew," *Commentary* 14 (August 1952): 157-163.

4. Ibid., p. 163.

5. Louise Laser, "The Only Jewish Family in Town," *Commentary* 28 (December 1959): 489-496. Also see Alexander and Lillian Feinsilver, "Colchester's Yankee Jews: After Half a Century," *Commentary* 20 (June 1955): pp. 64-70.

6. Brad Burston, "Jews in Exotic Lands," *Davka* 5 (Summer 1975): 36-37, 47.

7. Robert Shosteck, *Small-Town Jewry Tell Their Story* (Washington, D.C.: B'nai B'rith Vocational Study, 1953).

8. Ibid., p. 4.

9. Joseph Greenblum and Marshall Sklare, "The Attitude of the Small-Town Jew Toward His Community," in Marshall Sklare, ed., *The Jews: Social Patterns of an American Group* (Glencoe, Ill.: The Free Press, 1958).

10. Benjamin Kaplan, *The Eternal Stranger: A Study of Jewish Life in the Small Community* (New York: Bookman Associates, 1957).

11. Ibid., p. 158.

12. Peter I. Rose, "Strangers in Their Midst: A Sociological Study of the Small-Town Jew and His Neighbors" (Ph.D. diss., Cornell University, 1959).

13. Eugen Schoenfeld, "Small-Town Jewry: A Study in Identity and Integration" (Ph.D. diss., Southern Illinois University, 1967).

14. Peter I. Rose, with the assistance of Liv Olson Pertzoff, *Strangers in Their Midst: Small-Town Jews and Their Neighbors* (Merrick, N.Y.: Richwood Publishing Co., 1977).

15. Eugen Schoenfeld, "Jewish Identity and Voting Patterns Among Small-Town Jews," *Sociological Quarterly* 9 (Spring 1968): 175. Also see his "Intermarriage and the Small-Town: The Jewish Case," *Journal of Marriage and the Family* 31 (February 1969): 61-64, and his "Small-Town Jews' Integration into Their Communities," *Rural Sociology* 35 (June 1970); 175-190. In the intermarriage article, Schoenfeld notes that despite a high rate of intermarriage in small towns, those small-town Jews who do intermarry prefer to maintain an active involvement in the Jewish community.

16. Schoenfeld, "Jewish Identity and Voting Patterns."

17. Whitney H. Gordon, "Jews and Gentiles in Middletown—1961," *American Jewish Archives* 18 (April 1966): 41-70.

18. Daniel J. Elazar, "The Geography of American Jewish Communal Life," *Congress Bi-Weekly* 40 (January 26, 1973): 10-13.

19. Ibid., p. 11.

20. *Jewish Heritage* is published by B'nai B'rith Adult Jewish Education, 1640 Rhode Island Avenue, N.W., Washington, D.C. 20036.

21. Susan Rebecca Brown, "As They See Themselves," *Jewish Heritage* 15 (Winter 1974): pp. 5-8.

22. Peter I. Rose, "Small-Town Jews and Their Neighbors in the United States," *Jewish Journal of Sociology* 3 (December 1961), pp. 174-191.

23. Schoenfeld, "Small-Town Jews' Integration," pp. 175-190.

24. Eugen Schoenfeld, "Problems and Potentials," *Jewish Heritage* 15 (Winter 1974): 14-18. The discrepancy between the "resident and stranger" findings continues. Ruxin, in a recent attempt to "reconcile this 'resident' or 'stranger' question in the context of one rural Jewish community" concluded that it is easy for the American Jew to become part of the American rural tradition "without sacrificing one iota of his Jewishness." See Robert H. Ruxin, "The Jewish Farmer and the Small-Town Jewish Community: Schoharie County, New York," *American Jewish Archives* 29 (April 1977), pp. 3-21.

AS THEY
SEE THEMSELVES

SUSAN REBECCA BROWN

Small-town Jews feel neglected and forgotten—or at best unappreciated. When the call went out to small-town Jews to attend a conference, they responded, "It's about time someone recognized us." And they prodeeded to the big city to make themselves heard and understood. They came to demonstrate the strength of Jewish commitment in their communities. Contrary to large-city opinion, many of them seemed to be saying, the small community often offers a richer Jewish life; there is a distinct desire to retain identity which in large cities is too often lost because it is taken for granted. They also came to meet each other and to sensitize the Jewish community to the pressing needs in their communities back home. For one burden particular to the small-town Jew is his feeling of isolation.

OUR ISOLATION . . .

"Ours is a diaspora within the diaspora," one of the delegates stated. Leonardtown and Lexington Park, Maryland, for example, together make up a Jewish community of slightly more than forty families. Jewish communities of this size can be found all across the country, sharing the same basic problem of numbers. "It's difficult to find your Jewishness with only a very few individuals in the community": variations of this theme were repeatedly heard. Too few for graded Hebrew school classes, too few for dating and marriage, too few for cultural and educational activities. Fellowship, community *ruach,* is vital to Jewish survival in these areas: but "too few, too few."

On the positive side, however, the very isolation sometimes offers a greater sense of responsibility for group survival, stretching beyond the periphery of the locale.

"Most important is our constant awareness that there is a world of Jews and that we are very much a part of the entire Jewish community of the world," was the way Michael Bienn, a graduate student from Brookings, South Dakota, summed it up. "The Conclave gave us an opportunity to be together and to find out that we're not alone," another affirmed.

Yet isolation in numbers is not the only problem. The forty Jewish families of Lexington Park and Leonardtown describe themselves as a "speck in the eye of their county," which has a population of about 50,000, mostly Catholic. Theirs is a kind of minority isolation which is simply not in the experience of metropolitan Jews. For example, one member of their community used the term "Judaism" in a radio interview, and the M.C. asked him the meaning of the word. In another town—in the Bible Belt area—one woman reported trying to put a paid ad in her local newspaper during the recent Israeli crisis only to be told that the available space had to be used for a story about raising ducks. There is underlying sentiment that this very visibility to Christians causes the Jew to become more visible to himself. "In the Bible Belt it's the Christians who shamed the Jews into being Jewish," one Southern Jew quipped. "They came to us and asked, 'You gave us the Bible but where are your houses of worship?' So the Jews built shuls and started activities there. . . ."

OUR IDENTITY . . .

There is adversity and there is isolation, but there is also the fact that Jews in many of these towns can trace their family histories back over several generations. They are proud of their continued Jewish identity and they are also proud of their position in the town: "We have a small but active Jewish community [Clarksburg, West Virginia] which dates back to 1875; it is highly respected because of our Jewish identity and because we've always been a credit to the entire community for the leadership we've provided to our city." In Lexington Park, Maryland, "several families go back before the turn of the century. They came down as shopkeepers and their descendants are still here and very definitely a part of this community. One gentleman, for example, was the Justice of the County Court here, the highest political position you could get." In fact, Jewish political power is more easily wielded in some of these towns because of their history of personal contact with the local congressmen and senators.[1]

Pride in their Jewish identity is very real. A conference delegate from Williamsport, Pa., tells us he feels the Jews in the small towns are *the* Jews: "The Jews in the big cities are so large in number they obviously make an impact, but if you take them one by one you'll find that two-thirds of them don't identify themselves with being Jewish. At the High Holidays they hire halls and theaters for places to pray and, obviously, if those Jews go to those places, they must not belong to anything, but in Williamsport you are identified—you belong and if you don't, you can't live there."

The strong sense of Jewish identity rooted in these towns, however, is as threatened by modern assimilation as is urban Jewry—only more so. If ten families out of forty "don't attend shul on Friday night in favor of the country club," the synagogue attendance is diminished. And what about intermarriage? "In a small town where there might be one or two Jewish boy or girls, this is a problem. We feel it's not right to forbid our children to date non-Jewish if it means staying at home." Apathy and defection of the young—these are problems which small-town Jews share with their urban brothers. Yet, in a certain sense, there is hope for retaining Jewish identity in the small town which is missing in the urban cities. That hope springs from the nature of the small town—its smallness and isolation, which tends to bring the community together and offers more opportunity for meaningful human contact, for fellowship. Some metropolitan areas are, in fact, trying to create this "small-town" atmosphere by forming *chavurot*, small intimate groups within their megalopolis synagogues.

A QUESTION OF SURVIVAL . . .

Small-towners are divided in their opinion as to whether they will survive. On hearing about the small-town conclave, several wrote and asked why B'nai B'rith is "wasting its money" on Jewish communities that are dying out. One Southerner predicts that "in the next twenty-five years there will be small towns without Jews in the South." On the other hand, there are communities reporting growth: Springfield, Missouri, gained twelve Jewish families, bringing their number up to seventy-five; the two towns in Maryland report that while "their numbers have gone up and down tremendously over the last twenty years"—sometimes being left with barely a minyan—they are at an all-time high now and, what is more, over half the members are under forty. This optimism is documented by demographic experts gathered recently to discuss "The Future of the Small Town": "The dying American small town, once the backbone of the new nation and more recently the heralded symbol of the death of our national innocence, may not be dying at all," they report. "While the suburbs continue to be the place most Americans say they want to live, small towns are next—and are the clear favorite for bringing up children."[2]

Small-town Jews are aware of the advantages of their lifestyle. "Big-city people are at first amused at the provincialism of the town," they say, "but if they stick it out, they wouldn't go back to the city." They claim a "greater opportunity to become actively involved in Jewish life, to play a vital role." So the question they ask themselves is: "How can we attract young people who are fed up with problems of ecology, crime, with all the things that you have in abundance in the big cities—how do we attract these young people who want to live a cleaner, a more peaceful, happier and healthier life, to come to us? We need Jewish doctors, teachers, rabbis—how can we get them to join us? Job opportunity may be one answer, and several communities have already begun an aggressive campaign to attract members through special employment incentives. Charleston actually placed an advertisement in the Anglo-Jewish press listing the attractions of "living in the hollows of West Virginia."

The advantages of the small-town Jewish community given, the problems still remain and must be faced, not only by those who live there but by urban Jews as well. All Jews have a tremendous stake in the preservation of these communities; their quality of life and their quality of *Jewish* life is vital to our survival.

But when all is said and done, the future of small-town Jews is dependent on their own will to survive. That such a spirit does exist is evidenced by the words of Armand J. Cohodes, a delegate from Michigan City, Indiana, who in reporting back to his own community, summed up the mood of most conference delegates:

> We must keep the Jewish community going. We must decide among our-
> selves whether we want a Jewish community or we don't. If we don't,
> then let's close up this temple and sell. It would probably make a nice
> discount store or gasoline station. But if we don't want to close it for lack
> of feeling and lack of attendance and lack of involvement, then let's do
> something about it. . . . Judaism is not all religion, it is not all fundraising,
> and it is not all putting up buildings. It is a feeling and a desire, and it is a
> tradition, and it is a way of life. We really are something special. So we
> have to work together to keep this something special going. Besides, no
> one has shown us a better way of life than a Jewish life.[3]

NOTES

1. See Herman Edelsberg, "The Small Town in Politics," pp. 56 ff.

2. *The New York Times,* November 6, 1973.

3. A full text of Mr. Cohodes' report together with specific proposals is available on request. [Write B'nai B'rith Program Division, 1640 Rhode Island Avenue, Washington, D.C. 20036.]

SMALL-TOWN JEWS
AND THEIR NEIGHBORS
IN THE UNITED STATES

PETER I. ROSE

For many years social scientists and historians have been trying to piece together a composite portrait of American Judaism. Owing to their predominant pattern of city residence, research has been focused on the urban dwelling Jews; and the Jews of the United States have been characterized as a metropolitan people. There is, however, a scattered minority of American Jews living in little hamlets and rural villages who do not fully fit this urban image. Such people do not reside in old style ghettos, in ethnic neighborhoods, or in modern homogeneous suburbs. Unlike their urban co-religionists, they are not members of on-going Jewish communities. They are strangers in alien territory.

Critical examination of Jewish life in the small community would seen to be a logical extension of research in the study of American Judaism and the nature of Jewish-Gentile relations. Yet, while the literature offers a wealth of information about the urban Jew in America, there is a dearth of published material about his "country cousin." And what there is is limited to sketchy life histories, journalistic descriptions, and anecdotal recollections of the experiences of individuals who have lived in, visited, or passed through little villages appearing in such publications as *Midstream, Commentary,* and *Congress Weekly.*[1]

It was, therefore, in an attempt to add to the general literature on Jewish life on the American scene, to assess Jewish-Gentile relations in this neglected setting, and to re-examine the ubiquitous concept of "marginal man" that an extensive study of the small-town Jews of New York State was conducted in 1958.[2] Because the small-town Jew is so often cast in the role of being an ambassador of "his people" to the Gentiles, a parallel study was simultaneously carried out with non-Jewish small-towners also living in upstate New York.

Data were gathered to seek answers to several questions. To what extent do group traditions persist in cases of relative isolation? Does identification wane when unsupported by fellow members of one's own group? How intensive are relationships between the stranger and the world in which he has chosen to live? What kinds of adjustments does he have to make? And, finally, to what extent does interpersonal contact with an isolated minority member influence the stereotypic conceptions and misconceptions held by the majority group members about him?

THE RESEARCH DESIGN

Investigation was confined to one particular area of the country: "rural" New York State. Operationally, "rural communities" and "small-town Jews" were defined as follows:

> Rural communities are those communities with fewer than 10,000 permanent residents, in non-metropolitan counties of New York State, excluding all towns in the Catskill mountain region, in Westchester county. and on Long Island.
> Small-town Jews are persons identifying themselves as being Jewish living in "rural communities" having 10 or fewer Jewish families.

The first of the two studies was an attempt to document and analyze the background, beliefs, and behavior of small-town Jews and to study and record their attitudes relating to the communities where they reside. We were particularly anxious to explore the areas of religiosity, community satisfaction, associations, and patterns of socialization.

Respondents were located through initial contact with twenty individuals who were known to the writer; each lived in a small town in one of twenty different counties. These persons provided the names of all the Jews they knew who fit the criteria established for designating "small-town Jews." These persons, in turn, supplied additional names. This technique, called "pyramiding," provided 180 names in two weeks.

Of the 180 names twenty names were randomly selected; and these individuals and their families, together with the original key informants, were personally interviewed in the Spring of 1958.

The 160 in the remaining group were mailed detailed questionaires which asked a number of questions about origins, family life, satisfaction with small-town living, religious beliefs and practices, organizational affiliations, and attitudes about their relative isolation.

In *every* instance—whether in the interview setting or in responding to the survey —respondents were told that research was being conducted on Jews living in small towns and that *their* help was needed to tell *their* story accurately. In no cases did those to be personally interviewed refuse to co-operate; and in the case of the mail survey, 80 percent responded.[3]

The second study was designed to gather information on the impressions and attitudes of small-town community leaders about themselves and their images and attitudes about minority groups. Data were collected on the relationship between generalized prejudices and attitudes toward Jews, Negroes, and "foreigners"; the extent to which isolated Jewish persons might influence stereotypes; and the nature of interpersonal contact and socialization between Gentiles and Jews in rural communities.

The names of community leaders were obtained by writing to the mayor or clerk of each village selected and asking that a form designating 25 statuses of leadership— in business, the professions, in government and politics, in education and social service, and in agriculture—be filled out with the appropriate names and returned.

Twenty towns were included in this second survey. All had fewer than 5,000 residents. Ten towns had from one to three Jewish families; the remaining group had *none.*

In all, 315 questionnaires which complemented those sent to Jewish participants were mailed. With two follow-up appeals a total of 60 per cent were returned.[4]

JEWISH LIFE IN THE RURAL COMMUNITY

Dealers and Doctors

Almost to a man the Jews of New York's rural areas are outsiders and not native sons. Most are urban-emigrants who settled in small towns after having spent the early part of their lives in American or European cities. Only 4 per cent were born in the communities where they now live. Of the remaining majority half were born in one of the large American metropolitan centers and 12 per cent in middle-sized cities in the United States. Thirty per cent were born in Europe, many of them refugees from Nazi-dominated Germany and Austria.

How did these urban Jews happen to settle in such hamlets? Two-thirds came for business reasons. These respondents are, in the main, second generation East European immigrants. Many began their careers as travelling salesmen and peddlers who settled down and started a little general store in one of the towns along the circuit. Here they remained and here they prospered.

In addition to these "dealers," the other major group are refugee physicians who fled to America only to find it difficult to establish practices in urban areas. A large number of such doctors were placed in small towns by refugee agencies or professional groups..

Besides these two major groups, there are several lawyers, teachers, insurance brokers, cattle dealers, and farmers to be found within the sample group.

When asked to place themselves into the upper, upper middle, lower middle, or working class, 74 per cent marked "upper middle." Only three respondents felt they were "working class": two teachers and one tenant farmer. It was from the ranks of the professional people that the greatest percentage of "upper class" self-ratings came.

The high self-evaluation of socio-economic status is reflected in the relatively high incomes of the small-town Jews. In response to the question "Roughly, what was the total income for your family last year?" 30 per cent said their income exceeded $20,000, 37 per cent gave $10,000-$20,000, 30 per cent $5,000-$10,000, and only 3 per cent indicated that they made less than $5,000 per annum.

Owing to the large proportion of professional Jews in the sample (36 per cent), it is not surprising to find a high level of education. Seventy per cent of those questioned hold at least a Bachelor of Arts degree or its European equivalent. The small-town Jews indicated, however, that only 11 per cent of their parents had college diplomas and 56 per cent said that their parents had gone to the eighth grade or less. As for their own children, nine out of ten parents in the sample indicated that one or more of their children would (or did) obtain at least a college degree.

When asked about their political affiliations 27 per cent said they consider themselves Republicans "in most political matters"; 29 per cent are Democrats and the rest marked "independent." However, it is interesting to note that a number of "Republicans" wrote in the margin of the questionnaire saying that they were "registered Republicans whose loyalty lies in the Democratic camp."

Finally, respondents were asked the following question: "Basically, do you consider yourself more a rural person or more an urban person?" Two-thirds of the group said "urban."

Once a Jew . . .

Eighty-six per cent of the small-town Jews placed themselves in some "Jewish" category: orthodox, conservative or reform. *All* expressed some feeling of religious and/or cultural identity with Judaism. Those who said they did not fit into any of the three categories are not apostates as their response to this particular query might appear to suggest. Rather they tended to qualify their answers with statements like: "I'm a liberal Jew," "My family are ethical Jews," or "We're Jews, that's all."

Three-fourths said they belonged to some religious congregation. At the same time almost all persons said they "rarely" or "never" attend religious services since the synagogue to which they belong is too far away. (Estimates ranged from 15 to 100 miles.)

While they are too isolated to establish some form of Jewish communal existence, many keep traditional observances at home. For example, over half celebrate the Passover holidays, 25 per cent never serve bacon or ham, and 15 per cent maintain strictly kosher homes, importing meat from distant cities. The attempt to maintain the traditions of the faith is found in both the "immigrant" and "refugee" groups. The latter, however, is less likely to display Jewish and Israeli artifacts in the home.

The deep-seated sense of Jewish-identification is evident in the following random excerpts from several interviews:

> I came to this community from New York. There I was raised in a real ghetto. All my friends and associates were Jews. I went to *heder,* to *shul,* etc., like everybody else. This was our way of life. Although I wanted to get out of the city and away from the ghetto, I never wanted to forget I was a Jew. This is my fate and I try to live up to it in every way.

Another respondent phrased it this way:

> Although I was born in the city I have lived in a small community practically all of my life. Here there are few Jewish families, but when you get right down to it I'm sure I prefer being with people of my own religion. I guess being a Jew is in my blood and in my soul.

And a third:

> Most people like us are city-folk living in rural areas. While our homes are here, our roots are somewhere else. . . . We bring the past with us when we go into upstate communities like this. Part of this past is our religion. We see ourselves as Jews and so does the community. . . .

All told, most small-town Jews maintain some affective connection with their religion even when they leave the geographic boundaries of the urban Jewish community.

A housewife summed up the expressions of many when she said:

> We're not what one might call observant Jews. Yet there are certain traditions we like to keep. We have a *mezuzah* in the doorway and a *menorah* on the mantle. We celebrate some of the holidays like the High Holy Days and Passover. We light the *Shabbas* candles and things like that. And, I must say I like a good piece of *gefilte* fish when I can get it. Yet we eat pork, work on Saturday . . . why sometimes I even go to Midnight Mass with my friends.

"Irrespective of whether you follow religious practices or attend synagogue, do you consider yourself a religious person?" Each person answered this question by placing himself somewhere along a continuum of "very religious" to "not religious at all." Five per cent considered themselves "very religious," while 62 per cent felt that they were "moderately" so. Thirty-six per cent said "somewhat religious" and 7 per cent said they were "not religious at all."

A strikingly high correlation appears when one compares the degree to which a person considers himself religious with the extent to which he practices religious observances, and with the nature of affiliation, that is, whether orthodox, conservative, or reform. Taking these three items together we constructed the Religiosity Scale[5] which allowed us to simplify analysis by using this single measure or "traditional" religiousness. Respondents were broken into three groups: high, medium, and low on religiosity.

In communities having several Jewish families the presence of co-religionists tends to reinforce religious identity and to support religious practices. Table I graphically illustrates the fact that in towns with more Jews, religiosity is higher among Jewish respondents.

Table 1

Religiosity and the Number of Jews

Religiosity	Number of Jewish Families in Town			
	1	2	3-5	6-10
	%	%	%	%
Low	66	62	59	42
Medium	27	32	26	26
High	7	6	15	32
	100	100	100	100
	(31)	(21)	(44)	(24)

In addition to this demographic factor it was found that religiosity is correlated with several background factors. Those highest in socio-economic status (by self-rating and income) are lowest in religiosity. In relation to occupation, those in the medical arts (mainly of the refugee group) are most apt to be low in this expression of religiousness, while those in agriculture tend to be the highest. This was borne out in the interviews. We spoke to the daughter of an immigrant from Russia, a man who became a cattle-dealer in a small upstate community where he raised his family She related:

> Our religion was very important to us. We sang Hebrew songs and spoke Yiddish in the house. I couldn't speak English until I first went to school.

. . . To my father the family was the core of Jewish life and so we learned about Jews and our religion through discussions at home, through books, through stories. We were always very Jewish.

And a Jewish farmer had this to say:

It's funny, but though we're really out of touch with Jews we're the ones who try to keep up the traditions. . . . We think of ourselves as more Orthodox than anything. You know, the Gentile farmers around us are pretty religious too. If you can't go to church, then you have to bring religion into the home.

Furthermore, we found that small-town Jews who are low in religiosity are more apt to see themselves as more "urban" than "rural" even though these very people live, most often, in the tiniest hamlets. And those low in religiosity tend to feel Gentile members of the community consider them "different from" rather than "typical of" most Jews while those highly religious stress the reverse; they feel non-Jews think they are typical of Jewish people.

Although respondents were asked the difficult question of telling how they felt others saw them, it seems that they answered mainly in terms of their own self-images. Among those who said they felt they were viewed as "different" the following kinds of reasons were given: "don't conform to stereotypes," "better assimilated," "differ in physical features," "gentler and less crude," "quieter." Most of the adjectives were related to personal demeanor. Moreover, this group felt that Gentiles considered them as "unique" Jews and suggested that they were more likely to be seen as exceptions to commonly held beliefs.

Those who felt they were seen as "typical" tended to give quite opposite reasons which were related to *positive* stereotypic images. "I'm wealthy and well-educated," "I still maintain the traditions and practices of Judaism," "have a Jewish name." In other words, these people felt they were viewed as recognizably Jewish, and most expressed the belief that their behavior was, for Gentiles, typical of Jews.

Ambassadors to the Gentiles

Being strangers in a Gentile world, many respondents appear to be more conscious of being Jewish than do their urban cousins who live in the centers of ethnic communities. In one form or other *every* respondent indicated that there are times when he is called upon to represent *the Jews*. Here, as several stated, they are "ambassadors to the *goyim*." Most often this occurs when interfaith functions are held in the community. There the local priest and minister are accompanied by the Jewish merchant to "give balance to the program."

Frequently the Jew serves as a "representative of his people" in less formal settings. He is called upon to give "the Jewish point of view" or to explain why Jews do one thing and not another. When the townsfolk turn to the Jews for information, the respondents related that they often feel a deep sense of responsibility and of inadequacy.

For example, one man told me:

> You know, we're curiosities around town. The people always heard about Jews but never met one. Then we appeared. Real live Jews. After some hesitancy they began to ask us all kinds of questions. . . . Often I wished I could answer all of them. . . .

A housewife allowed:

> My children have been asked to explain about *Chanukah*, to tell the story of Moses, to explain what the *Mogen David* is. They wanted to know and my kids were the likely ones to ask.

And a merchant had this to say:

> "I can't understand it. As kids we learned that the Jews killed Christ. Tell me, [respondent's name]," he says to me, "is it true?" As a Jew, and the only one this guy ever knew personally, I'm supposed to have all the answers.

Small-town Jews were asked: "Are you most conscious of being Jewish when you are with other Jewish people or when you are among non-Jews?" Those who were most conscious of being Jewish when with non-Jews were those most isolated, that is, those in small communities having few, if any, other Jewish residents. "Religious or not," said one real isolate, "we're curiosities around here."

Friends among Neighbors

In small towns Jews find that there are few limitations on formal and informal social participation and interaction. All but 17 per cent indicated that they were members of some mixed organization. Over 45 per cent said they belonged to professional, business, and social groups. In addition, one-third are members of fraternal orders like the Masons or Elks.

When asked which organization (national or local) gave them the most satisfaction, almost every respondent listed some local (thereby non-Jewish) group. A druggist had this to say:

> I think I've been a member of every damn organization in this town. From member of the volunteer firemen to president of the school board. Discrimination? Not in any organizations, that's for sure.

And the owner of a small chain of department stores said:

> This is my community. These are my people in many more ways than Jews
> are. After all, our neighbors are friendly, all the organizations accept us,
> so we make friends here. This is home. When I join an organization they
> know they're taking in a Jew but it doesn't make any difference. . . . I've
> been President of Rotary, on the Chamber of Commerce, a member of
> the Masonic Lodge, and Secretary of the Rod and Gun Club.

This reflects the attitudes of most people interviewed.

We asked questions about discrimination against Jews. Eighty-seven per cent
said they could not think of any community organizations they would not wish
to join because of antisemitic feeling. In addition, 81 per cent said they knew of
no discrimination of any kind being practiced in their communities.

However, it is important to note that while most say they personally have not
experienced antisemitism, many are of the opinion that they are being exempted
from commonly held stereotypes about Jews. Many respondents feel that latent
antisemitism exists among some community members, but that Gentiles view *them*
as being "different from other Jews." Fortunately we are able to compare these
expressions with those of non-Jews. In the second study we found that what the
Jews feel as the true pulse of community sentiment is not always the reality of
the attitudes of Gentiles.

In predicting what we would find along the lines of socializing between Jews
and non-Jews we hypothesized that close proximity to Gentile neighbors and the
lack of opportunity to have day-to-day contact with members of a Jewish community would lead to a degree of intimate interfaith socializing unparalled in
larger communities. The majority of persons who were interviewed substantiated
this prediction. For example:

> Everyone has close friends. In the city Jewish people tend to cling to-
> gether. But in the rural village, when you are a minority of one, you as-
> sociate completely with Gentiles. While it's rare in the city for Jews and
> Gentiles to be invited to one another's home for informal visiting, this
> is an everyday occurrence in the little community.

In the small town Jews are more than participants in formal functions. In most
instances they are an integral part of the social life of their towns. For the adults
this includes such activities as parties, trips, dances, bridge clubs, and just plain
"dropping in." For the children this often means playing together, going to parties,
and frequent instances of dating.

In over 50 per cent of all cases small-town Jews designated a Gentile person as
their closest friend. Yet, 30 per cent said they feel "more comfortable" with Jews
than with non-Jews, especially in social situations. Those highest on religiosity,
identifying most strongly with traditional Judaism, are more apt to feel this way.

And the Next Generation

That the strength of identification with Judaism plays a major role in determining patterns of and feelings about informal socializing with Gentiles becomes even clearer when we examine the attitudes of Jewish parents toward their children. Since 90 per cent of our respondents are parents, we were able to get reactions to a number of questions; reactions which indicate a firm conviction that Jewish identity should not only be maintained but intensified. Thus, while a high degree of informal interaction is practiced, the small-town Jews, like their urban co-religionists, are anxious for their children to keep the faith and marry Jews. As a result they send them to Jewish summer camps and, when they are through with high school, encourage them to attend large, metropolitan universities. And, although they themselves are satisfied with rural living, few expect their children to return to the small town after graduation.

Here is the opinion of a retired business man:

> We've lived here ever since the children—I have three—were born. They grew up among Gentile people. I don't think they ever met another Jew until they were fifteen or sixteen. In no case were they ever discriminated against. My son was captain of the basketball team and played ball for the local Alter Boys Baseball Club. My daughters always went around with local kids and dated boys from school. I can't say I was happy about this, but I didn't try to stop them. Yet, despite a number of crushes on certain fellows, they never got real serious about any of them. . . . When they graduated from high school they all went to college in the city. There they met Jewish people. . . . I'm really happy that my children all married Jews. It's easier that way.

It seems safe to say that the small-town Jew is similar to the city-dwelling Jew to the extent that he wants his children to remain Jews. He is firmly opposed to inter-faith marriage. To him this represents either the confrontation of too many social problems or alienation from Judaism; both are considered highly undesirable. Complete assimilation into the Christian community is not the goal of the American Jew. This means giving up a part of himself, a part that sometimes even he cannot explain. Rather, the Jew in New York and "East Nothing" wants to remain a hyphenated American, sharing the "best of both." No better example of this is to be found than in the rural hamlet.

The Best of Both

Stonequist, Park and others have characterized the Jew as a disturbed marginal man,[6] an eternal stranger[7] unable to reconcile the traditions of his people with the counter-forces of the majority world; "one whom fate has condemned to live in two societies and in two, not merely different, but antagonistic cultures."[8] One might expect to find ample support for such a definition among the small-town Jews who live away from the mainstream of Jewish life. Yet, rather than being on the periphery of two cultures, the ex-urban Jew seems to have internalized the best of each. He is more a part of his community than he is apart from it. He is far more assimilated to the Gentile milieu than his urban cousin. But, as indicated above, he remains a Jew.

While he strongly identifies with fellow Jews—a reference group he can "feel" rather than "touch"—and in many ways expresses a feeling of kinship with his people, he has adapted himself to the folkways of the small town in a variety of ways. He enjoys the advantages of sharing two "cups of life" and, in a word, is bi-cultural. This duality (rather than marginality) causes the majority of respondents to come to agreement with one who stated:

> You see, we feel we have the best of both . . . Judaism with all its tra-
> dition, its stress on culture, on learning, on freedom. . . . And the fact
> that we live in a small town with nice people and good, clean air. . . . We
> wouldn't trade either for the world.

All told, those who can reconcile the past with the present find that they can share a little of each of their different cultures. Those who find satisfaction in the small community generally seem to agree with one woman who said:

> It's funny. I never thought a city girl like me would like small-town
> living. But I've changed. I honestly enjoy the lack of sophistication at
> Home Bureau meetings, the knock-down-drag-out fights at school meet-
> ings, the gossip that never escapes anyone. I love the scenery, the sim-
> plicity, and the lack of formality here. Sometimes I miss the city. A
> good play, a concert, a corned beef sandwich! But we get away each
> year and spend a few days in New York. After about three days I've
> had enough. I'm ready for home. I want to go back to . . .

And with a lawyer originally from New York City:

> I guess having been raised in the city makes you appreciate a com-
> munity such as this even more than if you were born here. It's just nice
> not to have to be on the go all the time. . . . There was a time when I
> would have laughed if somebody suggested that I might wind up in the
> sticks. But here I am and loving every minute of it. People accept you
> for what you are, not who you are. . . .

Naturally those who gave such enthusiastic testimonials for small-town living were among the most satisfied with their lives in the rural community. Yet only

14 percent of all respondents expressed true dissatisfaction. Two main reasons were most frequently given for disliking the small town. First, there was general dissatisfaction with rural living. "This town is too provincial for me." "Progress is nil. I just wish we could get out." "I'd take the impersonality of the city any day over the gossipy closeness of this burg." The second kind of dissatisfaction related to isolation from other Jews. "Frankly I would be much happier if we could be with Jews more often." "My wife is not happy here. She'd much rather be some place where she can pick up the phone and talk to the girls. We miss Jewish contacts." "If I had it to do over again, I surely wouldn't move out to the sticks. I'd rather be where there are more Jewish people."

Why do they not move out? The answer is provided by a merchant:

> We always plan to leave here for a larger community. My business keeps me here, as it furnishes me with a good income. If I could leave, I would. The small town is too backward for me.

It must be remembered that the dissatisfied residents are deviant cases. The majority of respondents express some degree of satisfaction with their communities. They were either "very satisfied" (50 percent) or "somewhat satisfied"(36 percent).

Satisfaction seems to depend upon whether or not town people are cordial and accepting of strangers. In most cases isolated Jews are, as several interviewees put it, "curiosities and strangers." Generally the burden is on the Jew himself; at least he thinks so. If he accepts the ways of the rural village in which he resides, that is, if he joins the local lodge, contributes to the funds, buys his food and some clothing in town, takes an interest in community affairs, he is "in." According to a storekeeper:

> The secret of a Jew living in a small town—happily—is to assimilate as soon as possible—but, always to remember he's a Jew.

And a doctor said:

> In small rural towns one is accepted for what he is. Religion plays a minor fact in your being accepted. If one is honest and equitable in his dealings with others, you are placed in the forefront of things. . . .

Minority Adjustment

The brief descriptions of the findings of our study of Jewish life in the small town are but excerpts from the original report. Yet it is hoped they shed some illumination on the life of the isolated member of one minority group and indicate the role of the ethnic ambassador. From this first study several generalizations are suggested. (1) Those who leave the confines of the ghetto or ethnic community are frequently anxious to seek economic and social betterment, to find acceptance in the new setting without loss of ethnic identity. (2) Once the minority member enters the new "alien" situation, he finds himself in the position of representing his "people" to the community at large. As a stranger his ethnic identity becomes particularly salient to the community and to himself. More often than not, consciousness of minority membership increases when one becomes an isolate. (3) The minority member who lives in the milieu of the majority has infinitely greater opportunity to adapt himself to the folkways of the dominant group than does one who lives in the middle of the ethnic community.

OPINIONS OF COMMUNITY LEADERS

For that part of the research which was designed to tap the attitudes of the majority group we chose to get reactions of community leaders. Such individuals were selected because it was felt that they would have the greatest opportunity to have contact with the widest number of persons in their towns. In addition, being in positions of formal leadership in such small villages (average population 2,500) meant that these same persons would most likely play informal leadership roles as well; they would be the pace-setters for community opinion. It also seemed logical to assume that a higher percentage of community leaders would have closer contact with Jews than rank and file citizens.

Many of the same kinds of questions used in the first section of the study were asked of respondents in the second. In addition, a number of items referred directly or indirectly to attitudes about Jews and other minority group members.

Piecing together the varied comments of several different Gentile opinion leaders, all of whom live in one village in central New York State, we have a rough image of "native" small-towners, their attitudes toward the community, general prejudice, and the effects of contact with minority representatives.

> I have lived in this town all my life. . . . I feel that in the small, rural community people are friendly to one another. A common greeting is "Hello Joe". . . . truly a warm feeling, one of belonging. . . . I love it here.
>
> Well, I'm an American, since before the War of 1812. I guess I feel this makes me a little better. I'm not prejudiced. I just prefer to be with my own kind and I'm sure they'd [Jews, Negroes, and foreigners] prefer to mix together too. . . .
>
> There are only two Jewish families here and they are highly regarded— one man is a business man. The other is a very fine attorney. No comparison with New York City Jews. They're different. . . .
>
> I run a store and come into contact with salesmen of different races. I have three Jewish salesmen, all three are good men. There is none of this pushing and trying to sell you stuff you don't need like in the city. . . .

The Natives

While the small-town Jew is generally an outsider who migrated to the rural communtiy, most of the Gentile respondents were born and raised in their towns or in similar villages. Only one-fifth of the total group were born in cities and a mere 2 per cent were born abroad. Like the Jews, some who came from outside came for business reasons. But unlike the Jews, most "newcomers" settled down in small towns because of marriage to a community member, because of cheaper housing, or for health reasons.

These people are mainly of old "Yankee" stock with 38 per cent claiming that their families—that is, their father's father's family—came to America before 1800. Members of this group tend to call themselves "American," "Scotch-Irish," or "Holland-Dutch" in their self-descriptions. Those whose families immigrated during the nineteenth century are more apt to be of German or Irish descent. The most recent group are most often of Italian origins.

The occupations of these respondents are widely varied, ranging from farmers to bankers, from ministers to mill-hands. Like the Jewish small-towners, most place themselves in the upper middle class. Their average annual family income is, however, half of that of the Jewish respondents, i.e. $7,500. Half of the Gentile participants are self-employed as compared with 80 per cent of the Jewish group.

Thirty-nine per cent of the Gentiles said they had a college education or had gone beyond college; 64 per cent had at least a high school education. Like the Jews they too have high aspirations for their children. Seventy-six per cent of these persons are Protestant (the remainder Catholic); two-thirds are Republicans; and two out of every three see themselves as more "rural" than "urban."

When asked about satisfaction with their communities the most typical response was "This is home." By and large the respondents were highly satisfied with their communities (68 per cent) and an additional one-fourth expressed moderate satisfaction. For this group community satisfaction is dependent upon such variables as length of residence, the ties one has to one's home town, and the progressiveness of the community.

When asked for comments a highly satisfied respondent wrote:

> This is a small, rural, closely knit community where newcomers have to make every effort to become an insider. The effort, however, I feel is well worth it. We are not too far from a large city (but far enough to be away from the clatter), our school is excellent and religious relations in this community are excellent. While this town is pretty conservative, I find a great deal of satisfaction in the slow, easy-going pace. I've lived here since I was a boy and wouldn't leave for anything.

For contrast here is the comment of a dissatisfied resident of the *same* community.

Passivity, complacency and a sheer lack of or neglect of economic intellect in this community has been responsible for the apparent degeneration of atmosphere and attitude in all things related to even a reasonable degree of progress. This, of course, offers nothing of value to the high school generation. It offers nothing to newcomers. All in all, a community which was once great is slowly but most certainly annihilating itself.

Ethnocentrism and "The Good Old Days"

In some instances dissatisfaction with one's town is unrelated to whether the community is a good place to live and work or not; rather it seems to depend upon the image of what the town itself should be (or what it might have been) and what it has become.

Although the lack of change or progress appeared the most significant factor for dissatisfaction with community life, there were some residents who have *become* dissatisfied precisely because changes have occurred. Not the least of these changes is the influx of outsiders to a number of small towns. In almost every village included in our sample there were two or three respondents who longed for the old days, who resented the intrusion of newcomers, who could not accept change as progress.

Several examples serve to illustrate their attitudes:

I am sure foreign people make a mistake in keeping customs of their own land alive and featured in this country. If this country meets their expectations, they should forget the folklore of Europe, St. Patrick's Day Parades, German Days, and get behind American things. If they can't do this they should be returned to the land they love. This country is supposed to be the world's melting pot. If they won't melt, they should not belong.

We have a lot of foreigners here. . . . They're all right, keep in their own place, go to their own church. But I must say it isn't really the same any more. This town has a great heritage, it was settled before the Revolution. . . . I don't mean to imply that I am prejudiced or that I dislike foreigners. We all have our place in this great country of ours. I just think it a shame that outsiders like those who live here, have to keep their old ways. It makes it harder for them to be accepted.

These persons were among a small group of respondents (21 per cent) who agreed with the following statement: "This country would be better off if there were not so many foreigners here." They were also in agreement with "Religions which preach unwholesome ideas should be suppressed," as were 56 per cent of the sample group; and with the statement "Americans must be on guard against the power of the Catholic church," with which one-quarter of all respondents also agreed.

Such attitudes indicate ethnocentric thinking. A Scale of Ethnocentrism[9] based upon responses to the first two questions cited above and one which stated "Some people say that most people can be trusted. Others say you can't be too careful in your dealings with people. How do you feel about it?" was used to assess general prejudice.

A high degree of ethnocentrism is, in most cases, highly correlated with poor paying jobs, low educational attainment, small-town origins, occupations involving working with "things" rather than "people," and "old family" status. If one is ethnocentric, one tends to be more "success-oriented" and less apt to want to be "independent." The highly ethnocentric individual is more likely to indicate a need to belong and express a strong desire to be accepted by others. Those who see them selves as being *upper class* and those who feel they belong to the *working class* are higher in their distaste for outsiders than "middle class" individuals. Little differenc is found between Catholics and Protestants or along political lines.

Does the opportunity to interact with minority members affect the general prejudice expressed by the small-town Gentile? Without a panal study over time it is virtually impossible to answer this query. However, the data do indicate that contact is related to the amount of generalized ethnocentrism one feels, but *only* when this contact is close enough to permit social interaction to occur. As will be noted in Table 2, those who have close association with Jews and Negroes have a much lower degree of ethnocentrism than those who rarely communicate with members of these two groups or have no contact in the community at all.

Attitudes towards Jews and the "Exemption Mechanism"

Prejudice against Jews is more prevalent in the attitudes of the Gentiles (at least among community leaders) than the Jews themselves imagine. Many of the community leaders subscribe to traditional stereotypes about Jews. For instance, 83 per cent agree with the statement "Jews tend to be more money-minded than most people"; 80 per cent agree that "Jews tend to be shrewder business men than most people"; and 77 per cent agree that "Jews tend to be more aggressive than most people." These figures are *not* significantly altered when the nature of contact—"none," "impersonal," "personal"—is used as a control.

Thus most of the respondents feel that Jews in general possess these "characteristic traits." Whether or not a Jew lives in town is not crucial for changes in stereotyping. Merely buying in a "Jewish store" or visiting a Jewish physician may only perpetuate generalized images of Jews. Many of the small-town Jews in New York State do, in fact, fulfill several of the classic stereotypes, especially for those who never get to know them individually. As a group, they are frequently in business. They are more liberal politically. They do tend to possess an urbane demeanor and are thus natural recipients of the traditional suspicions of "city slickers." And their

Table 2

Ethnocentrism and the Nature of Contact with Jews and Negroes Living in the Community

Degree of Ethnocentrism	Jews			Negroes		
	NO CONTACT[a]	IMPERSONAL CONTACT[b]	PERSONAL CONTACT[c]	NO CONTACT[a]	IMPERSONAL CONTACT[b]	PERSONAL CONTACT[c]
	%	%	%	%	%	%
High	32	33	10	30	50	13
Medium	34	32	36	36	14	31
Low	34	35	54	34	36	56
	100	100	100	100	100	100
	(88)	(46)	(39)	(124)	(14)	(39)

[a]"No Contact" means that respondents say there are no members of this group living in their community and also includes those who "don't know" whether or not the group is represented in their town.

[b]"Impersonal Contact" refers to respondents who say they know members of this group but only "to speak to" or someone they "see around."

[c]"Personal Contact" refers to respondents who say they know members of this group who call *them* by their first names, to whom they can say what they really think, or close friends with whom they can discuss confidential matters.

children, being strongly motivated, do tend to do especially well in school. Here is ample support for the "kernel of truth" hypothesis.

Yet expressions of attitudes and actual behavior are sometimes contradictory. Close examination of the data disclosed the fact that when interaction takes place at an *equal status* level, community leaders, even those with negative images of Jews as a group, tend to accept individual Jews as exceptions to the rule. They see them as being "different."

In general, respondents who have personal and intimate contact with local Jews view their close acquaintances as less clannish, quieter, less flashy, and less radical than they imagine Jews to be. Here are three excerpts of statements appearing on the last page of the mailed questionnaire.

> My experience as to Jewish residents of this community is probably not typical. A high-class, wealthy, cultured, refugee Jewish family came here in 1940 and we have been very close friends ever since then, both professionally and socially. They seem, to me, very different from most Jews.

> Frankly, I'm not too fond of Jews. I've heard too much about how they stick together, how they can chisel you, how they try to get ahead. Yet, here in —— there is a Jewish family who are not at all like this. They are fine, intelligent, honest citizens and very close friends of ours.

> When the —— came to this community everyone was suspicious. We knew what Jews were like and we didn't like what we knew. After a while we found that they were pretty nice folks. We looked at them as a different kind of Jew. They didn't seem the Brooklyn type. Thinking about it now I have the feeling that our children build their image of what a Jew is supposed to be from the contact they have with the children of this Jewish family. Sometimes we have warped ideas about what we think is true. . . .

Repeated *personal* and *informal* contact in the home and around town can serve as a significant factor leading towards the ultimate reduction of prejudice against Jews. Exemption is perhaps an important intermediate step in breaking down predispositions towards minority groups.

One further statement serves to illustrate this proposition:

> When a Jewish family first moved in we wanted them to prove themselves to us. It must have been hard on them but they came through like troopers. They became an important part of the community. They showed us a different kind of Jew. No Shylock. Knowing them for twenty years

now when I think of Jews I think of them. I used to think about some mean, hook-nosed character.

Majority Reaction

The following generalizations are tentatively offered based upon the study of the community leaders of twenty small towns in New York State. (1) In the small community the minority group member is constantly in direct contact with the majority group. As he gets to know their ways, they cannot help but get to know him. He stands upon the threshold of influencing deep-seated images. He can reinforce such images or aid in the recasting of these by those with whom he interacts. (2) The isolated minority member rarely constitutes a threat to the established order and community members are often willing to accept the individual outsider despite articulated expressions of prejudice. (3) Repeated and intensive contact and personal association often tend to change the mental picture of the isolate from being "different from" to being "typical of" the group he represents. Exemption is viewed as an instrumental step in the ultimate reduction of prejudice.

A FINAL NOTE

On the basis of the two studies reported here, it is logical to predict that increasing interaction with Jewish "representatives," especially those who have spent their early years in the small town, would have a decided effect on changing the overall attitudes of Gentiles toward Jews. A study of the children of small-towners would provide the information needed to test this hypothesis. But any research of this kind would necessarily have to be conducted in the very near future.

As is stated in the summary of the original report:

> Another prediction is, unfortunately perhaps, in order. With the tremendous rate of post-teen out-migration on the part of the offspring of Jews living in rural communities we wonder whether the small-town Jew is, in reality, a disappearing type in the spectrum of American Jewry. Most Jews who settled in small villages did so prior to World War II. Since that time few have chosen to live in such communities. Now the children are grown and rapidly leaving the nest to live in larger centers. Although some children will return to run the business, our studies suggest that small as it now is, the population of American Jews living in small communities will increasingly diminish in the years to come. . . .[10]

NOTES

1. See, for example, Toby Shafter, "The Fleshpots of Maine," *Commentary*, 7 (January-June 1949) 60-7; Earl Rabb, "Report from the Farm," *Commentary*, 8 (July-December 1949)

475-9; Harry Golden, "The Jews of the South," *Congress Weekly,* 31 December 1951; Lee J. Levinger, "The Disappearing Small-Town Jew," *Commentary,* 14 (July-December 1952) 157-163; Louise Laser, "The Only Jewish Family in Town," *Commentary* (December 1959) 489-96; and a letter to the Editor from Gerald M. Phillips, "Jews in Rural America," *Commentary* (February 1960), 163.

2. This research was sponsored by The Anti-Defamation League of B'nai B'rith, 515 Madison Avenue, New York City. The original manuscript is entitled *Strangers in Their Midst, A Sociological Study of the Small-Town Jew and His Neighbors,* Cornell University, 1959. The project title was that of "Cornell Community Studies." (Permission to use Cornell's name was granted by Vice President for Research, Theodore P. Wright.)

3. Approximately 25 per cent of those who did not respond were randomly selected and attempts were made to interview each. Of this group two persons claimed they were no longer Jews and refused. Both were German refugees and had married non-Jews *prior* to their immigration to America. Two persons were deceased. The remaining group all identified themselves as Jews. Four permitted themselves to be interviewed and the information gathered was consistent with that of the less reluctant respondents. One individual refused to be interviewed and expressed the general feeling that such a study could do little to enhance Jewish-Gentile relations.

4. That slightly less than two-thirds responded suggests the possibility of a selective bias in the second part of the study. Time and budget did not permit the personal follow-up of non-respondents similar to that in the first study. At present efforts are being made to gather data from a selected number of these reluctant participants.

5. The Coefficient of Reproducibility is 98.

6. Everett V. Stonequist, *The Marginal Man: A Study in Personality and Culture Conflict,* New York, 1937; and Robert E. Park, "Human Migration and the Marginal Man," *American Journal of Sociology,* 33 (1928), 881-93.

7. Georg Simmel, "The Stranger," *The Sociology of Georg Simmel,* Kurt H. Wolff, trans., Glencoe, Illinois, 1950, 402-8; and Robert E. Park and Ernest W. Burgess, *Introduction to the Science of Sociology,* Chicago, 1921, 286.

8. Park, "Human Migration," op. cit., 891.

9. The scale itself breaks down in the following manner. Those "high" on ethnocentrism have a low faith in people and agree with the statements that America would be better off without so many foreigners and that some religious groups are inferior. Those "medium" were negative on one of the three items. Those "low" did not agree with the latter two and were of the opinion that "most people can be trusted." The Coefficient of Reproducibility is 96.

10. Rose, op. cit., 279-80.

SMALL-TOWN JEWS' INTEGRATION INTO THEIR COMMUNITIES

EUGEN SCHOENFELD

There is a persistent conception in literature in general that Jews do not integrate into their communities; that though they reside in communities they are never a part of them; that they are individuals whose roots in the community, if any, are shallow; in a word, that they are "strangers." Previous sociological literature has dealt primarily with Jews who reside in large cities, in metropolitan areas. In this article I will consider the question, Do Jews who reside in small communities manifest similar characteristics; Do small-town Jews, though they represent only a minute fraction of total Jewry in the United States, maintain this separatist tendency? Or do they assume rather the "resident" characteristics of the general populace?

SAMPLE

The data for this research were gathered among Jews living in 12 small towns in southern Illinois. The population of these towns ranges from 4,400 to 16,000. Dispersed in these towns live approximately 90 Jewish families, ranging in size from as few as 3 members to as many as 12 in the largest city. To get the names and addresses of the Southern Illinois Jews, I contacted the Jewish Federation of Southern Illinois, which gave me its mailing list. Because that list, however, represented only those Jews who had institutional affiliation, I used in addition a "snowball" method to get the names of four unaffiliated Jews. Altogether I contacted 89 families, from which I interviewed 83 adults. In six instances where the husbands were not available their wives were substituted; in two instances I interviewed self-supporting single women. Most of the sample (66 of the 83 respondents) are migrants from nearby urban centers who left the city because they saw increased economic advantages in small towns. However, because migration into small towns ceased years before this investigation[1] and the unsuccessful migrants have left, the present Jewish population is comprised of economically well-to-do individuals. Almost three-fourths of the males in the sample are entrepreneurs, primarily in retail ready-to-wear businesses, and the others are professionals and white-collar employees.

PROBLEM: STRANGER OR RESIDENT?

The problem central to this research is whether small-town Jews manifest the attitudes of "strangers" or of "residents." By the term "stranger," following the conceptualization of Simmel (1950), I do not refer to an individual (or a group) who comes to sojourn for a brief period without intending to settle, one who comes today and leaves tomorrow. Instead, says Simmel, "The stranger . . . is the person who comes today and stays tomorrow. He is, so to speak, the potential wanderer; although he has not moved on, he has not quite overcome his freedom of coming and going" (p. 402). The rootlessness of the stranger, his lack of commitment to a particular place, his desire not to have objects or conditions which would tie him to a locality, all make him "by nature no 'owner of soil'—not merely in the physical sense but in the figurative sense." Given this fact of freedom of mobility, Simmel finds it quite natural that the occupation of the stranger should be that of a trader. He writes: "Throughout the history of economics the stranger everywhere appears as the trader, or the trader as stranger. As long as the economy is essentially self-sufficient, or products are exchanged within a spatially narrow group, it needs no middleman: a trader is only required for products that originate outside the group" (p. 402).

With increased technology and consequent division of labor, there arose an increased need for a more permanent form of economic exchange. However, as traditional values are the last to change, land and handicraft were divided among the residents, and primary production, at least, historically remained within the domain of the resident. "Trade," writes Simmel (p. 403), "was therefore indicated for the stranger, who intrudes as a supernumerary, so to speak, into a group in which the economic positions are actually occupied: the classical example is the history of European Jews. . . ."

Another significant characteristic of the stranger, observes Simmel, is his objectivity. The quality of this objectivity is his freedom from "collective prejudice," from a given value system, and from ideologies which influence the residents' interpretation of reality. Objectivity, Simmel observes, "may also be defined as freedom: the objective individual is bound by no commitments which could prejudice his perception, understanding, and evaluation of the given" (p. 405).

These phenomena place the stranger in a peculiar position vis-à-vis the community in which he resides. On the one hand, his constant interaction and association with the community, even though this association is secondary, leads to a certain

closeness.[2] On the other hand, his freedom and objectivity serve to maintain a
kind of "strangerness," which is manifested by the other residents' perception of
his group as "they." It is thus, says Simmel, that the stranger is "not conceived as
individual but as stranger of a particular type. . . . He is not perceived as an individual
[who is a] bearer of certain objective contents" (p. 403) but is instead viewed as
a member of a particular group whose status has been already predetermined.

Park (1950) also perceives the Jew as a stranger and a trader, but adds another
characteristic: that of the cosmopolite. He writes: "Most, if not all the characteristics of the Jew, certainly his preeminence as a trader and his keen intellectual
interest, his sophistication, his idealism . . . , are all characteristic of the city man,
[the] man who ranges widely, lives preferably in a hotel—in short, the cosmopolite"
(pp. 354-355). The cosmopolite does indeed manifest some of the characteristics
of the stranger as depicted by Simmel, such as his freedom from local ideologies.

In sum, "the stranger" is an individual whose relationship with the community
is primarily instrumental. He is a cosmopolite whose reference group is not the
community in which he resides, whose ideologies are not those of the community,
and who judges its residents in stereotyped particularistic terms. The "resident,"
on the other hand, manifests characteristics just the opposite of these.

To differentiate between the characteristics of the "stranger" and those of the
"resident," I constructed a "stranger-resident" scale. This scale consists of ten
items, the first five of which were taken from the "localite-cosmopolite" scale of
Dobriner (1958: 133), insofar as his items are relevant to my concepts. Dobriner
checked the validity of his items through what he called "logical validation[3] . . .
[and] the reliability of the scale was checked . . . by administering the scale to
selected groups of college students and comparing similar groups for consistency
in score" (p. 136). The second half of the scale consists of items representing the
characteristics of the stranger as conceptualized by Simmel. The validity of this
half was also checked by the same method which Dobriner used. In addition, I
administered these items to Jewish faculty members and graduate students who
had lived in the local small towns less than two years. The items which showed
the greatest consistency were selected for the scale. A score of zero (0) was given
if the subject responded as a stranger and a one (1) was given for a resident-like
response. The possible range of scores ran from 0 to 10. I have arbitrarily defined
those scoring from 6 to 10 as residents.

In addition to this scale, I measured integration or nonintegration into the community, that is, "resident" or "stranger" characteristics, by membership in voluntary social organizations. Both small-group and community studies indicate that
the web of interaction differentiates the integrated members from the isolates
and strangers. On the community level, the patterns of inclusion and exclusion
are revealed if one examines the status stratification of that locality.

Social stratification in America is said to be based upon class and status factors.
The class factor represents a differentiation based on the impersonal setting of
the market place, and in this sense is purely an economic variable; the status factor

represents hierarchical differentiation of honor granted in a context of interpersonal association. It was in the realm of class stratification, because of its noncommunal quality and impersonality, that the first advancements by minorities were made. But, in the realm of status honor, minority groups have made little headway, for here a specific style of life is mandatory. Hence, if minority groups are to be accepted into the status groups of the dominant culture, they must reject their previous style of life in favor of that of the status group (Weber, 1958: 186-189).

Although acceptance into and participation in non-Jewish voluntary associations are valid indicators of integration, they do have some limitations. On the one hand, acceptance into social organizations in small towns does not necessarily indicate decreased social distance between non-Jews and Jews; Jews may be accepted into such organizations because they represent money, both in dues and in contributions. On the other hand, Jewish attendance does not necessarily indicate that an ethnic cleavage has disappeared or that, by joining and attending, Jews have transferred their affective and expressive relations to non-Jewish associations. The latter, however, is indicated by examining the small-town Jews' friends, or, more specifically, by asking whether they limit their primary associations to Jews only. If they do, then one can assume that their voluntary association with non-Jews is primarily utilitarian and instrumentally defined.[4]

To gather information about the small-town Jews' friends, I asked the respondents the following two questions: "(1) Think for a moment of the people you see most often. I am interested in the people *you* see, not necessarily those your family sees. Of these, who is your closest friend? (2) Now, we would like the same information about the family with whom your family is closest." These questions were repeated to solicit information about three of their best friends in both categories. The reason for dichotomizing friendship was that I believed that males, because of their business and professional activities, would have personal friends apart from those whom he considered as "family friends."

FINDINGS

The stranger-resident scale

Table 1 shows that the majority of small-town Jews in my sample scored in the range indicating "resident" characteristics. More specifically, 67 percent of the respondents scored in the range designated as "residents" and 16 percent scored in the middle range; only 15 percent scored in the range designated as "stranger."

Compared with urban and suburban Jews, these small-town Jews are more attached to their community. Dobriner (1958: 139-140), examining the localite-cosmopolite orientation of the residents of Huntington, a suburb in Long Island on the periphery of the New York metropolitan area, found Jews, regardless of their length of residence, to be more cosmopolitan than the other residents. On a 10-item scale, the median score of old-time Jewish residents was 3 compared to a median score of 11 for old-time Protestants. A similar difference, though not such a large one, was found between Jewish newcomers and all newcomers. The median score was 3.6 for Jewish newcomers and 5.0 for the total newcomers sample.[5] Although Dobriner's scale and the one used in this research are not the

Table 1

Distribution of respondents by scores on the "stranger-resident" scale (N=83)

Scores	Percentage of respondents in score categories
6-10	67.3
5	16.8
0-4	15.9
Mean=6.2	Median=6.0
Chi-square=42.1	$p < 0.001$

same, there is enough similarity in the conceptual variable which the scales were measuring that a useful comparison of the findings can be made. Thus, the data given by Dobriner (1958) show that the Jewish score in the urban sample not only is lower than the non-Jewish score but also is lower than the mid-score that could be achieved on the scale. Although I do not know the range on the Dobriner scale,[6] even if we take the highest reported median score of 11 as the maximum, the median Jewish score of 3 is still far below the hypothetical 5.5 mid-range. In contrast, the median score of our sample was 6, which is higher than the mid-score of 5. One thus could assume that small-town Jews have closer ties to and identification with their community than do urban Jews.

Stranger and resident as ideal types

In the interest of clearer understanding, I have postulated the "stranger" and the "resident" as ideal types defined by specific behavior in the following five areas: (1) economy, (2) reference group, (3) small-town ideology, (4) localism-cosmo-politanism, and (5) perception. Although the responses to the questionnaire indicate that small-town Jews are predominantly "residents," they still do not show which of the five areas are most responsible for this integration. It seemed, therefore, that an analysis of the individual factors, indicating the different effects which these factors have upon integration, would afford greater insight into this aspect of the investigation.

Economy

Both Simmel (1950: 402) and Park (1950: 354-355) stress the importance of the relationship between economic orientation and the role of the "stranger." To re-iterate, the stranger's relationship with his community is said to be contractual; he perceives those outside of his ethnic group in primarily utilitarian terms, that is, as potential customers.

The three items in Table 2 which occur in the stranger-resident scale are used to differentiate among small-town Jews with regard to their economic orientation to the community. The data are not very conclusive, for half of the Jews in my sample perceive their residence in the community primarily in economic terms. But placing primary emphasis upon income and economy in general among small-towners is not an exclusively Jewish characteristic. The extent of non-Jewish emigration among the younger group indicates that even those who come from long lines of established residents do leave the community when such a move seems economically advantageous.[7] But it is significant that over 50 percent of the respondents conceive their relationship to the community in terms of personal relationships rather than of economic factors.

Table 2

Frequency of positive responses to economic commitment items (N = 83)

Item	Percentage of respondents giving positive responses
(a) The most rewarding organizations a person can belong to are local organizations serving local needs.	52.4
(b) If I did not earn my living in this town I would just as soon live some place else.	51.2
(c) If one can better himself economically by leaving he should not consider friendship as a reason to hold him back.	39.0

Reference group

An important determinant of one's sense of belonging is his reference group, the group which influences his action in any situation (Merton, 1957: 225), whose norms he obeys, and upon whose judgments he places primacy. To determine the locus of small-town Jews' reference group, I wished to examine two factors: first, the extent to which Jews dissociate themselves from the Jewish community as their reference focus, and second, the extent to which they accept non-Jews, or, more specifically, their neighbors, as their reference group. The items in Table 3 were used for this purpose. The data indicate that small-town Jews reject the Jewish community in general as their primary reference group. Jewish norms and values and concern with other Jews' opinions are not of paramount importance to their way of life; they are concerned with their neighbors' opinions, because it is

Table 3

Frequency of positive responses to reference-group items (N = 83)

Item	Percentage of respondents giving positive responses
(a) What my fellow Jews think of me is more important to me than what the other townspeople think.	8.5
(b) What my neighbors think of me is very important to me.	76.8

with their neighbors that they associate, and, above all, because it is their neighbors who, as their customers, provide them with a comfortable living. Thus, one might speculate that Jews' relationships with their community and their acceptance of it as their reference group are probably manifestations of an organic solidarity in the community, resulting from reciprocal interaction. As Malinowski (1959: 41) suggests, "The man who would persistantly disobey the rulings of law in his economic dealings would soon find himself outside the social and economic order—and he is perfectly well aware of it." For whatever reason, it is evident that small-town Jews do accept their communities as their reference group and thus that they become both more concerned with their neighbors as judges of their behavior and more dependent upon their communities. By becoming so dependent, they also begin to shed the characteristics of the "stranger," for by accepting community values as their frame of reference, small-town Jews lose their objectivity (described by Simmel [1950: 405] as one of the chief marks of the "stranger") and assume the characteristics of the "resident."

Small-town ideology

Inasmuch as small-town Jews accept their community as their reference group, we can also expect them to incorporate the small-town *Weltanschauung.* The two items in Table 4 were used as indicators of small-town ideology among Jews in small towns.

The discrepancy between responses to the two items is curious, especially in view of the fact that the second item is considered to be an important small-town value (Vidich and Bensman, 1960). Although 63 percent of the respondents perceived the small town in its traditional image, as the backbone of America, only 27 percent perceived it as a locus of morality where children grow up to be better citizens than children raised in the cities. This discrepancy can perhaps be explained if one considers that most of the respondents were born and reared in large cities and could not deny that they themselves were good citizens. However, the bulk of the respondents who were born and reared in small towns did agree with item *b* of Table 4.

Table 4

**Frequency of acceptance of
small-town ideology (N = 83)**

Item	Percentage of respondents giving positive responses
(a) Big cities have their place, but when you get right down to it, the local community is the backbone of America.	63.4
(b) Children raised in small towns grow up to be better citizens than those who are raised in large cities.	32.9

Localism-cosmopolitanism

Important aspects of the resident-stranger dichotomy are those qualities which Merton (1957: 394) refers to as "localite-cosmopolite." There are two important characteristics which distinguish "localites" from "cosmopolites": (1) They have different conceptions of the significance of news. The "localite" thinks of news almost entirely in terms of its implications for himself or his associates. The "cosmopolite," on the other hand, considers news in relation to national and international problems. (2) They have different attitudes toward acquaintance with people in the community. The localite typically wants to know as many people as possible; the cosmopolite, on the other hand, is interested in the quality, not the quantity of the people he meets. My hypothesis that small-town Jews would tend to exhibit the characteristics of "residents" led me also to expect that they would tend to be "localites."

The data in Table 5 indicate inconsistencies. Most of the respondents (89 percent) thought that it was essential to have many friends, yet only a few (30 percent) thought that local news was more interesting and important than international happenings. Though lack of data does not permit a more detailed analysis, it might be suggested that occupation, education, and world condition have an effect on people's attitude toward news. In view of the politically tense situation of the present day and the fact that many events which effect the local community and its businesses take place outside the community, we can assume that the small-towner tends to become aware of and concerned with national and international happenings. Furthermore, it is logical to assume that increased education is related to reading, both in quality and in quantity (the level of education among the small-town Jew is high—52 percent attended college); one would therefore expect small-town Jews to manifest a concern with world affairs.

Table 5

Frequency distribution of "localite" orientation (N=83)

Item	Percentage of respondents giving positive responses
(*a*) National and international happenings rarely seem as interesting and important as events that occur right in the local community in which one lives.	30.5
(*b*) Many personal relationships and contacts with other people in the local community are essential in life today.	89.0

However, in regard to their personal relations, small-town Jews do show "localite" tendencies. Knowing many people is an important and widely held value, and many of the respondents made deliberate efforts to join voluntary organizations as avenues for meeting the citizens of the community.

Perception

One of the characteristics associated with the "stranger" is that he is judged by the dominant group, not as an individual, but rather as a member of a particular group. The reciprocal is also true, for the "stranger" perceives the individuals of the majority group in terms of a stereotype. Thus, Jews in the past have looked upon goyim in particularistic terms and ascribed to them certain common character istics. Small-town Jews, however, differentiate among non-Jews and view them in universalistic rather than particularistic terms. All except two of the respondents saw the non-Jews of their community as individuals in their own right and, thus, as possessing individual characters.

Associations

Membership in organizations

Because of their communal qualities, minority groups have made little headway in status mobility. Kramer and Leventman (1961: 181-183) reported that the urban Jews in their study had not been successful in gaining entry into organiza-

Table 6

**Small-town Jews' membership
in voluntary associations (N=83)**

Organizations	Percentage of respondents who were members
Inclusive	
Business Association	22.0
Chamber of Commerce	39.0
American Legion	22.0
Veterans of Foreign Wars	15.9
Parent-Teachers Association	7.3
Women's Club	7.3
Scouts	6.1
YMCA	4.8
Exclusive	
Elks	58.5
Country Club	40.2
Masons	31.7
Eagles	13.4
Lions	11.0
Rotary	9.8
Shriners	8.5
Kiwanis	6.1
Moose	3.7
Athletic Club	3.7
Garden Club	2.4
Others	13.4

tions stressing the norm of exclusiveness. Similarly, Dean (1958: 307) found that in middle-sized communities "there has been a growing participation by Jewish leaders in general civic causes and community service activities," namely in organizations stressing inclusiveness. In contrast, he found that Jews were "most seriously limited from assuming leadership role[s] in the community at large where . . . roles entail membership in groups governed by the norms of exclusiveness" (p. 310). Thus, Junior Leagues and exclusive country clubs exclude all Jews, and the Rotary and Kiwanis clubs have discriminatory practices that limit participation to a select few. However, I hypothesized that the prevalence of the values of *Gemeinschaft* and neighborliness in small towns would break down the barriers of status, and that, as a consequence, small-town Jews would join clubs and organizations which stress exclusiveness.

The data in Table 6 indicate that the majority of small-town Jews in my sample, unlike Jews in the city, do belong to clubs which specify exclusiveness. Table 6 shows, for example, that the Elks, a club representing an orientation to exclusiveness, has more than twice the Jewish membership of the Business Association, the number-one inclusiveness-oriented club. Small-town Jews' preoccupation with status is further evidenced by their joining organizations which they consider most prominent. The data in Table 7 indicate that the three clubs most frequently joined by small-town Jews are also considered the most prominent, that is, they are the societies to which the wealthiest and most socially esteemed people belong.

Table 7

Organizations considered most prominent by small-town Jews (N = 83)

Organizations	Percentage of respondents designating organization as prominent
Elks	76.8
Country Club	65.9
Masons	51.2

By and large, Jewish people in small towns seem to manifest the middle-class characteristics of the "joiner." All except five respondents, who are either in their twenties or in their late sixties, belong to some voluntary association, either Jewish or non-Jewish (Table 8).

Excluding the temple, most Jews belong to at least one Jewish organization, even if only nominally. The organization to which most belong is the B'nai B'rith (83.3 percent), which itself exists (in this area) only nominally and whose mem-

Table 8

**Membership in Jewish and
non-Jewish organizations (N = 83)**

Number of Organizations	Percentage of respondents belonging to specified number of Jewish organizations[a]	Percentage of respondents belonging to specified number of non-Jewish organizations
0	16.7	6.0
1	67.6	9.6
2	14.9	14.5
3	—	10.8
4	1.3	12.0
5		24.1
6		9.6
7		8.4
8		3.6
9		1.2

Chi-square = 3.96

a. Exclusive of temple or synagogue.

bers are merely "dues payers."[8] The function of B'nai B'rith seems to be symbolic: small-town Jews use their membership to reaffirm their allegiance to world Jewry, because this organization is concerned with Jews on both the national and the international scale.

Jews are also active participants in non-Jewish organizations. When asked the reason for joining non-Jewish social organizations, the majority of the respondents

Table 9

Reasons for joining non-Jewish organizations

Reason given	Percentage of respondents giving specified reasons (N = 83)
Sociability	48.8
Community needs	45.1
Good effect on business	25.6
Invitation to join	13.4
Other	4.9

said that their primary intention was sociability; only 25 percent were motivated to join both social and business organizations because such joining was "good for business" (Table 9). In fact, most small-town Jews joined local business organizations because they felt that their help was needed to make the community become more prosperous by bringing in new industries. Unlike association in urban areas, where Jews have little informal contact with Gentiles (Dean, 1958; Kramer and Leventman, 1961), Jewish-Gentile association in small towns seems to be extensive, both in business and in social life.

Friendships

Considering the involvement of small-town Jews in voluntary associations, one can expect a high frequency of interaction between Jews and non-Jews. Small-town Jews (unlike the first-generation Jews, who responded to traditional Jewish values and ideologies and stressed the importance of separate existence) attach great importance to homogeneity and integration into the community, an emphasis which is further reinforced and supported by small-town *Gemeinschaft* ideology. Consequently, I hypothesized that there would be no significant difference in the number of Jewish and non-Jewish friends which small-town Jews have. The data in Table 10 support the null hypothesis: 77 of the respondents in my sample have at least one Jewish friend and 78 have at least one non-Jewish friend.

Table 10

Numbers of respondents reporting specified numbers of
Jewish and non-Jewish personal and family friends (N = 83)

Number of friends reported	Number of respondents reporting specified number of Jewish personal friends	Number of respondents reporting specified number of non-Jewish personal friends	Number of respondents reporting specified number of Jewish family friends[a]	Number of respondents reporting specified number of non-Jewish family friends[a]
0	60	38	28	49
1	12	14	11	14
2	8	11	18	11
3	3	20	25	8

a. N = 82 in this case because one respondent was single.

A comparison with Dean's findings indicates that urban Jews have a smaller proportion of mixed and completely non-Jewish friends than small-town Jews.

Only 3.6 percent of my small-town Jewish sample reported that three of their best friends are Jewish, but 75 percent of the Elmira Jewish sample reported that they socialize predominantly with Jews (Dean, 1958: 310). On the other hand, 24 percent of the small-town sample reported that all of their best friends are non-Jews, but only 10 percent of the Elmira respondents reported participation in predominantly non-Jewish cliques (Dean, 1958: 311). Surely, this difference in Jewish versus non-Jewish associations is a function of the number of Jews in the community. In urban areas, the size of the Jewish community makes it possible for a Jew to choose friends among people who share not only his religion and culture but also his occupation or profession. Unlike the Jewish professional in an urban community, the lone Jewish physician or lawyer in the small town who wants to interact with others in his profession must turn to non-Jews.

However, if we look at the pattern of association between families, we find a greater proportion of interaction between Jews. Whereas in the category of "personal friends" we find only 3 respondents who have only Jewish friends, in the "family friend" category 28 reported that their friends are all Jewish. Furthermore, although 20 respondents indicated that all three of their closest personal friends are non-Jews, only 8 respondents reported similarly with regard to their family friends.

This difference between personal friends and family friends, I believe, can be accounted for by the difference in those who made the choice of friends. My sample consisted chiefly of men, and their personal friends were their own selection. Men whose business activities are carried on predominantly with non-Jews, whose professional colleagues and business associates in the small town are predominantly non-Jews, will tend naturally to choose non-Jewish friends. On the other hand, family friends are selected primarily by wives, who have fewer opportunities to meet non-Jewish people. Although Jewish and non-Jewish males have business interests in common, women's contacts are usually purely social and involve friends whom they meet through the temple and its sisterhood. Considering the fact that the wives are the social secretaries of the home and arrange for social gatherings, one can easily see why "family friends" may tend to be Jewish.

This variance also has been observed by Dean (1958:310). He reports that only 12 percent of the Jewish men whom he interviewed belonged to Jewish organizations but that 48 percent of their wives did so.

The Jews of southern Illinois, when asked about the qualities they seek in friends, rejected being Jewish as the primary and most important criterion for selecting friends. Seemingly, being Jewish is neither necessary nor sufficient ground for association. Friends are selected according to universalistic criteria; common interests, education, and, above all, personality factors are given the most attention. However, occupational similarities of the friends indicate that class and status are additional factors in friendship selection among small-town Jews.

CONCLUSION: RESIDENTS, NOT STRANGERS

Considering small-town Jews' attitudes toward their communities, the types of organizations to which they belong, and their interpersonal associations, one can conclude that Jews in small towns tend to assume the characteristics of the non-Jewish population. Unlike "strangers," these Jews tend to manifest "localite" tendencies and are on the whole concerned with their community. Though there is still an ethnic factor involved in their interpersonal associations, it is apparently of less than general importance, and personal friends are selected on the basis of universalistic rather than particularistic criteria. Small-town Jews generally profess that religion and ethnicity make no difference in their selection of friends (Table 11), and one could hardly expect a different attitude among them, considering that (1) there are very few Jews in small towns, a fact which automatically reduces the number of Jews from whom they can select friends, and (2) small-town Jews accept the small-town ideology, which stresses, above all, personal worth (Vidich and Bensman, 1960). It is the latter above everything else which Jews in small towns use to justify their selection of friends. It is not "who one is" that counts, but "what one is."

Table 11

Friendship preference among small-town Jews (N = 83)

Preferences	Percentage of respondents reporting specified friendship preferences
Prefer Jews	38.5
Make no distinction between Jews and non-Jews	61.5

Generally, then, we may conclude that small-town Jews do not manifest the characteristics of the "stranger," but rather those of the "resident." The small-town atmosphere and limited scope of community relations combine to affect both their mode and their degree of integration into their communities, so that in these two respects the Jewish residents of small towns in southern Illinois do not differ appreciably from non-Jewish residents.

NOTES

1. The last massive migration (over 26 percent of all migrants) came during and just after World War II.

2. Homans (1950) points out that increased interaction between two social units leads to increased sentiment.

3. Logical validation "refers to either theoretical or commonsense analysis which concludes simply that, the items being what they are, the nature of the continuum cannot be other than it is stated to be. . . . [Such validation] springs from the careful definition of the continuum and the selection of the items" (Goode and Hatt, 1952: 237).

4. I am cognizant of the fact that personal association is a reciprocal phenomenon; in this research, however, I was limited to one aspect of personal associations: namely, the extent to which Jews claim non-Jews as their friends.

5. The total newcomers sample also included the Jewish sample. Consequently, we must assume that if the Jewish sample were omitted the median score would be higher.

6. In view of the fact that 11 was the median score, it should follow that the maximum attainable score must be higher.

7. For instance, a breakdown of the southern Illinois population of persons 20 years of age and older shows that the age group between 20 and 30 comprises only 14.5 percent of the total population.

8. In the three years during which I belonged to this organization, only one meeting was scheduled.

REFERENCES

Dean, John P.
> 1958 "Jewish participation in the life of middle-sized communities." Pp. 304-320 in Marshall Sklare (ed.), The Jews: Social Patterns of an American Group. New York: The Free Press.

Dobriner, William M.
> 1958 "Local and cosmopolitan as contemporary suburban character type." Pp. 132-143 in William M. Dobriner (ed.) The Suburban Community. New York: Putnam.

Goode, William T., and Paul K. Hatt
> 1952 Methods in Social Research. New York: McGraw-Hill.

Homans, George C.
> 1950 The Human Group. New York: Harcourt, Brace.

Kramer, Judith, and Seymour Leventman
> 1961 Children of the Gilded Ghetto. New Haven, Connecticut: Yale University Press.

Malinowski, Bronislaw
> 1959 Crime and Custom in Savage Society. Paterson, New Jersey: Littlefield, Adams.

Merton, Robert K.
> 1957 Social Theory and Social Structure. Glencoe, Illinois: The Free Press.

Park, Robert E.
> 1950 Race and Culture. Glencoe, Illinois: The Free Press.

Simmel, George
> 1950 "The stranger." Pp. 403-408 in The Sociology of George Simmel. Translated, edited, and with an introduction by Kurt H. Wolff. Glencoe, Illinois: The Free Press.

Vidich, Arthur J., and Joseph Bensman
> 1960 Small Town in Mass Society: Class, Power and Religion in Rural Community. New York: Anchor Books.

Weber, Max
> 1958 From Max Weber: Essays in Sociology. Translated and edited by H.H. Gerth and C.W. Mills. New York: Oxford University Press.

PROBLEMS
AND POTENTIALS

EUGEN SCHOENFELD

In the conclave recently held under the auspices of B'nai B'rith and B'nai B'rith Women about Jewish life in small towns, three major concerns were voiced by representatives of small-town Jewry. These concerns dealt with: (a) the vanishing small-town Jew, (b) the sense of isolation that is experienced amidst integration and, (c) the maintenance of Jewish identity.

THE VANISHING SMALL-TOWN JEW

Jews are disappearing from small towns. Once thriving Jewish communities in small and medium-sized cities have become merely the skeletal remnants of their former self. Although this is of great concern to Jews living in small towns it is not, however, limited to Jews alone, but is experienced by all small towns in general.

The one problem that differs is that young Jewish people tend to emigrate in a greater proportion than do non-Jews. That exodus of young Jews is related to the fact that these towns and villages are no longer considered as places which might provide an adequate future for them. With the great emphasis on education among Jews, sons especially leave for college to become professionals, and, upon completing their studies, move to large metropolitan areas.

Daughters, like the sons, attend universities, meet and marry young men, and settle with their husbands in the larger cities. Young professionals move to the city because it offers greater opportunities for advancement, and also because their more extensive education leads them to find the small town confining and barren. For instance, the young physician finds that the large city, in contrast to small towns, offers him not only a great variety of personalities and professional orientations from which to choose friends and associates, but also affords a greater number of hospitals with more sophisticated equipment, which is important to his professional fulfillment. In the non-professional side of life the city offers the greater variety of experiences to which he has become accustomed during his college years. Business advantages which drew Jews into small towns in the first place have now lost importance. Entrepreneurship has given way to the department stores, and very few young men now seek their fortunes by starting small businesses.

ISOLATION AMIDST INTEGRATION

The Jew living in small towns is a relatively integrated member of his community. He appears to be less of a stranger than are his brothers in the large urban communities. Because of a lack of Jewish population density they cannot develop a total sense of being Jewish. They feel something lacking—an undefinable quality which comes perhaps from being surrounded by a large number of one's kind, a quality which emerges only in a high Jewish density.

Unlike the urban Jew, who sees himself as a cosmopolitan, a small-town Jew is a localite. He feels, for instance, that the most rewarding organization a person can belong to is a local one. Like his non-Jewish neighbor, he perceives the small town to be the backbone of America. He joins non-Jewish organizations primarily for sociability and/or because of the community's need. (In fact, in Southern Illinois, 94 per cent of the Jews belonged to one or more non-Jewish organizations.)[1]

And yet, amidst this high degree of integration and belonging, small-town Jews also indicate a sense of isolation and alienation. They belong—but not quite completely; they are a part of the community—but with reservations. While they may belong to Rotary, Kiwanis, and/or the country club, they are also identified as "the Jew"—and as such they feel isolated, not only from the Gentiles, but also from total Jewry.

This is not to say that Jews in small towns do not get together, or that they lack synagogues or temples in which to associate. Synagogue membership, the support of Israel, and membership in B'nai B'rith (over 90 per cent of Jews in Southern Illinois are dues-paying members), while necessary, is not sufficient to create a sense of Jewish belonging. Jewish life and the feeling of being Jewish must also be gratified by the human senses—by hearing, by smelling—in a word, by being. The non-religious Jew who does not belong to a temple or synagogue and, more likely, not even to any Jewish social group, will continue to feel Jewish if he lives in a highly dense Jewish area. For there he may hear Yiddish, he will see and read Jewish papers or books, he will smell the aromas from kosher or kosher-style restaurants and delicatessens. It is this aspect of Jewish life that the small-town Jew lacks and which leads him to develop the sense of isolation. He knows that he is Jewish but he does not feel it. He is alienated from the totality of Jewish life.

IDENTITY

The concern for one's identity and its transmission is inherent to all people regardless of ethnic and religious background. On the one hand, people are concerned with sustaining their identity because of a sense of responsibility to maintain their kind; on the other hand, and more importantly, there is a concern to transmit that identity to one's children as a way, consciously or unconsciously, of combatting the sense of nihilism which is a part of the human fear of death. No one wants to cease to exist; everyone wants to be part of a continuous chain that links the individual both to the past and to the future.

In other words, each person seemingly wants to assure that his existence is neither temporary nor without hope for a future. But how can one assure such continuity of existence? Through the children, obviously. Not through their biological existence, although that is a necessary pre-condition, but by developing them into mirrors of one's self. Descartes once declared, "I think, therefore I exist"; similarly, parents declare, "My children think as I do, therefore I continue to exist, and with it I can assume the continuous existence of my people." In Jewish terms, by transmitting their people's values and thoughts, Jews assure the transmission of Jewish values and thoughts.

The fear of identity-loss among small-town Jews is not centered in the adults' identity but in that of their children. The Jewish adult's identity is a fait accompli. About three-quarters of the subjects interviewed in Southern Illinois, when asked to respond to the question, "Who am I?" indicated a strong Jewish identity. This was even true for those who had intermarried. Concern for their children's Jewish identity is exemplified in the following incident. In an interview with a Jewish physician who had married a loyal Methodist, the physician expressed extreme joy because his son, now enrolled in his own alma mater, not only had decided not to become a missionary, but had joined Hillel and was seriously contemplating a conversion to Judaism.

The loss of identity among the young in small towns is perhaps attributable to two major factors: lack of reinforcement and intermarriage. The young Jew in small towns lacks Jewish associations in and outside of the home to reinforce and support his image of being Jewish. At home his parents have, because of necessity, many non-Jewish friends. For instance, out of 82 respondents I interviewed, only three reported that their three best friends were Jewish. When I asked the respondents about the qualities they sought in friends, being Jewish was rejected as the primary, most important criterion. Seemingly, being Jewish is considered neither necessary nor sufficient ground for association. Friends are selected according to universal criteria, common interests, education; above all, personality factors are given most attention. The lack of Jewish association for the young is a fact of life in schools which may have only three or four Jewish students.

In cases of intermarriage, the loss of the children's identity is even more drastic. Such considerations, however, are often minimized prior to entering into a mixed marriage. Very often, a person about to marry someone outside of his or her faith attempts to minimize the act or its consequences by declaring that their intended spouse is not religious or that he or she does not follow the religion of his birth. Yet, a lack of commitment to one's religion does not insure that their progeny will have a Jewish identity or that such a home will have a Jewish atmosphere. Even if one's partner does not practice his or her religion, more likely than not, the fact of intermarriage also minimizes the practice of Judaism.

WHAT OF SOLUTIONS?

It has to be stated that many problems cannot be solved. At best one can recommend certain activities which may temporarily alleviate the intensity of the problem. For instance, it is not within the power of any Jewish organization, whether B'nai B'rith or Federations, to alter the economic conditions which led toward the centralization of production and distribution and consequently made entrepreneurship an anachronism. One cannot rejuvenate small-town economy so that it might attract Jewish businessmen—that is a thing of the past.

No plan can or should be unilateral. Just as small towns differ, so do their problems and solutions. For instance, there are towns devoid of young people or children, towns where Jewish life will exist for a short period and cease—no matter what. Conversely, there are towns with thriving Jewish communities, which must be treated differently from those that have no future. Similarly, towns with large Jewish populations have different needs than towns with intermediate and small Jewish populations. In order to make correct and rational decisions, therefore, more information is necessary about Jewish life in small towns. We must know their population characteristics as well as their economic needs and trends. In short, there should first be a concentrated effort to gather information.

While B'nai B'rith and other groups may attempt to provide help to solve the concerns of small-town Jews, there are some things which can be initiated by those Jews themselves. This self-help program can exist particularly in the areas of home and marriage.

The importance of the home in the formation of identity is almost axiomatic. It is the home where the child's personality is formed and the relative strength of his identity is determined. The child's future identity is determined by what he absorbs of religious rituals, and the manner in which they are performed. When rituals are presented not as an essential or normal life style, but rather as part of a show, designed for the children, children will sense they are inevitably seen as unimportant and rejected along with the rest of Judaism. Observances and practice in the Jewish home, if they are to have an impact on identity, must be performed *l'shem shmoh,* that is, for their own sake.

In this area of home and family, Jews are noted as a family-oriented group. The idea of *mishpochah* as an extended family consisting of people who interact and have a sense of responsibility to each other might well be reintroduced into small-town life. It does not necessarily have to consist of people related to each other through kinship but could rather consist of a number of families who want to share common Jewish and personal experiences. Such associations could effectively combat the growing sense of isolation and alienation. Moreover, this form of *mispochah* could become the nucleus for the observance of Shabbat, Passover, Sukkot, and so on. The extended family might also provide the children with a means of reinforcing their Jewish identity through their association with other Jewish children and with members of the older generation who can function as adopted grandparents, and who will be an important source of oral history and transmission of tradition.

A new attitude to intermarriage is also necessary. The high rate of intermarriage in small towns is a reality, and one destined to persevere if not accelerate. Because of their fewness of numbers (often not more than two or three to a high school) Jewish students depend on non-Jews for dates. The old approaches are no longer functional. While traditionally, the parents of a child who married "out" declared him dead and sat *shiva,* such an approval would hasten the demise of Jewish life in small towns. Small-town Jews must deal with this reality by providing mechanisms for integrating the non-Jewish spouse. The motto should be cooptation instead of ostracism, conversion instead of exclusion.

Obviously, this cannot be achieved without the help of rabbis and their willingness to reinterpret the Halakhah or traditional laws. One of the necessary changes should include the idea that marriage constitutes a legitimate reason for conversion. We cannot and should not indulge in a puristic value which specifies that only a true and deep commitment to Judaism can justify conversion, and therefore all prospective converts must be discouraged three times before being accepted.

Since the Jewish people in small towns represent less than one per cent of the Jewish population in the United States, the question naturally arises: Why spend effort and money to alleviate such a small problem? The truth is that the problems experienced by small-town Jews merely foreshadow (if not already mirror) the problems that exist among urban Jews. Intermarriage, loss of identity, and declining populations are hardly problems exclusive with small-town Jews. If solutions can be found for the latter, they may be equally useful for American Jewry in general. Small towns thus not only presage what is happening to Jewish life, but they can also serve as a proving ground in developing solutions. They serve an indispensable function that may insure the continued existence of the Jewish people.

NOTES

1. See author's earlier article "Small-Town Jews' Integration into Their Communities," *Rural Sociology,* June 1970, based on a study of Jews living in 12 small towns in Southern Illinois.

2

SOUTHERN JEWS

Little sociological attention has been given to southern Jews. A number of books and articles have been written on specific southern Jewish communities,[1] but most of the former have been historical and most of the latter have been informal observations.[2] A few informal observations from a more general orientation have also helped to describe the situation for southern Jews. Golden, in "Jew and Gentile in the New South" in 1955, stated that there was very little real anti-Semitism—and "even a solid tradition of philo-Semitism"—in the South because of the Anglo-Calvinist character of southern Protestantism and its devotion to the "Old Testament and Hebrew prophets."[3] He noted that the small-town southern Jew was "our" Jew to small-town southerners —well established financially and readily accepted socially—but that Jews in southern urban areas were socially segregated by Gentiles despite middle-class status. He further noted that acquaintance with and acceptance of "our Jews" often did little to change negative stereotypes toward Jews in general. Kertzer, in his 1967 book, included a chapter "Magnolia Judaism."[4] He noted that the southern Jew is "an alien element in a homogeneous, Anglo-Saxon, Baptist-Methodist society, which has not quite made peace with the idea that a person who worships God either as a Catholic or a Jew can be authentically American. . . . Yet the southern Jew, while less integrated in the religio-cultural life of the community is, paradoxically, more at home socially."[5] Killian, in his 1970 sociological book, concluded that southern Jews have largely assimilated to southern mores but that southern Jews may become "less southern" as they increase in numbers.[6]

Empirically oriented studies have also appeared on selected southern communities—for example, Reissman's study of New Orleans,[7] Fishman's study of "Southern City,"[8] Lowi's study of "Iron City,"[9] and Lebeau's study of Waycross, Georgia.[10] Mehling included an insightful essay on the "Jewishness" of Miami Beach in his 1960 book, but no in-depth empirical study has yet been made of the Jewish community in metropolitan Miami even though over 40 percent of southern Jews live in this area.[11]

Beginning in the 1950s, a number of articles appeared on problems southern Jewish communities faced in regard to the racial integration controversy. Perlmutter, in "Bombing in Miami" in 1958, for instance, noted the fundamentalist envy, scorn, and hostility of the rural Floridian toward the big city as exemplified by the "pleasure domes of Miami Beach" and the threat the rural Floridian felt from the "vibrations of south Florida urbanization" and a "remote" government in Washington.[12] Shankman, in "A Temple Is Bombe —Atlanta, 1958" in 1971, noted that the bombing of several southern synagogues in 1958 caused a number of southern Jews to "wonder whether they would soon become the targets of religious bigotry." Southern Jews were in a dilemma, he said, with some favoring segregation, many being indifferent to the black's struggle for civil rights, and a significant number tending to sympathize with the civil-rights movement but fearful "that making strong statements in favor of integration would lead to their economic ruin and social ostracism."[13] Levy has noted the more general dilemma for American Jews—being considered as "Jews" by whites but as "whites" by blacks.[14] Ringer concludes, however, that more research is needed on these topics before the situation can be known with accuracy.[15]

Research literature on southern Jews has remained rare;[16] it was not until 1973 that the first book was published that put together a comprehensive view of southern Jewry—an anthology by Dinnerstein and Palsson, *Jews in the South.*[17] In the same year, *The Provincials: A Personal History of Jews in the South* by Evans was published.[18] While not an empirical work, *The Provincials* is more than a personal history; it is an insightful depiction of the life of southern Jews. Ronald Bern's *The Legacy,* although a novel, also presents sociological insights into the problems of a Jew growing up in a small South Carolina town in this century.[19] In October 1976 research on southern Jewry was furthered by a Conference on the History of Southern Jewry held in Richmond, Virginia, and sponsored by the American Jewish Historical Society, the Richmond Jewish Community Council, and the Department of History and the Judaic Culture Committee of Virginia Commonwealth University, with the support of the National Foundation for Jewish Culture. A number of papers and several special addresses calling for more research on southern Jewry were presented at the conference. Edited by Melvin Urofsky, these papers will be published as *Shalom with a Southern Accent: Essays on Southern Jewry.*

The selections in this section discuss southern Jews. First is an article by Lavender that presents the "problem" of being a Jew in the South.[20] The article by Lowi discusses the division between the "two communities"—"old" and "new" Jewish families—that still exists in some southern Jewish communities.[21] The selection by the anonymous "Jewish southerner" presents an extreme response to the dilemma for southern Jews concerning the racial integration controversy and is included partly because of its rarity and partly because of its firsthand account.[22] The article by Mehling describes the Miami of an earlier time and gives a good background on the largest Jewish community in the South—a community that comprises over 40 percent of southern Jews but that has not yet been studied empirically.[23] The final article by Wolfe discusses the future of southern Jewry.[24]

NOTES

1. Historical studies are needed, of course, and make a valuable contribution to understanding the origins and backgrounds of communities. They usually do little, however, to describe the current situations of communities. Some studies that provide factual information are: Mrs. David J. Greenberg, *Through the Years: A Study of the Richmond Jewish Community* (Richmond: Richmond Jewish Community Council, 1955); Herbert T. Ezekiel and Gaston Lichtenstein, *The History of the Jews of Richmond from 1769 to 1917* (Richmond: privately published, 1917); Charles Reznikoff and Uriah Z. Engelman, *The Jews of Charleston* (Philadelphia: Jewish Publication Society of America, 1950); Bertram W. Korn, *The Early Jews of New Orleans* (Waltham, Mass.: American Jewish Historical Society, 1969); Julian B. Feibelman, *A Social and Economic Study of the New Orleans Jewish Community* (Philadelphia: Jewish Publication Society of America, 1941); and Ira E. Sanders and Elijah E. Palnick, *The Centennial History of Congregation B'nai Israel* (Little Rock: B'nai Israel, 1966). A more recent work is Mark Elovitz, *A Century of Jewish Life in Dixie: The Birmingham Experience* (University, Alabama: University of Alabama Press, 1974). A number of studies of more specific aspects of a particular Jewish community have been published, as for example, Janice O. Rothschild, *As But a Day* (Altanta: University of Georgia Press, 1967), and Melvin S. Harris, *The Columbia Hebrew Benevolent Society* (Columbia, S.C.: Columbia Hebrew Benevolent Society, 1947).

2. Articles based on informal observations also make a valuable contribution to understanding communities but usually need to be supplemented by empirical studies. Some insightful articles are: Calvin Trillin, "U.S. Journal: New Orleans," *New Yorker* (March 9, 1968): 138-143; and Harold Mehling, "Is Miami Beach Jewish?" in *The Most of Everything* (New York: Harcourt, Brace and World, 1960), pp. 129-144.

3. Harry Golden, "Jew and Gentile in the New South," *Commentary* 20 (November 1955): 403.

4. Morris N. Kertzer, "Magnolia Judaism," in *Today's American Jew* (New York: McGraw-Hill Book Company, 1967), pp. 265-280.

5. Ibid., p. 265.

6. Lewis M. Killian, *White Southerners* (New York: Random House, 1970).

7. Leonard Reissman, "The New Orleans Jewish Community," *Jewish Journal of Sociolog* 4 (June 1962): 110-123.

8. Joshua A. Fishman, "Southern City," *Midstream* 7 (September 1961): 39-56.

9. Theodore Lowi, "Southern Jews: The Two Communities," *Jewish Journal of Sociology* 6 (July 1964): 103-117.

10. James Lebeau, "Profile of a Southern Jewish Community: Waycross, Georgia," *American Jewish Historical Quarterly* 58 (June 1969): 429-442.

11. Mehling, "Is Miami Beach Jewish?" Some preliminary findings on the Miami Jewish community are found in Gladys Rosen's "A Case Study: The Role of the Rabbi in Miami." Paper presented at the Conference on the History of Southern Jewry, Richmond, Virginia, October 24-25, 1976. For a copy, contact Dr. Rosen at American Jewish Committee, 165 East 56th Street, New York, N.Y. 10022.

12. Nathan Perlmutter, "Bombing in Miami: Anti-Semitism and the Segregationists," *Commentary* 25 (June 1958): pp. 498-503.

13. Arnold Shankman, "A Temple Is Bombed–Atlanta, 1958," *American Jewish Archives* 23 (May 1971): 125.

14. Eugene Levy, " 'Is the Jew a White Man?': Press Reaction to the Leo Frank Case, 1913-1915," *Phylon* 35 (June 1974): 212-222.

15. Benjamin B. Ringer, "Jews and the Desegregation Crisis," in Charles Herbert Stember et al., *Jews in the Mind of America* (New York: Basic Books, 1966).

16. Alfred O. Hero, Jr., *The Southerner and World Affairs* (Baton Rouge: Louisiana State University Press, 1965), pp. 636-637. John Shelton Reed has noted the problem of studying southern Jews and has begun to correct this lack of research somewhat. See "Needles in Haystacks: Studying 'Rare' Populations by Secondary Analysis of National Sample Surveys," *Public Opinion Quarterly* 39 (Winter 1975-1976): 514-522. Also see his "Ethnicity in the South: Some Observations on the Acculturation of Southern Jews," in *Ethnicity,* forthcoming

17. Leonard Dinnerstein and Mary Dale Palsson, eds., *Jews in the South* (Baton Rouge: Louisiana State University Press, 1973).

18. Eli N. Evans, *The Provincials: A Personal History of Jews in the South* (New York: Atheneum, 1973). As noted, *The Provincials* is not empirically based and has a few flaws. Nevertheless, it is a valuable contribution to understanding southern Jewry. As Rothschild states, "Despite these flaws, *The Provincials* is basically a great book. As history, we must think of it as impressionistic—valid but primarily vivid material, to be felt rather than dissected. Eli Evans has not written a textbook. He has gathered a significant armful of our heritage and packaged it glowingly for mass consumption." See Janice O. Rothschild, "Southern and Jewish." *Hadassah Magazine* 55 (November 1973): 22.

19. Ronald L. Bern, *The Legacy* (New York: Mason Charter, 1975).

20. Abraham D. Lavender, "Shalom—with a Southern Accent." Published in *Contemporary Jewry: A Journal of Social Inquiry* 4 (Fall/Winter 1977) as "Shalom, Y'all: Accent on Southern Jewry."

21. Lowi, "Southern Jews: The Two Communities."

22. Anonymous, "A Jewish View on Segregation," Association of Citizens' Councils of Mississippi, Greenwood, Mississippi. This is a thirteen-page pamphlet, undated but published in the time of intense debate over integration in the South. It was published with the instructions to "read and pass on"; few copies are available today. Appreciation is expressed to Arnold Shankman for helping this writer obtain a copy.

23. Mehling, "Is Miami Beach Jewish?" Seymour B. Liebman, author of a number of scholarly books on Jewish topics, president of the Jewish Historical Society of South Florida, and a long-time resident of and participant in the Miami Jewish community, is probably the person best qualified to do a scholarly study of the community. To date there has not been encouragement (through funding) for such research.

24. Jerome A. Wolfe, "The Future of Jews in the South," original for this volume.

SHALOM-WITH A SOUTHERN ACCENT:
An Examination of Jews in the South

ABRAHAM D. LAVENDER

Much has been written about a "southern ethos" and a "Jewish ethos" and even about a "southern mystique" and a "Jewish mystique."[1] These terms may be overstatements, but sociologists have well documented the existence of a "southern subculture" and a "Jewish subculture."[2] Each of these can have strong effects on its members, and yet the two can interact with each other—and those individuals who are members of both can react in several possible ways, depending on the values and power of both.[3]

Only a small amount of research has been done on the interaction of the southern and Jewish subcultures.[4] The purpose of this essay is to suggest some values basic to each of these groups, to examine how the two have interacted in the past and how this has affected individuals who are members of both and to suggest questions for further research about the future of this interaction.

THE SOUTHERN SUBCULTURE

The writing about the South has varied from historical and sociological studies such as those of W.J. Cash and Lewis Killian,[5] to objective and subjective "participant observation" and impressionistic works of native sons and daughters such as Willie Morris,[6] to novels such as those of William Faulkner and Thomas Wolfe.[7] The results have been mixed, but there are several themes that are common to most of these writers: the Anglo-Saxon background, fundamentalist Protestantism, and the ever-present white-black problem.

Anglo-Saxon Background

The Anglo-Saxon background of the South is one of its strongest characteristics. Throughout its colonial period and early years, the United States was heavily formed

by the power and predominance of Anglo-Saxon values, and it "was in this atmosphere that the South developed."[8] But as the remainder of the nation continued
to grow and absorb other peoples and other values, the South remained basically
Anglo-Saxon in composition and values. With a few exceptions, non-British settlers
in the South—particularly French Protestants and German Protestants—were absorbe
into the Anglo-Saxon culture. The South today remains the region of the country
with the highest percentage of native-born, Anglo-Saxon, Protestant residents—the
"most homogeneous section of the country, that region where, except for the distinct separation of the white and black races, there has been greatest assimilation
of all persons into the political, social, and cultural pattern of the existing dominant
group."[9]

It was this "Anglo-Saxon, Nordic, North European, Celtic, Teutonic" culture
that provided the springboard for the spreading to other parts of the world the religious values of Puritanism and Calvinism, the social values of the Protestant ethic
and social Darwinism, and the emphasis on rationalism. And it was in the United
States that the frontier spirit and the overwhelming presence of the racial issue were
added and—especially for southerners—were to join with these other values to mold
the southern way of life and value system.

Fundamentalist Protestant Influence

The fundamentalist and absolutist morality of Puritanism and Calvinism is
also a major characteristic of the South. As Lillian Smith has said, "Nothing was
too small to be the concern of these moralists."[10] "By the time we were five years
old we had learned, without hearing the words, that masturbation is wrong and
segregation is right, and each had become a dread taboo that must never be broken,
for we believed God, whom we feared and tried desperately to love, had made the
rules. . . ."[11] It was a religious influence that also affected their economic behavior—
"They were self-reliant individualists and hardy fighters, sustained in their Calvin-
istic conviction that they had been called by the Lord to subdue the earth."[12] This
influence permeates the life of the South—if not religiously then socially and culturally—partly by its ideology that it is "the only right way" but also simply by its
size and numerical predominance. As Lillian Smith, among others, has explained,
"We cannot understand the church's role as a teacher of southern children without realizing the strength of religion in the lives of everybody, rich and poor. . . .
Church was our town—come together not to kneel and worship but to see each
other."[13] One may disagree with the social versus spiritual reasons for church attendance, but it is a fact that "few societies in modern Christendom can compare
with the American South for proportion of religious affiliation or intensity of religious conviction."[14] Not all writers believe that it has always been that way or that
intense. Alston and Flynt argue that this pervasiveness is a relatively new phenomenon, that there was more intellectual openness and social involvement in the past
than recognized.[15] Nevertheless, even these writers state that Protestantism in the
Bible belt has usually concerned itself with "such issues as the morality of dancing"

while "American society has been grappling with the problems of war, race, and justice," that it has concealed the issues of God and man so successfully as to enable men to live in the midst of injustice and oppression without thought of revolution."[16]

Anglo-Saxonism, Fundamentalist Protestantism, and the Race Factor

The Anglo-Saxon background—with its emphasis on rationalism, social Darwinism, and the work ethic—combined with the influence of fundamentalist Protestantism—with its "born-in-sin" concept of human nature, its belief in being "the only true way," and its absolutist morality—to mold a belief system in which it is difficult to separate these two influences. Factors such as "poor education, rural underprivileged childhood, low social status, passive resignation to fate, laissez-faire economics, political conservatism, and a general pessimism concerning human nature" have been so interrelated with fundamentalist Protestantism that it is "often difficult to distinguish fundamentalism from the whole ethos of the religion."[17] The "dogmatism and pride of a people already stern, hard, and proud" has been increased by a "strict and limited moral and theological education."[18] It was a system that molded people who were "not interested in humanistic education, and their introspection was dogmatic and logical, not spiritual. As their passage through successive frontiers lessened their education and increased their individualism, they became increasingly moralistic,"[19] a moralism that encouraged them to "think in dogmatic, over-simplified ways, to apply black-and-white moralism to social and political issues."[20]

As Anglo-Saxonism and fundamentalist Protestantism combined to intensify each other, so these resulting intensified values spread to influence nonfundamentalists and the entire region. Attitudes toward education are perhaps indicative of this interaction, for just as education "was low on the list of priorities held by Southern churches, being absolute anathema in the eyes of some,"[21] so it sometimes was expanded to the point that education was discouraged (or at least not encouraged) by middle and upper-middle classes. For example, it is not uncommon for parents in the South who are economically comfortable to require their college-age children to work part-time for meager wages while attending college—even when this work negatively affects the child's college accomplishments and chances for further education—to help finance expenses. This is partly due to the work ethic—that hard work and sacrifice build character and strength. It is also due to the lack of importance put on formal education and exposure to "alien" and "impractical" values. But it is also due to the fear of pretension, the fear that the child will "think he knows more and is better" than others. As Anson has perceptively explained, "You don't want to do anything that will make you too different than anyone else in town. You see it here. A kid can be smart but he doesn't want to seem too intellectual, and he especially doesn't want to seem like a grind. Being too intellectual is identified with pretension."[22] It is easier to be accepted as a success in other ways—for example, in sports, politics, or business. In these areas also one must always be on guard not to be perceived as being "better" or "stuck up," but education—at least formal higher education—remains an area with fewer rewards and more dangers.

It is a value system that emphasizes lack of pretension, honesty in relations with others, loyalty to one's family and friends, and self-confidence in one's worth and one's values. But it is also a system that often allows that loyalty to close out those who are not family or friends and to have strong feelings against one's enemies, a system where confidence in one's values as absolute leads one to provincialism and intolerance. It is a system that encourages individualism and independence, although that individualism can lead to insensitivity toward the less fortunate. It is a system that often allows more openness across different economic strata than in other regions of the country but where "within our own breed of whites and Protestants . . . we would never have given thought to the possibility of any other variety being there."[23] It is a system where that intolerance of variety, added to loyalty to one's own, sometimes extends to violent excesses—as when the trial of two white men charged with the kidnapping and murdering of a fourteen-year-old youth, Emmet Till (because he had allegedly "wolf-whistled" at a white woman in 1955) was "quickly transformed from one of murder to one of the defense-of-an-embattled-white-Mississippi."[24] As Workman says, "Despite a reputation for quick temper, the Southerner is amiable, friendly, and tolerant of all save those who would interfere with his family life. Southerners will wrangle among themselves . . . but they will draw together in quick resentment against the non-Southerner who proposes to alter conduct by compulsion of word or deed."[25]

The southern subculture is much concerned with "good manners," hospitality, and "helpfulness, courtesy, and amicable relations"[26] where even nonacceptances are "covered by gentility, good manners, and [smiles]"[27] and where "to call a southerner inhospitable is comparable to calling him un-Christian."[28] But this is a value system that is more likely to label disagreement as lack of loyalty and lack of manners and where criticism of the status quo is more likely to be labeled as lack of appreciation for hospitality. This "to criticize is to be disloyal and ill-mannered" ideology is illustrated by the perhaps extreme response to an outsider who had criticized unequal facilities for blacks in a small southern county in 1973: "People of quality do not have to push in where they do not fit; they do not lie down in the streets and demonstrate; and most of all, they do not make demands. . . . Farewell. And please don't come again. We love our quiet, lazy, peaceful, loving way of life. Take your rebellion, your dirty mind to the foot of the Cross and get them cleaned up. . . . You betrayed your good friends here."[29]

There is a loyalty to the land in the South, a loyalty perhaps "in affection only a step removed from motherhood itself."[30] This value is expected in others. As Anson has said, "Where are you from? It is the question you always hear in the South, asked not only of Yankees but of other southerners." As Anson continues, the northerner would more likely say he was from "Pennsylvania" or "New York" or even "not anywhere in particular," but "a Southerner would never say that. He would always be specific . . . narrowing it down as much as he could so you would know him better and feel more at ease."[31] The South is a land where the past matters, where memories of things long past and persons long dead are meaning-ful,[32] but where the past is often worshipped "without giving alternatives of change a chance." It is a system that—at least until recently—could probably still be sum-marized by W.J. Cash's description of the "ninety-nine per cent pure Anglo-Saxon" who was "extraordinarily on the alert to ward off the possibility that at some future date [this purity] might be contaminated by the introduction of other blood-streams than those of the old original stock."[33]

The South has been a subculture where "any differences [have] always stood out with great vividness."[34] This differentness has been particularly obvious and harmful for the black, but it has also been harmful—to a lesser degree—for other outsiders: the Catholic, the Jew, the foreigner, and others.

Although scores of thousands of individual southerners do not fit the above description and although there are places in the South—such as Miami—that are different in many ways, this white-Anglo-Saxon-Protestant value system has been pervasive enough to mold the overall ethos of the South, so that even those out-posts such as Miami are engulfed—or at least hemmed in—by it. It is a value system that is not limited to fundamentalists, but where Protestant "denominations have generally tended to become more conservative and less socially aware as they be-come more middle-class"[35] and where "both lower and upper class status white Protestants in the South have become more conservative in recent years,"[36] and where even "moderate" or "liberal" WASPs—Brooks Hays of Arkansas, Charles Weltner of Georgia, Frank Graham of North Carolina, Claude Pepper of Florida—practicing their definition of Anglo-Saxon and Protestant values have been rejected by their fellow-WASPs.[37]

THE JEWISH SUBCULTURE

Into this southern subculture "where all differences have stood out with vivid-ness," we now place the Jewish subculture. Jews have long been in the South. The first Jewish settlement of considerable size in the South was in Georgia in 1733.[38] Throughout the colonial period the number of southern Jews was small, and they were largely of the more relaxed and casual Sephardic orientation. In the middle decades of the 1800s increasing numbers of German Jewish immigrants spread into small communities in the South.[39] In the 1900s, and particularly as the children of the East European migration began to attain middle-class status and spread throughout the United States largely following World War II, the southern Jewish community increased. The size has always remained small, however, with southern Jews comprising less than 1 percent of all southerners.[40] In most southern states, Jews comprise about .25 to .50 percent of the population; Florida is the exception: 3.7 percent of the population is Jewish.

In some ways these southern and Jewish subcultures are similar: Jews also know the importance of an attachment to a land; tradition sometimes is a major factor in perserving group values; and values such as group loyalty and a "feeling of be-longing to a group" and "pride in . . . having a tradition worthy of being passed on

to others"[41] are important. There are some similarities in practice—although resulting from different causes—that make for conflict. Just as southerners are fearful of
outside influences—but from a position of dominance and desire to preserve their
society (although we must recognize that some of the effects of being subjugated
in the Civil War and Reconstruction era still remain)—so many Jews have a distrust
of all outsiders as a result of hundreds of years of Crusades, pogroms, forced conversions, and inquisitions at the hands of Christian Europeans. The Sephardic experience has been different, for most Sephardim have not lived in the "either-or"
(either assimilation to Christianity or life largely enclosed in the ghetto) world of
Christian Europe as have the Ashkenazim. Nevertheless, most (about 97 percent)
American Jews are from the Ashkenazic background and have been molded by
this distrust.[42]

Social Justice, Knowledge, Nonasceticism

Despite these similarities, however, there are major ways in which Judaism differs
from Anglo-Saxon-influenced fundamentalist Protestant ways. Judaism teaches
that "man is just a little lower than the angels" rather than that man is "born in
sin." Hence, the Jew has a more optimistic and less ascetic view of human nature.
For example, the social Darwinist predilection to view economically unproductive
individuals as negligent, shiftless, and imprudent is not as likely to be accepted,
and neither is the belief in strong "law and order" as necessary for limiting one's
"evil" impulses.[43] Judaism is a "this-world" oriented religion, and this has influenced it to stress the importance of social justice in this world rather than accepting this world and preparing for the "next world." Zedakeh (charity, but really
meaning "social justice" rather than "giving alms") has been a major concept of
Judaism. The high conception of human nature, the emphasis on this world, and
the emphasis on social justice—along with the Jew's own practical experience as a
marginal man and outsider—have all been suggested as having influenced the Jew
to be liberal on political, economic, and social matters regardless of whether he is
directly benefited.[44] He has been influenced to favor a big government in areas
of social justice and to hesitate to align himself with the political right even in
those few cases where the right is philo-Semitic.[45] Ringer reports that many Jews
believe that to be a "good Jew" one must "promote civic improvement" in the
community,[46] and these beliefs have been put into practice as Jews have consistently voted liberal and participated in social and cultural causes far beyond their
representation in the population.[47]

Judaism has accepted much of the Protestant ethic in regard to the work ethic,[48]
and American Jews have made rapid upward mobility[49]—but the social Darwinist
reverse idea that not "making it" is a result of laziness has not been accepted.
Partly because of the strong commitment to helping others and a strong sense of
belonging to the family and the community, the laissez-faire individualism and
independence that accompanies the Protestant ethic has not been accepted. Judaism
has traditionally given its highest status to the scholar and continues to put much

emphasis on learning.[50] The Jewish family is child centered, and this—partly because of its being combined with a higher concept of human nature—has led to belief in the child as a person "whose opinion has been taken seriously, whose wishes have helped determine the actions of adults around him and the nature of his environment. . . ."[51] This approach, mixed with the love of learning and a certain amount of the Protestant ethic, makes a subculture where parents strongly encourage their children to be "my son the doctor," where the parents sacrifice and even suffer (it was not unusual for newly arrived poor imigrants to hold extra jobs so that their children could go to "good" colleges and even join the "best fraternities and sororities") so that the children can improve themselves rapidly, and where parents receive much self-reward (nachus) from their children's accomplishments.[52] These values, combined with experiences and acquaintances in various parts of the world, have encouraged the Jew to value highly cosmopolitanism over provincialism, and formal education and culture over lack of these.

Nonfundamentalism

Judaism also has absolute values, and a moral system similar to—although not as ascetic as—Christianity's. In many ways traditional Judaism is as fundamentalistic as fundamentalist Protestantism. "The doctrines of Orthodoxy . . . are more precise [than Conservative and Reform Judaism] and are by definition beyond compromise or even the appearance of compromise. . . . It is fair to say that the entire belief structure of American Orthodoxy still finds verbal expression within the bounds of a rather narrow fundamentalism."[53]

But American Jews—and particularly southern Jews—have been much less affected by Jewish fundamentalism than American Protestants—and particularly southern Protestants—have been affected by Protestant fundamentalism. Consequently, there is more likelihood that the Jew will be flexible in his interpretations and applications of the specific "moral" rules—to think in "it depends" rather than in "either-or" terms. Because Jews "do not consider their bodily appetites as sinful, their behavior in matters of sex, drink, and food is affected accordingly. . . . Jewish proscriptions are generally against the excessive use of bodily appetites, not against their use at all."[54] For example, Jews are more likely than non-Jews to be liberal toward moderate use of alcohol and drugs such as marijuana but less likely to become alcoholics or drug addicts.[55] The same principle holds in the area of sexual morality. For example, a recent National Opinion Research Center poll indicated that 76 percent of white Protestants thought that extramarital sex was "always wrong" and 2 percent thought it was "not wrong at all," while only 22 percent said "almost always or only sometimes wrong"—that is, "it depends." For white Baptists, by far the largest single religious group in the South, the corresponding figures were 82 percent "wrong," 1 percent "not wrong," and 17 percent "it depends." For Jews, however, the corresponding figures were 24 percent "wrong," 7 percent "not wrong," and 69 percent "it depends." That this attitude extends not only to common behavior but also to rarer "victimless behavior" is indicated by the figures for attitudes toward homosexuality. Here there is even more of a contrast between the "either-or" and the "it depends" ideologies for Protestants and Jews. The figures for attitudes on homosexuality for Protestants were 79 percent "wrong," 8 percent "not wrong," and 13 percent "it depends." For Baptists, the figures were 88 percent "wrong," 5 percent "not wrong," and 7 percent "it depends." For Jews, the figures were 32 percent "wrong," 38 percent "not wrong," and 30 percent "it depends."[56] And yet, most research suggests that Jews are more likely than non-Jews to marry, more likely to value having children, and less likely to divorce.[57] But, of course, what is "community spirit, social justice, liberalism, and practicality" to some are "rabble-rousing, socialism, communism, permissiveness, and immorality" to others.

THE INTERACTION

With a mixture of such values, some conflict and marginality for Jews is inevitable. To the Jew, much of what has been described here as southern is actually gentile, even though as Dabbs's discussion shows there are some major differences even between southern Protestants and New England Protestants in such things as the latter's greater interest in passionate introspection and humanist education.[58] However, since attempting to enter the modern world in the last few centuries, Jews have found that "the various societies, together with their traditions and memories, are still Christian—at least as far as the Jews are concerned. However secular these societies have been from one perspective, they have not been secular in the sense of being neutral between Christianity and Judaism, Christians and Jews."[59] As a result of this, there has probably been a tendency from the Jewish perspective to give too much homogeneity to Protestantism—and particularly to Christianity, for many ethnic Catholics are much closer to Jews than they are to Protestants on many issues.[60] Nevertheless, just as the South is a more intense and more absolutist version of Gentile and Christian America, so the problems Jews face in the South have been intensified, and this has affected the interaction of the two subcultures.

There are a few issues on which Jews and Southerners agree. Southerners are more likely than nonsoutherners to be pro-Israel. Southern Baptists and other fundamentalists in particular support Israel "almost mystically because their own interpretations of the Bible include a Second Coming of Jesus Christ in the land of the Chosen People, Jews."[61] But this is not translated into an acceptance of Jews as Jews, into a policy that allows diversity. A 1966 study by the Anti-Defamation League, for instance, showed that 97 percent of southern Baptists agreed with the statement that "belief in Jesus Christ as Savior is absolutely necessary for salvation," and 80 percent agreed with the statement that "the Jews can never be forgiven for what they did to Jesus until they accept Him as the True Savior."[62] Hence, the same religionists who support Israel also have an absolutist belief system that teaches that Christianity is the only true religion and that it is the duty of a "good Christian" to convert "nonbelievers" (including Jews) to Christianity. The result has been an unrelenting pressure on Jews to convert. This started early and continues—with ebbs and flows—today. When the first group of Jews settled in Georgia in 1733, the Ashkenazim and Sephardim did not join together because the Ashkenazim were rigorously traditional in their observance while the Sephardim were "more relaxed in their Judaism, keeping the spirit rather than the letter of Hebrew law."[63] However, within a few years the Christians converted a member of the Jewish community, and the "assimilated Sephardim and the ghettoized Ashkenazim put aside their difference to come together in a rude hut which passed for a synagogue."[64] Few Jews in the South (and elsewhere, but especially in the South) have not been approached time after time by a would-be proselytizer trying to "save souls," often with an intensity and tenacity approaching harassment. A story in a weekly newspaper in 1976, for example, tells of the effort over a twenty-year period to convert a Jewish man in a small southern town. He was a good man "but Jewish." Whenever this Jewish man "heard of anyone in our town who was in any kind of trouble, he tried to help. . . . And he went to synagogue regularly." For twenty years, his fishing buddies (a next-door neighbor who wrote the article and two ministers) took advantage of every opportunity to "slip in a witness" to Jesus. As the author states, "Since he was my next-door neighbor, I'd drop by and visit him whenever he got sick. And I'd always ask for permission to pray, but he wouldn't let me. . . . 'No, your belief is different,' he answered. 'I don't want to hear any more about Jesus.' " But the buddies continued until finally when he was hospitalized and his buddies were still trying to get him "to realize that as a man of integrity he couldn't refuse the claims of Christ," he converted.[65] This is an extreme case, and most individual southerners would not spend this much effort to convert someone, but it nevertheless illustrates the situation in the Bible belt. Even when there have not been efforts to convert individually, the Jew has been permeated with Christianity. As Eli Evans has said, "That was the shame, the oppressive burden of Christian history. Some Jews in the South crumble under it and others try to ignore it; some slink and hide, others despair, but most absorb it and block it out, and survive. All of us in the South had to face it in one way or another."[66]

If the difference between Anglo-Saxon and Jewish values, and the difference between Christianity and Judaism, have made the life of the Jew in the South precarious or at least uncomfortable, the race issue has made it almost unbearable at times. As Killian notes, "Some prosegregation propaganda has stressed the strong support rendered the NAACP by Jewish philanthropists, suggesting that all Jews must be integrationists."[67] As Circuit Judge (and vice-president of the Mississippi Bar Association) Tom P. Brady wrote in 1954, "It is lamentable that attention should be called to the alarming increase of Jewish names in the ranks of Communist-front organizations of this country. Of all the nations which have ever been on this earth, the United States of America has been the kindest to the Jew. Here he has suffered but little ostracization—and he has brought most of this upon himself. . . . Hungry, naked, thirsty and homeless we took him in, and made him one of us. . . . The loyal American Jew, on his own volition, should take steps to stop this disloyalty and sometimes outright treason. We know he is embarassed by and regrets these incidents."[68]

As with the response to Anglo-Saxon values and Christian values, the Jewish responses to the race issue have varied. Hero notes that discouraging pressures on all white racial moderates and liberals have been virtually overwhelming, but that they have usually been even more compelling for Jews than for Gentiles of such persuasion and concludes that the responses have varied from intimidation to outspokenness.[69] Responses range from that of the anonymous "Jewish southerner" who wrote in the era of heightened racial tension that there were many Jews who "realize, as I do, that any white Southerner, Christian or Jew, must do all he can to help maintain segregation,"[70] to that of "tending toward thoughts sympathetic to the Negro" for the "vast majority" of southern Jews.[71]

THE JEWISH RESULT

The southern Jew is not the only southerner who has been marginal in the South; the Catholic, the black, and the liberal native WASP have also been marginal and ambivalent. Brooks Hays, president of the Southern Baptist Convention and congressman from the Little Rock, Arkansas, area for sixteen years, tells about a time in 1928 when campaigning for governer (unsuccessfully): "Their [a number of Negro listeners silently pondering the improvements he promised and wondering if they would be included] faces haunted me."[72] One reads of W.J. Cash's "love-hate intensity" of feeling, his "dedicated concern," his "personal anguish."[73] Bass and DeVries, in a commendable recent book on southern politics, tell of the change in a Louisiana legislator who fought vigorously for segregationist measures in the 1960s, but who by 1972 had changed because "I did not want to leave my children with the legacy that their daddy was a bigot and a racist."[74] Willie Morris writes that the longer he lives in New York the more southern he seems to become, "the more obsessed with the old warring impulses of one's sensibility to be both Southern and American. . . . we love it and we hate it, and we cannot turn our backs upon it."[75]

But if the white southerner is sometimes torn between being a southerner and an American, so much more is the southern Jew torn between being an American southerner and a Jew. Eli Evans has perhaps expressed this most succinctly: "I am not certain what it means to be both a Jew and a Southerner—to have inherited the Jewish longing for a homeland while being raised with the southerner's sense of home. The conflict is deep in me—the Jew's involvement in history, his deep roots in the drama of man's struggle to understand deity and creation. But I respond to the Southerner's commitment to place, his loyalty to the land, to his own tortured history, to the strange bond beyond color that Southern blacks and whites discover when they come to know one another."[76]

The Jew in the South is a person in the middle: marginal, more liberal that the southern Gentile, but less liberal than the Northern Jew. He has rarely converted to Christianity, and his Judaism has been influenced very little by Christianity. Indeed, if anything, within himself he has probably recognized even more the historical contrasts between Judaism and the Anglo-Saxon-influenced version of Protestant Christianity.[77] At the same time, a lack of Jewish mates—particularly in the small towns—has encouraged a high rate of intermarriage and loss of one's children as part of the Jewish community through assimilation.[78] Hero has suggested that he is probably closer to the southern Gentile on the issue of race relations in the South but probably closer to the northern Jew on issues that are not as salient and intimidating to his everyday life in the South.[79] Lowi's study has at least suggested that Jews who live in the South for a long time have "customs, aspirations, and general life-styles" that differ from those of recent northern Jewish migrants to the South[80] (and that presumably differ even more from those of northern Jews). The southern Jew, for example, is likely to put less importance on expensive bar mitzvahs and on economic status symbols in general, is likely to be less assertive and more casual in his interpersonal relationships, and is more likely to have intimate Christian friends and interact in a Christian atmosphere without fear of assimilation. At least until recently, his educational and occupational goals were relatively more likely to lead to business (or law) than to academia and the liberal professions such as psychoanalysis and psychiatry.

But just as the southern Jew does not necessarily view himself as any less southern because he has some Jewish values, so he does not necessarily view himself as any less Jewish because he has been influenced by and reacted to some southern values. Much of what is perceived as Jewish actually has European or non-Jewish origins, and many Jewish values are a reaction either positively or negatively to the past and present environment. The northern Jew's definition of Jewishness is a modification of "the" Jewish culture, just as the southern Jew's is a modification in a different way—and in some ways the southern Jewish modification may be closer to the Jewish culture of the prediaspora and preghetto eras than the northern Jewish modification. While the northern Jew is probably closer, for example, in such things as his concern for social justice and political liberalism, the southern Jew is probably closer in his commitment to an easier-going life-style and a more moderate concern with economic status.

THE CHANGING SOUTH: ECONOMICS, BLACKS, AND "OUTSIDERS"

This essay has discussed the South as if it were monolithic, but of course it is not. There is a difference between the Atlantic seaboard South that "experienced the liberal eighteenth century, and, though it fell from grace as it took its place in the Cotton Kingdom after 1800, . . . has never entirely forgotten its early history," and the Gulf South that "never having had this history, succumbed more completely to the violence inherent in the slave system."[81] There is a difference that sometimes extends to hostility between the provincial and fundamentalist rural South and the "pleasure domes" of the big cities.[82] This essay proposes, however, that despite the nonmonolithic character—and despite many scores of thousands of individual exceptions—the Anglo-Saxon-fundamentalist-Protestant values have been pervasive enough and exclusive enough to mold the overall character of the region.

There is a "new South"—the latest in several "new" Souths since the Civil War—largely resulting from the shift from agriculture to industry and the "vast ramifications for southern life" this shift has.[83] But even this newest "new South" has different meanings. Sometimes it means a land where millions of previously disenfranchised people now vote, a land more just in its treatment of blacks, a land that "will solve the racial problem long before the north does," a land more accepting of diversity and outsiders, and a land determinedly moving toward lessoning the three "P"s of provincialism, prejudice, and poverty. It is a South that has gained much attention with the rise to national prominence of Jimmy Carter.[84] But other times this newest "new South" is the South of the economically conservative laissez faire attitude of the oil industry, the anti-unionism of the textile industry, and the primacy of large defense installations—a land that now represents the "new ideological heart of the Republican Party," the new core of the battleground for the preservation of "individual initiative and free enterprise and the battle against the 'drift toward socialism.' "[85]

There are approximately eleven million southern blacks, comprising about one out of five of all southerners. In the past most discussions of southern blacks dealt with their victimization, but that has begun to change. They are a powerful new economic and political force. Their enfranchisement and rising economic status are causing extraordinary changes in the South, and they will be a major part of the current "new South." Southern blacks are predominantly Protestant, and many belong to fundamentalist denominations. But southern black Protestantism is different in major ways from southern white Protestantism. Southern black Protestants have not had dominant power, have not desired to maintain the political and economic status quo that has oppressed them, and have not had to justify racial segregation in religious terms. While often fundamentalistic, southern black Protestantism has not been molded by an ascetic "suffer-for-the-sake-of-suffering" (there was enough suffering for practical reasons) outlook, and has been less stern and harsh with "violators of 'the' morality." Blacks have been the victims—rather than the molders and economic benefactors—of social Darwinism and laissez-faire economics and hence have a greater commitment to social justice. While having an attachment to "home" probably as deep as the southern white has, as a marginal person in his own land the southern black has not become as provincial and unquestioningly loyal as the southern white. Whether these difference are sufficient—and whether the black influence will be sufficient—to affect the overall values of the region, including the historic southern attitude toward Catholics and Jews and other outsiders who are different—and who are increasingly moving to the South—is a question still to be answered. Allied with liberal and moderate whites who only a decade ago were "communists" because they were in favor of racial equality and antipoverty measures, they can be a permanent new force for change on many issues. The extent to which southern Jews and southern blacks will be allies in this "new South" is another question to be answered, but there is no question that both blacks and Jews will be more comfortable in a less absolutist and more tolerant South.[86]

There has been little scholarly research on the Jew in the South. Hopefully, this essay will stimulate more attention to this area—not only to the influence of the South on the Jew but also to the Jewish influence on the South.[87]

NOTES

1. "Ethos" refers to the complex of beliefs, standards, and ideas that characterizes a group. As used by laypersons, the concept is actually quite similar to the sociological concept of "culture" but usually also implies an additional "solidity" or "mystique" not implied by the sociologist's usage of "culture." "Mystique" implies not only that there is a complex of beliefs, standards, and ideas, but that this complex is unfathomable to outsiders and perhaps even to insiders. See Howard Zinn, *The Southern Mystique* (New York: Simon and Shuster, 1964); Tom Mathews and others, "The Southern Mystique," *Newsweek* (July 19, 1976): 30-33; and Ernest van den Haag, *The Jewish Mystique* (New York: Dell Publishing Co., Inc., 1969).

2. "Culture" has a number of meanings, but in broad sociological terms it means "the changing patterns of shared, learned behavior that humans have developed as a result of their group experiences." See David C. King and Marvin R. Koller, *Foundations of Sociology* (San Francisco: Holt, Rinehart, and Winston, 1974), p. 46. Subgroups within the cultural group that differ on some traits and that have an identity as a specific subgroup as well as a part of the larger cultural group are referred to as "subcultures." In this sense, the southern subculture is a part of a larger American culture, and the Jewish subculture is part of a larger Jewish culture. Whether a group is a culture or a subculture to some extent depends on one's point of departure. One could speak of a southern "culture" and a southern Jewish "subculture," but that is not the thesis of this essay.

3. There are a number of typologies to describe these possible interactions. See, for example, William M. Newman, *American Pluralism* (New York: Harper & Row, 1973).

4. This point has been made by several writers. See Leonard Dinnerstein, "A Note on Southern Attitudes Toward Jews," *Jewish Social Studies* 32 (January 1970): 43-49; Alfred O. Hero, Jr., "Southern Jews, Race Relations, and Foreign Policy," *Jewish Social Studies* 27 (October 1965); and John Shelton Reed, "Needles in Haystacks: Studying 'Rare' Populations by Secondary Analysis of National Sample Surveys," *Public Opinion Quarterly* 39 (Winter 1975-1976).

5. W.J. Cash, *The Mind of the South* (New York: Alfred A. Knopf, 1941); Lewis M. Killian, *White Southerners* (New York: Random House, 1970).

6. See, for example, Willie Morris, *North Toward Home* (New York: Dell Publishing Co., 1967) and *Yazoo* (New York: Ballantine Books, 1971).

7. William Faulkner's books are numerous and will not be listed here. For Thomas Wolfe, see especially *You Can't Go Home Again* and *The Hills Beyond* (New York: Harper and Brothers, 1941).

8. William D. Workman, Jr., *The Case for the South* (New York: Devin-Adair Company, 1960), p. 2.

9. Ibid., pp. 3-4.

10. Lillian Smith, *Killers of the Dream* (New York: W.W. Norton & Co., 1949), p. 79.

11. Ibid., p. 70.

12. James McBride Dabbs, *Who Speaks for the South?* (New York: Funk & Wagnalls Company, 1964), p. 85.

13. Smith, *Killers of the Dream*, p. 83.

14. Samuel S. Hill, Jr., et al., *Religion and the Solid South* (Nashville: Abingdon Press, 1972), p. 25.

15. Wallace M. Alston, Jr., and Wayne Flynt, "Religion in the Land of Cotton," in H. Brandt Ayers and Thomas H. Naylor, ed., *You Can't Eat Magnolias* (New York: McGraw-Hill, 1972), p. 102.

16. Ibid., pp. 101, 111.

17. Ibid., p. 107.

18. Dabbs, *Who Speaks for the South?* p. 89.

19. Ibid., p. 90.

20. Alston and Flynt, "Religion in the Land of Cotton," p. 107.

21. Ibid., p. 104.

22. Robert Sam Anson, "Looking for Jimmy: A Journey Through the South, Rising," *New Times* (August 6, 1976): 34. Of the large number of popular-magazine articles on the South since Jimmy Carter's rise to national prominence, this is one of the best. This was a special issue devoted to the South.

23. Morris, *North Toward Home*, p. 21.

24. James W. Vander Zanden, *Race Relations in Transition* (New York: Random House, 1965), p. 23.

25. Workman, *The Case for the South*, p. 2.

26. Hill, *Religion and the Solid South*, p. 25.

27. Anson, "Looking for Jimmy," p. 21.

28. Thomas D. Clark, *The Emerging South* (New York: Oxford University Press, 1961), p. 138.

29. Billy Spigner, "Ramblin' 'Round Clarendon: Farewell Betsy, Sorry About That!" *Manning Times*, (South Carolina), August 15, 1973.

30. Clark, *The Emerging South*, p. 7.

31. Anson, "Looking for Jimmy," p. 25.

32. Workman, *The Case for the South*, p. 10.

33. Cash, *The Mind of the South*, p. 305.

34. Ibid., p. 342.

35. Alston and Flynt, "Religion in the Land of Cotton," p. 115.

36. Norman H. Nie, Sidney Verba, and John R. Petrocik, *The Changing American Voter* (Cambridge, Mass.: Harvard University Press, 1976).

37. For individual examples, see Brooks Hays, *A Southern Moderate Speaks* (Chapel Hill: University of North Carolina Press, 1959), and Charles Longstreet Weltner, *Southerner* (Philadelphia: J.B. Lippincott Company, 1966). For a more general discussion, see V.O. Key, Jr., *Southern Politics* (New York: Alfred A. Knopf, 1949), and Jack Bass and Walter DeVries, *The Transformation of Southern Politics* (New York: Basic Books, 1976). The latter book notes recent changes but also indicates how much of this change on the part of a minority of white southerners has been opposed most strongly by southern white Protestants.

38. Leonard Dinnerstein, Introduction to Leonard Dinnerstein and Mary Dale Palsson, eds. *Jews in the South* (Baton Rouge: Louisiana State University Press), p. 3.

39. Rudolf Glanz, "The Spread of Jewish Communities Through America Before the Civil War," *Yivo Annual of Jewish Social Science* 15 (1974): p. 38.

40. Alvin Chenkin, "Jewish Population in the United States, 1974," in Morris Fine and Milton Himmelfarb, eds., *American Jewish Yearbook* (New York: American Jewish Committee, 1976), pp. 229-238.

41. Abraham D. Lavender, "Disadvantages of Minority Group Membership; The Perspective of a 'Nondeprived' Minority Group," *Ethnicity* 2 (March 1975): 99-119.

42. For a brief discussion of this, see Abraham D. Lavender, "The Sephardic Revival in the United States: A Case of Ethnic Revival in a Minority-within-a-Minority," *Journal of Ethnic Studies* 3 (Fall 1975): 21-31.

43. Scott Cummings and Richard Briggs, "Catholic and Jewish Immigrants and American Politics: An Historical Analysis of the Roots of Urban Liberalism" (Paper delivered at the

Annual Meetings of the American Sociological Association, September 2, 1976, New York City). This paper utilized data from the 1972 election study conducted by the Survey Research Center at the University of Michigan.

44. Mark R. Levy and Michael S. Kramer, *The Ethnic Factor: How America's Minorities Decide Elections* (New York: Simon and Schuster, 1973). See "The Jews: Forever Liberal Wherever They Are," pp. 95-121.

45. See Lucy S. Dawidowicz and Leon S. Goldstein, "The American Jewish Liberal Tradition," in Marshal Sklare, ed., *The Jewish Community in America* (New York: Behrman House, 1974), p. 299; and Seymour Martin Lipset, "Intergroup Relations: The Changing Situation of American Jewry," in ibid., p. 334.

46. Benjamin B. Ringer, "Jewish-Gentile Relations in Lakeville," in ibid., p. 343.

47. Levy and Kramer, *The Ethnic Factor*, pp. 95-121.

48. Gerhard Lenski, *The Religious Factor* (New York: Doubleday and Company, 1961).

49. Marian K. Slater, "My Son the Doctor: Aspects of Mobility Among American Jews," *American Sociological Review* 34 (June 1969): 359-373.

50. Lawrence H. Fuchs, *The Political Behavior of American Jews* (Glencoe, Ill.: The Free Press, 1956), p. 179.

51. Nathan Glazer, "The New Left and the Jews," in Sklare, *The Jewish Community*, p. 307.

52. Marshall Sklare, *America's Jews* (New York: Random House, 1971), p. 87.

53. Charles S. Liebman, "Orthodoxy in American Jewish Life," in Sklare, *The Jewish Community*, p. 140.

54. Fuchs, *The Political Behavior of American Jews*, p. 183.

55. Clyde B. McCoy and Jerome A. Wolfe, "A Comparison of Jewish and Non-Jewish Addicts in Institutional Treatment Programs," *Jewish Sociology and Social Research* 2 (Spring-Summer 1976): 10-15; and Joel Fort and Christopher Cory, *American Drugstore* (Boston: Little, Brown, 1975), p. 24.

56. Jon P. Alston, "Review of the Polls: Attitudes Toward Extramarital and Homosexual Relations," *Journal for the Scientific Study of Religion* 13 (December 1974): 479-481.

57. Sidney Goldstein and Calvin Goldscheider, *Jewish Americans* (Englewood Cliffs, N.J.: Prentice-Hall, 1968), pp. 101-136.

58. Dabbs, *Who Speaks for the South?* p. 90.

59. Milton Himmelfarb, "Secular Society? A Jewish Perspective," in William G. McLoughlin and Robert N. Bellah, eds., *Religion in America* (Boston: Beacon Press, 1966), p. 283.

60. Although they do not discuss this specific issue, see Charles H. Mindel and Robert W. Habenstein, eds., *Ethnic Families in America* (New York: Elsevier, 1976), for a general discussion of "ethnic" versus "WASP" values. This book covers fifteen ethnic groups and is one of the best readers available. The specific "Jewish-Ethnic-WASP" continuum I suggest is in need of further research.

61. Richard Reeves, "Is Jimmy Carter Good for the Jews?" *New York* (May 24, 1976): 12.

62. Note that there are three implications here: that the *Jews* of that time are to blame; that "Jews" today share that blame; and that Jews will not be forgiven for this "blame" until they stop being Jewish. Figures are from Charles Y. Glock and Rodney Stark, *Religion and Society in Tension* (Chicago: Rand McNally, 1965).

63. Harry Golden, *Travels Through Jewish America* (Garden City, N.Y.: Doubleday and Company, 1973), p. 174.

64. Ibid.

65. Bill Walker as told to Muriel Larson, "Conversion Results from Prayer," *Manning Times*, May 26, 1976.

66. Eli N. Evans, *The Provincials: A Personal History of Jews in the South* (New York: Atheneum, 1973), p. 124.

67. Killian, *White Southerners*, p. 80.

68. Tom P. Brady, *Black Monday* (Winona, Miss.: Association of Citizens' Councils, 1954). p. 57.

69. Alfred O. Hero, Jr., "Southern Jews," in Dinnerstein and Palsson, *Jews in the South*, pp. 217-250.

70. Anonymous, "A Jewish View on Segregation," published by the Association of Citizens Councils of Mississippi, Greenwood, Mississippi, n.d., p. 9.

71. Allen Krause, "Rabbis and Negro Rights in the South, 1954-1967," in Dinnerstein and Palsson, *Jews in the South*, p. 363.

72. Hays, *A Southern Moderate Speaks*, p. 3.

73. C. Vann Woodward, "W.J. Cash Reconsidered," *New York Review of Books*, December 1969.

74. Bass and DeVries, *The Transformation of Southern Politics*.

75. Morris, *Yazoo*, p. 148.

76. Evans, *The Provincials*, p. x.

77. This statement refers to beliefs regarding Judaism. In actual practice, the southern Jew has been influenced by the southern emphasis on religion. For example, "Southern Jews have been more inclined than Northern ones to be affiliated with and active in synagogues, as part of the general Southern involvement in organized religion; . . . the rabbi has been a more central figure in most Southern Jewish communities than in most Reform groups in the North. See Hero, "Southern Jews," p. 246.

78. For example, see Benjamin Kaplan, *The Eternal Stranger: A Study of Jewish Life in the Small Community* (New York: Bookman Associates, 1957).

79. Hero, "Southern Jews, Race Relations, and Foreign Policy," p. 230.

80. Theodore Lowi, "Southern Jews: The Two Communities," in Dinnerstein and Palsson, *Jews in the South*, p. 277.

81. Dabbs, *Who Speaks for the South?* p. x.

82. Nathan Perlmutter, "Bombing in Miami: Anti-Semitism and the Segregationists," *Commentary* 25 (June 1958): 498-503.

83. Vander Zanden, *Race Relations in Transition*, p. 13.

84. For example, see Anson, "Looking for Jimmy," pp. 18-66; Mathews et al., "The Southern Mystique," pp. 30-33, Susan Fraker et al., "Carter and the Blacks," p. 29, and Joseph B. Cumming, Jr., "Plains Tries to Adjust," p. 32, all in *Newsweek*, July 19, 1976; Reeves, "Is Jimmy Carter Good for the Jews?" pp. 10, 12; and Johnny Greene, "The Dixie Smile," *Harper's* (September 1976): 14, 18-19.

85. Haynes Johnson, "South Now Ideological Heart of GOP," *Washington Post*, August 18, 1976.

86. In discussing the amount of nonactivism by southern Jews on behalf of civil rights for southern blacks, it is necessary for perspective to note that southern Jews have often not stood up for their own civil rights because of fear. As Hero has noted, "Jews in some communities have been willing to declare themselves against irresponsible views only when under direct attack themselves—they have been afraid even to criticize overt anti-Semitism by racists" ("Southern Jews," p. 248).

87. Most of the concern expressed so far has been with the southern influence on the Jew, rather than with the Jewish influence on the South. This is to be expected, considering the relative size and influence of the two. However, there are indications that there has been some Jewish influence on the South. As Evans and others have shown, one of the strongest characteristics of the southern Jew has been his cosmopolitanism—his contacts with individuals and media from outside his region. As Hero notes, "The presence of a few Jewish families has helped to limit the natural provincialism of many Southern towns and to make life more tolerable for the few Gentiles of similarly broad horizons" ("Southern Jews," p. 249); also see p. 220 for a discussion of "The Most Cosmopolitan Southern Ethnic Group." This role of "mediator with the outside world and distributor of culture from the outside world" is a role that the Jewish community has often played in history—sometimes to its detriment.

SOUTHERN JEWS:
The Two Communities

THEODORE LOWI

INTRODUCTION

An attempt was recently made by Peter Rose to add another piece to the puzzle of the life and ways of American Jews.[1] One can only agree with Dr. Rose that the image of Jewish life portrayed by life in the eastern metropolis is incomplete indeed. Not all the conditions of life in the big city extend to non-metropolitan environments where many Jews live. Thus, Rose argues, "Critical examination of Jewish life in the small community would seem to be a logical extension of research in the study of American Judaism and the nature of Jewish-Gentile relations."[2]

Rose's survey of two small towns in upstate New York adds, as he hoped, a few pieces to the puzzle, but its limitations are as suggestive as its contributions. First of all, he is dealing with a very small segment of American Jewry, and he is leaving out a large slice of life in the larger but non-metropolitan towns and cities, particularly in areas outside the Northeast. Second, in many aspects the small-town rural New York Jews are really very special cases in comparison with all *but* the metropolitan Jews of the Eastern seaboard. By Rose's own count, over 90 per cent of the Jews in his two rural towns were fairly recent immigrants from other parts of the eastern United States and abroad. Only 4 per cent were locally born and bred; over 60 per cent hailed from other American cities; and 30 per cent were refugees from Nazi-dominated European countries. Beyond the fact that so many were newcomers, identification with and commitment to the town were quite weak; many in all age groups displayed strong aspirations for residence elsewhere. Rose has an interesting subject and some significant findings, but his base for generalization is limited. At least it leaves one wondering whether truly non-metropolitan Jews, particularly in groupings sufficiently large to constitute sub-communities, are in any way significantly different.

The study offered here is not meant to be a description of all Southern Jews. This would hardly be possible. It is, rather, a participant-observation inquiry into some of the peculiar consequences of the adaptation of Jews in the South. The case involves the entire community of Jews in a middle-size Southern city. The issue was perceived by all the participants as one of the few vital issues ever faced by them as Jews; their behavior confirmed their assessment that the stakes were high and the outcome a matter of intense interest. Given this degree of importance attributed to the issue by the participants themselves, I became convinced that the case was sufficient to reveal some of the basic attitudes of the Jewish community as well as to suggest some of the major attributes of its social structure.

Conditions in Southern towns are in many respects quite special. They are clearly unlike conditions in all American metropolitan centers, and are probably equally dissimilar from those of towns of the same size outside the South. And in these towns the Jewish community, while always a fairly small unit, is a substantial one both in numerical and economic terms. Many of the Jewish families have been located in the South for two, three, even four generations. Along with them are Jewish families much more recently Southern. They live together in a common social and usually identical institutional milieu. Yet they also live apart from one another, sufficiently apart to be thought of as constituting not one but two communities; and there is a clear pattern in this living apart. What is the basis of the two-community pattern and what are its causes and its consequences? What is its significance for our notions about Jewish life in particular and ethnic and other types of identification in general?

The Setting

Iron City[3] is a steel, rubber, and textile town of some 60,000 people. Located in the hilly north of one of the Deep South states, Iron City is blessed with many natural resources but not with much new investment in the past decade. Its population has for some time been stable both in number and composition. The white community is homogeneous, particularly in comparison with non-Southern and Southern seaboard cities. Jews and Catholics are recognized as white minorities. However, their minority status is seldom a problem, the reason perhaps being that Negroes constitute about 30 per cent of the population. Until quite recently even relations between Negroes and whites were stable. Except for some labor violence in the distant past, Iron City has little in its past to cast doubt upon the civic boast of the civic boosters.

The Case

Early in 1958 on quiet Saturday night the city of Birmingham, Alabama, was shaken by a blast which tore off a wing of its largest synagogue. Most of the residents of Iron City reacted with mild shock and short-lived indignation. But the Jews of Iron City were deeply disturbed by the bombing, the first such dese-cration close to home in any of their recollections. All felt strongly that some-thing ought to be done, but there was little agreement among them as to what should be done. After many weeks of informal discussion, the entire congrega-tion—for all Jews in Iron City were members of one congregation—was crystal-lized around a proposal made by two brothers, the Kahns, owners of a prosperous retail store. The Kahns sponsored a motion to make a contribution, in the name of the synagogue, to the Birmingham reward-fund, which by that time had ac-cumulated many thousands of dollars. The Kahns got their motion on the agenda of the third regular monthly meeting of 1958 and were quietly campaigning in its favor.

Practically every member of the congregation of fifty to sixty families attended the meeting. Fully aware that the congregation treasury was almost empty, owing to recent expenditure on redecoration, the Kahns proposed to give the sum of $250 to the treasury on condition that it be sent to Birmingham in the name of the Iron City synagogue. As the Kahns' proposal would cost the congregation or an unwilling member not so much as a dollar, there would seem hardly to have been any issue at all. But every Iron City Jew knew that there was a most impor-tant issue to be settled, and that issue came through as simply and clearly as if it had been so stated in the motion: Resolved [in effect], that the Jews of Iron City identify themselves as Jews and as a congregation of Jews with the Jews of Birming-ham and elsewhere outside of Iron City. Aye or Nay?

The debate opened with a short but impassioned speech by Kahn the elder. It was essentially a for-whom-the-bell-tolls speech, stating firmly that to maintain the respect of the Gentile community as well as their own self-respect, they must all take their stand as Jews. The opposition, even more impassioned, was voiced first by the owner of the largest retail clothing store in town and then by the wife of the owner of the third largest retail clothing store in town. They were self-ap-pointed spokesmen, for there was no opposition caucus prior to the meeting but only a strong awareness of consensus in the majority. The opposition recalled the Ku Klux Klan horse-whippings of some Jews and Catholics in the 1920s and stressed a well-enough-alone philosophy, which at the time of the debate was very well indeed. The proponents argued that German Jews had suffered because of their lack of identity as Jews. The opposition answered, with equal conviction, that for years they had been "treated all right"; in fact, relations with non-Jews would suffer to the extent that Jews identified with other Jews rather than with their home town as home-towners. The opposition cited such matters as equal treat-ment in the country club, the high school football teams, and other matters of social significance.

The case for the motion was altogether remote, academic, hypothetical; that against was immediate, concrete, compelling. The question was not called; a vote was never taken. At a point close to violence the brothers Kahn withdrew their

motion. The meeting was gavelled to a close amidst considerable shouting. As it
was strictly a civil ceremony, the rabbi did not attend the meeting.

Not unlike the United States Senate, the congregation was seated strictly along
party lines, the opposition on the right well beyond the center, the proponents
in the remaining seats to the left. As there was no isle separation, the demarcation
line was made by two almost unbroken columns of husbands running elbow to
elbow from the Chair backwards to the rear of the room. For debate, this is a
natural arrangement; however, it is made noteworthy by the fact that the columns
of husbands also separated the "old" Jews from the "new" Jews. As far as could
be determined during the meeting and for days thereafter, there were no exception
The new Jews favored the motion and sat on the left; the old Jews without exception opposed the motion and sat to the right and center. Here were the two communities in congregation assembled.

As the analysis proceeds, I hope to show, first, that there are two separate socia
structures among the Iron City Jews and that the separate social structures both
reflect and maintain some quite profound differences in what it means to be a Jew
Second, I hope to show that these differences exist within an even stronger set of
identifications common to all Jews. Both propositions and the fragmentary suppo
to follow should provide a basis for hypotheses about Southern Jews in particular,
and American Jews, minority relations, and value systems in general.

SOME FEATURES OF SOCIAL STRUCTURE:
HOME, CLUB, AND CAMPUS

The distinction between old and new is not an easy one for an outsider to draw
but although it is implicit, the Iron City Jews appear to understand it well enough
to behave accordingly. Roughly, there are two dimensions in the distinction, one
of time and one of place, and both are vague, shifting, *ad hoc*, fortuitous. Not all
the old Jews have been residents of Iron City for over a generation; and many of
the new Jews can at least claim to have seen the Depression come and go in their
present businesses. In composite form, an old Jew is one whose family has lived
somewhere in the *South* for as far back as memory serves and whose family has
been at least self-supporting and free of bankruptcy for a generation (perhaps
longer, for one does hear of stories about such-and-such an old Jew whose father
or grandfather was a "four-flusher"). The new Jew, in contrast, is one who himself came to town from "the North." (Very few in the past forty years or so came
to town directly from Europe, except for three young German refugee men in the
early 1940s who stayed for only a short time and were considered arrogant and
rather zany.) The new Jew and his family may claim twenty-five years or more
of respectable residence in the town, but he came directly from some metropolitan center outside the South, his speech is not so colorful with local drawl and
patois, and he has hosts of relatives in New York, Chicago, and the like. Jews of
Eastern Europe ancestry are more likely than not to be of the community of new
Jews, but this is not an important factor distinguishing the communities. The basi
distinction is in the degree of Southernness. By virtue of immigration patterns,

most of the Jews in both communities are of German origin with a few of Iberian ancestry among the old Jews and a few of Eastern European ancestry on both sides, according to degree of Southernness. There is, then, a middle group, perhaps Eastern European but definitely Yankee, who at least were born in the South, probably around the First World War or after. They are acceptable as old Jews if they are in acceptable businesses and are thought not to be too "pushy" or too "kikey." (One of the most prominent Jews in town, for example, was of German origin with strong Southern ties, but had lived in New York, had strong business ties to New York textile interests, was involved in some union trouble, and was owner of an incorporated business. He was an old Jew but one towards whom other old Jews were always strongly ambivalent.)

It may be difficult for the outsider to understand how two communities could be based upon so superficial a distinction as degree of Southernness. But I think it should be clear from the reward-fund debate, or it should become clear presently, that over the years many quite profound differences were related to the quality of Southernness or actually developed as a consequence of Southernness. The separation into two communities probably arose out of superficial differences of culture and personality traits (a direct connotation of the term "Southernness"), and the separation is maintained by the friendship patterns that arose as a consequence. And, as the separate friendship patterns emerged, largely owing to the resistance if not outright hostility of the established old Jews, they acted in the manner of a self-fulfilling prophecy to maintain the differences. Over the years the differences have congealed.

Only a superficial acquaintance with Iron City Jews is necessary to detect two separate communities in ordinary social activities. The most reliable index is the frequency of exchange of social calls among and between old and new Jews. It is difficult to find cases of frequent exchanges of social calls between an old and a new Jewish household. There must certainly be numerous instances, but they are clearly exceptional. An old Jew will often identify the name of a new Jew (when presented to him in conversation) as that of a friend; but, when pushed, he can seldom recall the last time their families gathered in each other's living rooms. If one could draw a flow chart between old and new Jewish families, shaded and sized in terms of frequency of exchanges of social calls, the arrows between sets of new Jewish families would be wide and dark, between old Jewish families the same, and thin and wan across community lines. The arrows would converge from both sides on a scant two or three families, one by virtue of the personality of a wife in an old Jewish household and the other families probably by virtue of an "intermarriage" of an old and new family. If these particular households are channels of amity and communication, they are not the sources of leadership. Each community has its spokesmen for issues such as choice of rabbi, teaching of Hebrew, etc., and the congregation presidency tends to alternate between the two, although this office is often filled on a "most available" basis.

Since there is only one country club in town, many Jews are members; a few are actually charter members. Thus, one possible manifestation of separateness is hidden. However, there was an attempt some years ago to start a Jewish country club which failed after several unsuccessful attempts to enlist the support of a number of the old Jews. Many said they could not afford to be members of both clubs and were unwilling to give up their stake in the non-sectarian one. On the other hand, in one of the larger Deep South cities there is but one Christian country club and two Jewish clubs whose membership is divided along the lines of "old" and "new." Years ago, so the story goes, one of the "pushier kikes" was blackballed from the established Jewish club. Being a man of some means, he started another. In those Southern towns large enough to support more than one synagogue, the difference in composition of membership tends to be "old" versus "new."

Differences in the marital patterns of the two communities are more difficult to discern because they become submerged in extremely strong family solidarity and hidden from the observer. However, a few things are known. There are more marriages outside the faith among children of the old families, but the greater significance here lies in their small numbers and the reaction of the old Jews to such marriages. More will be said on the latter presently. The gulf between the two communities is best indicated in this respect by the rarity of marriages that connect old Jewish families *of Iron City* with new Jewish families *of Iron City.* When a marriage does take place between children of old and new Jews, one of the partners is almost without exception an "import."

Families in both communities have many connections in other Southern towns, some far beyond their home base. When they visit another Southern town, the Jews of Iron City are expected to stay with or to look up and spend some time with an Aunt Sophie or a Cousin Abe or some friend-called-cousin. Wherever they go in the South, particularly the old Jews whose roots in the South are so deep, they almost never really leave the family. Thus, not only do there appear to be two communities in town after town, but this phenomenon is extended beyond to create a *dual Southern Jewish society.*

Besides family ties beyond Iron City, there are certain institutions that have helped maintain a dual Southern Jewish society. For example, such annual events as the Falcon Picnic in Montgomery, the Jubilee in Birmingham, and other events of the same sort in Atlanta and New Orleans were supported precisely for the purpose of having nice boy meet nice girl, usually by arrangement among families of old Jews. These were most often intensive four-day affairs over the Fourth of July, Labor Day and other holiday weekends. And gala and elaborate affairs they were, with tea dances, formal dances, garden parties, and the like, involving the country club (of the old Jews) and the finest Jewish houses. For many of the new Jews—but far from all of them—the elaborate Bar Mitzvah has performed the same function.

That the annual "picnic" has declined in importance is probably due to the more efficient functioning of the college fraternity through which the two communities maintain and extend their separateness. Zeta Beta Tau and Phi Epsilon Pi were always sought after and pledged by sons of the old Jews from Houston to Savannah. It is significant that these two fraternities are rarely found on the same Southern campus competing for the same types of boys. Note on the chart

Zeta Beta Tau and Phi Epsilon Pi Fraternities:
Specialization among Southern Campuses

States of the Old Confederacy

State	Campus	Zeta Beta Tau	Phi Epsilon Pi
Alabama	U. of Ala.	1916	—
Arkansas	Auburn	—	1916
	U. of Ark.	—	1932[1]
Georgia	U. of Ga.	—	1915
	Ga. Tech.	—	1916
Kentucky	U. of Ky.	1942	—
Louisiana	Tulane	1909	—
	LSU	1911	1933[2]
Mississippi	U. of Miss.	—	1935
North Carolina	U. of N.C.	1927	—
	N.C. State	—	1949
	Duke	1935	—
South Carolina	U. of S.C.	—	1928
Tennesee	U. of Tenn.	1942	—
	Memphis St.	—	1949
	Vanderbilt	1918	—

Border States

State	Campus	Zeta Beta Tau	Phi Epsilon Pi
Florida	U. of Fla.	—	1960
	Miami U.	1946	1929
Maryland	U. of Md.	1948	1959 or 1960
	Johns Hopkins	1958	1920
Texas	Houston	—	1956
Virginia	U. of Va.	1915	1915
	W. and L.	1920	1920

1. Discontinued 1941.   2. Discontinued 1958.

that among States of the Confederacy there has been only one campus where
chapters of both fraternities co-existed, and Phi Epsilon Pi abandoned that campus
in 1958. (It had probably been on the decline for some years before 1958.) It is
only in the Border States that the specialization of campuses does not appear.
(Note that even in the case of Florida, the fraternities co-exist only on the north-
ernized campus. At the University of Florida, in the northern, therefore "south-
ernmost," campus, only one of the fraternities has a chapter.) The trustees of
both fraternities are from similar backgrounds and, apparently, have had no will
to compete for the same types of boys, much less the incentive to recruit *all* Jewish students on the campus.

There is another order of fraternities for the sons of new Jews. These have
been, among others, Tau Epsilon Phi and Alpha Epsilon Pi, houses for the new
Jews and what was in times past referred to by sons of the old Jews as the "new
money" or the just plain "kike Yankees." Perhaps in the middle somewhere one
finds an occasional Sigma Alpha Mu or Pi Lambda Phi chapter with some "nice
Southern boys and the better class of Yankees." Friendship and dating patterns
as well as prejudices towards the "others" are passed along these channels. Girls
tend to be known as and identify as "ZBT" girls or "TEP" girls. (Similar distinctions can be found among Jewish fraternities on Northern campuses, but, in the
guise of animosity toward New York, the distinction has a much stronger flavor
of Western versus Eastern European ancestry.) Admittedly the system was never
rigidly adhered to, but the differences are sufficiently distinct to contribute to
the maintenance of the dual society and the two communities.

TWO IDEOLOGIES

The Jews of Iron City are politically unimportant. They do not live in one part
of town, they do not constitute a majority in any district, and they are not though
of politically as a distinguishable unit. No individual Jew speaks politically as a
Jew, and there is no single—or double—voice for Iron City Jews as a group. And
there is no sign of change. To illustrate the point, practically all Jewish sons and
daughters (old and new) of Iron City go to college, *but in a generation not a single
one has studied for the law.* In fact, there are no Jewish lawyers at all in Iron City;
the one Jewish holder of the LL.B. is an "import" who by marriage is owner of
the *second* largest retail clothing store in town. A check in several other small
towns in the area revealed that an occasional Jew does go to law school, but his
practice is found to be in Birmingham, Atlanta, or some other large metropolitan
center. The Jews of Iron City have thus avoided the one profession which typically
becomes charged with controversy—not only political controversy but controversy
over estates, divorces, and the like that can be so noticeable and divisive in small
towns. No Jews have ever sought or held public office in Iron City or beyond,
and it is rare to find Jews publicly committed to a candidate in a wide-open
election. Candidates seek their support, and they are often contributors to campaigns, but quietly.

The Jews of Iron City are politically silent. Many hold strong opinions, and many enjoy positions of informal opinion leadership without regard to religious affiliation. But they are silent. And for much the same reasons they are conservative. Iron City is a "redneck town." A large part of its population, attracted by jobs in the textile, steel, and rubber mills, migrated completely unequipped from nearby farms not more than thirty years ago. Local prohibition and a hundred neon-crossed tabernacles bear witness to their fundamentalist majority. As they are virtually all merchants, the Jews of Iron City are especially susceptible to reprisal by informal conspiracy, and they justifiably fear the unpopular view. But the same would be true of the Christian with liberal tendencies.

If all the Jews of Iron City displayed considerable anxiety about politics and open controversy, it would still be too easy to overdramatize the "dilemma of the Southern Jews." Practically all Jews in Iron City are publicly conservative, but easily a majority are privately conservative as well. Thus, it is difficult to gather firm evidence for assessing the differences in ideology between the two communities that both reflect and maintain the spirit of two communities. The old Jews probably enjoy higher status in the social structure of Iron City proper, but there are no gross economic disparities between old and new Jews that would invite jealousy and continuous conflict. More important, the manifest values of Jews, as suggested above, are homogenized under the pressure of Southern consensus on the most important political and social issue of all. One must, then, look for differences in propensities and predispositions, the distributions of which are always matters of scholarly controversy. With these problems in mind, let us look at some rough indices of difference.

On matters of partisan politics, the Jews of Iron City reflect the Southern tradition. Almost all of them are Democrats, and both communities are predominantly liberal on economic questions. Further in harmony with recent Southern trends is a growing Republican sentiment among the younger fathers, particularly in old Jewish families. The development was cut short in 1962 because the entire Jewish community of Iron City was repelled by a Republican state-wide candidate of that year. This home-grown product had paid the bail for the juvenile bomber of Iron City's own synagogue in 1960, and his campaign was intensely racist. Less rabid Republican candidates in the future could, however, restore the trend among many of the young educated old Jews.

The best indices of contrasting ideology, however, can be found in the rare instances of conflict among Jews themselves. Probably the only such conflicts before the 1958 reward-fund debate were those over Zionism from time to time before and during the struggle for Israel. Internal cleavage then was the same as in 1958 and for precisely the same reason: all of these controversies involved the question of the nature and meaning of identification with Judaism. Even more than the reward-fund contribution, Zionism *would define the Jew by his ethnicity*. To support a Jewish homeland or to react with uncommon sympathy to a remote synagogue bombing is virtually to expose the fact (or, to the old Jew, *create the spectacle*) of the Jew as somehow separate from home town and local traditions. Deep in the idiom of the intelligent old Jew is the distinction "Judaism is a religion, not a nationality." Zionism has become a dead issue with the founding and success of Israel. But the meaning of Judaism, or Jewishness, still divides. Perhaps here is the whole mystery of the two communities in a nutshell. Certainly it shapes ideology, propensity, and predisposition.

As all of this should suggest, the new Jew reveals the greater capacity to identify with Judaism as such, to define himself as "minority" and to generalize, however incompletely, about "minority." As a consequence, the new Jew has the more liberal tendencies on a variety of issues. On the question of segregation the political sentiments of the two communities differ, although again it would be too easy to overdramatize and misrepresent it. Since the passing of Zionism, it is here that the old Jew most willingly shows his hierarchy of identifications, as Southerner first, Jew second, and "minority" or "ethnic group" last (if such a concession is made at all). Typically, the new Jew can be pushed to concede the inevitability of desegregation; the old Jew can only be pushed to anger. Not a man on either side would join or otherwise condone a White Citizens Council (knowingly referred to as the "Klan in the Gray Flannel Suit"). But an old Jew, regardless of age, will use the rhetoric of states' rights, of Plessy v. Ferguson, and, if pushed, of race superiority and biblical sanction. The new Jew will not. The old Jew either bears no sense of guilt on the matter, or he deeply represses it. The new Jew is distinguished by a concern with an only poorly repressed sense of guilt about Negro problems. The old Jews will make the inevitable adjustment to integration more easily and more quickly than their white Christian brethren, but they will verbally support segregation to the end. New Jews are less likely to give verbal support to segregation but will never openly support integration. However, private expressions of guilt or concern for an underprivileged minority serve still further to separate the two communiti

ONE IDENTIFICATION

It seems to me, therefore, that there is enough evidence to suggest the existence of two communities or subcommunities of Jews in Iron City and probably in other non-metropolitan Southern cities. Further, it appears that the phenomenon has important consequences in ideology or predisposition which, in turn, support the dual structure. Impressions suggest further differences in customs, aspirations, and general life-style, but to elaborate them would call for more systematic study.

However, it must be added immediately that there is at least as much to suggest that above and beyond the two communities is a set of identifications strongly held and shared by all. Factors in this phenomenon are as significant for theories of value maintenance and minority adjustment as was the earlier section for theorie of American Jewry. What is significant is not that the new Jews maintain certain identifications but that the old Jews do as well. It is for this reason that the present section emphasizes most particularly the patterns of identification among the old Jews.

If the reward-fund debate or any related indices were interpreted as a case of strong versus weak identification, it would be totally misrepresented. New Jews may favor more strongly the teaching of Hebrew, the observance of a larger number of holidays annually, the contribution to the Birmingham reward-fund. They may have a slightly better record of attendence at Friday night services. They definitely appreciate Yiddish and old country humor more than old Jews. But more vital evidence suggests that the old and new Jews differ only slightly, if at all, in strength of identification. The difference between them—and the crux of the argument of the last section—*lies in what the identification means.* The one is no less a Jew than the other.

That there is great strength of identification in both communities can be seen clearly in marital and related patterns. There are more marriages outside the faith among old Jewish families, but the greater significance lies in their rarity and in the reaction of old Jewish heads of family to such marriages. While one seldom finds any conserted opposition by old or new Jewish parents to a mixed marriage of son or daughter, both communities seem to require some later act of identification—for example, sending the children to Sunday school. (Rarely does one find Saturday schools in non-metropolitan Southern cities.) Old Jews as well as new are capable of "losing touch" with youngsters who prefer a Unitarian or Episcopal life, and, at the risk of overemphasis, strong if unspoken hostility can be permanent. No members of either community ever seem to forget who the Jews are no matter how long ago the conversion took place. There is at least one instance in which the third generation, descended from converted and intermarried old Jews, were still regarded as Jews although few if any Gentiles were aware of the ancestry. In two other cases, Jewish men married Christian girls and allowed their children to be brought up as Christians. On High Holidays one of them comes alone to services, sits alone, and leaves alone. Both have had cordial business relations with other Jews; one, in fact, could not have started his business in Iron City without the substantial support of an old Jewish merchant. But neither was ever truly a friend of any other Iron City Jew.

There is a real workaday permissiveness in the Iron City majority toward white religious minorities. The fundamentalism of the lower class Christian sects is convertable into antisemitism, and theologically there is little tolerance among them for the Jews' not accepting the Gospel. Yet few local Jews can recall any overt expression of community antisemitism in Iron City. This is why the 1960 bombing attempt on the Iron City synagogue came as such a shock, especially among the younger generation of old Jews to whom antisemitism as well as dietary laws and observances was something in history books. Yet the old Jews are no less Jews. Iron City and other Southern cities are receptive to conversion, and there are sufficient examples of acceptance as a non-Jew to encourage conversion. This only emphasizes how rare indeed are instances of old (and certainly new) Jews discarding their identification. The arm's length at which old Jews hold new Jews is not a rejection of Judaism or Jewishness. To cite an extreme example, there is one very small town in Mississippi where, although there is only a single Jewish family (dating back into the mid-nineteenth century), there is a small synagogue which has been used for the High Holidays, weddings, and funerals. In the past a rabbinical student or young rabbi was imported for these occasions, and they were attended by the few other Jewish families from nearby smaller towns and the open country. Even here the one conversion, now over a generation past, is remembered; figuratively there remains a sign upon the doorpost of the Christianized descendants.

Old Jews are on the average more active and prominent in the noncontroversial civic and philanthropic affairs of Iron City, but this is merely a function of their greater average length of residence. Furthermore, the fact of their Jewish identification is never hidden; old Jews do not use the civic group as a channel of assimilation (in the pejorative sense). And, while old Jews exchange house calls with Christian families more frequently than do the new Jews, neither is this assimilative (in the pejorative sense) if the Christian families know them as Jews. If the old Jew is free to assimilate, he chooses not to do so, or else the possibility never occurs to him. Liberal Christians more readily accept Judaism as a religion that can be changed than do the old Jews themselves.

CONCLUSIONS

Southern Jewry is a special phenomenon both in the particular context of American Jewry and the general context of group relations. The old Jews are cut off from the mainstreams of Jewish culture by more than two generations. They live in relatively small numbers dispersed throughout city and open country in a social milieu which is hostile to Judaism but not to Jews or to conversion. And they are deprived through isolation, disuse and, in many cases, rejection of all but the most superficial of the rituals and ceremonies. Yet the old Jew maintains much of his Jewishness and his Jewish identification.

Here we have a situation of strong identification in the absence of many of those factors presumably necessary to its maintenance. Most conspicuous and interesting in its absence is ritual—the repetition of symbolic acts. The proposition, a negative one, that most immediately springs to mind is that *ritual functions as a value- or identification-maintaining force only where it has functioned in that manner for some time*. In fact, ritual may be important for value maintenance only where treatment of the minority is severe.

Identification can obviously be maintained and reinforced in many ways. Ritual is an institutional force usually attached to a church as a manifest function of a church. The fact that ritual and church have not constituted an important reinforcement for old Jews in Iron City suggests, then, a second propostition: *where the reinforcement of identification is institutionalized or is otherwise made a mani-fest function of some structure, group identification may come to depend upon the institution.* Since no such pattern of reinforcement is found in this particular case and identification remains strong, we must look to other, informal or latent factors. In the case of the old Jews, the family seems to be the reinforcing factor. Commit-ments among old Jews to "being different" were made when their ancestors were newcomers in the nineteenth century and were passed down as part of the family structure. In many respects, the function of family among old Jews is probably not dissimilar from that of the ancient Jewish family before the latent function of family was replaced by the manifest function of synagogue and ritual. This latent function of the old Southern Jewish family, the maintenance of identification, is probably also one of the underlying conditions of its solidarity. Institutions, from churches to big city machines and trade unions, gain solidarity as they add functions, and conversely.

The identification of Southern old Jews turns out in reality to be an ethnic rather than a religious experience. Old Jews display virtually every feature of ethnic-ity save its acceptance. Ironically, the old Jew is a living refutation of his own argu-ment that "Judaism is a religion, not a nationality." Religion is quite superficial to him, but Jewry is not.

The phenomenon of the two communities is the more significant because it does not arise out of rejection of Jewry or Jewishness by the old Jews. In fact, the debate and all of the related materials present a fairly clear picture of a social system char-acterized at one and the same time by *strong identification and low solidarity*. The differences arise over what the identification means; the difference between old and new Jews lies not in the direction or focus of the identification but in the *sub-stance* of the identification. The general proposition suggested by this is that *iden-tification and solidarity (or cohesion) are independent factors which may be closely related under some conditions and entirely unrelated under others.*

It is commonly assumed in political sociology that the cohesion of groups is based upon shared attitudes and common goals. Professor David B. Truman, for one, has gone so far as to define *group* as a bundle of shared attitudes.[4] Karl Mannheim in *Ideology and Utopia* hypothesizes that as groups lose homogeneity they also lose solidarity, which gives rise to more vigorous theorizing towards the re-discovery of common goals.[5] Certainly there are many cases to support these hy-potheses, but there are also many contradictory cases. The best type of case is the group based upon "log-rolling" relations. Here the members have absolutely nothing in common; in fact, the very basis of their solidarity is the dissimilarity of ultimate aims (identification). The "farm bloc" in the United States, highly cohesive in the 1920s and 1930, was essentially a series of corn-cotton-wheat "log rolls." The Southern Democratic-Conservative Republican coalition is an even better example of strong solidarity made possible by the fact that the Southerners have cared little about the economic aims of the mid-West and the mid-West has cared little about

the social aims of the South. In contrast, many groups based upon shared attitude
or identifications display real pathologies in organization. This was clearly true of
the Jews of Iron City.

An awareness of the different consequences of identification and variations in
the bases of group formation opens up many new avenues of theory about group
life and group solidarity. It also opens up new possibilities for refining the predic-
tors of public opinion. For, while group membership and identification are func-
tionally related to opinions, the connection is not nearly so simple or straightfor-
ward as opinion studies have assumed. When ethnic group or trade union member
are found to be concentrated 70 per cent or 80 per cent on one side of an issue,
many important questions are avoided by stressing only the dominant characteristic. The 20 per cent or 30 per cent "deviant" cases may or may not be "cross-
pressured"; they may be reading the symbols of identification differently.

EPILOGUE

About two years after the Birmingham attack, the synagogue in Iron City was
victim of a bombing attempt. It was a spectacular attempt. For the first time, the
attack occurred while Friday night services were taking place. Moreover, it was a
dedication service for the new wing. The Mayor, the City Commission, many Protestant ministers, and Christian friends were in attendance. After the bombing
attempt failed the young madman stood across the street and beseiged the place
with an automatic rifle before driving away. The younger Kahn and one of the
old Jews were shot as they ran out enraged to respond. The injured old Jew, spea
ing afterwards for the entire congregation, insisted that there be no pictures, no
wide press coverage ("Magazine interference has already done the South enough
harm."), and, once the bomber was captured, no special grand jury. The argumen
of the Kahn brothers had been fully vindicated in the attack, and the entire Jewi
community suddenly became aware of its unity. But four years later, the two co
munities remain.

NOTES

1. Peter I. Rose, "Small-Town Jews and their Neighbors in the United States," *Jewish
Journal of Sociology,* III (no. 2, December, 1962). My thanks to Professors Nelson W. Polsby
E.H. Mizruchi, L.A. Froman, and Lieut. Bertram H. Lowi, USN, for careful reading and
criticism of earlier drafts.

2. Ibid., 1.

3. The names of the town and the participants in the case have been changed to avoid
embarrassing my friends on both sides of the issue. Otherwise the events and data are as
accurate as possible.

4. David B. Truman, *The Governmental Process* (New York, 1951), 24 and Chap. 2.

5. Karl Mannheim, *Ideology and Utopia* (New York, 1955), 131.

A JEWISH
VIEW ON SEGREGATION

ANONYMOUS

"Dedicated to the maintenance of peace, good order and domestic tranquility in our community and in our State, and to the preservation of our States' Rights." On this magnificent motto stands the Association of Citizens' Councils of Mississippi.

What makes one Jew a better Jew than another Jew? Is a rich Jew a "better" Jew than a poor one? Is a Republican Jew a better Jew than a Democratic Jew? Is a Northern Jew a better Jew than a Southern one—or an Eastern Jew better than a Western one? Is an American Jew a better Jew than a French, or English, or Polish, or Russian Jew? Is a Jew who advocates integration better than one who favors segregation? Or vice-versa?

We Jews are so subject to the hurts and humiliations of the generalities uttered as truths or facts by the non-Jews that it is unthinkable that we should be willing to generalize about each other. What Jew living anywhere, anytime in the more than 5000 years of our history has not smarted under such as this: "Jews are lucky." "All Jews stick together." "All Jews are rich." The expression "Jew him down" is understood and used from one end of this country to another. Yet, every Jew knows he is an individual. Not richer or poorer or luckier or unluckier or greedier or more open-handed because he is a Jew, but because of the sort of an individual he, personally, is. The sort of individual he is depends in large measure on his background, his family, his culture, his education, his social and economic status, the community in which he lives and other environmental considerations.

I, personally, am a "Jewish Southerner," not a Southern Jew. I am also a "Jewish American," not an American Jew. I was born and reared in Mississippi, educated here and in the neighboring State of Alabama. Lest you be tempted to indulge in a "generalization" at this point on Mississippians and their total ignorance and lack of education, let me make a statement of statistical fact. THERE ARE MORE COL-LEGE GRADUATES PER CAPITA AMONG THE WHITE POPULATION OF MISSISSIPPI THAN IN ANY OTHER STATE IN THE UNION. In case you are interested in another less vital fact, there are also more Cadillacs per capita in Mississippi than in any other State. I do not happen to own one. Many negro citizens in Mississippi do.

As a Jewish Southerner, I objected, and still do object, to the stand taken by national (?) Jewish organizations, and most particularly B'nai B'rith and the Anti-Defamation League of B'nai B'rith, in connection with the segregation decision. I accord every person in America, Jew or non-Jew, colored or white, the right to form an opinion on this controversial subject and to express it. That is the American way. While I may disagree violently with your opinion, I will defend your right to express it—as an individual. But, with an organization, especially a national organi-zation, there is a difference.

National Jewish organizations such as B'nai B'rith and the American Jewish Congress, and others, each purport to speak for all American Jewry. Each is con-stantly striving to give the impression that that particular organization speaks for all Jews in the United States, regardless of locality. Nothing—nothing could be further from the truth. Most of these so-called National Jewish organizations have no Southern Jewish membership whatsoever. I doubt whether the strongest of these groups from the standpoint of Southern membership, the B'nai B'rith, can lay valid claim to having in membership a majority of Southern Jews. When the Anti-Defamation League of B'nai B'rith took the position it did in filing a brief as a friend of the court, urging that segregation in public schools be ruled uncon-stitutional, the organization did so in the name of American Jewry, including Southerners. I find it hard, if not impossible, to believe that 100 per cent. of these Southerners, just because they are Jews, subscribed to or in any way en-couraged or even condoned the stand taken by B'nai B'rith on the segregation issue.

The same thing happened to Southern Christians—both Catholic and Protestant. They, too, are refusing to "go along" with what they consider unrepresentative national action by their church groups.

The thinking of the leaders of Jewish organizations is fairly clear to me. They surely feel that since Jews have always and will always be a "minority" group, we must be vocal in the fight by another "minority" group in its efforts to achieve "Status." And as far as that thinking goes—north of the Mason-Dixon Line—it may be accurate. The negro may be a minority group in the North. In many sections of the South the white people are the minority group.

As a case in point, take my own State, County and Town. Statistics show that 45 per cent. of Mississippi's population is negro. But that does not give an accurate picture of the distribution of this negro population. There are many of the "hill" counties with little or no negro population. Yet in my own county, there are about 20,000 white people and 40,000 negroes. In this county, there are 4,000 white children of educable age—6 through 21—and 8,722 colored children of the same ages. In my own town, there are 500 white children in the white consolidated 12-grade school. There are over 1,000 colored children in the colored consolidated 12-grade school.

Should integration come (personally, I don't think it ever will), there would be two colored children to every white child in every grade in school. My own 10-year-old daughter, who is in the upper section of her class, will be in the 5th grade this year. In that 5th grade, in an integrated school, the class would be something like this (assuming half boys and half girls): 5 white girls, 5 white boys, 10 colored girls, 10 colored boys. The white boys and girls would all be 10 or 11 years old. But what of the colored boys and girls? Our records show that the rate of failures among the primary students is very, very high. The colored boys and girls in that 5th grade room would range in age from 12 to 15. Given the same economic, social, moral and financial backgrounds, it would still be considered unwise in many educational circles to mix such a varied age group. But when you add to the variance in ages 10 to 15—the difference in cultural, moral, economic and educational backgrounds, I find it impossible to see this as the way to assure the advancement of Mississippi's negro boys and girls.

The one thing which General Nathan Twining found most distressing and disturbing on his recent visit to Russia was the fact that they are going to win the "classroom" war in the race to produce more and better scientists in the coming generation. This fact has long been known to professional educators and lay leaders who have concerned themselves with schools and their problems. Now the military has caught on. In the interests of national defense, isn't this a very poor idea to undertake an integration program which would inevitably result in fewer and less adequate scientists when the crying need is for more and better trained people? If you think I'm "just whistlin' Dixie," to use a Southern expression, I advise you to study the facts and figures which have been brought out in the investigation of the deterioration of the public schools in Washington, D.C., the nation's capital, as a direct result of their hasty and ill-considered determination to make the Washington system a model of integration for others to follow. This investigation should be doubly interesting to American Jewry, or Jewish Americans, as you prefer, in view of the fact that the attorney heading the investigating committee is Mr. Will Gerber, of Memphis. Mr. Gerber is a Jewish Southerner.

I am wholeheartedly in favor of the advancement of the colored people of the State of Mississippi, the South and the Nation. I am wholeheartedly opposed to the thinking of those who claim it can be achieved by integration.

Where then can I go to implement my sincere desire to help the negro advance, as they desire to do, yet not at my expense and at the expense of my children? In other words, how can I help them to help themselves educationally, economically, culturally at their own rate and at the pace best suited to their capacities? It can only be done through continued segregated facilities. By expense, as used above, I do not refer to financial expense. This I gladly assume. The expense I referred to was moral, educational, cultural. What group could I join that would speak out for the preservation of segregation and at the same time lend the Mississippi negro a hand in advancing? There was such a group and I joined it. The Citizens' Council—dedicated to the preservation of segregation, but not "against" the negro. Not opposed to his achievement or advancement. Just dedicated to the proposition that that achievement and advancement could best come about through continued segregation.

But, some have said, the Citizens' Council is a renewal of the KKK. Nothing could be further from the truth as regards Mississippi Councils. Any community anywhere, large or small, which has a so-called Citizens' Council that is accused of emulating KKK tactics, has only itself and its so-called "best citizens" to blame. Where community leaders have assumed their rightful responsibilities of leadership and where the lawyers, doctors, business leaders and educators have organized Councils, there you have peaceful, harmonious relations with no remote resemblance to the KKK. While Klansmen hide their faces, members of the Citizens' Council proudly proclaim their membership.

But, some have said, the Citizens' Councils are anti-Semitic. Nothing of the sort. Where prominent Jewish leaders have enrolled as members and taken an active part in the duties of the Council, there is no chance of anti-Semitism creeping in. There are communities where Jewish leaders have flatly refused to join, although in these same communities prominent Catholic and Protestant men have joined, despite the stands taken on segregation nationally by their church groups. Who can blame them for feeling a bit bitter against white Southerners who try to stay "neutral" on such an issue? The white person who lives and works in the South has got to realize, from first-hand knowledge of the situation, what integration would mean, and he can do one of three things: He can realize it, and do all in his power to keep it from happening. He can realize it, and still feel that it is the thing to do and therefore be in favor of it. He can realize it, and desire earnestly to be "neutral" and let happen what will—but his will be a false neutrality in the eyes of his neighbors who will figure that "silence gives consent," because if everybody decided to be "neutral" the silence would be pure and simple consent. So the Jew who attempts to be neutral is much like the ostrich. And he has no right to be surprised or amazed when the target he so readily presents is fired upon.

Because I have always manifested such respect for my own religion, my fellow-members of my local Citizens' Council would not for one moment entertain though of turning the Council's activities into anti-Semitic channels. This pattern is, I am confident, being repeated in all the towns and cities where respected and self-respec ing Jewish Southerners have felt as I feel—that segregation must be maintained and that membership in the Citizens' Council will help to maintain it. I speak from first hand knowledge when I say that there are many Jewish members of Citizens' Coun cils both here and in Alabama. They realize, as I do, that any white Southerner, Christian or Jew, must do all he can to help maintain segregation. When integration comes to the South, the white Southerner will have to leave.

In many parts of the country, organizations are springing up which have adopted the obvious, famous and popular name "Citizens' Council." Some are well led and have the support of the finest elements in their community. Some may not be. In a movement of this magnitude it is natural that some of these organizations would not be well led and that opportunists would seek to take advantage of the chaos and confusion caused by the "Black Monday" decision of the Supreme Court.

Each Citizens' Council and its leaders will have to be judged according to their actions and deeds. Each Council in Mississippi and in most other States is a separate, independent, autonomous group which elects its own officers and maintains its own treasury. They are not responsible to nor for any other group or individual. The fact that the movement has grown spontaneously under these conditions proves the righteousness of our cause, brought about by popular resistance of good citizens to the obviously political "Black Monday" decision of the Supreme Court. Since this movement is based on public opinion, it is hoped that public opinion will eliminate unworthy, self-seeking rabble rousers who attempt to acquire personal publicity and who mistake notoriety for support.

Here in the South, particularly in smaller cities and towns, we cannot give lip service to integration as is done in the North and avoid having it by zoning laws, restricted neighborhoods, and such subterfuges. In the hundreds of small towns which comprise these Southern States, there is no such thing as zoning. Two or three schools will serve the whole town and those families living within a radius of 15 to 20 miles outside of the towns. Colored and white people live on "both sides of the tracks." Colored farmers live side by side with white farmers. No, the only way we can have segregation is to say so openly and frankly and let everybody know where we stand—and where he stands.

The NAACP would have the world believe that the million negroes in Mississippi and the millions of others in other Southern States are solidly united in their burning desire for advancement. Statistics on school attendance tell a different tale. Nationally, about 50 per cent. of the boys and girls who enroll in the first grade complete the full 12 grades and graduate from high school. In Mississippi, among the white students, the State average is 33 per cent. Among the negro students, this average is 3 per cent. In our home county, the average among the white students is 20 per cent. and among the negro students is 2 per cent. It would seem to be that the larger the negro population in a town or county, the fewer complete their high school education. This is true despite the fact that in some sections of the State, notably in the rich Delta country, colored students are enjoying a full nine months of school, in newly built, modern buildings that are far better staffed, offer a longer school term and more varied curriculum than many white students enjoy in poorer sections of the State.

. Yet, we venture the opinion that the negro in the South in general, and Mississippi in particular, has done more "advancing" than those in the so-called integrated States. We have today in Mississippi 14 negro college presidents. We have 191 negro college professors. There are 1531 negro men and 841 negro women working in the negro colleges of the State of Mississippi. There are 2889 negro teachers holding Bachelors degrees or Masters degrees in the State of Mississippi. These teachers hold either the A or AA certificate. We have 7030 negro teachers in the State of Mississippi. How many negro college presidents do you find in New York State? In Illinois? In Michigan? How many college professors? How many negro classroom teachers?

I have a strong feeling that the people of B'nai B'rith who spoke so boldly and so loudly for integration are the people farthest removed from the problem not only here in the South but in their own back yards. They are, by virtue of education, profession, financial status and the rest of the factors involved, the least in position to be faced with the problems of integration affecting them directly. So they fall into the category of the "Let's you do it" integrationists. I wonder how many negroes live in the neighborhood of the presidents of so-called National Jewish organizations? How many belong to their Kiwanis, Lions, Rotary or Exchange clubs? How many belong to their Synagogues? How many will be found in the schools attended by their sons or daughters, grandsons or granddaughters, nieces or nephews? Ask these same questions with regard to the other leaders in Jewish organizations. Then ask yourself what about the stand of the less fortunate Northern Jew who finds himself in an economic status that throws him into the integrated neighborhoods and schools. Did he encourage the B'nai B'rith to take the stand it did? Somehow, I don't think so.

If Southern Jewry were of a mind to indulge in a little "finger pointing" we could sit here in the ivory tower of our isolation from the large and terrible problems of the labor unions, labor racketeers, Communists in organized labor and the like which fill the papers daily. We could recoil in horror from the thought that a Jew could be a member of such groups, could condone the thing done to so fine a man as Victor Reisel. We could urge Northern Jewry to break away from affiliation with such undesirable groups and elements. We could piously point out that the good which would result from such an upheaval would surely make it up to them for their loss of life, limb and property. However, we realize that we are somewhat removed from the scene. So in a spirit of tolerance and sympathy, we leave the Northern public, including Northern Jewry, to settle their own labor problems, dishonesty, racketeering, communism, bossism, graft, corruption and the rest.

Is it too much to ask that they leave us to the solution of our own problems? Any jackass can be a Monday morning quarterback, an armchair general. Any idiot can successfully rear the other fellows children or make a go of his marriage or solve his financial difficulties. But it is the smart man who knows that each person has not only the right but the obligation to settle his own problems to the best of his ability.

I am engaged, through the Citizens' Council, in attempting to solve the negro problem in a way that will be to the benefit of all Southerners, colored and white, and will not be to the detriment or determent of any. The way to do this is through continued segregation. Any Mississippi negro who wants to advance can do so. He can have the best advantages of a good grammar school, high school and college education. He can return to his home as a doctor, lawyer, teacher or minister and make good. If he is really interested in the advancement of his people, he can help them enjoy the same advantages that he enjoyed. The negro cannot be advanced by legislation. He cannot have advancement poured on him from the outside. He has got to have an inner desire to be advanced before he can be helped to advance.

Much criticism was leveled against the Citizens' Council in their early days of organization because it was rumored that they advocated and used economic pressure. Recent events have proven that the only organized economic pressure which has been applied has been by negro groups. These boycotts have solved nothing, have bred ill will and bad feelings. They have cost jobs and large sums of money. They have deprived many citizens, both white and colored, of public conveyances which they could ill afford to lose. Where is the criticism of economic boycott when employed by a negro group or labor unions? The Federal Government uses economic pressure to enforce race-mixing in all phases of Government endeavor. Is economic pressure only to be criticized when white Southerners employ it?

"Dedicated to the maintenance of peace, good order and domestic tranquility in our community and in our State and to the preservation of our States' Rights"—something worth working for—worth fighting for through the real Citizens' Council.

IS MIAMI
BEACH JEWISH?

HAROLD MEHLING

"Their people wouldn't be comfortable with ours."

During a conversation with an old hand in the Miami Beach hotel industry, I generated an outburst of impatience. I remarked that several persons had noted the Beach's overwhelmingly Jewish composition during the winter months and had felt an attempt should be made to broaden the tourist group. My informant exploded.

"I'm sick of hearing that," he said. "We made Miami Beach a corned-beef and dill-pickle stand and that's the way it's going to be!"

I do not believe many other remarks could have made me feel quite so uncomfortable.

There is probably no way of dealing with Miami Beach's "Jewishness" without incurring a variety of displeasures. Earnest friends and respected acquaintances have urged me to avoid the subject. Some contend that its mere statement carries an anti-Semitic implication. Others maintain that the topic is valid but should not be discussed in public because it might invigorate latent anti-Semitism. In addition, certain persons who consider themselves gracious feel that the subject is crude; they have suggested that I file and forget it.

Obviously, then, this is a delicate matter, which means that for years it has been treated like the problem of Aunt Emma—the one who had to be put away. Aunt Emma is only talked about within the family; outsiders are either lied to or told that she is visiting a cousin in Cincinnati. As a result, Emma's condition is discussed in gossip, with a dearth of facts that usually succeeds in distorting her condition and her problem.

I have decided, therefore, not to suppress this part of the Miami Beach story—for suppression is what its omission would amount to. The question is more or less constantly discussed as a fact of life on the Beach. A psychological consultant has even asked hotel owners whether vacationers "would prefer a resort which was more representative of the character of the country as a whole." The subject is so ubiquitous that it is sometimes expressed in special humor; a local newspaper, commenting on the naming of a hotel bar, said that "a wag has suggested that the lounge be called the 'Mais Oui' in the summertime and 'Oi Vay' in the wintertime." Jews have contributed to this peculiar inwardness, too. One, for example, wanted to name a restaurant "Kleine Momser," which in English means "Little Bastard." He was talked out of his notion by an outraged rabbi.

And sometimes the subject is treated in even more openly racial terms—vicious and ugly terms.

The basic facts are that while Jews make up a fourth to a half of Miami Beach's tourist population during the summer, they comprise at least 90 per cent of it during the winter. Inasmuch as the winter percentage is grossly disproportionate to the number of Jews in America, it becomes interesting to discover the reasons for it.

It is a sad fact of South Florida life that the most informative way to discuss its Jews is with a review of the region's lengthy history of anti-Semitism. Intolerance has periodically thrived and lain dormant along the entire Gold Coast, but at its peaks of popularity, it has been pursued like tournament golf—industriously, with gusto and constant practice.

There is a chapter of the Florida boom, for example, that is considered bad form to repeat these days. That bustling period dovetailed with an era of Jew baiting that was not equaled in Florida until the synagogue bombings of 1958. The targets of the 1920s were the binder boys, the land sharks who tied up lots with small binders and then speculated in binders as their value rose with the inflated price of land. A large number of the binder boys were Jews who had come to Florida with many others to turn a $100 bill into a quick fortune. The Jews were singled out for derision by native and other good Christian fortune hunters, and soon Miamians found a way to express their sentiments. While a flashing electric sign in midtown New York read: "It's Always June in Miami," local folk mounted emblems on their automobiles that read, "It's Always Jew'n in Miami."

Fort Lauderdale is a community that has never lost a mania for anti-Semitism. Today it is a pleasant town for Christians, and for Jews who knuckle under by Anglicizing their names "for business reasons." As recently as 1959, a Lauderdale hotel wrote, in fractured but nevertheless explicit syntax: "We have a restricted clientele regarding pets, children under 12 years of age and the Hebrew Religion." An establishment not far up the coast reports: "Although Del Ray Beach is a Gentile resort, please don't consider us bigoted or stuffy." One of Del Ray's lot-sales advertisements has described it as "the only city on the East Coast fully re-

stricted as to Gentiles. . . ." And Palm Beach, as Cleveland Amory pointed out in
The Last Resorts, is what inspired Otto Kahn to define the word *kike:* "A Jewish
gentleman who has just left the room."

The exclusion or badgering of Jews has been no less vigorous a practice in
Miami Beach—in which, to this day, *there is not a single golf or dinner-dance club to
which a Jew can belong without hiding the fact that he is Jewish.* (And such de-
ception is not unknown, or, at least, not unsuspected.)

It all began, as most things did, with Carl Fisher, the man of blinkered vision.
Fisher practiced a curious policy under which any Christian could buy land if he
had the requisite amount of money, a Jew only after he had proved himself "the
right kind of Jew." However, a Beach resident who was associated with Fisher
for a score of years presents an explanation for his colleague's attitude that is
meant to clear up misunderstanding. "Fisher wasn't anti-Jewish," he explains. "He
was anti-kike. Some of his best friends were Jews."

Under the "anti-kike" policy, some land was sold to Jews who, presumably,
were the right kind. One was John D. Hertz of Chicago, founder of the Yellow
Cab Empire. Another was Albert D. Lasker, head of the U.S. Shipping Board
during the Harding Administration and president of Lord and Thomas, a Chicago
advertising agency.

If the recollection of Fisher's associate is sound, and indications are strong that
it is, "the right kind of Jew" can also be credited with an anti-Semitic assist in
Miami Beach. The day is recalled when Hertz approached a Fisher employee with
the dismaying news that "the wrong kind of Jew" was trying to buy property;
Hertz said that he and Lasker would consider it a favor if Fisher refused to sell.
Since the price of the land in question was a formidable $100,000, the employee re-
layed the delicate problem to Fisher. The Prest-O-Lite King, who had never previously been offended by money, agreed not to sell. (From that day to this, a
number of Jews have adjusted and accommodated themselves to anti-Semitism
in Miami Beach; as recently as 1959 some encouraged it "for business reasons.")

As an indication of how these practices were ground-laying and self-expanding,
consider that when Julian W. Mack, a Jew and a United States Circuit Judge,
came to Miami Beach, he was unable to register at Fisher's Flamingo Hotel—and
that until its recent demolition, Jews would still have spent some interesting
moments trying to get their luggage past the desk clerk. And when Julius Fleischmann, the yeast king but a Jewish king, visited the Beach, he was able to play polo
with Fisher but could not enter Fisher's clubhouse despite all his family had done
to banish teenagers' hickies. (If Fleischmann was insulted, he showed it only by
securing land and erecting his very own mansion. He was so obliging, in fact, that
when he climbed down from a polo pony and died of a heart attack one day, he
provided Steve Hannagan, Fisher's publicity man, with an opportunity to get the
first Miami Beach dateline in northern newspapers.)

Fisher was not alone, of course. John Collins' son-in-law, Tom Pancoast, barred
Jews from his hotel, and Newton Roney excluded them from the Roney Plaza.

Until the late 1930s Jews were barred from almost all ocean-front hotels above Lincoln Road; it was not until after World War II that a law banned display of restrictive signs, such as "No Jews or Dogs."

When Jews began to break through these barriers and vacation on the Beach in significant numbers, both Roney and Pancoast sold out, and the bars fell rapidly. Which is not to say, however, that apartheid had vanished. "Gentiles Only" signs persisted until their public display was outlawed in 1949 in the City of Miami Beach, two years later in adjacent Surfside. But not all the signs vanished, either. Some were moved inside, to reassure guests in a more discreet manner. One Beach landmark operated as a club and effectively barred Jews in that way. And despite occasional losses from empty rooms, the restricters felt their policy was worth it. They did not agree with William Wrigley, Jr., who is reported to have said, when asked if he would bar Jews from his Arizona hotel, "Why should we? Jews chew gum, don't they?"

But with an open-door policy established at the Roney and the Pancoast, it was clear that the dam had broken. And inasmuch as large numbers of Jews lived in residential clusters and enjoyed close association, the jungle-telegraph system was effective in spreading the word. More Jews were attracted to Miami Beach, for reasons that were extremely logical. Some were attracted because they had been discriminated against elsewhere and, regardless of a disposition to fight back, did not want their vacation atmosphere marred by bitter rows and strain. If Jews could go to Miami Beach and feel comfortable, that was the place to go.

But another feature of the Beach's attraction was a curious kindredness, based on age. South Florida's toasty climate has always exerted a strange pull on the middle-aged and elderly, and this age factor had much to do with the nature of life that developed in Miami Beach. The Jewish people who responded to the attraction belonged to a generation that had either been born in Europe or, if born in the United States, had spent its childhood in a Jewish milieu that has largely broken down. They were more observant of cultural traditions—much more the products of Jewish environments than are their children and grandchildren of today.

So it was that many of the Jews who visited the Beach lacked "American ways." They were conspicuously Jewish in their accents, their dietary customs, and their methods of worship. A number conversed in Yiddish and many relied on younger people to write their letters because sons and daughters at home could not read Yiddish. Kosher meat markets opened, synagogues and Hebrew classes appeared, and more Jews became involved in the conduct of the resort-hotel industry.

When World War II ended, however, Miami Beach was still a fairly well-balanced city. But then came the hotel-building mania, and a huge and ever-growing increase in the number of vacationers required to keep the new rooms filled. Competition for guests became intense, whereupon the hotel owners embarked on a deliberate policy of selectivity. They aimed their promotion at cities with large Jewish communities—New York, Boston, Philadelphia, Chicago. And soon, as inevitably as the sun rose warm and comforting on Miami Beach, they had made it a Jewish resort city. Some hotel men will explain that they were simply seeking the best return for their advertising dollar by "concentrating their promotion," by appealing to a "built-in" market. Others will supply a note of altruism by maintaining, "We gave our people a place to go." But it strains charity to accept that premise; there is not enough evidence on which to sustain a strong suspicion of humanitarianism.

In any event, Miami Beach's reputation as an almost exclusively Jewish winter resort became so widespread that, shortly after the Fontainebleau opened, this knowledge was expressed in a revealing incident. In the words of my informant:

> "The Shah of Iran was coming over, you see, and the State Department worried that a lot of people thought he was anti-Semitic. I was over at State talking to a friend when I heard about it. So, since I was the press agent for the Sans Souci, I said, 'Why not send the Shah down to us?' That sounded fine—the Shah going to the Beach and mingling with Jews and all that. 'Good,' they said. 'We'll send him to that new one—the Fontainebleau.'
>
> "I gasped. 'It just opened,' I said, 'and it takes a hotel a year to get the bugs out. You wouldn't want the Shah to eat his soup with plumbers plumbing over him, would you?' So they sent him to the Sans Souci.
>
> "We painted a big lion crest on the door of his suite and on his cabana, too. And we got some Woolworth diamonds and banged them in for the lion's eyes. The Shah had a hell of a time. Oh, he tried to water-ski up a sharp coral rock, but he recovered and when he left, he was a happy Shah."

It is questionable how many Jews Mohammed Reza Pahlevi mingled with during his happy time in Miami Beach, but it is significant that the Beach had become so "officially" Jewish that the press agent's stunt dovetailed with the quaint diplomatic needs of the State Department.

By now, inevitably, a fake caricature has been woven into the fabric of the Beach—so much so that an airline proclaims that blintzes, cheesecake, and celery tonic from Lindy's Restaurant are available on flights from New York to Miami. And if the stereotyped vacationer has not had enough blintzes by the time he is ready for his return flight, the airline will provide a fresh batch from Wolfie's of Miami Beach.

If this all represents some sort of grotesquerie, it passes unchallenged in Miami Beach.

One might suppose that the presence of a large number of Jews would foredoom closed-door practices in the Miami Beach area. It has not. If anything, numerous clusters of hard-core Anglo-Saxonism have developed in hotels and residential

areas. The apartheid hotels are the Christian watchtowers, and their operators
and inhabitants have evolved a rationale for their attitude. "It's a question of
taste," they are fond of saying. "Jews flaunt their money and their Jewishness,
and they're noisy." I do not have decibel measurements, but I am aware from observation that differences in deportment on the Beach are less a function of nationality than of *nouveau riche* gaudiness. The anti-Semites flaunt money and "nativism."
Their jewelery is as ostentatious and their mink just as redundant in the balmy
warmth. ("Yes," smiled an ocean-front philosopher, "but haven't you noticed
that *their* minks aren't Jewish?") The fact is that if it takes a rich Jew to live it
up in Miami Beach, it takes a no less rich Christian to do the same.

Some restricted hotels make an added attraction of their policy. Few are public
about it, but if the jungle telegraph operates among Jews, it operates no less sensitively among people who wouldn't be found wet in the same swimming pool
with a Jew. (Yet restricters would be surprised to know how often their lobbies
serve as a private meeting place for Jewish businessmen who wish to discuss a deal
in secrecy.) Sometimes, as along motel row, where a splashy establishment practices
as much exclusion as it can, a Jewish manager retaliates with roadside justice.

"Every so often," this resourceful man explained, "we get odd ones—mangy
characters with parrots on their shoulders, or obvious deadbeats. We have to turn
them away, but we don't send them off without help. We direct them to that god-
damned restricter. I'd give the price of four rooms to see his face every time the
deadbeats say we recommended the place."

Moving the observation post south, we discover that the city of Bal Harbour is
a "club," and that the membership-club device has become a favored method of
excluding Jews from residence. The Bal Harbour Club members, however, sold
their ocean-front land for millions of dollars to Jews who constructed and now
operate open-door hotels. But that is not universal practice in this city. The
Kenilworth, for instance, has been known to state bluntly, "As always, restricted
clientele." Today the Kenilworth's owners maintain that the swank establishment
bars no Jews. Other Bal Harbour hotels cannot—even would not—say the same.
And in Surfside, the Coronado Hotel recently expressed itself in an advertisement
that pointed out, unmistakably, that it is "catering only to a carefully restricted
clientele." Now that Carl Fisher's Flamingo has been demolished, no hotel or
motel within the City of Miami Beach itself is known to be restricted, but if one
should develop a notion to be, its identification would be simple. Its chatter items
would be sent only to the society columns, not to the entertainment pages, of
the local newspapers; it would set itself apart.

(I have not mentioned hotel policies regarding Negroes. Surprise: They are
accepted as convention delegates in Jewish-owned establishments—thus far without incident. But as more organizations with Negro members learn of this policy,
and the number of Negroes increases, it is likely that a challenge will emanate
from elsewhere in Florida, probably from a rural politician. Such an attack may

take a particularly ugly form, too. A recent gubernatorial candidate [unsuccessful] showed voters how far integration has already progressed by exhibiting films, via television, of Negroes eating in a Beach restaurant; among all the restaurants at which the film might have been made, the one chosen displayed a Star of David on its window.)

Meanwhile, it will be revealing to inspect the social climate that has been created by at least the Caucasian Standoff, in which Jews go to their hotels, Christians to theirs, and battle lines stand in bold relief in the South Florida sun.

It can be stated as a rule with few exceptions that the Jewish hotel and motel operators of the Miami Beach area have made little effort to break down the institution of discrimination. As a peculiar defense for their inaction, it may be said, with truth, that they are fairly powerless in any event; they have no real standing in the Greater Miami community and are almost divorced from it. But a good deal of their detachment is self-imposed. It is rare when they exert themselves on behalf of anyone but themselves. Some insist on minimizing the extent of the closed-door policy. Others turn their eyes toward the ceiling, sigh, and mumble in embarrassment. A number defend the practice, and more than one is known to have engaged in it himself.

Recognition that anti-Semitism thrives is usually expressed in a defensive form of humor employed by hotel entertainers. Since they function on the assumption that they are playing to an "intimate," i.e., Jewish, crowd—or that someone will fill in the gaps for the unknowing—they may spin a yarn about the "Jewish Air Force." This is their designation for the small planes that skim the Beach, trailing banners that advertise, "7-Course Kosher Dinner, $1.35." The comedian says, "I hear the Jewish Air Force lost two planes over Bal Harbour today. They've got anti-aircraft up there." Or, singling out a hotel known to be restricted, he quips, "They think they've got it made. Wait till they find out we put sour cream and boiled potatoes in the foundations!"

Occasionally, the tone of a joke matches the viciousness of the situation it depicts. Example:

A man walked into a restricted hotel and said, 'I'm Joe Goldstein."

The clerk replied, "Sorry, Mr. Goldstein, but we don't take *your* kind here."

"Oh, I don't want to register," Mr. Goldstein said. "I just want to pay my mistress's bill. (Pause.) She's *your* kind."

A veteran of the Beach scene dissents from the thesis that this is grisly humor. "Don't get sensitive about the wrong crime," he said. "If it's sad that such a story can bring down the house, it's tragic that conditions make it possible for the story to be told at all."

A more serious problem may lie in the desire of some Jews to defend and apologize for Miami Beach apartheid. Sometimes the defense is based on the proposition that Jews are incapable of talking to, eating with, or otherwise socializing with non-Jews. "There's some justice in those restrictions," a hotel executive told me. "In a way, they're right. Our people wouldn't be comfortable among *their* people, and their people wouldn't be comfortable with *ours*."

That outlook pales to blandness beside others that are frankly based on business considerations. As we shall see, the hotel industry on the beach is facing some bleak days, and ways to delay their arrival are frantically being sought. The basic problem is that the area is tremendously overbuilt, but there is always an extra wrinkle to a Miami Beach problem. One hotelman defined it this way. "By directing such an exclusive appeal to Jewish people, we have narrowed our tourist market to about six per cent of the American population. So every time the dog days come and rooms are empty, a lot of us say it plainly: 'We've run out of Jews.'"

Assuming the validity of this rather earthy analysis, one might forsee attempts to broaden the Beach's homogeneous tourist group by an investment in wider promotion. But only one piece of evidence of such an approach has been made public, and I blush to quote it from a newspaper column: "Morris Lansburgh, who operates the largest number of hotel rooms of anyone here . . . spoke boldly on a subject that already has been discussed in hush-hush circles. Lansburgh, during a discussion of tourism, said that he would like to see something done to attract other than Jewish visitors to Miami Beach. He went so far as to express his desire to see some restricted hotels here again. Should this column evoke conversation, just bear in mind that I'm merely reporting what Morris Lansburgh said. I have reviewed this with him and it is being used with his knowledge and consent."

But a few Jewish hotel operators—just a few—have gone even further. One tried to discourage Jews from patronizing his establishment and, after a bitter dispute, agreed to delete offending phrases from his promotional material only if the organization that protested would pay the printing costs. Another leased a hotel to an operating concern that is unquestionably known to exclude Jews. And a third greets motorists entering Florida with brochures that locate his motel "near churches." Those who believe this phrase is merely informational should understand that this motel owner was enjoying an occupancy of 90 per cent while his neighboring competitors were scratching for guests. But he does not devote all his time to his booming business; he is also prominent in the affairs of a Miami Beach synagogue.

It is conceivable that, on the record, many people may conclude that the moral smog of the Miami Beach area does not discriminate; it envelops many Christians and many Jews. The atmosphere calls to mind the famous *New Yorker* cartoon depicting a drunk at a bar, shouting, "I hate everybody, regardless of race, creed, or color!"

In the City of Miami Beach, the exclusion of Jews has retreated to a handful of beautiful residential areas; this is the Custer's Last Stand of Anglo-Saxonism. The most interesting of these pockets consists of two of four oval, manufactured islets known as Sunset Islands Nos. 1 and 2, which lie on the Biscayne Bay side of the city.

Somewhat in the fashion of the Lowells and the Cabots, Sunset Island No. 2 can be contacted only via a bridge from No. 1, and No. 1 via a guarded bridge from the city itself. According to D. Lee Powell, Mayor of Miami Beach, the roads on these islands are public. That is not the impression, however, that was conveyed by a uniformed guard who flagged my car down when I attempted to reach the islands. After learning that my mission was rubbernecking, he declared, "Those are private roads. It's all theirs—the whole thing!" Persistent pleasantness overcame him, though, and ultimately he waved me on with an admonition. "Don't park and don't get out of your car."

I found the islands to be lovely—idyllic, in fact. Some residents grow bananas in their back yards while others display violently colorful flowers and resplendent lawns. I felt a keen desire to stop and rest my head against the carpet grass, but remembering the forbidding guard, I drove on and admired the homes, which weigh in at $50,000 to $150,000. The owners of these mansions, I found, are for the most part socialites and other elegantly moneyed devotees of sunshine and exclusivity.

When the Sunset Islands were developed during the 1930s, landowners formed an association known as Sunset Island Property Owners, Inc. For the most part, its by-laws covered standard points of interest to the nervous propertied, but one covenant was exceptionally meaningful. It specified that only "Caucasians," Christians, and non-felons could join in the association. And so, under this restriction, dozens of expensive homes were built and occupied by untainted non-felons

Into this tranquilly antiseptic situation barged—all unknowing—a somewhat cloistered millionaire from Kentucky. He was B.J. Harris, a thoughtful, soft-spoke personable Jew who had rarely if ever met anti-Semitism in his home town of St. Louis, at the University of Kentucky, at Notre Dame, or as a building contractor and banker in Louisville. Nor had Harris encountered lapses in brotherhood durin his service as a Naval officer during World War II. He had been affiliated with Jewish religious institutions, but he had never had occasion to differentiate himself from other Americans.

After a tragedy in his family in 1949, Harris moved to the Miami area and discovered that others would differentiate for him. Being a man of considerable mea he set out in search of suitable land on which to erect a comfortable home. But each time a site caught his fancy, friends told him he couldn't buy or build on it, because he was Jewish. There were ten such areas in all.

When he drove through the Sunset Islands one day in 1952 and noticed a desirable lot for sale, Harris bought it. He then obtained a lot-purchase form, the wording on the back of which introduced him to the association's devotion to white Christiandom. By this time, although he would not put it that way, Harris had had a snootful. He decided to ignore the association. But the property owners had evidently become suspicious, because when he reconsidered and tried to obtain a membership application, he found his letters ignored. Finally, he notified the association that he intended to build his house. The property owners abandoned their reserve long enough to tell him that he was ineligible for membership.

Harris does not consider himself a crusader, and at this point he thought he might drop the matter. But his forbearance had been strained. "I couldn't understand their opposition," he recalls. "I felt I had been as good a citizen as anyone. Then I started thinking about the Constitution, and I decided I would find out if it could be made to mean what it said."

He gambled and had the house constructed, whereupon the association offered him a $25,000 profit if he would abandon it. He not only refused, but discovered shortly afterward that the association had amended its by-laws, removing all restrictions against non-Gentiles, non-Caucasians, and felons. The sole new requirement was that of "good moral character." The barrier seemed to have been broken.

But Harris, who had never spent so much as a day in a traffic court, was again rejected. So, thoroughly aroused, he moved into his home in June, 1953. If the cordiality expressed by some neighbors toward himself, his wife, and his children was reassuring, the lull was temporary. For the association quickly brought suit and forced him to enter a protracted legal contest to sustain his right to live on Sunset Island No. 2, Miami Beach.

The court proceedings were complex and only occasionally amusing—as when it developed that Virginia Hill had been a member of the association. Miss Hill was the intimate acquaintance of Bugsy Siegel, whose business had been gangsterism before it was dissolved by bullets. An officer of the association testified, remarkably, that he was unaware of Miss Hill's reputation while she was a neighbor. He was also unaware of rumors that Bugsy's cash had purchased her charming Sunset Island residence. Under questioning, he did manage to recall that the Miami Beach police had visited Virginia a number of times and that, under pressure, she sold out and left after the Kefauver hearings had cast doubt on her "good moral character."

But the court chose to find that the sole issue was membership in the association. No membership, no right to live among the good moral characters of Sunset Islands Nos. 1 and 2. Harris appealed, however, and in 1959—seven years after he had bought his land—the Florida Supreme Court ruled that the Fourteenth Amendment to the Constitution applied to B.J. Harris, a Jew. No decline in property values has been noted on the Sunset Islands, and no taint is visible.

It is an interesting illustration of the nature of Miami Beach that few tourists, even among "repeaters," are aware of most of the events and conditions I have described in this chapter. Their lack of awareness is a tribute to the thoroughness with which fortress hotels succeed in insulating their guests from life.

THE FUTURE OF
JEWS IN THE SOUTH

JEROME A. WOLFE

Both past and contemporary sociological analysis of southern Jewry has been very limited. Given the absence of any appreciable sociological data bank on southern Jewry, it is extremely difficult to predict or project what the future holds for Jews in the South. Furthermore, much of sociological analysis is not particularly well suited to predicting complicated historical events. Unseen, historical contingencies always make long-range historical forecasts at best spurious. Nevertheless, there have been some major shifts in the economy, population, and technology of the South over the years, developing into what many writers characterize as the new technological South. These changes and the prospects they may have in the future for southern Jewry will be the focus of this analysis.

The first Jewish community in the South developed during the settlement of Georgia in 1733. Although Jews have lived in the South approximately 250 years, there have not been large numbers of them there. From colonial times to the present, they have comprised less than 1 percent of the whole southern population.[1] Current demographic estimates of the total number of Jews living in the South are approximately 521,090. Of these, 403,525 reside in the southern Atlantic states (Virginia through Florida), 61,055 in the southern Gulf states (Alabama, Mississippi, Louisiana) and tier states (Arkansas, Tennessee, Kentucky), and 66,510 in the western South (Texas).[2]

While there has been much written about local southern Jewish history, it has only been in relatively recent years that sociological studies have begun to focus on Jewish life in the South. And, most of these studies have tended to focus primarily upon selected southern communities, such as Lowi's study of "Iron City,"[3] Fishman's study of "Southern City,"[4] and Reissman's study of New Orleans.[5]

Unfortunately, the sociology of Jews in the South still awaits the application of a number of in-depth quantitative studies of southern Jewry.

In analyzing Jewish life in the South, Dinnerstein and Palsson suggest that there have been predominant factors in the past that have always affected the lives of southern Jews.[6] Agrarianism has been the first major factor; others are racism and the dominant religious element, fundamental Protestantism.

To some extent these factors have been present historically in other regions of the nation as well, but it was perhaps the special combination of these factors and the effects they had on southern life that has given a special meaning as to what it means to be a southerner, and particularly a southern Jew. To a large degree the elements of agrarianism, racism, and fundamental Protestantism have interacted to produce some regional differences between southern and northern Jews.

The predominantly agrarian society in the South helped conserve a typically American bias that favored the producers rather than the financiers.[7] Such attitudes occasionally militated against the Jews during the early days of the Republic and in the Populist movement of the 1890s. Fortunately these prejudices did not prevent the Jews from attaining a high standing in many southern communities.

The impact of slavery and the aftermath of racism in the South has affected the Jewish experience in many respects. According to Korn, the test of the southerner became his acceptance of black bondage.[8] Southern Jews, Korn notes, had no ambivalence on this score. Most either kept silent or gave wholehearted support to the southern ideology. In contrast northern Jews could be found on both sides of the issue. Korn's conclusion may be a rather gratuitous assumption, however, as it appears that a number of southern Jews' attitudes toward slavery were much more complex and convoluted.

During the civil-rights movement there was considerable ambivalence among southern Jews in their attitudes toward supporting civil-rights legislation. Although many southern Jews did endorse integration publicly, others feared that their endorsement would bring about economic and social reprisals. Most southern Jews preferred to remain inconspicuous on this matter.[9]

The last factor, fundamental Protestantism, as the dominant religious element in many parts of the South, especially more so in the interior part of the South, produced a certain type of religious intolerance. Unfortunately this religious intolerance often focused on the Jews.[10] Yet in many respects fundamental Protestantism conveyed a mixed attitude toward Jews in the South. Some writers contend that in parts of the South Jews were held in special regard as being authorities on the Old Testament and were shown a type of reverence because they were Jewish.

If these three major factors—agrarianism, slavery and its aftermath racism, and fundamental Protestantism—have been the primary ingredients affecting the Jewish experience in the South in the past, it is interesting to predict how some changes in these factors will affect southern Jews in the future.

The new technological South is no longer monolithic in its socioeconomic structure. Since Reconstruction the South has become more diversified. It is misleading to continue to view the South as having a uniform culture. The very term "the South" is increasingly becoming a meaningless one because the geographic and cultural regions of the South are very vast and diversified.

Many southern cities—among them Atlanta, Memphis, and New Orleans—are already becoming highly industrialized and urbanized. Jews in the South have always tended to concentrate more in urbanized areas, and we should expect this trend to continue. If there are any reversals in this trend as there have been in the national population statistics of some people moving to smaller communities, we should still expect Jews in the South to live near highly industrialized urban areas. Of course, the Jewish experience in the South will always reflect to some extent the size of the community Jews live in, the length of time Jews have lived in that particular community, and the occupational structure of the community. But industrialization seems to have a way of homogenizing many aspects of a region, and the differences in attitudes in the future between Jews in the North and South will probably reflect not so much regional differences as it will whether one lives in a predominantly metropolitan or non-metropolitan area. If Daniel Bell's assumptions about the postindustrial society are correct that services will continue to expand and eventually dominate the economy, this should have a relatively high value for Jews in the future, since many Jews aspire educationally and occupationally to types of positions that will be vital for a postindustrial society.[11]

The future of race relations in the South and how it will affect southern Jews is very difficult to pinpoint. It is dependent on a multiple of factors such as the state of the economy and local and regional politics of various southern communities. Over the last two decades the South has moved from de jure segregation to de facto segregation. During this period the attitudes and feelings many southern Jews and non-Jews had about integration have been highly tested. Although it is highly speculative, it may be this type of racial confrontation that will in the long run have a positive effect of improving race relations in the South. Anti-Semitism in the South as in other regions of the country has been periodic and uneven. It is always difficult to isolate the intensity of anti-Semitic feelings. However, it may be that hard-core anti-Semitism in the South has already decreased appreciably, but more discrete forms of anti-Semitism will continue to exist in the South, as well as in other regions of the country.

Although many parts of the South will continue to be described as fundamentalist in religious outlook, this does not necessarily mean that it will have an adverse effect for Jews in the South. Harry Golden insists that the South, especially the rural South, has had a tradition of philo-Semitism, regarding the Jewish citizen almost with reverence.[12] As religious tolerance increases in the South, we should expect the rise of Jewish status in southern communities.

Attempting to predict the future of Jews in the South involves many restrictions and limitations. To be southern and to be Jewish have been vital and interesting parts of the American process. Whatever the future of the South is to become, southern Jews will be a dynamic part of that development.

NOTES

1. Ira Rosenwaike, "An Estimate and Analysis of the Jewish Population of the United States in 1970," *Publication of the American Jewish Historical Society* 50 (1960): 34.

2. Alvin Chenkin, "Jewish Population in the United States, 1974," in Morris Fine and Milton Himmelfarb, eds., *American Jewish Yearbook* (New York: American Jewish Committee, 1976), pp. 230-231.

3. Theodore Lowi, "Southern Jews: The Two Communities," *Jewish Journal of Sociology* 6 (July 1964): 103-117.

4. Joshua A. Fishman, "Southern City," *Midstream* 7 (September 1961): 39-56.

5. Leonard Reissman, "The New Orleans Jewish Community," *Jewish Journal of Sociology* 4 (June 1962): 110-123.

6. Leonard Dinnerstein and Mary Dale Palsson, eds., *Jews in the South* (Baton Rouge: Louisiana State University Press, 1973).

7. John Higham, "American Anti-Semitism Historically Reconsidered," in Charles Herbert Stember, ed., *Jews in the Mind of America* (New York: Basic Books, 1966), p. 248.

8. Bertram Wallace Korn, *American Jewry and the Civil War* (Philadelphia: Jewish Publication Society of America, 1951), chap. 2.

9. Leonard Dinnerstein, "Jews and the Desegregation Crisis in the South," *American Jewish Historical Quarterly* 65 (March 1973).

10. William J. Robertson, *The Changing South* (New York: Boni and Liveright, 1927), pp. 98-99.

11. Daniel Bell, "Notes on the Post Industrial Society," *The Public Interest* 1-6 (Winter 1967), and 2-7 (Spring 1967).

12. Harry Golden, *Forgotten Pioneer* (Cleveland: World Book Publishing Co., 1963).

3

POOR JEWS

Little attention was given to the Jewish poor until the publication of Wolfe's controversial "The Invisible Jewish Poor" in 1971[1] and a number of articles after that criticizing Wolfe's findings, including articles by Kaplan[2] and Rice[3] in the journal in which Wolfe's article had appeared. Welner's "A View of Jewish Priorities"[4] illustrates the broader questioning of priorities that occurred in the Jewish community, while Barbaro's "Ethnic Resentment"[5] discussed some changes that occurred in the Jewish community's position on antipoverty programs. Barbaro noted that the American Jewish Committee released a report criticizing black control of the antipoverty program and stating "unequivocally" that only a small amount of the large sums of money spent in governmental antipoverty programs had gone to help the Jewish poor.[6] The executive vice-president of the American Jewish Committee stated that American Jewish organizations had to intensify their moral and financial support of the Jewish poor, and the committee published a booklet —The Other Jews: Portraits in Poverty by Rabinowitz[7]—"as part of its effort to focus attention on the plight of the Jewish poor."[8]

A number of grants were made by governmental units and by Jewish agencies following the attention given to Jewish poor. In New York City, for instance, the Federation of Jewish Philanthropies voted in April 1972 to set up neighborhood service centers and to create the Metropolitan Coordinating Committee on Jewish poverty.[9] After the Office of Economic Opportunity and resources-administration studies had supported complaints by the Association of Jewish Anti-Poverty Work "that Jewish poor were often being left out of the antipoverty effort," a $250,00(Federal Office of Economic Opportunity grant was made to New York City in 19 to help the poor in ethnic groups outside the largely black and Puerto Rican official poverty areas.[10] The Metropolitan New York Coordinating Council on Jewish Poverty, in what was termed a "historic occasion," received $250,000 from the city to help establish community action programs for assisting the Jewish poor who were not cared for under governmental antipoverty programs.[11] In 1973 an Office of Economic Opportunity grant for $300,000 created the Jewish Legal Services to provide free legal services for indigent Jews. The Hasidic Corporation for Urban Concerns (which, despite its name, provided services for all Jews) received a grant for $198,542 for job training and counseling services for the poor in ten neighborhoods in New York City.[12] In 1974, after legal counsel of the Commerce Department's Office of Minority Business Enterprise ruled that the Satmar community of Williamsburg was a socially and economically disadvantaged group, the community was given $300,000 to help its members set up small businesses.[13]

Project Ezra on the Lower East Side of New York, financed by the Jewish Association for College Youth and donations, and the Chaver program sponsored by the University of Miami, also illustrate projects that help elderly Jews—many of whom live on poverty-level fixed incomes—to overcome some of the limitations of their age and income.[14] Special services have also been provided in other cities. In Los Angeles, for instance, the Jewish Federation Council of Greater Los Angel began a six-month experiment in home delivery of kosher meals to feed up to thirty-two persons two meals a day, five days a week, after a task force study showed more than 25,000 Jewish poor living in the Central Los Angeles area, with many being over sixty and virtual shut-ins.[15]

A number of cities distributed reports on projects for helping the Jewish poor, among them, Miami[16] and Baltimore.[17] In addition, a number of articles focusing attention on Jewish poverty have appeared in Jewish-oriented magazines such as *The National Jewish Monthly* and *The Times of Israel.*[18] The first book on the Jewish poor, *The Poor Jews* by Levine and Hochbaum, was published in 1974.[19]

The selections in this section describe the poor Jews. First is Wolfe's article,[20] followed by Kaplan's criticism[21] and Rice's criticism,[22] and Wolfe's reply.[23] Also included are two short articles that describe the situation for the Jewish poor in Miami[24] and New York City.[25] The article on New York City also includes a discussion of programs in some localities.

NOTES

1. Ann G. Wolfe, "The Invisible Jewish Poor," *Journal of Jewish Communal Service* 48 (Spring 1972): 1-7.

2. Saul Kaplan, "Comment: 'The Invisible Jewish Poor,' " *Journal of Jewish Communal Service* 48 (Summer 1972): 348-352.

3. James P. Rice, "Comment: 'The Invisible Jewish Poor,' " *Journal of Jewish Communal Service* 48 (Summer 1972): 352-353.

4. Barbara Welner, "A View of Jewish Priorities," *American Zionist* 62 (December 1971): 33-34.

5. Fred Barbaro, "Ethnic Resentment," *Society* 11 (March-April 1974): 67-75.

6. Ibid., p. 72.

7. Dorothy Rabinowitz, *The Other Jews: Portraits in Poverty* (New York: Institute of Human Relations Press, 1972).

8. Irving Spiegel, "Study Urges Aid for Jewish Poor," *New York Times,* January 30, 1972, p. 25.

9. Peter Kihss, "City Undertakes Extensive Study of Help for Poor: In Effort to Widen Program, Jewish and Italian Groups Are Asked for Council." *New York Times,* September 3, 1972, p. 19.

10. "City Gets an O.E.O. Grant to Assist Ethnic Groups," *New York Times*, September 4, 1972, p. 19.

11. Murray Schumach, "City Gives $250,000 to Aid Jewish Poor," *New York Times*, November 7, 1972, p. 39.

12. "Poverty Grants to Aid Jews Here," *New York Times*, August 12, 1973, p. 58.

13. "Hasidic Sect Gets $300,000 U.S. Loan for Small Business," *New York Times*, September 25, 1974, p. 41.

14. "Project Gives Remnant of Lonely Jews on Lower East Side New Motivation," *New York Times*, April 15, 1974; and pamphlet "Chaver" distributed by Hillel Jewish Student Center, University of Miami, Coral Gables, Florida.

15. Mike Goodman, "Kosher Meal on Wheels Aid Aged," *Los Angeles Times*, September 29, 1973.

16. Welfare Planning Council of Dade County, Florida, "Socio-Economic Diagnostic Study of the South Shore Area of Miami Beach, Florida" (November 1968), pp. 1-102. This is a study of all individuals in the area, including (heads of households) Protestants, 9 percent; Catholics, 18 percent; Jews, 60 percent; others, 3 percent; no answer, 9 percent. See p. 33.

17. Associated Jewish Charities and Welfare Fund of Baltimore, "Report on Services to the Jewish Poor and Near Poor in Baltimore," Social Planning Department (January 19, 1972), pp. 1-9.

18. See Elinor Horwitz, "Jewish Poverty Hurts in South Beach," *National Jewish Monthly* 86 (January 1972): 33-40; Mark Effron, "Left Behind, Left Alone," *National Jewish Monthly* 88 (April 1974): 14-24; Bruce Felton, "Down and Out in New York," *Times of Israel* 1 (October 1973): 67-71; M. Hirsh Goldberg, "The Jewish Poor," *Times of Israel* 1 (February 1974): 70-71; Ena Naunton, "South Beach: The 'Other' Miami Beach," *Times of Israel* 1 (March 1974): 47-50; and Louis Trubo, "Los Angeles Is a Shocker," *Times of Israel* 1 (May 1974): 55-56.

19. Naomi Levine and Martin Hochbaum, eds., *Poor Jews: An American Awakening* (New York: Transaction Books, 1974).

20. Wolfe, "The Invisible Jewish Poor."

21. Kaplan, "Comment."

22. Rice, "Comment."

23. Wolfe, "Reply: 'The Invisible Jewish Poor,' " *Journal of Jewish Communal Service* 48 (Summer 1972): 354-359.

24. Horwitz, "Jewish Poverty Hurts in South Beach."

25. Effron, "Left Behind, Left Alone."

THE INVISIBLE JEWISH POOR

ANN G. WOLFE

The difficulty of addressing oneself to the subject of Jewish poverty has to do with its invisible nature. Some seven years ago, America was startled to learn that there were, among us, 30 million poor people living below a level that was considered the poverty line by government standards. It took a man of insight and vision, Michael Harrington, to alert most of us to the fact that we were a country in which poverty, in its extreme, existed side by side with affluence.[1] For a reason that is not altogether clear, the Jewish community did not recognize the relevance of this phenomenon to its own people. To be sure, from time to time, we would read about a group of Jews living in extreme poverty, but these groups seem to be few and far between, and with an occasional exception, did not arouse either passion or anxiety. It is difficult to explain why it took so long for us to come to the realization that we too, have our poor—our "others"—a situation which now presents us with a new and urgent challenge.

The April 22, 1971, issue of *Jewish Week*, an Anglo-Jewish publication has as its lead editorial, an item with the caption, "Belated Recognition of a Problem." In it the editorial states:

> Better late than never is the utmost of enthusiasm earned by the announce-
> ment of the Central Conference of American Rabbis (Reform), that its in-
> coming President, Rabbi David Polish of Evanston, Illinois, is proposing
> a far-reaching program of service to the Jewish poor in America.
>
> It is not merely neglect that the American Jewish poor have suffered.
> They have been the victims of prejudice and discrimination as well, and
> they have suffered from these attitudes at the hands of fellow Jews. Lest

the Reform rabbis be allotted a disproportionate share of the blame for past error because of their present decision to take action, let it be recorded that the whole of the affluent Jewish community, including even much of the Orthodox establishments, is to blame.

Because the myth that the American Jew has conquered poverty has been generally accepted by the affluent Jewish majority, we do not even have reliable statistics on the extent of Jewish poverty.

The publication carries a news item that quotes from Rabbi Polish, to the effect that thousands of Jewish poor families do not have a place in the Jewish community, and he went on, "we have swept the Jewish poor out of sight and acted as though they didn't exist."

In order to understand the dynamics of change that characterizes the Jewish community in the United States, a look at our history is illuminating. From the end of the 1900's to the mid 1960's, the Jewish population increased rapidly. In 1880, American Jews numbered less than 250,000, and represented less than one-half of one percent of the total population. By 1970, the Jewish population had increased twenty-five times in 90 years, compared to a four-fold increase for the total United States population during the same period. Now, at the beginning of the 1970's, the American Jewish community is the largest concentration of Jews in the world, more than two and a half times the number of Jews in Israel, and accounts for half of world Jewry.

Secondly, look at the *source* of our population growth. The tremendous increase in the number of Jews in the United States was not the result of natural growth, as was true for most of the rest of America, but was rather due to heavy migration of Eastern European Jews between 1890 and 1924.

Before the 1870's the American Jewish community was composed largely of first and second generation German Jews, who had come to these shores between 1820 and 1870, with the remainder—some of Sephardic origin—descendants of the original Spanish and Portugese settlers of the colonial period. There were smaller groups from central Europe who were descendants of a pre-19th century migration. As a result, the striking feature that defines the character of the American Jewish community evolved out of the Jewish immigration from Eastern Europe at the turn of the century. However, the character of the American Jewish community is now changing, as a result of internal forces at work among native-born American Jews. The transition from a foreign-born, immigrant group to an Americanized second and third generation community has important consequences for the structure of the Jewish community, and for the ways in which American Jews live. For the first time in the history of the American Jewish community, a third generation Jewish population faces the American scene without large-scale outside reinforcement. We are now on our own, so to speak. It is this that sets the framework for an understanding of the phenomenon of our Jewish poor, and the invisible character of Jewish poverty.

Another interesting historical fact should be noted. In part of his study of the social and religious history of the Jew, Salo Baron observed that as early as the middle 17th century, it was already noticeable that "great destructive forces, contagious diseases, and wars, seem to have claimed fewer victims among the Jews than among their gentile neighbors." Whether the health and mortality differentials noted by Baron for the mid 17th century characterizes the American Jewish community today has not been fully explored. However, what skimpy data are available from some community studies indicate that there do appear to be differences that exist in the survival pattern of Jews from that of the total white population. There appear to be lower death rates of Jews at younger ages. The lower birth rate in the Jewish families results in a Jewish population today with a larger number of elderly than in the general population. One out of 10 Jews is over the age of 65.

We have no up-to-date scientific data on many of the characteristics of the Jewish population in America. We have pieces of information on income, occupation, age distribution, education, etc. Studies done at different times in different cities; surveys of special functional agencies, census reports—these help us put together the pieces of the puzzle. Hopefully, more accurate information will be forthcoming from the national population study, currently being conducted by the Council of Jewish Federations and Welfare Funds.

So, age is an important and basic demographic feature. At the present time, and until the national population study of the CJFWF is completed, the only national information on the age composition of the Jewish community is the 1957 census survey. Changes have undoubtedly occurred since then. However, the data clearly indicate that the Jewish population is, on the whole, older than that of the general white population of the United States. The youngest age group, under 14, makes up 23 percent of the total Jewish population, compared to 28 percent of the total white population. Also, there is an interesting figure in the 1957 census—28 percent of U.S. Jews are in the age range of 45 to 64, as against 21 percent of the U.S. white population in that age group. We can expect, therefore, that the Jewish population in the next decade will continue to have an *increasing* proportion of older people.

In American society, the problems associated with an aged population are serious. During the next few decades, such problems may be even more serious for the Jewish community than for the population as a whole. It is expected that the proportion in the Jewish population, 65 years of age and over, will increase from 10 percent, at the present time, to 17 percent in 1978.

Overall, therefore, it would seem that the Jewish age structure requires continuous assessing, not only for its impact on births, deaths, and the economic structure of the community, but also because of its broader sociological implications and because of the need to plan services for the future. In an as yet unpublished demographic profile of the American Jew conducted for the American Jewish Community,[2] Dr. Sidney Goldstein of the Department of Sociology at Brown University states as follows:

While recognizing that the general trend is toward an aging population, with its associated problems of housing, financial crises resulting from retirement, more illness, one must also be aware that changes are taking place at other points in the age hierarchy and that the needs for schools, playgrounds, camps, and teenage programs also vary as the age profile changes. Too often, the Jewish community has been guilty of planning its future without taking account of the basic considerations of the probable size distribution and age composition of the population.

The years of the past decade have moved along with increasing technological advances, leaving behind institutions and people who have become both out of fashion and ill-equipped to deal with changing needs. Some of us believe that many of our most serious national problems stem from the failure of our institutions to adapt to change. In the Jewish community, we see a larger aging population unable to adapt to a new and different society, and if we are candid, the same failure of national institutions to take cognizance of these changes, holds true for some of our Jewish institutions.

Part of the blame lies with the institutions, but the greater blame lies with us. For more than a decade after World War II, until the 1960s began to shake us out of our complacency, many of us were content to sit back and take comfort in the fact that we never had it so good. It was during this period that *we* became aware, and the country as a whole was convinced of the affluence of the Jewish community; it often created problems for us. All the statistical figures on income showed the Jewish community enjoying higher average incomes and a higher media income than that of the general population.

The researcher encounters the greatest difficulty in collecting information on income. Not until 1940 did the federal census include such a question. Of the large number of Jewish community surveys, very few collected information on income, and some of the information which was collected is often questionable. However, a small number of national surveys did include such questions. These clearly documented the fact that the income level of Jews is above that of the general population. A study conducted at the University of Michigan over ten years ago[3] indicated that 31 percent of Jewish families then had incomes of $7,500 to $15,000, compared to only 16 percent of the general population. The National Opinion Research Survey at about the same time had similar data.[4] The median income for heads of Jewish households was just under $6,000 compared to just over $4,000 for the total population. Somehow, these facts hid some others less pretty.

It is in these studies that we find significant indications of the extent of poverty in the Jewish community. The National Opinion Research Survey on income related to religion reported that 15.3 percent of Jewish households had incomes under

$3,000 a year; 15.6 percent of Catholics had incomes under $3,000 a year; and 22.7 percent of Protestants had incomes under $3,000 a year.[5]

Who are the Jewish poor? Who are those in the Jewish community who have not made it, who are not making it, and who live their lives in quiet desperation, out of the mainstream of the Jewish community?

We have blind spots in our vision of ourselves and it time to look at the facts. An interesting example of a blind spot relates to "wealthy" Miami Beach. In a study done in that community called South Beach,[6] it was learned that 40,000 people were clustered in an area of some 30 square blocks. Of these, 80 percent are over 65, and 85 percent are Jews. The average annual income is $2,460; thousands are living on less than $28.00 a week for rent and food.

Elderly Jews, the remnants of the vast immigration of the beginning of the 20th century, constitute the largest group of Jews living in poverty. In spite of all the figures I have given, we do not know, accurately, what proportion of the poor in our community is elderly. The 8 or 9 community studies which we have reviewed reveal that something like 60 to 65 percent of Jews living in poverty are over 60 or 65 years of age. An impressionistic look at the needs of the elderly poor discloses that the major problem facing the elderly poor is housing. Their living conditions are often inadequate, homes in various stages of dilapidation or disrepair. Frequently, they need help in improving their current housing, or assistance in relocating. They often find themselves the last hold-outs in areas that have ceased being Jewish. Loneliness and isolation are perhaps the most poignant characteristics of old age and these are reinforced for the Jewish elderly who are locked in to neighborhoods that no longer offer them the support and security they need. More than emotional insecurity is the sense of physical fright that the deteriorating neighborhood induces.

The aged often live alone (one report says two out of three do) as widows or widowers, in housing arrangements that do not allow for much meaningful social contact with others. In the survey of the Miami Beach area, to which I referred earlier, the people need financial help. They need to be able to pay the skyrocketing rents and have some money left from the Social Security check so that they can eat adequately. In addition to this they ask for simple things. Some said the best thing would be to get a hot lunch in a congenial setting where they could meet others and spend a few pleasant hours. Some of these people who were interviewed said they might have some group activities that were not, as one man put it "children's games for old people." One man who was interviewed said rather matter-of-factly that he had come to Miami Beach for a "warm death bed" and now found himself on a picket line protesting the increasing rents in the area.

An unpublished study conducted in Los Angeles revealed that there are about 8,000 elderly Jews receiving public assistance and that a very large number would be eligible but did not apply for a variety of reasons: pride, lack of knowledge of what is available, physical inability to get to the welfare office. Over 18,000 indigent elderly Jews live in households with incomes below $4,000 a year.

We owe a great debt to the present population of the elderly in our community. They were the ones who helped build our community. The vast numbers managed on their own—some had some help, but for the most part they were a vigorous, powerful, independent force. It should be possible for them to live out their years involved and cared for, and we should make it clear by what we do that we value their lives, their experience, the work of their hands, their humor, and their constant hope.

In a recently published book about the elderly Jews in an old age home,[7] this hope is etched sharply by one resident of the home who said:

> I don't want to talk about the past . . . I don't want to think I am getting older. I want to think about living. Now the world is altogether different. I like to know about the future. I want to look through a window to see how it will be after I am gone. I want to know about this world.

The aged who make up about two-thirds of our poor are perhaps easier to see, and evoke sentiments that all of us feel. But there are significant numbers of poor who are not old folk, and I think it is important to explode the myth that the Jewish poor are all the Jewish old.

There is less sympathy for this other group—30-35 percent of our poverty group —which is made up of single, unrelated people or families, many with young children some headed by one parent. There are Jewish families receiving Aid to Dependent Children, a fact that is usually greeted with disbelief. In New York City alone it is estimated, although here, too, we wonder why it has not been possible to get more accurate statistics about the Jewish poor, that one quarter of a million Jews subsist below a level of $3,500 a year, and another 150,000 live at near-poverty on incomes below $4,500. A study undertaken in 1963 and '64 by the Columbia University School of Public Health and Administrative Medicine[8] shows that 10 percent of the Jewish population is sustaining itself on $3,000 a year or less. For the foreign born Jews in New York City, this figure rises to 15.7 percent, a figure fairly similar to the Puerto Rican community where 16.3 percent are living under $3,000 a year. 75 percent of the foreign born Jews in New York are 50 years of age and older, but in addition to this aging population, there are Orthodox and Chassidic poor, many of them with young families. There are 80,000 Chassidic Jews in New York City, and this group is the third largest poverty group in New York.

Philadelphia, a study conducted by the Jewish Employment and Vocational Service of that city,[9] reveals what some of us have long suspected—that we are like anybody else. Unemployed Jews who came to this agency reflect the same problems that the poor of any group have. The study covered a sample of Jewish men and women representing an active caseload of more than 700 persons. The age range was from 17 to over 65 years, and about half of them were in their prime work period, in the ages between 21 and 50. One-third of the persons coming for help with employment had incomes in the previous year below $2,600, and one in six had an annual income of $4,000 or more.

Up until the very recent past we have had a long period of full employment in America. During such periods, jobless persons are usually people with severe problems of a personal nature, or were those against whom society discriminated. In the Philadelphia study, it appeared that six out of ten of the Jews coming for help with employment had disabilities classified as primarily emotional, but this group overlapped another group of four out of ten who had problems relating to aging or physical health. Limited education was found to be an important factor among poor Jews, half of the job seekers having less than 11 years of schooling, and one in five with less than an eighth grade education. Here, too, our blind spots operate. Because of the high proportion of young Jews in college today, and our tradition as the "People of the Book," we tend to overlook the earlier generation that has had a less impressive education.

In commenting on this study the Executive Director said:

The conditions of impoverishment in spirit as well as economically, which is typical, and the social dependency among other minority groups which stems from exclusion, rejection and chronic failure are operative in the Jewish population as well. . . .

It seems apparent that—in the case of Jewish Employment Vocational Service clients, at least, vocational handicaps underlie their separation from the mainstream of the self-respecting, self-supporting members of society.

One might consider too, current situations of economic recession and rising unemployment and its effect on that part of the Jewish community which lives marginally.

In summarizing the problem of the Jewish poor—estimated at 700,000 to 800,000 in the United States—we must make the point that their problems are common to all poor, but that there are problems peculiar to Jews, problems in inter-group relations, problems related to a Jewish identity which exist in a society whose image of the Jew is not altogether accurate, an image which the Jewish community persists in perpetuating. The problems include poor housing, inadequate medical care, neighborhoods that are undesirable in terms of emotional and physical security and outside the Jewish cultural mainstream.

There are special needs in the Orthodox community to which we must pay attention. There are demands which Jewish ritual makes—the need to buy kosher food, for example. The Chassidic community has a built-in resistance to secular education, particularly at the high school and college levels. Few Chassidim have a college degree, an impediment to benefiting from the economic advantages which higher education normally brings. Jewish education for this group drains the resources of the Chassidic family. On religious grounds, the Orthodox and Chassidic communities are opposed to birth control and tend to have large families. In Williamsburg, in New York City, the median family size is 6.3 children, as opposed to the average Jewish family size of 2 children.

My thesis is a plea to "raise our consciousness"—a phrase borrowed from Women Liberation. What, then, is to be done and who is to do it?

Future historians may likely assess the pattern of Jewish community organization as the unique characteristic of 20th century Jewry. It has become a model for the structure of voluntary organizations of other religious and ethnic groups. Students from all corners of the globe come to study the complex of Jewish health welfare, and other agencies. We have the structure and the processes for rational planning. What may need some doing, in my opinion, is the use of our structures in a way more responsive to needs which we now perceive. And in moving towards this responsiveness, I suggest that some basic questions need to be asked:

Who decides what service gets how much money?
What process is used in making the decision?
Do all elements in the Jewish community share in this decision-making process?
How are priorities set? Where is the power?
Does the Jewish community need to re-order its domestic priorities?
Are we paying enough attention to our domestic Jewish needs?

In this process of finding answers to these and related questions, we may renew the spirit which motivated the formation of Jewish services during the early years, the underlying belief that we must care for each other and that the suffering and pain of any in our community affects us all.

NOTES

1. Michael Harrington, *The Other America; Poverty in the United States*, Baltimore: Pengu Books, 1963.

2. Sidney Goldstein, "American Jewry 1970: A Demographic Profile?" *1971 American Jewish Year Book*, Volume 72, pp. 3-88.

3. Bernard Lazerwitz, "Family Income by Religious Group," *Journal of American Statistic Association*, September, 1961.

4. *Distribution of Income by Religious Groups—1962*, National Opinion Research Center, University of Chicago, Illinois.

5. Ibid.

6. *Socio-Economic Study of the South Shore of Miami Beach, Florida*, Welfare Planning Council of Dade County, Florida, November, 1968.

7. Dorothy Rabinowitz and Yedida Nielsen, *Home Life*, New York: Macmillan, 1971.

8. J. Elinson, D.W. Haberman, C. Gell, *Ethnic and Educational Data on Adults in New York City 1963-64*. New York: School of Public Health and Administrative Medicine, Colum University, 1967.

9. Saul S. Leshner, "Poverty in the Jewish Community," this *Journal*, Vol. LIII, No. 3 (Spring 1967), p. 245.

COMMENT:
The Invisible Jewish Poor, I

SAUL KAPLAN

Three major points are made by Mrs. Wolfe in her article on "The Invisible Jewish Poor."

1. That the economic advances made by Jews in the United States have given rise to false beliefs about the negligible frequency of poverty among Jews. Although in general it is recognized that poverty may exist side by side with affluence, the "Jewish community did not recognize the relevance of this phenomenon to its own people."

2. That Jews are not unlike other ethnic or religious groups in the prevalence of poverty.

3. That Jewish poor in the United States are estimated at 700,000 to 800,000, which would mean that 11.9-13.6 percent of the Jewish population is poor. The lower of these two percentages is higher than the poverty percent for the white population in 1970 (9.9 percent) and the higher figure is greater than the poverty percent for the total population of the United States (12.6 percent).

Whatever the procedure used in arriving at an estimate of Jewish poverty, one must reject any result that places the extent of Jewish poverty at a higher figure than in the general population—in light of the well-known data about the higher income of Jews, which in turn are associated with their higher education attainment and their heavy representation in business and professional positions. Fortunately, as shown below, better data than scattered local studies are available for estimating the national extent of Jewish poverty.

HAS THE JEWISH COMMUNITY IGNORED
THE PROBLEM OF THE JEWISH POOR?

It is difficult to know exactly what is meant by Mrs. Wolfe's references to the Jewish community and its alleged brushing aside of the problem of Jewish poverty. It is, of course, easy for economically successful individual Jews who constantly associate with other Jews in the same economic strata to lull themselves into the illusion that the Jewish poor are no longer with us. The organized Jewish community, however, as represented by Jewish Federations and Welfare Funds (if this is what is meant by the Jewish community) has surely not operated under such illusions. One evidence of this fact is contained in Mrs. Wolfe's reference to a study conducted by the Jewish Employment and Vocational Service of Philadelphia (an agency supported by the organized Jewish community), which showed that unemployed Jews, many of whom are poor, constitute a large part of its clientele. The same thing is true for JVS's in other cities.

Jewish Federations and their affiliate agencies have never been unaware of the continuing problem of Jewish poverty. The Jewish poor and near-poor are much more likely to be served by Jewish Federation agencies than Jews higher up in the economic scale. In Chicago, we estimate that Federation and Welfare fund agencies provide services to about 90 percent of the economically disadvantaged Jews in the metropolitan area. These services, although they may be of great significance in enabling poor Jews to cope more effectively with problems related to medical needs, interpersonal adjustment, vocational adjustment, Jewish education, or constructive use of leisure time, do not directly lift the beneficiaries of such services out of their condition of poverty although they may sometimes help in enabling individuals to take steps in this direction.

Since the establishment of the present day public assistance programs in the 1930's, Jewish agencies have divested themselves of the responsibility of providing direct financial assistance to the Jewish poor—except for refugee families and certain emergency needs. Moreover, under Federal public assistance policies, it is not permissible for a private agency to supplement an assistance payment simply for the purpose of providing a family with a standard of living that is higher than the public assistance level. In at least one community (Chicago) the policy of non-supplementation of public assistance payments is being reexamined by the Board of Directors and staff of the Jewish Federation with a view to seeing whether there might be some practical ways in which poor Jews could be helped through supplementation of assistance payments that would be true supplementation, and not mere an offset against assistance that would otherwise be received from public funds.

ARE JEWS NOT UNLIKE OTHER ETHNIC AND
RELIGIOUS GROUPS IN PREVALENCE OF POVERTY?

The author cites a 1962 survey of the National Opinion Research Center which showed that 15.3 percent of Jewish households, compared with 15.6 percent of

Catholic households, had an income of under $3,000 a year. Although reference is made to the 1957 survey of the Bureau of the Census in connection with age data on Jews, no reference is made to this source in relation to income data on Jews. The 1957 survey of the Bureau of the Census (which is conducted on a much broader basis than the surveys of the NORC) showed that 13.6 percent of Jewish families, compared with 18.5 percent of Roman Catholic families had an income below $3,000 (although to be sure the gap between urban Jewish and urban Catholic families in this regard was narrower, 13.7 percent versus 16.0 percent). The crucial fact, however, which appears to be ignored in Mrs. Wolfe's analysis, is that poverty cannot be measured by reference to income alone. The estimation of poverty must take into account both income and family size. The percent of households with an income below some defined point for a family of four persons ($3,000 in 1960 or $4,100 currently) is not the same as the percent of the population below the poverty line. If 15 percent of the households of two population groups have an income below $4,100, the group with the higher average family size (for example Catholics) will have a much greater percent below the poverty line than is true for a group (for example Jews) with the lower average family size.

The truth of the matter, as shown in greater detail below, is that there is good reason to believe that poverty does occur less frequently among Jews than among any other religious or ethnic group in the country.

HOW MANY JEWS ARE POOR?

The number of Jews who are poor cannot, of course, be estimated without a precise definition of poverty. Although poverty cannot be defined in any absolute sense, the Bureau of the Census uses the concept that a family is poor if its total income is less than three times the cost of food under the economy food plan of the Department of Agriculture. In 1970, for nonfarm households, the dividing line between poverty and nonpoverty ranged from an annual income of $1,950 for a one-person household to $6,468 for a family of seven or more and a middle figure of $3,968 for a family of four (with 1971 prices the latter figure would be $4,103).

All of the estimates of poverty or near-poverty that have been published by the Bureau of the Census take into account income in relation to family size. In November, 1971 for the first time, the Bureau published poverty estimates by ethnic origin. For persons of Russian origin, the poverty percent was given as 4.5 percent, which is lower than for any other ethnic group in the country.

The Census has stated the following about persons of Russian origin: "Since very few persons have migrated to this country from Russia since 1930, when two-thirds of the Russian-born Americans reported that they had spoken Yiddish in their childhood, it is likely that most persons of Russian origin had a Jewish cultural heritage." One may thus apply data on persons of Russian origin to the Jewish population on the basis of (a) the known fact that most persons of Russian origin are

Jews and (b) the hypothesis that income data on Jews of Russian origin represent income data on all Jews in the country.

The poverty percent for persons of Russian origin indicates that the number of poor Jews in the country is about 264,000. The extent of poverty, however, is much higher for Jews living as unrelated individuals than for members of families, and it is also much higher for females than for males, ranging from only 1.0 percent poor in families with a male head to 30.1 percent for females living as unrelated individuals.

Mrs. Wolfe is correct in stating that elderly Jews constitute the largest group of Jews living in poverty. This is evident from the fact that among Jews, poor unrelated individuals (most of whom are aged) represent 61 percent of the total poor. The Jews are the only ethnic group among whom poor unrelated individuals outnumber those living in families; in the country as a whole, such individuals represent less than 20 percent of the poor.

It is possible, of course, that in estimating 700,000—800,000 poor Jews Mrs. Wolfe had in mind some definition of poverty other than the official definition used by the Bureau of the Census, for example, near-poverty, the dividing line for which is 25 percent greater that the poverty level, or the "lower standard" of the Bureau of Labor Statistics which came to $6,960 for a family of four in the Spring of 1970. Two comments are in order on this possibility:

1. The *Newsweek* article of March 1, 1971, quoted an estimate attributed to the American Jewish Committee that "There are nearly 800,000 Jews living at or below the poverty level of $3,743 annual income. . . ." Thus, the official poverty definition for a family of four appears to have been used and then applied without correction for family size variations to all Jewish households.

2. If some definition other than the official definition of poverty is being used, then the definition that is employed should be made explicit. Only confusion can result when figures are published about "poor Jews" without specifying whether the figure relates to the poor, the near-poor, the economically disadvantaged, or some other concept.

Mrs. Wolfe's article repeats the well-known fact that the median income of Jewish households is significantly greater than the median in the total population. This fact alone should have cast doubt on the proposition that Jews are not unlike other ethnic and religious groups in the prevalence of poverty. Although it is mathematically possible for two population groups to have the same frequency of poverty even though one group has a significantly higher median income than the other, it is realistically inconceivable that this would be true. The income data on ethnic groups published by the Bureau of the Census clearly establish the nature of the negative relationship between median family income and the percent below the poverty line. Invariably, according to the Census data, if the median family income for one ethnic group is higher than for a second group, the percent of persons below the poverty level is lower for the first ethnic group than it is for the second. These data are shown [in the table here].

Median Income and Percent Below Poverty Level, by Ethnic Origin

Ethnic Origin	Median Family Income, November, 1969, in Families Headed by Persons under Age 65		Percent of Persons below Poverty Level, 1970	
	MEDIAN	RANK	PERCENT	RANK
Russian	$11,554	1	4.5	9
Polish	8,849	2	5.3	8
Italian	8,808	3	6.1	7
German	8,607	4	8.57	6
English	8,324	5	8.61	5
Irish	8,127	6	10.5	4
Other	7,671	7	15.4	3
Not reported	7,264	8	15.6	2
Spanish	5,641	9	24.3	1

Clearly (as shown by the Census data on persons of Russian origin) poverty among Jews occurs less frequently than among any other ethnic group in the country. Jewish poverty, to be sure, has not been abolished, but fortunately Jews are poor less often than other ethnic and religious groups.

This brings us to the nub of the matter, for unless steps are taken to serve the Jewish poor more effectively, it makes little practical difference whether one's estimate of Jewish poverty is too high or too low. Effective social planning for the benefit of the poor must depend on realistic, not exaggerated, estimates of the size of the problem in relation to the resources that are or that may become available to help them with both material assistance and other needed services. The Jewish community needs sober enlightenment on the magnitude of Jewish poverty and the problems faced in coping with it. It does not need shock treatment from inflated figures, especially from a source that does not have and is not in a position to assume practical responsibility in dealing with the economic and social problems of the Jewish poor.

The Jewish poor are ill served if their numbers are overstated. The important task is to face up to the responsibility for the estimated 264,000 Jewish poor, many of whom are being aided by public agencies as well as by private Jewish agencies, but who are still poor. To meet their unmet needs is a sizable task for our communities, who must find new resources and define new priorities if our goal is to eliminate Jewish poverty.

COMMENT:
The Invisible Jewish Poor, II

JAMES P. RICE

It was gratifying that you requested Mr. Saul Kaplan, Research Director of our Jewish Federation, to publish his comments on Mrs. Ann Wolfe's article on the "Invisible Jewish Poor." Mrs. Wolfe's paper has been widely circulated by the prestigious and usually reliable American Jewish Committee, thereby giving credence to misleading estimates of the Jewish poor, which have been utilized by other Jewish organizations, and published widely in the general and Anglo-Jewish press.

As early as March 1971, when an article in *Newsweek* referred to an estimate of 800,000 Jewish poor by Mr. Milton Himmelfarb of AJC, we called the inaccuracy to Himmelfarb's attention. He immediately denied responsibility for giving that figure to *Newsweek*, stating that other AJC staff members had been responsible for it. After Mrs. Wolfe's report was made here in June 1971, we pointed out on several occasions, the essential inaccuracies of the AJC figures to both Mrs. Wolfe and Mr. Bertram Gold, Executive Vice-President of the AJC. After the new and definitive information on poverty among ethnic groups was released by the Census Bureau in November 1971, Mr. Kaplan reduced his own previous estimates of a maximum of 500,000 poor Jews to 264,000 or 4.5% of the Jewish population (the same as the published percent for persons of Russian origin, most of whom are Jewish).

Our statements to Mr. Gold and Mrs. Wolfe have been completely supported in several communications to Mr. Gold by the top staff of the Council of Jewish Federations and Welfare Funds. The CJFWF staff and executives of a number of Federations have also vigorously and carefully refuted the contention that Federation agencies ignore the needs of the poor. For example in Chicago we currently estimate (on the basis of agency data) that our Federation and Welfare Fund agencies are serving approximately 90% of the economically disadvantaged Jews of our community. Furthermore, in 1971 our Federation board authorized cash supplementation to Jewish clients of the Public Aid Department if threatened cuts in relief were put into effect. We are now undertaking an intensive study of all the Jewish poor of our community with a view to developing a program which would go beyond our present efforts.

A revealing development relates to the paper delivered by Dr. Erich Rosenthal of Queens College at the AJC Consultation on Jewish Poverty in December 1971, which was attended by approximately 85 community representatives from all over the country. In his paper, Dr. Rosenthal referred to a Jewish poverty rate that might possibly be as high as 24%—which, of course, would tend to support the higher figures being used by Mr. Gold and Mrs. Wolfe. On February 28, 1972, Mr. Kaplan received a copy of Dr. Rosenthal's report from Mrs. Wolfe, and immediately sent him as analysis to which Dr. Rosenthal, with true professional integrity, replied on March 14th that, *recognizing the validity of Mr. Kaplan's analysis, he was requesting Mrs. Wolfe not to include his presentation in the written report of the Conference proceedings.* As of this writing, the participants in the Consultation who heard both Mr. Gold's and Dr. Rosenthal's figures have not been informed that Dr. Rosenthal's report has been withdrawn, nor, up to the present time, has the AJC attempted to refute the figures presented by Mr. Kaplan.

Earlier this month, the AJC Institute of Human Relations Press published the monograph by Dorothy Rabinowitz "The Other Jews—Portraits in Poverty." In his introduction to the monograph Mr. Gold says once again: "On the basis of a number of estimates, which use various income levels as standard definitions of poverty in the United States, there is general agreement that the number of Jewish poor today lies somewhere between a minimum of 350,000 or 400,000 and a figure perhaps twice that." As I have pointed out to Mr. Gold, such loose statements still leave the impression of a huge percentage of Jewish poor, which cannot be justified by current data.

It is also to be regretted that neither Mr. Gold nor Dorothy Rabinowitz mentioned in the monograph that Federation agencies are taking responsibility for serving such families and individuals as part of their regular and ongoing responsibilities.

The AJC efforts have resulted in a kind of sociological "overkill," which is as unacceptable in our field as it is in the field of international relations. There is no doubt about the fact that there are Jewish poor, and our leadership in Chicago shares the view that we should give greater attention to their needs. AJC could have served a tremendously useful purpose by drawing attention to this issue on its merits but instead obtained national attention at the price of continually disseminating inaccurate and misleading statements, with inferential criticism of agencies who are trying to meet the needs.

It is disappointing that such questions arise about the organization whose "Yearbook" is justifiably regarded as an authentic guide about American and World Jewish affairs, and whose many special studies about American Jewish life are accepted with respect and trust. Fortunately, in Chicago, as in most other communities, AJC members cooperate fully as leaders of Federation agencies in programs to aid the Jewish poor, and in other Federation activities. They express their commitment by responsible involvement in an effort to solve the problems.

The readers of the *Journal* now have been given the opportunity to get a different perspective, which is indispensable to the central issue of our responsibility to reexamine the needs of the Jewish poor in the context of the total American Jewish priorities.

REPLY:
The Invisible Jewish Poor

ANN G. WOLFE

The flurry of reaction to the appearance of my article in the Spring issue of the *Journal* came as no surprise to me. There has been a continuing flurry of reaction to my Chicago speech of June 8th, 1971, that was the basis of the article. The original reactions, which ranged from surprise to dismay to anger to outright hostility is something of a lesson in what happens when a communal raw nerve gets touched. With it all, I have not yet been able to sort out the reactions. I can understand the surprise—that was to be expected, since I made the point about the invisibility of Jewish poverty. But the anger and hostility, expressed in letters and public utterances by Jewish professionals, leaves one with some questions about professional behavior. This is not the time, nor do I wish to divert our attention by pursuing this issue. Some time in the future, perhaps, there will be time and mood to get into this little-talked about concern.

I am delighted to have contributed to the excitement in the profession of Jewish communal service. It is difficult to recall the last time there was so much passion expressed about a domestic issue. During the 1940's many of us used to look forward to the annual meetings of the Conference, at which controversy was encouraged, and divergent views on serious communal questions were given open hearings. Unfortunately, over the past decade or more, there has been little excitement and hardly any passion. The last flurry, in my memory, occurred at that famous debate in Chicago (again, Chicago!) between Bruno Bettelheim and Isidore Chein on "Bringing up the Jewish Child." And, here, too, I say with some degree of pride, that the American Jewish Committee had something to do with it, since two *Commentary* articles—by Kurt Lewin and Bruno Bettelheim—formed the basis of that debate.

The present excitement over my paper seems misdirected, and the passion misused. I would have preferred more passion about the issue of poverty itself, rather than on the accuracy of the figures. However, let me address myself to how the estimates were arrived at. I take issue with Mr. Kaplan's rejoinder on a number of counts:

1. I do not believe that poverty can be definitively measured by the standards set by the Department of Health, Education and Welfare. I suggested to Mr. Kaplan, in a conversation with him, that a more realistic way of measuring poverty in the Jewish community might be the use of figures from the Bureau of Labor Statistics of the Department of Labor. The Bureau, from time to time, issues figures for three types of families, indicating minimum needs for each category: at a higher level, an intermediate level, and a lower level. Just this past week, as of the date of this writing, the Bureau issued figures for Autumn, 1971. To maintain a family of four at the lower level (in the New York-New Jersey area) $7,578 a year was needed. The budget-type family studied consists of a 38-year-old husband employed full time, a non-working housewife, a boy of 13 and a girl of 8. The lower level family lived in rental housing (without air-conditioning), performed more services for themselves, had fewer household appliances, used free recreational facilities. Fewer had cars, and those who did owned older models.

The Bureau issues figures for older couples and individuals, and since my review indicated that about two-thirds of the Jewish poor are old, these figures have a special relevance. The figures for Autumn, 1971 for older people at the lower level were not available from the BLS regional office at the time of this writing. They will be available two to three weeks hence. However, the 1970 figures, which are probably about 3-4 percent less than 1971 needs, indicated that an aged person living alone needed $2,300 a year; an aged couple needed $4,200. Hardly generous, but somewhat closer to real life.

My point is that one might reasonably conjecture that any young family of four living on an income below $7,578 a year, or any aged person with an income of less than $2,300; or an aged couple with less than $4,200 a year are poor. And since a substantial number of Jewish elderly maintain themselves on Social Security payments, it is likely that many of them are just plain poor people.

2. Mr. Kaplan takes issue with the survey of the National Opinion Research Center. By the way, this is the first time this point has been raised. For the most part, the studies and facts in the paper have been ignored. Mr. Kaplan, and his supervisor, Mr. Rice, have merely said they were wrong. The NORC is generally accepted as reputable and accurate. The Center has been used by researchers, sociologists, and political scientists. I cannot enter this debate, since I have no way of being on either side of the argument about NORC's methods.

But the issue raised seems relatively minor. The NORC survey in 1962 indicated that 15.3 percent of Jewish households, 15.6 percent of Catholic households, and 22.7 percent of Protestant households had an income under $3,000 a year. Mr. Kaplan prefers the 1957 figures of the Bureau of the Census for urban poor: 13.7

percent of Jewish families compared with 16.0 percent of Catholic families. (Using the NORC figures, based on an estimated Jewish population in 1960 of 5,000,000, there would be 765,000 Jews in poor households; using the Bureau of the Census figures for 1957, using the same population estimate there would be 685,000 Jews in poor households. Neither figure seems much out of line from my estimate of 700,000.)

I am not unaware of the fact that family size alters the degree of poverty in a family. My contention, however, is that even using the *smallest size* possible, any family living on such income is poor.

3. Mr. Kaplan bases the main point of his argument on the census data based on ethnic background. In his letter, he has explained clearly the basis for this rationale: Persons of Russian origin = Jews of Russian origin = all Jews.

This is a method used since the thirties, based on the fact that from the end of the 19th Century through the first two decades of the 20th Century the only Russians coming to America were Jews. The method may have been valid for the thirties and forties. I have doubts about its use to-day, and in these doubts I am joined by others, more knowledgeable than I in the ways of demography. These doubts were raised by several participants in the *Consultation on Poverty in the Jewish Community* convened by the American Jewish Committee in December, 1971. This method eliminates the large Hassidic community that came to America from Poland after World War II (or are Poland, Greece, Austria, Hungary, all counted as Russia by this method?). It eliminates all Jews of other national backgrounds, as well, by averaging them out. I believe this use of ethnic background that equates Russians with Jews has many dangers, let alone the question of its validity as a source of accurate information and indicates how difficult it is to change what may have been once valid, and is perhaps no longer.

4. Finally, Mr. Kaplan claims not to know what is meant by my "references to the Jewish community and its alleged brushing aside of the problem of Jewish poverty." In all of this discussion, it seems to me that this is the simplest and clearest part of it all, and possibly explains the reaction to my paper. I never said *nothing* was being done in behalf of the Jewish poor. I said little was being done, that for the most part Jewish poverty had been obscured by Jewish affluence, and that Jewish agencies needed to re-examine what they were doing and whom they were serving. I still think I was right. I don't doubt that Mr. Kaplan's figures are correct. He says that Chicago Federation and Welfare Fund Agencies serve two-thirds of the Jewish poor and near-poor in that city. It would be interesting to know in what ways. For example, in the "constructive use of leisure time," how many poor Jews are served? Does this mean attendance at a lecture? What proportion of the two-thirds are so served? But I am prepared to accept Mr. Kaplan's figures at face value and applaud the Chicago Federation for its advanced understanding of the problem. A final word on the figures. Many estimates have been produced, different ones, often by the same person. Mr. Kaplan first estimated that there were 500,000 poor Jews (note Mr. Rice's letter); then on June 1, 1971, just a

week prior to my visit to Chicago which had been announced and the subject
"The Invisible Jewish Poor" publicized, Mr. Kaplan estimated 372,000. His estimate has changed again. It demonstrates the difficulty of arriving at correct, precise figures.

I indicated in my paper that we looked forward to the information coming out
ʻof the demographic survey now being conducted by the Council of Jewish Federations and Welfare Funds. Already there have been some indications from Mr. Kapla
and others that we may not get the precise information on Jewish poverty we seek
because of the way the sample was chosen, and because of a high degree of non-
responses in some cities, New York among them. I would hope that we will continue to study the data and get as clear a picture of the extent, degree, and nature
of Jewish poverty as possible.

Now, to address myself to Mr. Rice's letter. If the *Journal* typesetter could
print Yiddish, I would start by using a Yiddish folk saying: *"Men zogt die tochter
nur men maint die schnur."* For those who don't know Yiddish, I translate: "They
say it's their daughter but they mean it's their daughter-in-law."

Mr. Rice is really angry at the American Jewish Committee, and his anger pre-
dates my speech in Chicago last June. His shrill letter impugns the motives of the
American Jewish Committee (which he calls "usually reliable") and since I am responsible for AJC's work in this area I cannot allow him to question my professional integrity without a challenge. When he accuses us of engaging in "scare"
tactics and sociological "overkill" he levels an attack which must be responded to.
I do this reluctantly, since, as I indicated earlier, I believe this is a diversion from
the major issues I raised in the paper, and to which Mr. Rice has not yet addressed
himself.

AJC has had a Social Welfare Division since 1968. We have worked to develop
social policy positions on welfare reform, national health insurance, child care,
and other issues. Our national committee, in October 1969, began to address itself to the question of the relevance of these issues to the Jewish community. It
was out of this study that our attention was drawn to the existence of poverty in
the Jewish community.

In May, 1970, we invited a national staff member of the Council of Jewish Federations and Welfare Funds to address a workshop at our annual meeting on the
issue of Jewish poverty and Jewish Services. The following year, we proposed a
joint staff conference of AJC staff from ten cities with Federation staff from the
same cities (Chicago and Mr. Rice among them.) We set a date in April, 1971, and
a place, and together with CJFWF staff drew up an agenda. Our purpose was to
develop guidelines for working harmoniously in communities, and to highlight
the issue of Jewish poverty as a way of engaging in joint activity. Unfortunately,
that meeting never came off, for a variety of reasons.

We then began to think of a way of raising the social policy issues on Jewish
poverty and asked CJFWF to co-sponsor a Consultation with us. They said they

would be unable to do so. We went ahead, and planned our own. It turned out to be a productive, serious exchange and we believe it advanced our knowledge of the nature and special problems we face. Many professionals in Jewish communal service across the country participated, including three Federation executives, social work educators, and communal workers in the Hassidic and Orthodox communities. It is interesting to note that the invitations to this Consultation had the fewest rejections of any in my own professional career. We invited 105—stretching the capacity of our facilities—90 accepted, and 87 came. For those who run meetings, this is a remarkable showing and attests to the high interest in the subject.

Mr. Rice is obviously irked because we have refused to engage in a debate of numbers with him, and will not do so now. I would suggest that energies expended might better be directed to the problem itself. And in response to Mr. Rice's support of Federation's work in behalf of the Jewish poor, I can only point out with great pleasure that Federations all over the country have strengthened and emphasized the need to give greater priority to this area of work. If this is mere coincidence that's just fine. And I cannot resist the impulse to ask Mr. Rice (although I will surely not participate in another round of letters!) about the figures in *his* letter. He says "Our Federations and Welfare Fund Agencies are serving approximately 90 percent of the economically disadvantaged Jews of our community." Mr. Kaplan just got through saying: "In Chicago, we estimate that Federation and Welfare Fund Agencies provide services to about two-thirds of the Jewish poor and near-poor in the metropolitan area."

Now, really, Mr. Rice! Who is "reliable"?

Mr. Rice makes a big point—"a revealing development" he calls it—about a letter sent by Dr. Erich Rosenthal to Mr. Kaplan (incidently, this letter was copied and widely distributed, without Dr. Rosenthal's knowledge). What does it "reveal"?

At the Consultation on Poverty in the Jewish Community, Dr. Erich Rosenthal read a paper entitled "The Income Distribution of the Jewish Population in the United States in 1969: An Exploratory Report." In it, the author attempted to assess the degree and magnitude of the problem of poverty, and indicated the difficulty because of the lack of precise measurements. He quoted the ethnic background census material referred to by Mr. Kaplan; he referred to the Bureau of Labor Statistics figures and related this to the age factor in the Jewish community. In his paper he writes:

Conclusion
The analysis of the 1969 U.S. Sample Survey revealed that in 1968, 76 percent of the Jewish families in the U.S. are clearly above the poverty level, or to be more precise are maintaining themselves on or above— mostly above—the "lower" living standards as defined by the BLS. The same survey also shows that 4.1 percent of Jewish families live in a state of poverty. On the basis of presently available data it is not possible to es-

tablish a maximum percentage of Jewish families in poverty. It might
be as high as 24 percent.

AJC had no interest in "pushing" one or another set of figures. On a visit to
Chicago, I gave Mr. Kaplan a copy of Dr. Rosenthal's paper. Mr. Kaplan wrote to
Dr. Rosenthal—an 11-page single space letter, indicating that Dr. Rosenthal's ethnic
figures were not up to date, and that figures, he, Mr. Kaplan, had secured over the
telephone from staff in the Population Division of the Bureau of Census would
change the ethnic estimate downward. Dr. Rosenthal subsequently phoned me to
ask that I not distribute his paper until he could make the up-to-date changes. He
did *not* ask me to change the rest of the paper. This is the "revealing" letter to
which Mr. Rice refers.

Mr. Rice is wrong, as Mr. Kaplan was wrong, in accusing us of contending "that
Federation agencies ignore the needs of the poor." As I indicated earlier, we did
not say that; it *is* our contention that the time for re-examination of the emphasis
and priorities in Jewish communal services has come.

Mr. Rice is wrong again in his criticism of the monograph *The Other Jews: Portraits in Poverty* by Dorothy Rabinowitz. The pamphlet was completed in September,
1971 and published in January, 1972 (not "earlier this month," as stated by Mr. Rice
in his *April* 18, 1972 letter.) The dates have some bearing on his criticism of Bertram
Gold's introduction which Mr. Rice quotes: "On the basis of a *number* of estimates,
which use *various* income levels as standard definitions of poverty in the United
States, there is general agreement that the number of Jewish poor today lies *somewhere between* a minimum of 350,000 or 400,000 and a figure perhaps twice that."
(emphasis mine—AGW) What's wrong with that? The figure of 350,000 or 400,000
is *Mr. Kaplan's* released by him in June, 1971. Mr. Rice is annoyed that we didn't
accept this as definitive.

Further, Mr. Gold makes the point in his introduction, and I stress it again:
"Some day soon, we hope, there will be more accurate data. But in the meantime,
we must not become overly preoccupied with numbers. It is sufficient to recognize
that there are altogether too many poor Jews—and then to concentrate on the nature of their poverty and what needs to be done about it."

Mr. Rice regrets "that neither Mr. Gold nor Dorothy Rabinowitz mentioned in
the monograph that Federation agencies are taking responsibility for serving such
families. . . ." Wrong again. Mr. Gold says clearly: "Now that our agencies are view-
ing the problem with a new perspective, a host of new programs around the country are being developed and existing ones are being intensified."

I am sorry Mr. Rice feels disappointed with AJC, and the national attention
drawn to the issue. Mr. Rice himself has been trying to draw some national attention as evidenced by his JTA press releases disputing our figures—among his other
efforts. He, of course, has every right to want national coverage.

Finally, I would like to return to the point of my article and the questions I raised. I believe these are the still unresolved issues in the Jewish community, and affect all areas of Jewish interest:

—Who decides what service gets how much money?
—What process is used in making the decision?
—Do all elements in the community share in the decision-making process?
—How are priorities set? Who sets them?
—Who has the power?
—Does the Jewish community need to re-order its priorities?
—Are we paying enough attention to our domestic Jewish needs?

And now, let's put the copying machines to rest. And go back to work.

P.S. I want to be sure that the readers of the *Journal* understand that I write this as a professional and an individual. I know that it is not always possible to separate out one's agency from one's own work. The AJC supports my work in this field, but I take full responsibility for my paper and its contents. There are other, more correct avenues for discussing differences between organizations.

JEWISH POVERTY
HURTS IN SOUTH BEACH

ELINOR HORWITZ

In the middle sixties when Lyndon Johnson invoked the poverty program few Jews imagined that he was speaking about problems that touched them. Yet in recent months Jewish leaders and observers have officially noted the existence of Jewish poverty throughout the nation. According to Rabbi Isaac Trainin of the Federation of Jewish Philanthropies who recently spoke at the B'nai B'rith triennial convention, the American Jewish community has been "living with myths about itself, including the myth that there are no poor Jews." He estimated that 800,000 Jews concentrated in urban areas, are existing on substandard incomes.

In "The Invisible Jewish Poor," a report prepared for the American Jewish Committee, Ann G. Wolfe cites that 15.3 per cent of Jewish households subsist on annual incomes of less than $3000 at a time when the federal poverty index is $3968 for a family of four.

Most of the Jewish poor are elderly. In New York City, for instance, it is estimated that most of its 250,000 indigent Jews are over sixty-five—remnants of the great European immigration of the early twentieth century, who have remained in their familiar neighborhoods although their children have moved away.

There are, of course, many who have migrated after retirement to tropical have in Florida and California, budgeting their modest needs on seemingly adequate fix incomes. Over the years, though, inflation has disastrously eroded their purchasing power.

One such community that has drawn the attention of observers this past year is South Beach, the southern tip of wealthy Miami Beach. Of the 40,000 residents of South Beach, 80 per cent are over sixty-five and 85 per cent are Jews. Their financial stresses have aroused concern, dissent and a wide range of response to the ancient question, "Am I my brother's keeper?"

"Journalists always take one-sided views," says the man from the city publicity bureau, making no attempt to moderate the level of his irritation. "The new luxury high-rises have plenty of elderly retirees—middle-class people with comfortable incomes who live well—but you don't want to write about *them*—just about poverty on South Beach. We didn't create that situation. This isn't *indigenous* poverty! This isn't Appalachia. These people put in their productive years in other cities and then they crowd themselves into the most valuable real estate in the country and cry, 'We can't live here on $150 a month!' We can't refuse people the right to live here, but we can't turn this into a welfare camp."

"Quote me, quote me," shouts David Taub of South Beach, banging his fist on the table in the crowded cafeteria. "I tell you the people in the hotel industry, the banking industry, the real estate industry and the developers' industry would like nothing better than to chase all the senior citizens off the beach. They feel they're a detriment to the tourist economy."

Max Serchuk, sixty-nine-year-old president of the Dade County Council of Senior Citizens, says: "The theory up to now was that there were no poor people in Miami Beach. But we have all the makings of a senior citizens' slum. Let me show you a picture of an old man looking for food in garbage pails." He begins searching his files.

"Reports of poverty are exaggerated," the man in the city publicity bureau says. "Here's the sort of thing that happens. A reporter sees one demented old man poking into a garbage can, photographs him and writes, 'In beautiful Miami Beach people are eating out of garbage cans!' It's as if you took a city with a million people and found two with leprosy and wrote, 'Leprocy stalks the city!' Now would that be fair?"

It is a valid point; an unfortunate choice of image. Under the languorously swaying coconut palms and the technicolor sunshine of Miami Beach there are two distinct and divided communities: the elderly with restricted incomes and the promoters and beneficiaries of tourism. Antagonism is rampant between them and personal accusation of the most damaging sort can be heard in South Beach gathering places, in the offices of bankers and businessmen and at Jewish charitable and philanthropic agencies. If one speaks to enough people, each leader, regardless of his particular persuasion, becomes transformed from hero into villain.

Problems of the elderly poor are not a local peculiarity but an urgent national issue. Twenty million Americans, representing one-tenth of the population, are aged sixty-five and above. Half these older men and women have less than $75 a week to live on. One in four is impoverished, subsisting annually on less than $1,954

designated by the federal government as the poverty line. The United States Senate
has a Special Committee on Aging and last month 3,400 delegates met in Washing
ton, D.C., for the White House Conference on Aging with the overall goal of estab
lishing a national policy on aging by the federal government. The first such confer
ence, held ten years ago, pushed for Medicare.

But comparisons of Miami's South Beach with other areas of the country seem
inappropriate because, as everyone tells you, Miami Beach is "not typical." The
expedients of a tourist-based economy mesh poorly with the needs of a senior
citizen haven. Miami Beach promoters fret over the recent loss of a beauty contest
shudder at news of oil slicks off distant beaches, ponder the implications of Disne
World and spend vast municipal sums on political conventions for publicity purposes.

Yet, in this fun-filled resort city, the median age is sixty-six—up ten years since
1960, and the highest in the country. Retirees, many on extermely modest incom
arrive from every state in the Union, lured by the healthful climate and social
warmth.

Even affluent retired folk are not avid resort customers. They shun the Bunny
Club and are indifferent to the revues and big name entertainers at the posh hotel
They oppose legalized gambling which presumably would woo tourists from Puer
Rico.

The growing number of aged poor in Miami Beach voice only contempt for the
city's 'glamor" and the question of whether it waxes or wanes. They want, most
of all, low rents in an area where rapid inflation is intrinsic to the economy. It is
not surprising that the question of building a public housing project or a marina
on a two-acre bay site has become a bitter controversy.

The South Beach area is divided from the rest of the beach by Lincoln Road
and extends south to First Street. Many of its residents have no source of income
other than social security, the national average for which is $98 a month. In South
Beach, a shabby one-room efficency apartment now rents for $100-$120 a month
up 100 percent since 1965. The only low-cost housing is a tiny, fifty-unit develop
ment at the extreme southern end of the island. By contrast, the middle- and high
income dwellers living north of Lincoln Road often buy $35,000-$100,000 two-
bedroom condominiums or pay upwards of $8,000 a year for luxury apartment-
hotels.

Those members of the South Beach community who are genuinely indigent
have become so through the erosion of their purchasing power by inflation. They
are men and women who retired ten or fifteen years ago on presumably adequate
but fixed incomes whose standard of living has been destroyed by rent increases,
chronic diseases and widowhood.

There is considerable disagreement about the extent of this poverty problem.
There are many non-poor who state that this is not "real" poverty, but the self-
inflicted deprivation of proud people who want to leave their savings intact, both
as emergency fund and legacy, and who are willing to go poorly-housed and ill-

nourished to do so. On the first few days of each month, an astonishing scene
occurs outside the several savings banks of South Beach. Elderly people line up
in the sun and wait literally hours to have the interest added in their savings books.
"They don't trust the bank and keep track of the $2.12 due them," says a banker.
A leader of one of the area's twenty-eight senior citizens' groups says that, on the
contrary, "They withdraw the interest to buy food."

In Ann Wolfe's report for the American Jewish Committee she writes of the
South Beach community: "The average annual income is $2,460; thousands are
living on less than $28 a week for rent and food."

Arthur Rosichan, executive vice-president of the Greater Miami Jewish Federation, says the study is exaggerated and inaccurate. "She had no facts," he says,
and a local rabbi visiting in his office concurs. "We tried to do a population study
on the aged and they simply wouldn't answer questions about income. You just
can't prove anything, so all these suppositions mean nothing."

Other experts—among them Bernard Baron, veteran case worker and director
of social services in Miami Beach—attest to the accuracy of the figures. Leonard
Helfand, senior attorney with the federally-funded Legal Services Senior Citizens
Center, estimates that about half the population of South Beach lives near or below the poverty line.

Asked to cite a typical case, Baron outlined the financial status of a widow who
receives $83 a month from social security. The county welfare department will in-
crease her monthly income to $114, the limit allowed for welfare eligibility. Her
monthly rent may be $90. His office—the only municipal welfare office in Dade
County—might grant her an additional $15-$20 monthly subsidy.

About seven hundred people are on welfare in Miami Beach, approximately
three-quarters of them Jews. The figures are considered meaningless since the
majority of indigent residents are prevented by shame and embarrassment from
applying—the familiar "I-should-take-charity!" syndrome.

Food stamps are now dispensed in Miami Beach and when the office opened a
few months ago two thousand residents applied. It is not at all necessary that recipients be on welfare. Individuals qualify by intricate criteria of "adjusted gross
income." Another highly successful new project is the subsidized hot lunch program, served in the Ida Fischer School cafeteria for 50 cents at the unlikely, but
only-available, hour of 4 p.m. About two hundred fifty elderly poor congregate
daily for a well-balanced and well-cooked meal, and another center is scheduled
to open soon.

A group of citizens from the high-rise apartment houses call their organization
S.O.S. (Save Our Seniors) and they also donate meals. Their program delivers food
to elderly invalids and supplies meal tickets which are redeemable at a cafeteria
and kosher restaurant in South Beach.

The major Jewish agencies have not been directly involved in financial assistance to the city's elderly poor. The Jewish Federation expresses its basic concern
for the well-being of the Jewish community with large donations to Mt. Sinai Hos-

pital ($120,000 allocated this year) and the Hebrew Home for the Aged ($250,00(

"If we assumed welfare payments," says Rosichan, "we would absolve the state
of its responsibility and we'd also have to drop our aid to Israel. The State of Florida has been incredibly low on welfare payments and if we contributed they'd sim
drop their contribution accordingly. There would be no additional benefit to the
recipients. The wealthy retired Jews in the community have little community iden
tification and are not eager to contribute to the philanthropic institutions they so
willingly supported in other cities in their productive years. We feel our money is
well spent in purchasing in-patient care for patients at Mt. Sinai who don't qualify
for public welfare. We also—and by we I mean the Jewish community of Miami
Beach—pay $330 per patient in the Home for the Aged because our state refuses
to pay the total cost, although many other states do."

Leon Fisher, executive director of the Jewish Family and Children's Services,
explains that financial assistance has never been a function of his agency. "It's a
public welfare responsibility," he says. "We provide some special temporary sup-
plemental assistance, but the essential programs of the family agencies are related
to counselling. We also cut the red tape by acquainting people with such resources
as housing, legal services, medical care. We help guide people into nursing homes
and contact their out-of-state relatives if they're seriously ill."

Many South Beachers feel that the agencies are not responsive to their needs.
YMHA is condemned for having closed down its Miami Beach facility.

It is for these reasons that the frustrated elderly join lobbying groups. Those
who wish it and those who fear it believe that if the elderly poor of Miami Beach
united and voted as a bloc they could have considerable political clout in municipal elections and vote in candidates sympathetic to their plight.

In comparison with virtually any low-income neighborhood in the country,
South Beach has a most convivial atmosphere. It is perhaps for this reason that
the problems of its residents are frequently underrated. Unlike the urban ghettos,
where the elderly often live in total isolation, fearful of crime in the streets and
kept indoors by inclement weather, South Beachers enjoy a vast spectrum of social and recreational facilities and the outdoor freedom of a tropical clime. There
are free talks, concerts, travel films, dances, choral groups, instrumental ensemble:
and adult education courses. There are popular 25 cent vaudeville shows and meet
ings at night in the donated board rooms of area banks. A new community center
will open soon. The area is small and the sidewalks are crowded with strollers
headed towards the beach in swim suits, light shirts and rubber sandals.

The Beach at 10th and Ocean, which stretches for many blocks, is an afternoo*
meeting place. Its deep expanse of white sand leads to the turquoise sea. Between
the beach and the road is Lummus Park—all manicured green grass and palms and
sea grape trees. It's a scene fit for a travel poster except for the shapes in the swim
suits. Men and women arrive, starting about 1 p.m. each carrying a light-weight
aluminum chair. A group gathers on the grass under a tree for the singing. A plum
lady begins with, "I Will Take You Home Kathleen," reading the words from a
spiral notebook. The audience is attentive and appreciative.

The call goes up for some Yiddish songs and a man of perhaps seventy-five is pressed to sing. He wears his thready drip-dry sport shirt with a distinctive grace and he smiles engagingly and protests a bit: He's rather hoarse, he sang yesterday, he cannot begin to match the performance of the lovely lady who rendered "Kathleen"—and then he assents. His voice is a rich baritone with color and control which bespeak a former professional career. He raises his right arm, palm upwards, on the high notes, in a distinctive gesture of old-time vaudeville. When a tiny ancient lady makes the *faux pas* of joining in, the others shush her. An hour later he's still complying with a long list of special requests.

Another gathering place is the Governer Cafeteria at 12th and Washington. An elderly couple enters. She leans against him, supporting herself on his arm. In his other hand he carries her large white pocketbook brightly decorated with a scene which blends a palm tree, an alligator and an orange into pure Miami Beach kitsch. She is explaining an intricate family relationship. "You see, part of the family is out of Brooklyn and part of the family is out of the Bronx and what happened, a Goldberg married a Hertzmark. . . ."

The cafeteria is jammed. The aromas are comforting and seductive. A sandwich man slices to order from a peerless succulent corned beef as his customers harass him. "Cut from the lean side, the lean side," a woman says irritably. Another eyes her impeccably trimmed sandwich and announces to the general public, "Pheh. Stringy. The meat is stringy." The sandwich man conveys aloof contempt with his eyebrows and then drops the hauteur and says, "So, don't take it. Go get something else, you think it's string. Eat blintzes, you're worried the meat is stringy."

In front of the cafeteria is a large new ambulance. On both sides it says in red paint: "Presented to the people of Israel by the American Federation of Senior Citizens. Miami Beach, Florida. U.S.A." Everyone who leaves the cafeteria pauses to admire it, peek in the windows, exclaim. One man leads another who is blind. He places the blind man's hand against the silken white enamel paint. "It's the ambulance. THE AMBULANCE," he shouts. The blind man runs his hand over the surface and nods. "Vunderful," he says. "Vunderful."

The owner of the cafeteria and president of the five-hundred member American Federation of Senior Citizens is short, intense, middle-aged David Taub. Taub arrived in Miami Beach in the late 1940s from Germany. On his muscular forearm a tattoo says A 18556. He talks about the ambulance, which will be shipped to Israel soon. "The money came entirely from social security South Beach people, one-two-dollar donations. We still owe $4,000 and they won't give us a license to solicit in the street. The ACLU has taken the case to federal court. The 'haves' (he points northward) contribute nothing unless they have their names attached and get credit. We sent them letters to help with the ambulance but got no response."

Taub is a very angry man. So is Max Serchuk of the Dade County Council of Senior Citizens. They criticize Jewish philanthropic organizations for forgetting their brothers on South Beach. They feel that the rabbis should have protested the suit brought against a public housing project which is now in limbo. Says Serchuk, public housing is "not the picture they (pointing northerly) want to convey to the public about Miami Beach."

The suit opposed a two-hundred unit low-cost housing development planned for two acres on South Beach bay front. Since, under the terms of the federal grant for this housing, the project could not be constructed on land on which buildings would have to be razed, the city allocated the only vacant lot on the beach—the waterfront side which had been used as a parking lot for garbage trucl

Although Miami Beach citizens did not oppose public housing, and a referendu approved the project, others in the community desiring to redevelop the South Beach area wanted to use the bayfront parking lot for a marina.

Soon after the referendum, the home owners' association of wealthy Palm Island filed a suit stating that the city had no right to sell recreational land at one-quarter its value. The suit was carried up through the judicial system and dismisse at all levels as senior citizens circled Palm Island with protest signs and chants. During the long delay, a freeze was placed on funds for the public housing at the Department of Housing and Urban Development's regional headquarters in Atlan Georgia.

"I was not in agreement with the suit, although I live on Palm Island," says Jack Gordon, president of Washington Federal Savings and Loan and publisher o the *Miami Beach Sun*. "We spoke out against it editorially in the paper," he note

The *Sun*'s allegations of racism—that some interests feared public housing wou attract blacks from Miami—were denied. But more likely causes for the suit were the ever-present desire of developers to promote tourism by construction of the marina and the feeling that public housing a few miles down the road from the expensive hotels is unesthetic. A promoter summed it up as "simply a bureaucra snafu."

It is difficult in Miami Beach to name the heroes and to pinpoint the villains. It is infinitely easier to recognize the victims.

LEFT BEHIND, LEFT ALONE

MARK EFFRON

A doorbell is rung. There is no answer. Repeated knocks echo through a hall-way littered with candy wrappers, beer cans and junk mail. The place smells of urine. Finally, a thin female voice can be heard from within. "What do you want? Go away!"There is fear in the voice, not anger. The once carnival red paint on the door is now chipped; the plaster around the frame is cracked. Sometimes the door is opened a few inches, the upper chain still secure. Other times, the door stays locked, and the sound of retreating footsteps can be discerned.

Close to 300,000 poor Jews live in New York City alone. Almost two-thirds of them are over 60. Many live behind locked doors that are easily penetrable—alone, without proper food or medicine. Some have caring relatives. Others have only four walls.

The Lower East Side is home for up to 20,000 Jewish poor, most of whom settled in the area in the first years of the twentieth century. Then, New York symbolized the American Dream. Now, for many, the city is the American Urban Nightmare.

HOME AND FRIENDS

Three women, all in their 70s, sit around a long table in a classroom at the Educational Alliance on East Broadway, a community center which specializes in helping immigrants. The three women have been in America for more than fifty years, but they keep coming to the Alliance, as do blacks, Chinese and Puerto Ricans. The women arrived early for a meeting of the Hospital Service Club. One of them, whom we shall call Mrs. Green—large-bellied, with skinny legs—cannot and does not try to conceal her rage.

"I was robbed in the toilet of my rent money and Medicaid card," she says. "I applied for a new card nine weeks ago. I'm still waiting. I was in the hospital and I have to see a doctor. But I can't. I keep signing my name over and over again. We senior citizens are treated like little children. . . . We can't talk correctly. . . . We need help."

She pounds the table as she speaks, as if the table is the bureaucracy which is withholding her all-important card. The woman finishes and sits upright, relieved that she's told her story. Her friend Mrs. Wolf is blind. Yet she looks straight at the person she is speaking with. Her face reacts to what others are saying. She is afraid of walking at night; even during the day, she is "thankful to God" that nobody has hit her.

For Mrs. Wolf, the club at the Alliance is home and friends: "When somebody is sick or in the hospital, I go to the hospital, but I can't see that person so I cry. Here, we care for each other. We have many clubs, and we hear beautiful stories and sing songs and hear lectures. We even put on shows." At this point Mrs. Wolf is interrupted by a plump friend who is sitting across the table. She says: "I was a chorus girl in our production of *East Side Story*."

It's eleven o'clock in the morning on Essex Street, near Delancey. On the streets the people talk and buy and kibbitz. Except, the people are no longer all Jewish. Chinese, Italians, Puerto Ricans and blacks now brush shoulders with the Jews. One sign is in Chinese, the next is in Hebrew.

Buildings that were dilapidated forty years ago stand next to *shuls* that are no more—windows are shattered, doors are boarded with random widths of warped wood, Hebrew letters are covered by Puerto Rican posters and announcements of wrestling matches. Garbage and glass lie in the streets, on the steps, in the narrow alleys that separate buildings.

Bernstein's Chinese Kosher Restaurant emits a strange aroma as the door is opened—part corned beef, part egg roll. Shops selling Jewish religious articles stand next to pickle stands and dairy restaurants. Hardware stores with Jewish names sell appliances to Chinese people who don't speak English.

In Seward Park, across the street from the Educational Alliance, old Jewish men and women sit, some with shopping bags at their sides. Four men play cards at a makeshift table. An old woman shivers from the cold.

Inside the Alliance, the guard at the reception desk directs people: black children to a kindergarten class, old Jewish people to a lecture.

Sonya Goldberg, a social worker, is a short woman in her late 50s. She is always on the move. It is around her that old and poor Jews congregate. She is a source of strength, a knowledgeable daughter. She has been at the Alliance for nineteen years. Her cramped office is filled with stacked flyers and decorated with a Jewish calendar and pictures of Sholom Aleichem and Martin Luther King.

"Many of these people are forgotten," she says while checking a date in a calender, writing down a number and looking for something else. "The children moved to the suburbs and made good. The parents stayed behind. We took a vote at one of our meetings. It was whether a parent should live with his or her children. Out of thirty people, only two thought they should live with their children. The rest wanted their independence."

Some of the senior citizens, most of whom live only on Social Security and occasional checks from relatives, see their children and grandchildren; others don't. One Alliance member sees her son only at the cemetery around Rosh Hashanah. Another woman was able to go to the upstate camp run by the Alliance because her niece paid.

During one of the programs at the upstate camp, a woman became very sick. Mrs. Goldberg telephoned the woman's daughter. "What do you mean, she's sick?" asked the daughter. "*You* are taking care of her. She's your responsibility. I can't be bothered."

The phone rings. A woman is inquiring about the Hanukkah party. She wants to know if she can get her money back in case she doesn't attend. "I can't promise anything," Mrs. Goldberg replies kindly. "We're having *challah*, potatoes, cole slaw." As she hangs up, another woman enters the office. (The door is always open.) She wears a grey coat and black open-toed shoes with thick heels. Her white hair is up in a bun. She has come in from Brooklyn for a meeting which was held last week.

"Why didn't you send me a card?" Her face creases and one hand grabs the other. "You let me know *now!* I shlepped so far and I'm not feeling well. . . ." Mrs. Goldberg calms her down by putting her hand on the woman's shoulder. "Lena, I'm sorry. We'll send you a card for the next meeting. Take care and we'll see you next time."

Sonya Goldberg feels that affluence has broken up families. The rich daughter or son can't be bothered with the poor parent.

"The older people are separated from their children both physically and financially. And when they do live with their children, the results can be devastating."

She cites the example of one woman who lived with her schoolteacher daughter. The mother stayed home and cooked and cleaned. But when the daughter had company, she would get rid of her mother by sending her to the movies. Mrs. Goldberg advised the woman that it would be better for her if she went on welfare.

Two classrooms down from Mrs. Goldberg's office, a group of elderly people sit around a table. Mr. Rabinowitz is translating into Yiddish the Hebrew poems of Chaim Bialik. His audience is quiet, reflective. Some rivet their eyes on Mr. Rabinowitz; others gaze out windows at a world filled with devastation. The poet's words, written after the Kishinev pogrom, echo in the large classroom: *walls with gaping holes . . . doors wrenched off their hinges . . . singed beams laid bare.*

As Mr. Rabinowitz reads, one woman reflects on her life: "It's changed from a lot of friendly people who cared for each other. Now, we're all strangers from

each other. We're no longer friends. Now it's big buildings everywhere. I guess the
buildings had something to do with it."

An old man who has overheard our conversation looks at us for a while and
then decides to come over. "We used to sleep in the park," he says with his heavy
Yiddish accent, "even in the nighttime. It was safe then. Now they rob you even
in the park. They wait for you. I saw, the other day, they robbed a lady who came
out of the supermarket and they even took the bag with the groceries."

Another man joins us. He says he is "past 75," but he looks younger. Some of
his hair is still brown. He disregards the realities of being old and weak on the
Lower East Side: "We don't take it any more! The Jews are fighting back. At one
time, they told you to turn the other cheek. Now it's an eye for an eye. They don't
take it any more! And that may save the Jewish race!"

And the words of Bialik filter through: *Whole lives of men . . . like broken
potsherds . . . past all mending.*

DOORBELLS, DOORBELLS

The apartment is small, neat. In the main room there is a bed covered by a
flowered spread—violets on bright yellow. Pictures of grandchildren rest on the
one table. The focal point of the room is the television. It can be viewed from all
parts of the room: the bed, the sofa, the chair.

The woman we shall call Mrs. Dubrow has white hair pulled straight back in a
bun. She wears a simple shift over her thin body. Her mouth twitches even when
she is silent, which is often. Her daughter, who lives in Queens, does most of the
talking.

"TV is my mother's only communication," she says. "She has no friends. If
you have friends, even if they say the same things over and over, it's better than
nothing. But here—in this building—they're all for themselves."

The mother nods. "When I got out of the hospital, nobody asked me if I needed
a container of milk."

The daughter interrupts. She is in her early 50s. Her brown hair is just beginning
to turn grey. She wears a chocolate brown pants suit. She says that the trip from
Queens Village took about an hour.

The daughter grew up on the Lower East Side. She recalls: "We were like gypsies,
we moved around so much. They'd tear down the building, or my grandmother
moved in and we'd have to move closer to a *shul*. Then we moved to Pitt Street.
There we stayed twenty-five years."

The mother is alone most of the week. She rarely goes out. When she does, it
is to buy some food or visit the same *shul* on Stanton Street that she has been going to for over forty years. She says she is diabetic so she doesn't participate in
senior citizen luncheons sponsored by different groups.

She watches television and thinks of all the things that have changed.

Apartment doors used to stay open all the time. Heavy and pungent aromas would escape from the open doors and mingle in the hallway. Neighbors would drift in for a glass of tea or a piece of cake.

Mrs. Dubrow remembers the feelings people once had for each other. There was little money, but there was that feeling! Neighbors would take care of their sick. On sunny days, the park would be filled with gossiping adults and noisy children.

Now the children are grown up and live in the suburbs—like her daughter. Mrs. Dubrow pushes back her white hair. Her daughter fidgets in the chair, checking her watch.

The daughter speaks again: "These days people feel they don't need each other. That makes me feel sad. In my childhood, we made do with what we had. Today, everything comes so easy. Sometimes I feel like I want to help the other old people in the building. But why should I take on *their* problems? Why should I accept their burdens? Nobody rings the doorbell to see how *my* mother is. Too bad. . . ."

Mrs. Dubrow says the older people in the building envy the fact that she has a daughter. During the spring, when the parks are filled, people come over, attaching themselves to the daughter, claiming a little of her.

Are these trips to the Lower East Side a drudge for the daughter? "There's no one else to take care of her but me," the daughter says. "She's lost in Queens and won't live there, so I make the trip."

One woman upstairs didn't have a daughter, Mrs. Dubrow says. "Nobody rang her bell. So, she jumped out of the window and killed herself. After it was all over, one woman said, '*I* rang her bell.' "

Mother and daughter look at each other. The daughter has a shopping bag full of her mother's dirty laundry to be cleaned in Queens. The mother eats food bought by her daughter in new supermarkets in the suburbs.

"The area didn't change," the mother says. "It's the people."

ORAL HISTORIAN

The *Forward* (or *Forverts*) building on East Broadway was once visible for miles in all directions. Now, it is dwarfed by blocks of highrises. But the newspaper is still a beacon to the tens of thousands of Yiddish-speaking residents of the area. (It can also be bought in Paris, London or Buenos Aires.) *The Jewish Daily Forward*'s city room is like that of any newspaper. Except everybody is Jewish and the typewriters have Hebrew characters.

Dr. Samuel Silverberg is frail, erudite, touching 80. He has lived in the area, on and off, for over fifty years. He is a retired physician who now helps out at the newspaper.

He is comfortable—not at all poor. But he started out poor and he is one of the many oral historians of the Lower East Side.

"The Lower East Side was once mostly Jewish," Dr. Silverberg says. "Maybe we weren't affluent, but we kept the area cleaner that the blacks and Puerto Ricans today. Sure, there were racial tensions. Then, the Irish were always drinking. But when they killed, they killed each other!"

He says a lot of older Jews who moved to the Bronx and Brooklyn are moving back into new co-ops in the area. He attributes this to the deterioration of neighbor hoods and housing conditions in the Bronx and Brooklyn. Also, emotional ties to the Lower East Side bring people back.

When asked about racial tension he says that "we don't mix much, and we get along, not overwhelmingly. If I get close to a colored or Puerto Rican, I feel the animosity. But they also feel our animosity. Decent people try to hide it, but we are born with it. I remember in Russia, during a Gentile funeral, my friends and I laughed and made fun. We felt a Gentile could die as long as a Jew lived. It was wrong. A liberal tries to suppress these things."

His soft hands move slowly and gracefully. He is warming to his subject now, and as the typewriters clack in the background, he speaks of old people and fear; how it affects meetings and synagogue worship.

"People are living in fear everywhere in the country," Dr. Silverberg says. "Colored people themselves live in fear. Jews go to *shul* in groups. They are afraid to go to meetings at night. Things start earlier so people can get home before they find themselves solitary passengers on empty streets."

Jewish poverty today confounds him—as does the despair that goes with it. He remembers the unbridled optimism fifty years ago. That's over now, he says.

As long as the family stayed together, there was no despair, he explains. "But the children left home and the parents stayed. The children don't visit the parents often enough. There's not the closeness of the olden days. The condition of life in America loosened the family. And, the Jewish establishment doesn't do enough for the poor."

As Mrs. Green put it, senior citizens are treated like children. But they are children in a family where there is little love and less respect—not enough for protection against the chill of constant fear and poverty.

It wasn't supposed to happen this way.

WHAT'S BEING DONE TO HELP

Project Ezra is a volunteer organization that aids the elderly on the Lower East Side. It evolved out of a 1971 attempt by twenty young Jews to move to the Lower East Side and become part of the Jewish community. The plan fell through, but three of the participants formed the nucleus for Project Ezra. There are now six full-time workers and sixty volunteers—mostly college students—each of whom spends at least one day a week visiting an old person.

One Ezra volunteer who visits a woman on East 6th Street said after her second visit: "Miss W. was glad to see me, happy that I kept my promise to return. She was still undressed, so I went out and did some grocery shopping for her. When I returned, I tried to give her the $4.00 in change. She refused. She pushed $3.00

back at me and told me to buy myself a blouse. We sat down and she served oranges and honey cake. We spoke about the weather, TV, the price of bread. She asked me to write her when I would come again. She walked downstairs with me, wrapped my scarf around my neck, took my hand and said goodbye." Case Supervisor Allen Gottlieb says that the volunteer was told to accept the money. Miss W. may have little to give away, but until the volunteer came, she had no one to give anything to. According to Gottlieb the program makes the elderly feel less alone, and the volunteers learn about a world they have only heard about. He tells of an old woman: "She was so shy at first. She hardly said anything. Soon, she started to smile, and before I knew it, she was rummaging through suitcases, eager to show me pictures of herself as an actress on the Yiddish stage 45 years ago."

Volunteer recruiter Pearl Beck went into a housing project in Chinatown. Practically each Jew told her the same thing: "There are no other Jews in this project. I'm the only one. I've been living here over twenty years. How can there be a social group if I'm the only Jew?" Beck discovered 150 Jews. "We start with a group of people messed up," Beck says. "Some have mental problems, others are widows and widowers, or never married. All are alone. Slowly, they meet and discover things to do, to talk about. After twenty years, they find people like themselves living right on the same floor."

Project Ezra operates on a budget of $35,000. About a third comes from the Jewish Association for College Youth; the rest from individuals and small groups. "We're not saving people," says Pearl Beck. "We're trying to change the quality of their existence."

B'nai B'rith has seventeen professional and industrial lodges in New York to collect and distribute clothing to elderly Jews.

A woman came to a lodge: Her husband just died, her son was getting *bar mitzva*, and she had no money to buy him a suit. She was considering canceling the ceremony. In time for the *bar mitzva*, both she and the child had new clothing.

Mort Greene, Director of Field Services for District One, is overall coordinator for B'nai B'rith poverty programs. "In New York, Passover food is desperately expensive," Greene says. "We have elderly Jews in the Coney Island section who have ninety cents a day to spend on food. We solicit food through our Teamsters and Harvest lodges. Last year, we went to manufacturers, distributors and jobbers, and we received over $2,000 worth of food. We gave Passover food to 255 people. This year, we're sending packages right to their apartments."

B'nai B'rith's Telephone Reassurance Program is run by 200 women volunteers. Once a week, they call shut-ins to find out about problems, to talk. An information Referral Service on Coney Island, staffed by members of Municipal and Welfare lodges, follows through on serious problems reported.

The East Side Council is one of seven community councils funded by the Metropolitan New York Coordinating Council on Jewish Poverty. The East Side Council has lawyers involved in housing litigation. They recently fought a court order restraining Jewish tenants from moving into a new housing development. The order awarded the apartments to a Puerto Rican group which claimed that since they were dispossessed by the construction, they had first rights. The Jews claimed that they lived in the old apartments before the Puerto Ricans, and only moved out when they heard that the buildings were to be condemned. In an out-of-court settlement, Jews, Puerto Ricans and other groups will move in. It is a victory for the East Side Council and the Jewish poor.

Rabbi Joseph Langer runs the East Side Council. A recent achievement: The federal government will subsidize a food stamp and Social Security officer for their East Broadway office. Rabbi Langer explains: "The elderly Jews feel stigmatized by the city welfare offices. There are the lines, the red tape, the humiliation. Many of these people don't speak much English. This way, they can come here, it's informal, they can speak Yiddish, get their food stamps, sign up for the newly legislated Supplementary Security Income and go home without feeling like they are accepting charity.

A week before Passover, Rabbi Langer has arranged for a group of 200 synagogue youth to come into the neighborhood and help the people prepare for a kosher Passover. A free communal *Seder* is scheduled at a *shul* on Delancey Street.

4

HASIDIC JEWS

Despite their recent arrival in the United States, Hasidic Jews are a segment of the American Jewish community that has not been neglected by students of the American Jewish community. Most of the attention has been given to the Satmars, however, and only a few articles have been empirically based sociological studies. Kranzler's *Williamsburg: A Jewish Community in Transition* was published in 1961.[1] Although not oriented specifically to the study of Hasidic Jews, it provided much data on the Hasidic Jews and their interaction with the larger community. Poll's *The Hasidic Community of Williamsburg*, a specific study of the Hasidic community, was published in 1962.[2] In this same period, two published articles that provided scholarly analyses of Hasidic communities were "The Modern Shtetl: A Study of Cultural Persistence" in 1962 by Freilich[3] and "Chassidic Community Behavior" in 1964 by Rubin.[4] (In 1972, Rubin published his *Satmar: An Island In the City.*)[5]

Hasidism has received much popular attention because of the neo-Hasidism of

Martin Buber[6] and because of the neo-Hasidism of a leading American rabbi, Abraham Joshua Heschel.[7] The best-selling novels of Chaim Potok have dealt both favorably and unfavorably with the Hasidic community.[8] Elie Wiesel, another best-selling author, also has dealt with Hasidic Jews in some of his books—particularly *Souls on Fire*—and suggests that the "preconditions are ripe for the revival of Hasidism."[9]

Hasidism has also received attention from academic and religious journals, in addition to the two specific studies mentioned earlier. *Judaism* devoted an entire issue to Hasidism in 1960, primarily covering philosophical and religious aspects. As Herman Leder, for example, noted, there were many articles about Hadisism in 1960 "on the occasion of the 200th anniversary of the death of . . . the founder of the Chassidic movement."[10] A 1969 article by Jacobs reviews some of the other books and articles on Hasidism, also primarily on philosophical or religious aspects.[11] Shmueli's 1969 article "The Appeal of Hasidism for American Jewry Today" is probably the best statement of "the astonishing acceptance of some Hasidic ideas, if not practices, by American (particularly Jewish) intellectuals today, and even by the wider public."[12]

A section on Hasidism was included in Kertzer's 1967 *Today's American Jew*[13] and several articles describing the life-style of different Hasidic communities have appeared in the last few years. For example, "In Williamsburg the Lines Are Drawn" and "New Square" appeared in 1974, both by Steinberg. Also in 1974 was "Hasid of Brooklyn" by Issacs and "The Call of the Ghetto" by Schultz; in 1975 "The Pious Ones" appeared; in 1977 "Brooklyn's Hasidim" appeared.[14]

A number of articles on the Hasidic community's functions, conflicts with the larger society, and outreach efforts have also appeared. A gathering of thousands of Hasidic Jews from all over the world who had come to receive new guidance from their spiritual leader and to observe Simhat Torah is described in a *New York Times* article and illustrates the influence of the rebbe (Hasidic rabbi) to Hasidic Jews.[15] "A 'Happening' in Williamsburg" describes a mobile job recruitment unit that recruited poverty-stricken Hasidic Jews as "tellers, clerical workers, key-punch operators, data processors and other positions that suit their training or for which they can be trained in an ongoing bank program."[16]

Problems resulting from a traditional religious outlook and life-style are also illustrated by an article in the *New York Times* that noted that Hasidic rabbis were advising Hasidic Jews not to use subways during rush hours because "the attire of many women in subways is unseemly and . . . the crush of men against women is often improper."[17] Other articles provide much additional information on areas of conflict. An example of an overt conflict with the customs of the larger society occurred in June 1973 over the attempt by Lubavitcher Hasidic Jews to close a service road outside their synagogue for sabbath gatherings. Three Hasidic Jews were arrested and eight policemen were injured when a physician trying to escort a patient through a gathering "was set upon in his car."[18] (A 1974 article distributed to policemen in Hasidic areas described some Hasidic customs in order to help police respond more sensitively to problems in Hasidic areas.)[19] In September 1975, a

Lubavitcher Hasid who had survived Auschwitz was killed in front of his apartment house in an attempted robbery even though he was carrying no funds because it was the Jewish sabbath. At his funeral procession, mourners were taunted with Hitlerite calls, and members of the funeral procession attacked the taunters.[20] In November 1975 Hasidic homes and religious schools were firebombed in the Satmar area of Boro Park.[21] Not all the conflicts have resulted in violence or in displays of anti-Semitism, however. In 1974, for example, the New York legislature proposed a reapportionment plan that would have greatly reduced the Hasidic community's voting power. The Hasidim, opposed by Jewish organizations as well as by the black and Puerto Rican communities, won a court review of the plans.[22]

A program of Hadar Hatorah, "one of a network of religiously oriented institutions maintained in this country and the world over by the Lubavitch Movement," is described by Spiegel,[23] as is a program whereby Jewish youth live a brief time with Lubavitcher Hasids in Crown Heights.[24] Spiegel also describes the network of Lubavitcher Chabad Houses maintained near college campuses for purposes of reaching "wayward and untutored" Jewish youth, and the policy of setting up sidewalk "synagogues on wheels" to reach less traditional Jews.[25] The Lubavitcher movement is also engaged in other activities such as welcoming Soviet Jewish immigrants to the United States and helping Israeli front-line soldiers to celebrate Jewish holidays.[26]

The selections in this section describe Hasidic Jews. First is the article by Rubin,[27] which gives a general and scholarly description of the Hasidic origin and life-style. The general characteristics of two Hasidic communities and the problems they face are then presented. Isaacs' article primarily discusses the Satmar Hasidic community in Brooklyn,[28] and Steinberg's article discusses the "Squarer" Hasidic community (one of the small movements) in Rockland County, New York.[29] The final selection by Spiegel—who has extensively covered Hasidic activities—describes some of the activities of the Lubavitcher movement and gives some idea of the future.[30]

NOTES

1. George Kranzler, *Williamsburg: A Jewish Community in Transition* (New York: Feldheim, 1961). Also see his *The Face of Faith: An American Hasidic Community*, with photographs by Irving I. Herzberg (Baltimore: Baltimore Hebrew College, 1972).

2. Solomon Poll, *The Hasidic Community of Williamsburg* (New York: Schocken Books, 1962).

3. Morris Freilich, "The Modern Shtetl: A Study of Cultural Persistence," *Anthropos* 57 (1962): 45-54.

4. Israel Rubin, "Chassidic Community Behavior," *Anthropological Quarterly* 37 (July 1964): 138-148.

5. Israel Rubin, *Satmar: An Island in the City* (Chicago: Quadrangle, 1972).

6. See, for example, Martin Buber, "Interpreting Hasidism," *Commentary* 36 (September 1963): 218-225. Buber has written a number of books that interpret Hasidism. The major one responsible for his association with Hasidism is *The Way of Man According to the Teaching of Hasidism* (London: Vincent Stuart, 1963). Others include *Tales of the Hasidism* (1947); *Hasidism and Modern Man* (1958); *The Tales of Rabbi Nachman* (1962); *Legend of the Baal-Shem* (1969); *I and Thou* (1970); and *The Origin and Meaning of Hasidism* (1972).

7. Gilbert S. Rosenthal, *Four Paths to One God* (New York: Bloch Publishing Company, 1973), p. 18. See Heschel's *A Passion for Truth* (New York: Farrar, Straus & Giroux, 1973).

8. See *The Chosen* (New York: Simon & Schuster, 1967); *The Promise* (New York: Alfred A. Knopf, 1969), *My Name Is Asher Lev* (New York: Alfred A. Knopf, 1972), and *In the Beginning* (New York: Alfred A. Knopf, 1975). Both Potok and Buber have been criticized by Hasidic Jews for some of their writings.

9. Elie Wiesel, *Souls on Fire: Portraits and Legends of Hasidic Masters* (New York: Random House, 1972). Some other books by Wiesel that reflect his philosophy are: *Night, Dawn, Legends of Our Time, The Oath, One Generation After, Gates of the Forest, Beggar in Jerusalem, The Accident, Zalmen or the Madness of God, Messengers of God,* and *Ani Maamin.* The specific quote regarding Wiesel's view on the future of Hasidism is from Alan L Berger, "The Sources of Hasidic Experience," a review of *Souls on Fire, Midstream* 19 (February 1973): 78.

10. *Judaism* 9 (Summer 1960). See Herman Leder, "The Story of Chassidism," *Jewish Voice Pictorial,* 1960, pp. 14-15, 30-32.

11. Louis Jacobs, "Hasidism," *Judaism* 18 (Summer 1969): 337-342.

12. Efraim Shmueli, "The Appeal of Hasidism for American Jewry Today," *Jewish Journ of Sociology* 11 (June 1969): 5-30.

13. Morris N. Kertzer, "The Hasidim," in *Today's American Jew* (New York: McGraw-Hi Book Company, 1967), pp. 158-172.

14. Harry Steinberg, "In Williamsburg the Lines Are Drawn," *The Times of Israel* 1 (Apri 1974): 48-52; Harry Steinberg, "New Square," *The Times of Israel* 1 (March 1974): 31-36; Stephen Isaacs, "Hasidim of Brooklyn," *Washington Post*, February 17, 1974; Ray Schultz, "The Call of the Ghetto," *New York Times*, November 10, 1974, sec. 6, p. 34; and Harvey Arden, "The Pious Ones," *The National Geographic* 148 (August 1975): 276-298 (with phot graphs by Nathan Benn); and Jerome R. Mintz, "Brooklyn's Hasidim," *Natural History* 86 (January 1977): 46-59.

15. Irving Spiegel, "Hasidim from Abroad Gather Here," *New York Times*, October 2, 1972, p. 41.

16. ADL Bulletin, "A 'Happening' in Williamsburg," *ADL Bulletin* 26 (November 1969):

17. Murray Schumach, "Lindsay Approaches Point of No Return with No Indication of a Change of Course or Mind," *New York Times*, August 13, 1973, p. 30.

18. Wolfgang Saxon, "Jews and Police Clash in Brooklyn," *New York Times*, June 3, 197 p. 21. Also see follow-up articles on June 4, 5, and 12.

19. "Police Studying Jewish Customs," *New York Times*, October 20, 1974, p. 47.

20. "Jew Carrying No Funds on Sabbath Slain in Holdup," *New York Times*, September 28, 1975, p. 43; Robert McG. Thomas, " 'Heil Hitler' Disrupts Rites for Jew Slain in Holdup *New York Times*, September 30, 1975, p. 41; Leslie Mattland, "A Guarded Racial Peace Follows Brooklyn Killing," *New York Times*, October 2, 1975, p. 43.

21. Alfonso A. Narvaez, "2 Synagogues and Homes Fire-Bombed in Boro Park," *New York Times*, November 12, 1975, p. 47.

22. "Hasidim in Williamsburg Gain High Court Review of Vote Suit," *New York Times*, November 12, 1975, p. 47; Gerald F. Lieberman, "Top Court Ruling Pleases Hasidim," *New York Times,* November 23, 1975, p. 111. The U.S. Supreme Court later ruled against the Hasidim. One should also note that there are internal conflicts among Hasidic sects—particularly due to the Satmars' opposition to Israel (see Isaac's article) and the Lubavitchers' positive involvement in Israel. (See, for example, note 26, below.)

23. Irving Spiegel, "Emphasis on Jewish Heritage Permeates Life of Youths at Speical School," *New York Times*, July 29, 1973, p. 54.

24. Irving Spiegel, "Program Brings Jewish Students to Visit Hasidim," *New York Times,* January 2, 1973, p. 16.

25. See the following articles, all by Irving Spiegel in the *New York Times*: "Where Women Go to Find Judaism—And Themselves," April 17, 1974, p. 48; "Collegians Aided by Hasidic Rabbis," August 10, 1974, p. 30; "Jewish Homes Aid Aimless Youths," August 24, 1975; and " 'Synagogues on Wheels' Explain Orthodox Rites," June 23, 1974.

26. Irving Spiegel, "Arriving Soviet Jews Celebrate Purim," *New York Times*, February 24, 1975, p. 12; Irving Spiegel, "With Book and Bottle, Hasidic Jews Mark Purim on Israel's Front," *New York Times*, February 27, 1975, p. 1.

27. Rubin, "Chasidic Community Behavior."

28. Isaacs, "Hasidim of Brooklyn."

29. Steinberg, "New Square."

30. Irving Spiegel, "The Rebbe: In His Torah There Is Room for All Jews," *National Jewish Monthly* 90 (March 1976): 11, 12, 14, 16, 17.

CHASSIDIC COMMUNITY BEHAVIOR

ISRAEL RUBIN

Chassidism, the pietist movement that originated among the 18th century East European Jews, has in recent years attracted interest in some intellectual circles—largely as a result of Martin Buber's writings—but has at the same time received little systematic attention from social scientists. What seems most intriguing about Chassidism is the fact that although it began as a revitalization movement, it has remained viable long after it had accomplished its task. Further, it has spread to environmental settings that lacked the conditions which favored its original inception. In fact, even today several dynamic Chassidic communities continue an apparently thriving existence in New York City, in Israel, and in several Latin American and West European cities.[2]

The present analysis is based on a field study of the contemporary Satmarer Chassidim of Brooklyn, New York, as well as historical research. After summarizing the circumstances that gave rise to Chassidism, we shall attempt to isolate two behavior clusters that seem to have characterized practically all Chassidic communities of the last two centuries, though with minor variations in actual form and relative emphasis. These behavior patterns, which became crystallized during what we may call—following Wallace (1956) and Weber (1946: 262-4, 297)—the routinization stage of the movement, shall then be viewed as the clue to the understanding of the lasting viability, as well as the wide appeal of the Chassidic culture.

BACKGROUND AND ORIGIN[3]

The Chassidic movement originated in an atmosphere of extreme stress. In the 17th century, the Jews of Poland and Ukraine underwent a series of disastrous ex-

periences that destroyed their centuries-old prosperous existence. In 1648-49, the
rebelling Cossacks who overran the greater part of Southern and Central Poland,
exterminated practically all the Jews who did not manage to flee. Soon thereafter,
a crisis of a different nature followed. Shabtai Tzvee, a Turkish Jew, proclaimed
himself as the Messiah, long awaited by Jews to usher in the ultimate era of bliss-
ful redemption that the Prophets foretold. He soon attracted a sizable following
throughout the Mediterranean basin. From there the movement spread to Poland
where many of the survivors of the Cossack onslaught clung in their misery to the
hope of the approaching redemption. The movement suddenly collapsed, and the
remnants of the once flourishing Polish-Ukrainian Jewry were left with nothing
but despair. Organized community life, the educational system, economic foundations, political security—all lay in shambles. Existence had to begin anew. However, the suddenness with which the onslaught came, the lack of mental preparation for the disaster, plus the dramatic rapidity with which the Shabtai Tzvee movement collapsed, seemingly combined to inhibit the disorganized survivors from
making a fresh start.

One of the inevitable outcomes of the prolonged period of disorganization was
wide-spread ignorance. The seemingly demoralizing effect of the situation is understandable if we consider that not long before that, Poland was the most prominent
center of Jewish scholarship, and that it was probably against the memories of the
glorious past that the Jews of the period of decline viewed their dismal present.

It was in this climate of despair, which lasted for several generations, that Chassidism made its appearance in the first half of the 18th century. The father of the
movement was Reb Yisroel, commonly known as the *Baal Shem Tov*, or in short:
the *Basht*, the Man with a Good Name.[4] His teachings were simple and encouraging.
At the foundation of the Chassidic ideology was the principle that in man's quest
for proximity to God, sincerity is a greater asset than scholarship. The latter is only
of secondary importance, especially when not accompanied by sincere inner piety.
Conversely, sincerity without scholarship may lead to the attainment of the highest
level of righteousness.

Furthermore, the way to attain this sincere desire to reach God is through joy,
not of a vulgar nature, but the kind which approaches holy ecstasy, a state in which
one rejoices in the privilege of serving the Lord. The following maxim, attributed
to the Basht, summarizes this basic idea of Chassidism: "There is no *mitzvoh* (religious command) to be joyous. Yet joy leads to more good than the execution of
any mitzvoh does. Nor is sadness mentioned anywhere as a sin. Being sad, however,
leads to more evil than the worst of sins."

These were ideas that the downhearted East European Jew eagerly embraced.
He no longer needed to feel inferior on account of his ignorance. All he had to do
was to search within himself for the dormant divine spark which every Jewish soul
is supposed to contain, rekindle it, and he might reach the same spiritual heights
as the scholar, if not even higher ones. Moreover, not only does it become unnecessary to brood over the present state of affairs, but to be optimistic and hopeful is

in itself a virtue, while sadness must be avoided.[5] It amounted to a legacy for beginning the process of rebuilding in a hopeful mood, regardless of the sad reality. It is then no wonder that in a relatively short time Chassidism became the dominant ideology among the Jews in Ukraine as well as Southern and Central Poland —the regions most affected by the Cossack uprising. It is equally understandable that the opponents of the movement, the so-called *misnagdim*, had their center in the North, especially Lithuania, where life was but little affected by the above-mentioned events, and where the new teachings were conceived as a threat to the Jewish value of learning.

After the death of the Baal Shem Tov (1760), his disciple Reb Dov Behr took over the leadership of the movement, and for the duration of his life he remained the recognized leader of all Chassidim. Already during his lifetime, however, some other disciples of the Basht, who accepted Reb Dov Behr's leadership merely on a *primus inter pares* basis, opened new Chassidic centers of their own. But the pattern of dispersion and decentralization fully unfolded after Reb Dov Behr's death (1773). As no central authority emerged, the local centers which now mushroomed throughout Eastern Europe, became fully independent.

This brings us to our main theme which focuses on Chassidism's continued vitality in its post-pioneer decentralized stage, its lasting popularity in Eastern Europe after the return there of a relatively normal state of affairs, as well as its expansion to such outlying regions as Hungary where no major crisis preceded its intrusion.

ROUTINIZED CHASSIDIC COMMUNITY BEHAVIOR

As a basis for isolating the essential elements of the Chassidic culture, we shall take the simple empirical fact that Chassidim have in all these two centuries been a clearly distinguished and distinguishable category, *i.e.*, there has never been any appreciable doubt in the mind of either Chossid or non-Chossid as to who does or does not belong in this category. We may then ask: on what grounds has the differentiation been made? Looked at from this angle, we find that Chassidim have differed from other Orthodox Jews in two main respects: they belonged to a peculiar *type* of community, and, closely related to it, they emphasized in their behavior the informal over the formal, or, more precisely, the expressive over the instrumental. We shall examine these in some detail.

Although it draws the bulk of its membership from the region within which the leader resides, the Chassidic fellowship has not been a geographical community in the usual sense, for residence—even in the very locality of the leader—does not compel one to belong.[6] It requires a voluntary decision to become a Chossid. Further, what draws individuals into the Chassidic community, are not common interests, economic or political, that are normally an outgrowth of common residence, but a number of rewarding experiences that await the joiner, catering to needs of a different and more universal nature.

The key to all rewards has been the characteristic figure of the Chassidic leader —the *tzadik* (righteous man) or *rebbeh* (master, teacher)—to whom the followers ascribe all the qualities they associate with the ideal man and leader. The tzadik is believed to have received at birth a soul of a higher order that enables his spiritual ascendance. It does not determine it, however. In order to realize his potentialities, one has to conquer the temptations of Satan, subjugate the impure desires of both body and mind, and become fully saturated with love of God and every Jew, even the simplest one.

When one has attained the level of a true tzadik, he is believed to have become capable of procuring spiritual and even material benefits for others. His prayers carry extra weight, for he prays not on his own behalf but on that of the entire Jewish collectivity. In this capacity he not only begs, but occasionally demands that God accede to the wishes of His people, who, after all, suffer only on account of their loyalty to Him and their stubborn refusal to trade this loyalty for a pot of lentils. God must grant this request, as the Talmudic sages put it: "The tzadik decrees and God confirms (or fulfills)."

He, the ideal man, and the atmosphere in his "court" constitute the main attraction for the Chossid, who from time to time leaves his routine existence with its petty worries at home and "travels" to the tzadik. There, a variety of soul-lifting experiences are in store for him. First, he would have an opportunity to pray together with, often under the leadership of, the tzadik. Then he would participate in the solemn public meals—the so-called "tables"—that the rebbeh "conducts." At the "table" only the rebbeh, members of his immediate family, and a few privileged Chassidim are being served, whereas the average Chossid would stand in awe, observing how his ideal man serves the Lord with even such a prosaic activity like eating, and waiting for an opportunity to partake in this extraordinary feast by grabbing or receiving a bite from what the rebbeh ordinarily leaves in each dish. At the "table" one also hears the tzadik "say Torah," *i.e.*, expound his particular brand of Chassidic teaching. Finally, there is mass singing and dancing—the concrete expression of the Chassidic positive valuation of joy.

Aside from these collective experiences, each Chossid has his high point of the court visit, his private few minutes with the man he trusts and admires, and with whom he would now share his problems and anxieties. The rebbeh would offer both advice and blessing. The Chossid would then leave with feelings of renewed faith and hope, ready to face again the prosaic reality that he had escaped when he went to the rebbeh, but which now, upon returning, appears less formidable. After all he is not alone. The tzadik keeps a protective fatherly eye on him, and with such help he, the Chossid, will somehow manage to pull through.[7]

The dynastic pattern of succession, which gradually replaced discipleship, leaving the latter to the opening of new territory or to cases with no suitable heir, has essentially two basic functions. First, it facilitates continuity, for loyalty to a tzadik is more easily transferred to his offspring than to a stranger. The ideological basis for the transfer was hinged to the above mentioned beliefs about the nature of the tzadik—that he possesses a superior soul and that he has succeeded in harnessing all his actions to the service of the Creator. It seemed then reasonable to assume that one born of "holy seed" is more likely to be a potential tzadik. For the father, himself a tzadik, no doubt eliminated from the sexual act the element of vulgar carnal pleasure and instead had in mind the fulfilling of a religious command and the bringing of "worthy sons" to this world. One born of such a pure relation is thus considered a logical candidate for the kind of soul that enables one to develop into a tzadik. Second, dynasticism made for the creation and perpetuation of local traditions, thus completing the process of decentralization and rendering each center fully independent of, and on a par with all others. This in turn promoted adaptation to local conditions, or, in case of several systems operating within one area, to the particular element that a given system catered to.[8]

In sum, the Chassidic community is locally adapted and colored, yet not tied to any particular locality, whereas focus and permanence is provided by the idealized image of the rebbeh. This floating but stable community, which is superimposed on the geographical community, may then be viewed as deriving its strength from giving its adherents a feeling of belonging to a fellowship the stability of which cannot be shattered by either governmental whim or just necessity to change locality of residence, a feeling of security that Jews in particular had difficulty in developing with respect to their community of residence.

The second cluster of Chassidic behavior patterns that provide an outlet for individualized expressive behavior grew out of the participation in the just described community, but exceed its boundaries. Not only is the very belonging a matter of choice, but the extent and mode of participation are largely unstructured, and, therefore, each Chossid can suit his own needs and temperament. He visits the rebbeh when and as frequently as he feels a need for it. When at the court, not only does each one have his personal moment that is in a way unique, but even the experience one shares with the others has a minimum of structure, allowing an almost unlimited range of valid modes of participation. At prayer, one has choice as to pace, pitch of voice, and amount as well as type of bodily movement. While the "table" is being conducted, one can stand in a solemn pose close to the rebbeh, be a few feet removed and engage in a light conversation, or at will, alternate between solemnity and informality. In addition, one may altogether absent himself from the table. The same goes for the singing and dancing. Thus, not only do these experiences provide socially sanctioned opportunities for expressive behavior, but they do so in a way that allows for individual differences.

Chassidim have carried these behavior patterns outside the rebbeh's court. When not at the rebbeh, Chassidim, typically, congregate in a *shteebl* (literally: little room), which they use for prayer, study, community feasts, singing, dancing, and occasionally even sleeping. The shteebl, in short, is a minor replica of the informal synagogue at the court, and thus provides an opportunity to practice at home the behavior patterns acquired during the court visits. Further, informality and expressiveness are being carried into practically all areas of activity. Chassidim have been notorious for their vociferousness as well as their lack of respect for punctuality or any other form of discipline. This is even so with regard to such discipline as synagogue decorum prescribed by Jewish law, but completely disregarded by Chassidim, and this despite the fact that Chassidim of all ages have been zealous and un-compromising Orthodox Jews.

In his by now classic article on revitalization movements Wallace observes that whether the revitalized culture will be able to maintain its vitality beyond a certain point "will depend on whether its mazeway formulations lead to actions which maintain a low level of stress" (1956: 279). It seems plausible to suggest that by institutionalizing ample opportunity for individually tailored expressive behavior, the Chassidic formula has led to considerable reduction of stress, which, in turn, has been one of the main factors in the wide-spread success and the lasting tenacity of Chassidism.

The above analysis departs radically from a half-century-old tradition that has its roots in the writings of the historian Dubnow (1931),[9] who regarded the creative phase of Chassidism as having ended with the death of the founder. What continued thereafter, Dubnow calls Tzadikism, a cult that features the exalted image of the tzadik, portrayed as basically an imposter who exploits the ignorant by performing miracles to them for a handsome fee. This view is based on the fact that in most courts the above-mentioned Chossid-rebbeh private meetings have also been the occasion for the Chossid to hand the rebbeh a sum of money, a so-called *pidyon* (redemption). Careful scrutiny of Chassidic lore and behavior, however, suggests that Chassidim themselves have considered miracle-seeking as the domain of the simple-minded who are unable to grasp the true nature of the Chassidic experience. As for the giving of redemption money, in some communities the custom has not existed altogether, in others it has been the practice of a minority, and even where it is universal, the sum one gives is—with few exceptions—not specified, frequently amounting to a mere token. Likewise, the portrayal of the typical rebbeh as an exploiting charlatan appears to be inconsistent with reality. Most of the twentieth century Chassidic leaders, for example, appear to have been highly revered by the leading non-Chassidic Orthodox scholars. In all, it is difficult to comprehend how an exploitative cult to which belonging is voluntary, could have retained its popularity for such a long period, in such a variety of settings. Our analysis is thus offered as an alternative to the Dubnowian view.[10]

As for general theory, all one may legitimately engage in on the basis of analyzing a single case, is speculation about its implications. Our case suggests the possibility of replacing the residential community when the stability of the latter is strained, with a type of social organization that fulfills the basic functions that community is believed to fulfill, but which derives its stability from foci other than residence.[11] Viewed this way, one wonders about the validity of the Romantic theme concerning the "loss of community" of modern man, a theme that found its classic expression in Toennies' formulation of *Gemeinschaft* and *Gesellschaft*, but which is still very much alive (ct. for example Coleman 1961, Nisbet 1962). Could it be that at least the more adapted urbanites, who because of their high geographical mobility find it difficult to maintain stable residential communities, have been replacing the latter with such structures as business and professional associations, the community character of which has, as yet, been little investigated? What is suggested here, in other words, is that the Chassidim may have inadvertently created a type of community that may—with different form and content, of course—prove to be highly adaptable to the urban-industrial setting.

NOTES

1. The field research upon which this paper is partially based, was conducted during 1960-61. It was made possible by an Andrew Mellon Fellowship awarded by the Graduate School of the University of Pittsburgh, as well as supplementary grants by the Conference of Jewish Material Claims Against Germany Department of Cultural and Educational Reconstruction, and the National Foundation for Jewish Culture. I gratefully acknowledge my indebtedness to these organizations. I am equally indebted to Professor George P. Murdock of the University of Pittsburgh for his invaluable advice and guidance. Thanks are finally due to my colleagues Professors David Cooperman, Edward Gross, and Gregory Stone from whose comments I have profited. I read a somewhat modified version of this paper at the 62nd annual meetings of the American Anthropological Association (San Francisco, November, 1963).

In transliterating Hebrew terms, I aimed at phonetic similarity to the Ashkenazic pronunciation which practically all Chassidim—being Askenazic Jews—have been using (an exception is *Shabtai* which resembles the Sephardic, for Shabtai Tzvee was a Sephardic Jew). The Hebrew letter with which Chassidim begins, has no phonetic equivalent in English. The *ch* we use should be pronounced like in the German *nacht*. The change from Chossid in the singular to Chassidim in the plural, is due to the fact that in the Hebrew they are spelled and pronounced differently: the singular is spelled with a letter which sounds like the *o* in moment, and in the plural it is replaced with a letter that resembles the *a* in bar. The retention of the Hebrew suffix *im* to denote plurality is customary, as its replacement with the English *s* would have made for awkwardness.

2. A number of studies of contemporary Chassidic life have been reported recently (Freilich, 1962; Kranzler, 1961; Poll, 1962)—all emphasizing viability and persistence. As for the writer's experience with the Satmarer Chassidim, he found them to be very much "alive," numerous newspaper reports notwithstanding.

3. The historical sketch is based on well-known facts of Jewish history that the writer has gathered from a variety of sources—primary source material, histories, living lore, etc.—in the process of both studying and living. Thus references seem both superflous and impractical, especially since the aim in this paper is not to present the history of Chassidism, but to attempt a theoretical analysis of the indigenous Chassidic culture patterns.

4. Some translate *Baal Shem Tov* as *Master of the Good Name*. However, it seems to the writer that *Man with a Good Name* comes closer to what Chassidim have understood the term to mean. The writer found this to be true among Chassidim he came in contact with during his upbringing abroad, as well as his recent study. (Though in the *Chabad* literature of the Lubawitsher Chassidim one finds an occasional interpretation of the Founder's Talmudic medieval Hebrew, and especially in Yiddish, there are numerous two-word terms that contain the word *baal* in the sense of *man with, man of,* and *man who has*. Examples are: *baal moom,* one who has a blemish; *baal tzedokoh,* man of charity; *baal-din,* man who has a judgment (a litigant). Translations of the above as, respectively, master of the blemish, master of charity, and master of judgment have an extremely unrealistic ring, and in the case of the last, it is definitely incorrect since a litigant is involved, but is not master of the judgment. One is therefore inclined to argue that instead of *master,* the basic meaning of *baal* may well be *one who has.* Thus one may have a house, a blemish, a litigation, a habit of giving charity, and—a good name. Consequently to render *Baal Shem Tov* as *master of the good name,* and

especially to read into this title an ability of manipulating God's name for the purpose of miracle-making (this is incidentally not what the Chabad interpretation refers to) seems to be far-fetched, and may well reflect the Dubnowian view of Chassidism as primarily a miracle-making enterprise, a view we shall discuss later.

5. One of the Basht's disciples, Reb Nochem Tshernobler, in his book, *Yiamach Lev*, points out that the Hebrew root *otzev* means both sadness and idol, and deduces hence that the two are related.

6. Occasionally, individuals who depended for their livelihood on Chassidim, or who could not endure the strains of social isolation in an all Chassidic locality, joined involuntarily. However, our concern is with the movement's widespread and long-lasting success, which can, logically, only be explained in terms of its appeal to voluntary enthusiasts.

7. At this point it may be of interest to trace the semantic transformations of the term *Chossid* that reflect the socioculture developments we have been discussing. Since biblical times the term had been used to connote "Pious beyond legal requirement." (For a relatively short period in the second century B.C.E. the anti-Hellenists were called Chassidim.) With the advent of the Chassidic movement, the term acquired the specialized meaning of one who belongs to this particular culture (and hence our use of capitals). After decentralization and the emergence of independent communities, it became necessary to add an adjective which consisted of the name of the rebbeh's locality and the suffix *er* which in Yiddish means *of*. For example, a Gehrer Chossid is not a Chossid who lives in Gehr, as the term literally suggests, but one who is a follower of the rebbeh who resides in Gehr, thus emphasizing the individual's community membership rather than his residence. The next step has been one of generalization as chossid came into wide colloquial usage as a synonym for follower, reflecting the personal Chossid-rebbeh relationship in addition to community membership and belonging to a cultural type.

8. A good example is the Chassidic system of Lubavitsh which was situated in the North in the vicinity of the critical scholarly Lithuanian misnagdim. In response, Lubavitsh developed an intellectualized brand of Chassidism with an elaborate literature on Chassidic theory and philosophy.

9. The essence of the thesis can also be found in any one of Dubnow's numerous writings that deal with the 18th century East European scene (1916: 220-241, for example). For a sample of contemporary uncritical acceptance of the thesis, see Sachar (1958: 74-80), and for a slightly modified slant, cf. Zborowski and Herzog (1952: 166-180).

10. Martin Buber's approach (referred to above) is basically philosophical and hence not amenable to adequate analysis within the epistemology that governs the enterprise of science and which limits the latter to more tangible concepts than "philosophical essence."

11. Earlier leads in this direction by Lindeman (1934), MacIver (1917), Schmalenbach (translated 1961), and Weber (translated 1946) are but occasionally mentioned in the contemporary literature (cf. Martindale 1960: 132-3). Goode's attempt to explore the community character of professions (1957) has remained an almost isolated effort.

REFERENCES

Coleman, James S.
    1961—Community Disorganization. In Merton and Nisbet (eds.), Contemporary Social
        Problems, 553-604. Harcourt, Brace & World.
Dubnow, S. M.
    1916—History of the Jews in Russia and Poland, From the Earliest Times Until the
        Present Day. Tr. I Friedman. The Jewish Publication Society of America.
    1931—Geschichte des Chassidismus. Berlin.
Freilich, Morris

1962—The Modern Shtetl: A Study of Cultural Persistence. Anthropos. 57: 46-54.
Goode, William J.
1957—Community Within a Community: The Professions. American Sociological Review 22: 194-200.
Kranzler, George
1961—Williamsburg: A Jewish Community in Transition. Philip Feldheim, Inc.
Lindeman, E. C.
1934—Community. Encyclopedia of the Social Sciences. Macmillan.
MacIver, R. M.
1917—Community. Macmillan.
Martindale, Don
1960—American Social Structure. Appleton-Century-Crofts, Inc.
Nisbet, Robert A.
1962—Community and Power. Oxford University Press. Appeared in 1953 under the title: The Quest for Community.
Poll, Solomon
1962—The Hasidic Community of Williamsburg. The Free Press.
Sachar, Howard M.
1958—The Course of Modern Jewish History. The World Publishing Company.
Schmalenbach, Herman*
1961—The Sociological Category of Communion. Tr. Naegele and Stone. Parsons et al., eds. Theories of Society I: 331-347. The Free Press.
Weber, Max*
1946—From Max Weber, Essays in Sociology. Tr & ed. Gerth and Mills. Oxford University Press. Reprinted in 1959.
Wallace, Anthony F. C.
1956—Revitalization Movements. American Anthropologist 58: 264-279.
Zborowski, M. and Herzog, E.
1952—Life Is with People, The Jewish Little-Town of Eastern Europe. International Universities Press, Inc.

---

*The publishing dates of Schmalenbach and Weber are misleading for they indicate the dates the English translations appeared, whereas the original German appeared in the case of Schmalenbach in 1922, and Weber's essays are taken from various publications scattered through the 1920's.

HASIDIM
OF BROOKLYN

STEPHEN ISAACS

New York—The Williamsburg section of Brooklyn, across the East River from Manhattan, was once one of the elegant resort areas of the East Coast. The Vanderbilts, the Whitneys, the Morgans and others used to ferry over to enjoy the concerts, the beer gardens, the fine hotels.

In the intervening years, Williamsburg has undergone great migrations. By now, most of the neighborhood has evolved into a festering urban cancer—a rundown collection of hovel-like apartments into which blacks and Puerto Ricans and other Hispanics are crammed. Unemployment and underemployment are endemic. The schools, beset by massive problems of vandalism and discipline, are barely, if at all, teaching.

But in the midst of this depressing slumscape reposes what is essentially a small, 18th Century East European village. This part of Williamsburg has no crime, no drugs, no venerial disease, no graffiti. "To us," says one leader of this enclave, "juvenile delinquency is a guy who gets caught watching a baseball game on a television set."

This community, hard by the old Brooklyn Navy Yard, is populated by an unusual remnant of Nazi Germany's insanity: 20,000 to 25,000 Hasidic Jews, fundamental religionists who are as remarkable in their discipline as the early Mormons or the Shakers or the Amish.

The Hasidim do not own television sets. They attend no movies. They dress—and think—like their forebears of more than 200 years ago. They pray like them, eat like them, wash like them. They believe they are the true continuum of the true Judaism. They refuse to compromise with the temptations of modernism.

Some Hasidic sects, like the Lubavitchers, do seek publicity. The Lubavitchers maintain a news service and send missionaries around the country and the world to try to convert less pious Jews who have not seen the beauty of Hasidism. Their embattled community in Brooklyn is in the Crown Heights neighborhood, another deteriorating, crime-ridden area about two miles south of Williamsburg.

But the more numerous Hasidim of Williamsburg—most of whom are Satmar Hasidim—seek no publicity, no fanfare. Indeed, among their strongest characteristics is a suspicion of the outside world, based partly on the inward intensity of their religion and partly on the horrors of their wordly experience.

Hasidism was founded in the early 1700s in the Carpathian Mountains by Israel Ben Eliezer, a teacher and clay digger who became a spiritual leader known as the Baal-Shem-Tov, or "Master of the Good Name." From the Baal-Shem-Tov spread the word that concentration on intellectual hairsplitting, which had become a mark of religiosity for Jews, was false. True piety was in the intensity of feeling put into study and prayer and commitment to God.

Hasidism ("Hasid" in effect means "pious") was a form of democratization, and it caught fire with millions of Jews in Eastern Europe. Ordinary Jews could suddenly be just as pious, just as worthy, as learned scholars. The Baal-Shem taught that "every person should be equal in a man's eyes whether that person lacks knowledge or whether he knows the whole Torah. How does one attain this attitude of equality? It is attained by constant clinging to God, for out of a constant concern to cling to God, one has no time to think of other things."

The late Rabbi Abraham Joshua Heschel, in a recent book published posthumously, wrote that one of the Baal-Shem's most important successors "urged a recognition of the sham, the emptiness and the folly of mundane pleasures, and therefore their depreciation, leading to independence from the world. One must stay away from the world's noise, its distractions and dangers. Then, and only then, can one serve God."

This accounts for one element of the Satmar Hasidim's reclusiveness. Hitler accounts for the other.

Of the 6 million Jews murdered by the Nazis, about half were Hasidim. They were easy prey because of their distinctive appearance, because they were unworldly and non-political, and because their way of life required that they stay in close-knit communities near their rebbes, or masters. They tended neither to assimilate at home nor flee to Palestine like the Zionists they disagreed with. (Hasidim, and especially the Satmars, oppose Zionism basically because they feel only the Messiah can create a rebirth of the Jewish nation; many feel the secular state of Israel interferes with the divine plans of the coming of the Messiah.)

Some Hasidim survived the Dachaus, Bergen-Belsens and Auschwitzes. Some straggled to Israel anyway. Most of those left were displaced persons who came to America.

In Williamsburg today, most older Hasidim wear their pasts in their psyches—in extreme paranoia—and on their arms, where the tattooed concentration camp numbers remain in pale blue.

The paranoia was evident when a reporter and photographer from *The Washington Post* recently visited the area. The streets bustled with Hasidim—everywhere, that is, except where the two newsmen went. It was as if these outsiders brought clouds of doom with each step.

At one point, the photographer stepped into a kosher drug store (even drugs are specially prepared) to use the telephone. The bearded pharmacist exclaimed over the equipment hanging from the photographer's neck, though he was not really that interested in the gear. "Are you an amateur?" he asked with a caution bred in a Holocaust atmosphere. When told whom the photographer worked for, the pharmacist refused him use of the phone. (In addition to this paranoia, many Hasidim believe that having their pictures taken violates the second commandment forbidding graven images.)

The Hasidim are scared, perhaps rightly so, and they are hurrying to repopulate the world with Hasidim. It is said that the Hasidic population of Brooklyn, concentrated in Williamsburg, Crown Heights and Borough Park, is doubling every five years.

This is not hard to believe when one sees the strollers and shoppers strung out on a sunny afternoon along Lee Avenue in Williamsburg or 13th Avenue in Borough Park, where another 25,000 or so Satmars live, along with up to 9,000 other Jews of various intensities and types.

The Torah frowns on birth control. Indeed, it insists upon abundant procreation, and Hasidic families of 10, 12 or more children are not unusual. For the older Hasidim, these often are second families, the first ones having been killed in Europe.

That is true, for example, of Rabbi Leopold Friedman, who was once a prosperous banker in Sevlus, Czechoslovakia. He was a pious Hasid and a close adviser of the Satmars' rebbe, Joel Teitelbaum. Rabbi Friedman lost all but one of his seven children, his wife and all of his other relatives in the Holocaust. He survived Warsaw, Auschwitz, Dachau. After the war, he was summoned to New York to help organize the Hasidim here by Rebbe Teitelbaum, who survived Bergen-Belsen. Friedman remarried, to a woman who lost all of her family, including five children, in the camps.

A son of Friedman's second marriage, Albert, is now a 25-year-old rabbi in Williamsburg. Albert Friedman talks of his father's accomplishments in Williamsburg, for Leopold Friedman created an institutional complex to abet the insularity of the Hasidim that is all but amazing. It includes:

—The largest private Jewish school system in the world, including about a dozen buildings, where every boy and girl (separately) learns Yiddish as well as English. The boys study Torah and the Talmud and its commentaries and Hasidic lore.

—A hospital and clinic, with women gynecologists so women can avoid having strange men touch them.

—An emergency ambulance and oxygen service.

—A synagogue that, on the high holidays, accommodates 7,500 worshippers, plu five other Satmar synagogues in Williamsburg and Borough Park.

—A private bus service that connects the communities in Williamsburg and Borough Park, and another private bus line that connects Williamsburg with Manhattan's diamond center on 47th Street, where many Hasidim work

—A special nursing service in which Hasidic men and women go to community hospitals to help feed fellow Hasidim who cannot care for themselves.

—One of the largest loan societies in New York, with interest-free loans to Hasidim who have business or personal financial need.

—A super kosher butcher shop.

—A bakery for matzah, or unleavened bread.

—An employment agency with contacts at 5,000 businesses.

—Summer camps in upstate New York.

—A publishing enterprise which prints a weekly newspaper, *Der Yid*, and books for the schools, among other things.

—A burial society for those who cannot afford such costs.

—What is said to be the largest *mikveh* in the history of the world.

A *mikveh* is a ritual cleansing bath. The immersion must be in natural, pure water. Hasidic men visit one every day, and there is one, tied to artesian wells, underneath their main synagogue, which is perhaps 50 feet from the fumy, bustling Brooklyn Queens Expressway.

Across the expressway is the new *mikveh* for the women, which cost more than $1 million (the entire expense borne by one Hasid) and which has 39 separate *mik vehs* for women. Hasidim follow orthodox commands that they refrain from sexu relations during menstrual periods and for seven days afterward. The women must immerse themselves before relations can resume.

At the synagogue on a recent Sabbath evening, the Williamsburg Hasidim celebrated the birth of 14 boys in the preceding week, as well as the impending marriage of eight young men the following week. Hasidim usually wed young, and the marriages are "match-made," either by the rabbis or by matchmakers.

Hasidic women ritually shave their heads after the marriages—so they will not be attractive to other men—and on the street they wear scarves or wigs. Women may not sit in the synagogue with the men, so as not to divert the men from the intensity of their prayers. When the women go, they sit in a separate balcony with a latticed screen that shields them from the men's view.

"Our divorce rate is about 1 per cent," says Rabbi Friedman, "and most of tho are for physical reasons."

All this is about as far as one can get from the women's liberation movement. "What should they want with women's lib?" asks Salomon Feder, who helps administer the school buildings. "They don't have to work. They are in charge of everything in the home, in taking care of the children, in giving love to the children. What is more important? They are the bosses at home, they make the supper, everything."

What distinguishes the Hasidim from strictly orthodox Jewry, however, is their super-orthodoxy, their absolute devotion to the Torah and its commands and teachings, their refusal to mix in the society and to submit to any of its temptations.

Last year, for instance, the rebbe ruled that his followers should refrain from riding New York's subways during rush hours because of the immodest apparel of non-Hasidic women and because, in the rush hour crush, men and women are often shoved into each other. Hasidic men and women, even husbands and wives, are never supposed to touch publicly.

The rebbe's views are revered by Hasidim. Each dynasty has its own rebbe and each dynasty usually is named after the European town in which its founder settled. Some Hasidim believe their rebbes have divine powers or are miracle workers, and all questions about how to live are taken to him.

The Satmars built a huge, Florida-style mansion with white columns for their rebbe in the midst of the decaying Williamsburg slum, complete with private chapel and with a high steel fence surrounding it. In his younger years, Rebbe Teitelbaum rarely slept in a bed, instead constantly studying, praying and advising his followers, occasionally dozing in his chair. Now near 90, he had a stroke several years ago and has cut down his activities, spending more time at his place in Belle Harbor, Queens, and with followers in Florida, where he is now.

The crush of inner-city life has taken its toll on many Hasidim, particularly those who suffered physically in the Nazi era and those whose rigorous religious schooling has precluded secular job skills. Many Hasidim are rich, but many are also poor. Money stretches hardly at all when there are so many children and when food costs more because it is *glatt* kosher or unquestionably kosher.

Marvin Schick, an orthodox Jew who was an assistant to former Mayor John Lindsay, has been struggling with the Department of Health, Education and Welfare to have the Hasidim declared a minority group so they can share in Emergency School Act money. The Hasidim feel strongly about their *yeshivas*, schools, and they voted as a bloc to defeat Allard Lowenstein when he tried to unseat Rep. John Rooney in the district in 1972. Lowenstein opposes federal aid to parochial schools.

Hasidic boys are sent to day school at 3. At 3½, the boys (whose side curls are never cut) start learning the Hebrew alphabet—Hebrew is reserved only for holy use—and at 4½ they start learning the Torah.

For an adolescent, the Torah is all. Six days a week, boys rise at 3 or 3:30 in the morning to go to the *mikveh*, are in school from 5:30 or 6 A.M. until nearly sundown, and then return to synagogue. After supper, they return to synagogue for the nightly study session. On Saturday, the sabbath, they are in synagogue almost all day.

Religious education often continues after marriage, with the wife's parents (or sometimes both sets of parents) supporting the young couple who immediately start producing offspring. This means many Hasidim are unprepared to earn a living in the secular world, and unemployment is high—about 15 per cent. When someone is without work, the community pitches in to help. Public welfare is so stigmatized to the Hasidim that many refuse to accept it even if they are near starvation.

A program to train Hasidim as computer programmers has had great success, taking advantage of the discipline in logic that develops with intense study of Talmudic commentaries.

Other Hasidim do vigorous work, such as driving trucks, and many are employ in such community services as the special kosher butchering trade or in making Hasidic garments. One New York rabbi, a Hasid says, "You know, you can't just walk into Macy's to buy those clothes." Still others work in Manhattan's garment district and in the diamond business which is a traditional trade for Hasidim.

While the Satmars and Lubavitchers are the largest Hasidic sects in America, many Hasidic sects and branches exist elsewhere in the country. Says Rabbi Friedman, "Wherever you find Jews, you'll find Hasidim."

Some Haisdim have found cities too corrupting and too oppressive. One sect, the Skvir Hasidim, built a community 40 miles north of New York City, calling i New Square.

The Satmars attempted a similar move in 1962, when they bought 500 acres i Mount Olive Township, N.J., 35 miles west of Manhattan, for 800 houses. But proper zoning for the housing was refused, primarily, the Satmars believe, because of anti-Semitism.

This April, the Satmars will try again with a small town near Middletown, N.Y Rabbi Sender Deutsch, who with Rabbi Leopold Lewkowitz has taken over the duties of the late Rabbi Friedman, says that "many families want to live outside the city. So 105 families will settle there in time for Passover. We've built 80 gard apartments and 25 single-family houses." There was no anti-Semitism this time. "We kept it quiet until we finished up everything," says Rabbi Deutsch.

Back in Williamsburg, meanwhile, Rabbi Lewkowitz arranged for half of the new high-rise apartments to have space on the lower floors (Hasidim cannot live high up because they cannot ride elevators or turn on any electrical device on the Sabbath), with 2,000 Hasidic families expected to occupy those.

Essentially, as one Satmar Hasid says, his people "just want to be left alone."

Many do not feel hospitable toward the Hasidim, including less orthodox Jew who find their insular and archaic ways offensive. But the Hasidim ignore them and go their own way, trying desperately to live their lives despite the horrendou conditions in Williamsburg, despite their burgeoning population, despite the fina cial problems of their schools, despite the need for more room to live and grow.

NEW SQUARE:
Bridge Over the River Time

HARRY STEINBERG

New Square, New York, is only 40 miles from the fleshpots of Manhattan, but it might as well be on another planet. Its spiritual locale is the East European shtetl, circa 1870. That is what the Squarer Hassidim have managed to resurrect in their self-imposed exile from the distractions and temptations of modern life.

High on the whitewashed wall of the synagogue the clock points to 1 A.M. Friday night has passed into Saturday morning. Below the clock, almost 200 men and boys dressed in the Hassidic tradition (black hats or the fur hats called *shtraimels*, black coats and white shirts without neckties) link hands and form a circle around the Rebbe and start chanting a *niggun*—a tune without words. They circle the table, the benches around it empty now; only the Rebbe, with his brother-in-law at his side, sits deep in thought, listening as his Hassidim chant and circle the synagogue.

This is not a description of life in some now-vanished East European backwater; this is New Square, a modern village in the heart of Rockland County, New York, less than an hour's drive from Manhattan. Population, 1300, the largest *incorporated* Hassidic community in the world.

Only 40 miles from Times Square, New Square is a world removed from the city. It is the place where the Squarer Hassidim, an ultra-orthodox sect, have chosen to live, away from the congestion and secular distractions of the city. It is a place where life is lived according to the strictest interpretation of the Torah.

In New Square—anglicized from Skvira, a village 20 miles from Kiev in the Ukraine—everything is done the way it was in Europe. The *shtetl* destroyed during World War II is alive again.

The first sign of its existence is the green-and-white sign on the shoulder of Route 45 which reads "New Square." A white arrow points to a narrow road— Washington Avenue—which meets the highway at right angles. The first houses are about 15 yards down the road; they look no different than any of the other houses in that part of Rockland County.

NO SIDEWALKS

The streets are paved and clean, but there are no sidewalks so the lawns of the Cape Cod houses run all the way to the pavement. The posted speed limit is 15 miles an hour and children wander the streets freely.

New Square was an idea conceived almost 20 years ago by a group of Hasidim in the decaying Williamsburg section of Brooklyn. They were tired of the robberie the muggings, the anti-Semitic incidents and the conflicts with their religious life that were so prevalent in the city. They wanted to raise their children away from "goyishe" influences.

Most of those who sought to escape were followers of Rabbi Joseph Jacob Twersky, the Skvirer Rebbe, whose family had supplied Rebbes back in Skvira for generations.

The site finally settled on was a dairy farm in the town of Ramapo, away from the distractions of New York, but still close enough to allow the men to commute And in the winter of 1957, the first 20 families moved in.

Their new life in New Square was filled with problems. For the first five years the streets were unpaved and treacherous during winter and spring. There were no shopping facilities, and because of strict Hassidic Kashruth requirements, food hac to be brought in from Williamsburg. There were no schools, so they were started in the basements of homes.

There were also construction problems. The Squarer, inexperienced home buye ran into difficulties with their contractor. "He took us for a ride for half-a-million dollars," says Rabbi Daniel Goldstein, the village clerk.

There were other headaches, too. At its inception, New Square was only a sub-division, subject to all the laws and ordinances of Ramapo, which passed restrictiv zoning rules, and eventually stopped issuing building permits.

"They wouldn't even let us finish our Synagogue," Goldstein said.

Among the zoning restrictions was one which required that only one-family houses be built, and that each house stand on one acre of land. But as the old Yiddish saying goes: *A yed gibt zich an eytseh,* (a Jew finds a way out). The one-family houses were built—extra large so they could be converted later to two-fami homes. In addition, the houses were built one to an acre, but each house was posi-tioned at the corner of its lot, to allow for denser housing in the future.

There were also disputes with Ramapo over the sewage system (which cost the residents $100,000) and the town started condemnation proceedings against the subdivision. At this point, the Rebbe suggested that the subdivision seek to incorp rate itself as a village, to gain freedom from the oppressive rules of Ramapo.

There is some dispute locally as to whether the restrictions were inspired by anti-Semitism. "You can't measure those things," says Rockland County Planning Board chief Aaron Fried, "but I would say it [anti-Semitism] was considerable."

Ramapo challenged New Square's right to incorporate and lost both the case and an appeal; and in November of 1961, with about 600 residents living on 135 acres, New Square was freed from Ramapo's control.

LIFESTYLE

The lifestyle of New Square can best be envisioned by describing the physical layout of the village. The center, where one would normally expect to find a business district, is occupied by three buildings around which life in New Square revolves: the Synagogue, the Rebbe's house and the boys' school. The shopping center and light industry facilities are in a corner of the village, near the cemetary.

The largest house in New Square is the Rebbe's. Owned by the community, it has a special rear wing which serves as both a reception room, and, with its sliding roof open, as a *sukka*. Rabbi Joseph Jacob Twersky was the first Squarer Rebbe to live in New Square. He was the founder of the community and its guide during the first difficult years. Upon his death in 1968, his only son David was chosen his successor.

The Rebbe does not rule in matters of law—another rabbi, called the Rav—does that. Instead, the Rebbe serves as the spiritual mentor and counselor to the villagers. Whether in matters of travel, marriage, business or health, the Rebbe's advice is sought and followed. But most of all, the Rebbe prays for his followers—intercedes with God on their behalf.

"To be a Rebbe means you have to give up your life. You belong to the people; you must feel everyone's problems just as if you were suffering," Rabbi Goldstein explains.

Though nominally supported by the community, the Rebbe contributes more than he takes from the village. On holidays and weekends a long stream of Hassidim from other communities come to seek his advice and prayers. In gratitude, they usually leave a gift which is spent either to support the Rebbe or for some charitable cause.

The Rebbe holds no official title, but even while his aides deny it, it is clear he plays an important role in the government of New Square. Just as Goldstein and Samuel Weissmandl, the mayor's aide—who run the village—wouldn't make a personal decision without consulting the Rebbe, neither would they make an official decision without his accord.

Comes election time, local politicians line up for an audience with the Rebbe. Ramapo Councilman Hyman Jatkoff, is a veteran of these preelection interviews. "You ask him if he can get his people out to vote for you, and he says he doesn't know," Jatkoff notes. Most of the talk revolves around local issues, he adds, "but the Rebbe never takes a position."

WELL BRIEFED

Jatkoff explains that the Rebbe appears to be well briefed on the issues and that the politicians—who visit in groups of four or five—participate in the interviews because "there are certain things on the American political scene that a candidate is expected to do. . . . It's a mark of respect." The Rebbe reportedly speak English, but all interviews are conducted in Yiddish. An interpreter stands by for those who do not speak Yiddish.

Goldstein and Weissmandl insist they never instruct villagers on how to vote, though they offer advise to those who seek it. "They ask us," Weissmandl says, "because we deal with the people [the politicians] every day." One villager, however, confided that most Squarers are not informed about local issues and they vote as they are told. "Our vote isn't our own," he says.

Rockland County election records also attest to a bloc of New Square votes. There are a few non-Squarer voters in the district, but most live in the village, and in 1972 the district went overwhelmingly for Richard Nixon 304 to only 34 for George McGovern. In 1970 Nelson Rockefeller outdistanced Arthur Goldberg 112 to 32 in the race for governor.

In local elections, New Square tends to go Republican. Some area residents point to the help the village received at the state level when the old Rebbe died (officials issued a cemetary permit on a Sunday, so he could be buried the same day, in strict accordance with Jewish law).

NO PEWS

The second building in the central tract is the synagogue, a two-story edifice, large and airy, but still furnished in the style of the Hassidic *shitbl* (house of worship) of the old country. Instead of pews in the main hall, there are long tables, flanked by low, backless benches. In the synagogue all during the week, young men sit and study the Talmud. Most of them are married, and in the Hassidic tradition, continue their studies with the support of their wives, parents and in laws.

There is another "synagogue" in New Square, one that has attracted attention in local newspapers. It is a bus and it leaves New Square each morning, carrying men wrapped in their prayer shawls and phylacteries to jobs in the city.

The third building in the central area is the boys' school—a girls' school is located about four blocks away. Here, from age three, the boys learn everythin from the alphabet to the most esoteric interpretations of the Talmud. From six to 13, they also study reading, writing and arithmetic for two hours a day. Histo and science are avoided for their potential conflict with traditional teachings.

From age 13 until they are married, the boys study the Talmud and Commentaries from 8:30 A.M. until 10 P.M., with breaks for lunch and dinner. There are no summer vacations, and the only days off are the Sabbath and the various Jewish holidays.

At the girls' school the curriculum is more liberal. The girls take secular courses through the 11th grade, and Rabbi Goldstein, who is also principal of the school, says they also get courses in current events, social studies and science (watered down). They are permitted to scan such periodicals as *Weekly Reader* and *Junior Scholastic*, after Goldstein has edited them to remove "objectionable material." Classes in sewing, typing and bookkeeping are also available.

"It's an error to teach them everything and let them choose. You have to dole it out to them in a baby food jar," he said.

"IT DOES"

Goldstein adds that the boys get all the secular knowledge they really need from the Talmud, which he claims includes discourses on history and law. Asked about the Talmudic assertion that the sun revolves around the earth, Goldstein replies: "It does . . . we asked the Rebbe about it, and he said the world is stationary and the rest [of the universe] moves."

The economy of New square is, at best, still weak. Weissmandle reports that perhaps 75 percent of the villagers receive either food stamps, Medicaid, or both. County officials, however, believe that only a half dozen Squarer are on welfare, and that most of these are seriously ill, or incapacitated.

"Many more are eligible for welfare," Weissmandl insists, "but their Jewish pride won't let them take it."

Without a doubt, the Squarer are much better off than the Hassidim of the old country. Their homes are more spacious and comfortably furnished and their kitchens have separate stoves and sinks for meat and dairy meals. Still, the Hassidim could hardly be considered candidates for the affluent society. The reasons include their large families (an average of eight), limited secular education, strict religious observance which circumscribes the days and hours worked, and in Rockland County, high real estate taxes.

The villagers of New Square pay the usual real estate levy to support the local school system (about $1,000 per house per year) despite the fact that they don't use the schools. On top of that, they must pay tuition for their children to attend yeshiva.

When their synagogue burned down several years ago, the villagers had to seek outside help to rebuild it. When their basement schools became inadequate, they had to turn to Joseph Gruss, a New York stockbroker, who donated $100,000 for each of the two school buildings.

Yet, despite financial hardships, Weissmandl says new square has never accepted money from Jews who were not *shomer Shabbos*—sabbath observers.

CLOSED ON SATURDAY

Recently, the Mobil Oil Co. leased a small area of New Square facing Route 45 for a service station, which will be closed on Saturday and the religious holidays. Mobil had tried for years to open a station in the area, but couldn't win a zoning change from Ramapo. So, Mobil turned to New Square, which controls its own zoning, and agreed to sign a lease which requires the station to close at sundown Friday, and stay closed until one hour after sundown Saturday. Donald Serniak, a Mobil real estate representative, described the lease as "extremely unusual" because the service station will be closed "when we normally enjoy our heaviest business."

The people of New Square live simply according to the dictates of the Torah and the customs of the old country.

"What is the purpose of life?" asks Abraham Loeffler, a tailor and one of the oldest residents. "To serve God," he answers.

As their forebears did for centuries in Eastern Europe, the Squarer often take in guests who have come for the Sabbath. They are open and friendly, almost fighting over the sanctified privilege of feeding and housing the visitor.

The predominant language in New Square is Yiddish—though it is quite heavily interlarded with English. Some Hungarian and Hebrew are also spoken.

Marriages in the village are arranged (boys and girls are strictly separated all through school) and usually occur at 18, though some have taken place as early as 16. The prospective bride and groom are introduced by friends or relatives, not only to each other, but also to the in-laws. Jewish law is opposed to forced match so either bride or groom can back out, but once they agree and a date is set, the couple doesn't meet again until under the *chupa*—the canopy under which the marriage takes place.

The Squarer generally keep to themselves, rarely leaving the village except for the morning bus ride by the breadwinners. "New Square could be a million miles away," says Rabbi Hillel Friedman who heads a nearby Conservative synagogue. One of the few remaining points of friction between the Squarer and the outside community is the village's perennial opposition to increased school budgets which would push taxes higher. Villagers have arrived en masse at school district election to oppose a higher budget.

As to the other problems which plague most communities, New Square knows little of them. Police and fire services are contracted out of the town of Ramapo, and there are no crime, drug, alcoholism, runaway youth or sexual promiscuity cases.

NO ARGUMENT

Though the Squarer women—by outside standards—would be considered secon class citizens, those familiar with the issue say that none of them are women's lib ationists. That's the way the Torah wanted it, the men say, and they get no argument from their women.

Television is strictly forbidden in the village. Its portrayal of non-Jewish behavior and "violence and filth" are considered destructive. Radios are permitted, but not encouraged; perhaps 25 percent of the villagers own radios.

The villagers don't know much about the world outside. They are interested in it and question outsiders carefully, but they just don't have the time to read newspapers with any degree of regularity. Major events such as news from the Middle East and space flights attract some attention, but that's about the limit of it.

As a community completely secluded from "worldly influences," New Square has its drawbacks. There are Squarer Hassidim, including Weissmandl, who refuse to live in the village because they find it "too secluded."

But for those Squarer who survived the horrors of the Second World War—and for their children—New Square is the rebirth of a way of life most of them thought they'd never see again or experience. And this time they are sure nobody is going to take it away from them.

THE REBBE:
In His Torah
There Is Room for All Jews

IRVING SPIEGEL

The Rebbe eludes us. To those who don't know him—and to those who do—he persists as a gray mystery.

He is Menachem Mendel Schneerson, a graduate of the University of Berlin and the Sorbonne, seventh in the lineage of spiritual leaders of the Lubavitch movement. But there is no simple way to explain how a 73-year-old talmudic scholar sets in motion the spiritual, educational, social and rehabilitative programs which inspire his followers the world over.

The Rebbe is a loner. Yet he commands a fastidious, filial loyalty. A nod from the Rebbe will dispatch a disciple to the remotest corner of the world. Let the Rebbe cast a pebble in the Crown Heights section of Brooklyn where the Lubavitch movement has its headquarters, and the ripples reach Melbourne, London, Casablanca, Los Angeles and Jerusalem.

He is an ascetic; his family life reclusive. Yet he is constantly surrounded by devoted students. He rarely leaves the confines of his synagogue-office at 770 Easter Parkway. But far from being isolated from the secular world, he is immensely knowledgeable about political and social affairs.

Like Winston Churchill, he is a night person, at his desk in the post-midnight hours. Two nights a week—Sundays and Thursdays—are reserved for *yehidus*— private audiences—with those who come from all corners of the world to report to the Rebbe, to seek his counsel, to bask in his blessing. The visitor might be a rabbi or a businessman, the President of the State of Israel or a housewife. The list is as wide-ranging as it is long.

No question angers him. His memory is photographic; his gift for remembering names and faces, encyclopedic.

Menachem Mendel Schneerson was born in 1902 in Czarist Russia, the great-grandson and namesake of Rabbi Menachem Mendel of Lubavitch, the third Rebbe of the movement since its founding in the eighteenth century. By the time of his *bar mitzva*, he was esteemed as an *illui*—a Torah prodigy. His abilities set him so far apart from his *cheder* classmates that he was taken out of school to study, first with private tutors, and, when they ceased to challenge him, with his father, Rabbi Levi Yitzchak, a renowned kabbalist and talmudic scholar.

He first met Joseph Isaac Schneersohn, his predecessor as Lubavitcher Rebbe, in 1923, in Rostov, Russia. Six years later, after Joseph Schneersohn escaped a Bolshevik death sentence through the intervention of foreign statesmen including President Herbert Hoover, they met again in Warsaw. There, Menachem Mendel married Schneesohn's second daughter, Chaya Moussia. The couple immigrated to the United States in 1941, and his father-in-law appointed him head of Lubavitch agencies, including the educational, social service and publishing arms. When Rabbi Joseph Schneersohn died in 1950, Menachem Mendel Schneersohn succeeded him as the Lubavitcher Rebbe.

There is strict obedience to the Rebbe's judgment among Lubavitchers. He is moral instructor and practical advisor; as much an activist as a preacher. He not only counsels but innovates in ways which—to quote a disciple—"bring the genuine meaning of Torah to the lost and the unlettered, to the alienated and the disenchanted."

Unlike other Orthodox Jews who want their sons to continue learning Talmud

---

Kathy, a diabetic, lost three babies in succession. Doctors advised her to have a tubal ligation because another pregnancy would endanger her life. Kathy kept postponing the surgery. On a trip to New York to inquire about adoption possibilities, husband Sandy accompanied a childhood friend to a *farbrengen*. Although he came from a secular background, Sandy was shaken by the Rebbe's discourse—the topic was the meaning of a Jewish home—and he decided to write him for advice.

The Rebbe responded promptly: Kathy should try bearing a child again, and they would soon find another and better doctor. Over their parents' objections and ridicule, the young couple followed the suggestions.

The Rebbe asked to be kept informed about Kathy's health. An aide telephoned the hospital after the delivery. He conveyed the Rebbe's message: Kathy and Sandy could have one more child and they should raise the children in *Yiddishkeit*.

The couple has two children; Kathy's health has never been better. They are now observant Jews. They do not think that a miracle happened to them. They believe that they were helped by the Rebbe's superior knowledge of medicine and by the competence of the doctors.

for many years after ordination, the Lubavitchers see Torah study as preparatory to a life of dedication to the propagation of Judaism.

Most Lubavitchers marry during their final year of rabbinical school. Then they do advanced work in Talmud for one year while their wives complete their studies as Hebrew teachers. During this year, the couple decides how they can best serve the Jewish people. For some, it is a personal commitment to Jewish law, while making a living as chemical engineers or artisans, plumbers or diamond cutters. For the select few, the choice is *shelichus:* the mission to spread Jewish values among the uninitiated, which will take the young couple far away from their familiar homogeneous community.

The Lubavitch network of Chabad Houses is a creation of the Rebbe. The term Chabad is an acrostic of *chochma* (wisdom), *bina* (understanding) and *da'at* (knowl edge). They are not proselytizing centers, and those who come—mostly wayward Jewish youth—are not asked to adopt hasidic lifestyles but are given a chance to "find themselves" under the guidance of Lubavitch rabbis. The Lubavitcher who, at the Rebbe's bidding, has taken up duties as a counselor-teacher in a Chabad House is likely to be as adept at discussing James Joyce or the presidential pros pects of Morris Udall as he is at interpreting Talmud.

An example of a Chabad House is the one in St. Paul. Set in a wodded dell, it was once the mansion of a brewery magnate. It is now a refuge for some fifty Jewish women who regard themselves as *ba'alot t'shuva*—returnees to tradition.

It is a uniquely feminine place. On Friday evenings, tradition glows in the mass

---

Rachel graduated from high school but could not decide what career to follow; her interests were in art and education. She took a friend's advice and wrote to the Rebbe for guidance.

She had been raised Conservative, but when the Rebbe told her to go to a Lubavitcher camp that summer, she did. At the end of that summer, again on the Rebbe's recommendation, Rachel enrolled in the Lubavitcher women's seminary, Bais Rivka. She studied half a day and taught the other half. By the time she reached 19, Rachel began to worry, seeing many of her friends becoming engaged. It seemed to her that every day some one announced that she had found her *zivik*, her divinely appointed partner.

She wrote to the Rebbe, requesting a blessing that she would marry. Instead, she was told to wait five months, until after Pesach. Although Rachel was dis appointed that she did not receive the blessing, she decided that it was not her concern any longer: If the Rebbe told her to wait, then it became his responsibility. The next five months were a relaxed time for Rachel. With out dating fears, she was able to con centrate on her studies. But as she was putting the Pesach dishes away, she turned to her roommate and said: "So where is he?" Three weeks later, it happened. Moishe was the first per son she dated after Pesach. By the end of the year, they were married.

kindling of the Sabbath lights, a radiance that had once been meaningless to the young women.

They are a diverse group, living and studying together: college graduates—Ph.Ds among them—and high school dropouts. Some had been involved with drugs. Others had flirted with the mystical beliefs of the Orient or the political tumults of the New Left. All had shared in a sense of aimlessness.

Their mentors are Rabbi Moshe Feller and his wife Mindelle, sent to St. Paul by the Rebbe "to help lost Jewish girls find themselves." The young women who come are usually sent by Lubavitch centers in other cities. "It means," an 18-year-old from South Africa told me, "that we are sent by friends to be cared for by friends."

"When a girl is referred to us by a Lubavitch office, that office still feels responsible for her," says Rabbi Feller. "They follow her progress here. They pay the hospital bills for girls on drug withdrawal programs if parents can't afford it. This feeling of responsibility is to see the girl all the way through—not just to start her out."

The girls live dormitory style. Their stay is for two to twelve weeks, living in an embracing Jewish setting and taking instructions in classical Jewish studies. None is asked to join the Lubavitch movement. But more than half of the 500 girls who have come to the St. Paul Chabad House since the program began in 1971 departed with a strong commitment to traditional Judaism.

"When I first encountered Lubavitch people, Judaism was the farthest thing from my mind," said Arlene, 28, a well-paid computer programmer who, in her words, "had everything: a busy social life, a Manhattan apartment, summers at Fire Island—and a gnawing feeling about the purposelessness of it all." *Shabbat* and *kashrut* had been a joke to her. "But I noticed how graceful and sincere the Hasidic lifestyle was. These people were genuinely happy. They won my admiration."

The story is repeated at Chabad Houses in Buffalo and Miami, Berkeley and San Diego, and in more than a dozen countries.

A *farbrengen*, a gathering at which the Rebbe lectures, attracts an international

---

Tom was stationed in Vietnam. After his first battle, he began to fear that he might not come back alive. A Reform Jew, Tom had heard of the Rebbe and thought that he might as well approach him for advice.

The Rebbe replied that he should always remember to wash his hands before every meal and say the *bracha*.

Perplexed, Tom nevertheless did as told. One day, he had to walk a good distance from the tent where his buddies ate to find a wash basin. As he was saying the *bracha*, a shell hit the tent and it went up in flames.

Upon his return to the States, Tom still says a *bracha* before meals and he has begun to observe *kashrut*.

audience to "770"—the Eastern Parkway house number is the familiar hasidic identity for his headquarters.

The Rebbe's idiom is classical Yiddish, and his discourse continues hour after hour—without notes. His observations embrace a broad spectrum of topics, from current events to *pilpul*—sprinkled with quotations from the Bible, the Talmud and other sources.

His themes have one constant thread: Wisdom rests in the study of Torah. "Turn it and turn it over again," he repeats from *Pirkei Avot*, "for everything is in it."

Besides those who listen raptly at "770"—professors, lawyers, businessmen along with the Hasidim—there are others in Chabad centers throughout the country and overseas who hear the Rebbe's words through special telephone hook-ups. The Lubavitchers operate a complex communications network which links followers to the Rebbe who has not stepped out of New York since 1947, when he traveled to France to bring his widowed mother to live near him.

Perhaps even more than the words, the experience of listening to the Rebbe on the telephone inspires. Even followers who understand no Yiddish find their faith strengthened by the Rebbe's voice and participation in the event. It is not rare to find a *ba'al t'shuva*—returnee to tradition—listening intently without having the faintest idea about the specific message being conveyed.

Comes an infrequent moment when the Rebbe pauses in his peroration, and his Hasidim seize upon it as a time for joyous declaration. They begin to chant, spiritedly, jubilantly. Here and there a Hasid lifts his cup of wine or tumbler of vodka in a gesture of *l'chaim* to the Rebbe. The Rebbe responds with a warm smile. His blue, deep-set eyes glisten. Suddenly his voice booms out in song, leading the others.

A favorite topic of conversation at "770" is the Rebbe's capacity to offer advice and judgment on myriad problems affecting the welfare of followers and friends. During one of my own audiences with the Rebbe, I asked how he could do so with confidence.

"I am not afraid to say that I don't know," he said. "And if I do know then I have no right not to answer."

He paused for a moment, stroked his beard, then tilted forward in his chair, the felt hat on his head a crown of authority. "When someone comes to you for help and you believe that out of your knowledge and experience you can help him, to do otherwise is to become a cause of his suffering."

He leaned back, smiled gently and added: "Perhaps it is my role to awaken among those who come to see me the potential that is in them ."

A visitor to "770" was the widow of the famous sculptor Jacques Lipshitz. A work by her husband that had been commissioned to be mounted on Mount Scopus in Jerusalem included a rendering of a phoenix. Several Jewish scholars argued that the phoenix originated in Greek mythology and therefore was inappropriate as a featured work in a Jewish setting. The Rebbe advised her otherwise. He cited a passage in Job and midrashic sources which speak of the bird known as the phoenix. The Lipshitz work now stands on Mount Scopus.

An American visitor to Moscow, after attending services at the Great Synagogue, found himself pelted with questions and *Shabbos* greetings from worshippers surrounding him on the steps outside the *shul*. It was mostly small talk, the Russians intensely curious about Jewish life in America. After the crowd thinned, an elderly man sidled up to the visitor and whispered in Yiddish: "Give him a regards."

The American was bewildered. "Give *whom* a regards?"

The old Jew stared for a moment. "Him, the Rebbe."

"Rabbi? Which Rabbi?" the American floundered.

The old Jew was incredulous. "You really don't know who I mean? The *Rebbe.* The *Lubavitcher*! Tell him we'll need *matzos* this Pesach!"

In my many varied journalistic assignments, covering the Rebbe has been something special. To a reporter who has been, at times, irritated by Jewish leaders who occupy a swivel chair with a placard "King of the Jews," the Rebbe is the one who has a unique mystic quality.

I stopped putting on *tefillin* some two years after my *bar mitzva*—about the time I joined *The New York Times* in the 1920s. Some five years ago, I put on *tefillin* again, to please the Rebbe. But then came the feeling that it was good to support the Rebbe in his campaign to have all Jews putting on *tefillin*. For some time now, I have been doing it regularly, and it has given me much satisfaction and a sense of *Yiddishkeit*.

During the past twenty-five years that he has been the Lubavitcher Rebbe, the outreach philosophy of Chabad and its goal of spreading *Yiddishkeit* took on new dimensions.

For instance, the Rebbe has set up hotlines. Law enforcement agencies are encouraged to refer to Chabad houses homeless and troubled young Jews in need of shelter, food and counseling. There is the "Jewish peace corps"—a summer program which sends Lubavitch students into hundreds of small communities to distribute *tefillin* and religious books. There are *mitzva*-mobiles—"our Jewish tanks," says the Rebbe—that are a familiar sight on metropolitan streets: mobile units with loudspeakers urging Jews to put on *tefillin* each morning, to affix *mezuza* to their doorposts; to have a Bible, *siddur*, Book of Psalms and charity box in their homes; to set aside time each day for Torah study. Do you need a *chumash* or *tefillin*? The Rebbe's team is delighted to present them to you as his gift.

"What the Rebbe is pushing for," says Rabbi Yehuda Krinsky, a literate, promotion-minded young man who is the Rebbe's administrative aide, "is the spread of *Yiddishkeit*. In a world rent with aimlessness and disenchantment he has made Lubavitch an anchor, a pillar of light and hope with which Jews of all classes and ages might identify."

The Hasid and the Torah scholar, the communal leader and the intellectual, the laborer and the tradesman, plain folk and hippie—the Rebbe seeks to reach out to them all. To do so are his *mitzvot*.

5

BLACK JEWS

Several impressionistic articles have been published on various black Jewish or quasi-Jewish groups. Among them are "Founder of Jewish Cult Has Promised to Rise in 60 Days,"[1] which appeared in 1931, and "The Voodoo Cult Among Negro Migrants in Detroit,"[2] which appeared in 1938.

There has, however, been little empirical research on black Jews in the United States.[3] Wolf's "Negro 'Jews': A Social Study"[4] was published in 1933, and Fauset's 1944 book (reprinted in 1970) *Black Gods of the Metropolis* had a section on black Jews.[5] Brotz's "Negro 'Jews' in the United States" was published in 1952.[6] In 1964 Brotz's *The Black Jews of Harlem* was published; it remains the only empirically based book that has been published on black Jews.[7] Brotz was primarily concerned with explaining black Judaism in the larger context of the black nationalism movements. Waitzkin's "Black Judaism in New York," published in 1967, describes in more detail the beliefs and rituals of black Jews.[8] Other recently published articles include Landes's "Negro Jews in Harlem"[9] (1967) and Ehrman's "Explorations and Responses: Black Judaism in New York" (1971).[10] The latter article was printed in slightly condensed form in 1972 under the more descriptive title, "Tracing the Beginnings of Black Judaism."[11] Lincoln's *The Black Experience in Religion* (1974) has a section by Shapiro on black Jews.[12] Safier's doctoral dissertation, completed in 1971, provided valuable information on the self-concepts of black Jews.[13]

Several articles describing the characteristics and problems of various black Jewish communities have been published in recent years. Polner's 1972 "Being Black and Jewish"[14] discusses New York City's black Jews, as does Felton's 1974 "Black Jews in New York."[15] Dwyer's 1974 article discusses "Chicago's Black Jews."[16]

A few reports have been published on specific conflicts that black Jews have faced. The expulsion of three black Jewish students from an Orthodox yeshiva in 1971 is discussed in Felton's article. Felton noted that the students were expelled "on the grounds that their orthodoxy was questionable" and that twelve white students were expelled on the same grounds.[17] Goldfarb pointed out, however, "that a white who claims to be Jewish is, in fact, a Jew unless there is reason to doubt his assertion," but that "in the case of blacks, there is no such general presumption."[18] Goldfarb further discusses the problem of conversion of blacks and argues that those "many blacks who, for whatever reasons, are close to Judaism spiritually and religiously and who feel part of the Jewish people even though their formal status as Jews has not been established according to the requirements of Jewish law" should be willing to give proof of their Jewishness or undergo a Halachah conversion.[19] Coleman has noted, however, that individual blacks who do undergo formal conversion to Judaism often continue to experience rejection after conversion.[20] (This experience of rejection is also often expressed by white converts, but Coleman is suggesting that it is more likely to occur for black converts.)[21] A 1973 article noted the denial of Israeli citizenship under the Law of Return to a group of black Jews from the United States.[22] Black Jews also argue that the American Jewish community gives only modest notice and help to the Falashas (black Jews) of Ethiopia, who now are accepted as authentic Jews by the Israeli government.[23]

Some attempts have been made in recent years by the larger American Jewish community to confront the problems of black Jews, and some of these attempts are described by releases and reports of the Synagogue Council of America.[24]

The selections in this section describe black Jews. First is the article by Ehrman, which traces the beginnings of black Jews in the United States and which also discusses in some detail the black Jewish community of New York.[25] The following two articles discuss specific problems of black Jews. The article by Ross[26] discusses the problem of migration to Israel, and the article by Goldfarb[27] discusses the problem of conversion to Judaism. The final article by Coleman—a black Jew by conversion—describes the probable future of these problems and describes some of the activities being undertaken to aid black Jews in gaining acceptance by the larger Jewish community.[28]

NOTES

1. "Founder of Jewish Cult Has Promised to Rise in 60 Days," *Amsterdam News*, July 1, 1931.

2. E. D. Beynon, "The Voodoo Cult Among Negro Migrants in Detroit," *American Journal of Sociology* 43 (May 1938): 894-907.

3. Some attention has been given to black Jews outside the United States. See, for example, *Falasha Anthology—Black Jews of Ethiopia*, ed. Wolf Leslau (New York: Schocken Books, 1969).

4. E. Wolf, "Negro 'Jews': A Social Study," *Jewish Social Services Quarterly* (June 1933).

5. Arthur Huff Fauset, *Black Gods of the Metropolis* (New York: Octagon Books, 1970), vol. 3.

6. Howard M. Brotz, "Negro 'Jews' in the United States," *Phylon* 13 (December 1952): 324-337.

7. Howard M. Brotz, *The Black Jews of Harlem* (New York: Schocken Books, 1964).

8. Howard Waitzkin, "Black Judaism in New York," *Harvard Journal of Negro Affairs* 1 (1967): 12-4.

9. Ruth Landes, "Negro Jews in Harlem," *Jewish Journal of Sociology* 9 (December 1967): 175-188. Landes's article was based on a 1933 paper that had been submitted to a German journal and was subsequently destroyed by the Nazis. At the suggestion of Howard M. Brotz, she had the paper published in 1967. Commenting on the work Brotz has done since her original research, she notes that Brotz's findings "contradict my view that the cult was bound to fail. However, this Judaism has never become significant in the Negro life of the United States or elsewhere; and it has been hardly more than a curiosity to American (white) Jews. It has made no impact on social institutions or values, though it can matter in some personal lives. The organization described in my account has disappeared entirely."

10. Albert Ehrman, "Explorations and Responses: Black Judaism in New York," *Journal of Ecumenical Studies* 8 (Winter 1971): 103-114.

11. Albert Ehrman, "Tracing the Beginnings of Black Judaism," *Jewish Digest* 18 (October 1972): 45-51.

12. Deanne Shapiro, "Factors in the Development of Black Judaism," in C. Eric Lincoln, ed., *The Black Experience in Religion* (Garden City, N.Y.: Anchor Books, 1974), pp. 253-272. The original source was Deanne Shapiro, "Double Damnation, Double Salvation: The Sources and Varieties of Black Judaism in the United States" (Master's thesis, Columbia University, 1971).

13. Arno Safier, "Dual Minority Status, Group Identification and Membership Conflict: A Study of Black Jews" (Ph.D. diss., New York University, 1971).

14. Murray Polner, "Being Black and Jewish," *National Jewish Monthly* 87 (October 1972): 39-43.

15. Bruce Felton, "Black Jews in New York," *The Times of Israel* 1 (February 1974): 53-56.

16. James Dwyer, "Chicago's Black Jews," *The Times of Israel* 1 (February 1974): 56-57.

17. Felton, "Black Jews in New York," p. 55.

18. Harold Goldfarb, "Blacks and Conversion to Judaism," *Jewish Exponent*, September 18, 1970.

19. Ibid.

20. Robert T. Coleman, "Black and Jewish—and Unaccepted," *Sh'ma* 4 (March 22, 1974): 74-76.

21. For some representative articles on white converts, see Marcia Falconer, "Conversion and Acceptance"; Jay C. Jacobson, "In Israel: It Begins With Love"; and Ethel Frisbie, "In America: Are You Jewish?" *Hadassah Magazine* 57 (May 1976).

22. "Israel Expelling Black Hebrews," August 11, 1973, *Washington Post*. This article states that the Israeli Interior Ministry had ordered the expulsion of fifteen members of a black Hebrew sect. All citizens of the United States, the fifteen had been in Israel for two

years and were living in the desert development town of Dimona. This article also observes that about this same time, two black Hebrew women from the United States were denied entry to Israel as Jews under the Law of Return.

23. Michael T. Kaufman, "Concern Is Voiced for Ethiopia Jews," *New York Times*, November 2, 1975, p. 27. Also see information papers published by the American Association for Ethiopian Jews, 304 Robin Hood Lane, Costa Mesa, California 92627. This series attempts to inform American Jewry "of the plight of our black brethren in Ethiopia." *Information Paper No. 3* (February 1976).

24. See, for example, a press release dated June 4, 1973, by the Synagogue Council of America concerning the National Conference on Black Jews, which was held on May 31, 1973. Also see the Annual Report of the Committee on Black Jews, 1973, of the Synagogue Council of America, 432 Park Avenue South, New York, N.Y. 10016.

25. Ehrman, "Explorations and Responses."

26. Frank Ross, "A Black Rabbi Looks to Israel," *New York Times,* June 10, 1973, p. 104.

27. Goldfarb, "Blacks and Conversion to Judaism."

28. Coleman, "Black and Jewish—and Unaccepted." For an example of a black American convert being accepted as a Jew in Israel see Larry Lewis, "Black American Soldier in the Israeli Army," *Sepia,* October 1975, pp. 18-24. For an example of Israel's current positive attitude toward Falashas see Ben Burns, "How Israel Welcomes Long-Lost Black Jews," *Sepia,* April 1977, pp. 56-63.

EXPLORATIONS AND RESPONSES:
Black Judaism in New York

ALBERT EHRMAN

Between 1910-1930, New York's Harlem presented a picture of seething ferment. During that period the Negro population of New York City increased by a phenomenal 181%.[1] Negroes from both the South and West Indies jammed into Harlem. There were English, French, and Spanish speakers among the new migrants. By 1933 there were already no less than an estimated 350,000 Negroes living in Harlem.[2] Why did they come? One factor, undoubtedly, was World War I. Thousands of young Negro men who had served with the American Armed Forces during World War I had gotten their first taste of big-city life as a result of their military service, and liked it. They would never again return to the sleepy rural homesteads whence they had come. But a far more pervasive reason was the cry for hands from the burgeoning new industries of the industrial North. For the first time in American Negro history, the direction of Negro life was being reversed on a mass scale, *viz.*, from the South northward. This same situation also held true for the West Indian Negroes who were also migrating in large numbers to the new American industrial centers in the urban North. Thus, two distinct groups of Negroes, one of American, and the other of West Indian provenance, both hailing from an essentially rural background, yet each possessing its own distinct character, outlook, and temperament, suddenly found themselves rudely thrown together into an environment that was at once both alien and hostile to their own native traditions. The time was propitious for hypnotic and charismatic "leaders" of the Negro masses to arise. And arise they did!

MARCUS GARVEY AND ARNOLD JOSIAH FORD

Without a doubt, the man who more than any other electrified the Negro masses during this period of turmoil was the Jamaican-born Marcus Garvey.[3] Garvey came to America in 1917 on the advice of Booker T. Washington. Garvey, a man of keen intelligence, dreamt of a land, nay a continent, which Black men could truly call their own, and where, more importantly, Black men ruled. Upon coming to New York, Garvey organized the *Universal Negro Improvement Association* (U.N.I.A.), the first mass movement among American Negroes. As choirmaster of the U.N.I.A., Garvey employed a talented musician by the name of Arnold Josiah Ford.[4]

Arnold Josiah Ford was a West Indian like Garvey. His father had been a fanatical evangelist in Barbados. But upon coming to New York, Ford repudiated all Christian doctrine and announced himself to be an Ethiopian Jew! Ford was eminently successful as Garvey's choirmaster and for a while his influence and prestige in the U.N.I.A. was second only to Garvey's. Ford tried to persuade Garvey to accept Judaism as the Negro's true and rightful religion. But Garvey rejected his counsel.[5] Seeing that he could accomplish nothing further in the U.N.I.A.,[6] Ford set out on his own as a "Rabbi" in Harlem.

When Ford entered upon his rabbinical career, he was by no means entering *terra incognita*. There already were at that time several flourishing Black Jewish cults in Harlem. There was, for instance, the colorful "Rabbi" Ishi Kaufman who headed the Gospel of the Kingdom Temple. Rabbi Kaufman, unfortunately, met a tragic end. While spraying his Temple with a gasoline spray gun to kill insects, his beard was ignited by a lit cigarette. Although 60 years of age, the Rabbi with his beard ablaze leaped 15 feet to the sidewalk. Firemen fighting the blaze had to physically restrain him from dashing back into the building to retrieve his money. The firemen cleaning up the debris of the totally wrecked Temple discovered $910 in bills which were partially destroyed by the flames. Rabbi Kaufman died soon thereafter.[7]

Then, too, there was the notorious Elder Warren Robinson, who claimed to be the Jewish Messiah, but who in reality headed a scandalous love cult. Robinson employed two sets of agents in his nefarious undertakings. One was composed of handsome well-educated youths who courted the daughters of wealthy Harlem residents, not for marriage, but to lure them into the cult to add to the already vast numbers of the "Messiah's" wives. The second group of agents were older men who adopted the characteristics of Orthodox Jews, e.g., they grew beards and spoke Yiddish. Robinson had hired a Jewish teacher to instruct these men in the Yiddish language and in the mannerisms of the Jews. The purpose of these older agents was to secure money from sympathetic white Jews. The money was then turned over to Robinson.[8] Upon his death on June 18, 1931, during the height of the depression, he was reputed to have amassed a personal fortune in excess of $8,000,000![9] Ford, however, was vastly superior in both character and intellect to these other competing "Rabbis."

Around 1924, Ford organized the *Beth B'nai Abraham* (B.B.A.) congregation of which he served as Rabbi. In this capacity, Ford propagated the following doctrines. All Africans are blood Hebrews. Indeed, Africans have never been Christian but traditionally Hebrew.[10] Even today, fragments of Hebraism persist among American Negroes,[11] although slavery has disturbed the native traditions and exposed them to the hostile influences of the Christian New World. Further, these native African Hebrew traditions can be taught only orally, being "Kabbalistic" in nature, and they contain secret knowledge that the White Jews have long since lost.

About six years after its organization the B.B.A. became acutely embarrassed financially, the members lost hope, and the Rabbi planned to abandon them. All but two of the men left him, complaining that he confined his attention to the women. But meetings continued. Another spurt of membership appeared briefly. There was a final collapse in 1930, and all the property was lost. Then Ford and his common-law wife, who had been his aide in the B.B.A., announced that they were sailing for Africa with no definite plans, except that they hoped to be converted to Islam! Howard Brotz, however, writing as recently as 1964,[12] did not believe that Ford and his common-law wife ever sailed for Africa. As the final collapse of the B.B.A. took place during the depression, passenger fare for Ford and his family would have been extremely difficult to obtain. Instead, Brotz believes, Ford migrated not to Africa, but to Detroit! In Detroit, Ford assumed the name of W. Fard and preached Islam to the lower-class Negroes of that city. And it was precisely in the year 1930, the very year that Ford disappeared from New York, that Elijah Muhammad, the present-day leader of the Black Muslims, claimed to have been taught his beliefs concerning the religion of Islam by the Prophet Wallace D. Fard.[13] But new evidence has recently come to light which would seem to controvert Brotz's attractive thesis. Howard Waitzkin[14] has discovered that a family of Black Jews by the name of Ford actually arrived in Ethiopia from the United States during the early thirties. In Ethiopia this Ford distinguished himself by his musical abilities which is congruent with what we know of Arnold Ford's musical activities in New York City. Recently, a son, Joseph Ford, has returned to America on behalf of a campaign to promote literacy in Ethiopia. Waitzkin is now trying to contact this Joseph Ford to learn if his father is, indeed, Arnold Josiah Ford, and, if so, to ascertain his father's latter-day history in Ethiopia.

Before we close our story on Arnold Josiah Ford, one last item of crucial importance must be noted. Before Ford disappeared from New York, he ordained another West Indian by the name of Wentworth Arthur Matthew as "Rabbi."[15]

WENTWORTH ARTHUR MATTHEW

Wentworth Arthur Matthew is today the Rabbi of New York's most prestigious Black Jewish congregation,[16] the *Commandment Keepers Ethiopian Hebrew Congregation*, located in handsome quarters at 1 West 123rd Street in a pleasant section of Harlem. Matthew is an alert, charming, and keenly intelligent man. Though he claims a D.D. as well as a Ph.D. degree, Matthew is, in reality, a self-educated man. His origins are shrouded in obscurity. He probably prefers this mystification for it adds to his charisma. His most fanciful account of his own origins was given in an interview with *News-Week* magazine.[17] At that time Matthew declared that he was born in Sierra Leone. In his teens he visited Egypt and Palestine. Then he crossed the Atlantic and went first to Haiti before coming to New York. Matthew has never repeated this story again. After careful investigation, the most we can say is that Matthew was probably born on June 23, 1892,[18] in Lagos (now Nigeria), West Africa. At an early age the family left West Africa and moved to St. Kitts, British West Indies. There Matthew spent the formative years of his early life.

In 1913, at age 21, Matthew came to New York City. During his first six years in New York, Matthew did odd jobs throughout the city, including professional boxing and wrestling.[19] But soon Matthew received his "calling" and in 1919 organized his own congregation with a nucleus of nine men (including himself). In those early days the differences between Judaism and Christianity were not quite clear in Matthew's mind. He called himself *Bishop* and *Rabbi* interchangeably. In fact, the first newspaper article that ever reported his activities carried the title: "Negro Sect in Harlem Mixes Jewish and Christian Religions."[20] His congregation was then known as: "The Commandment Keepers: Holy Church of the Living God." Services were advertised for Friday, Saturday, and Sunday with *Bishop* W.A. Matthew presiding. But soon after Ford left New York, Matthew came out squarely as a *Rabbi* and was soon denouncing Christianity as the Black man's worst enemy.

As had Ford before him, Matthew took some Hebrew lessons from an immigrant Jewish teacher to whom he had presented himself as a Jew. Matthew also acquired details of Orthodox Jewish ritual, the names of Jewish institutions, as well as a few phrases of Yiddish. Calling himself "Rabbi," he purchased Jewish ritual materials—an ark, Torah scroll, prayer shawls, and skull caps—and rented rooms on 131st Street in Manhattan where he established his "Synagogue" and "Rabbinical College." He put out a sign that Hebrew was taught, spoke on street corners, practiced healing, and preached the following doctrine:

> During slavery they took away our name, language, religion, and science, as they were the only possessions the slaves had, and they were pumped full of Christianity to make them more docile. The word Negro is a badge of slavery which comes from the Spanish word *niger* meaning black thing. Those who identify themselves with Negroes identify themselves with black things, not human beings. . . . All so-called Negroes are the lost sheep of the House of Israel which can be proved from Scripture, and they all have birthmarks that identify their tribe. Jacob was a black man because he had smooth skin.[21]

With this preachment Matthew effected his unalterable break with Christianity.

At this point we must ask ourselves, why did Matthew and his followers break irrevocably with Christianity and adopt Judaism? To this query we can offer three possible factors.

1) The Tradition of Extreme Protestantism—A most pervasive factor, in our judgment, is to be found in the lure that Judaism has always had for extreme Protestant groups and individuals, particularly in the English-speaking world. In describing the origins of Protestantism, Dr. Will Durant has written:

The influence of Judaism culminated in the Reformation. Theologically this was a reversion to the simpler creed and severer ethic of early Judaic Christianity. Protestant hostility to religious pictures and statuary was, of course, a return to the Semitic antipathy to "graven images"; some Protestant sects observed Saturday as the Sabbath; the rejection of "Mariolatry" and the worship of saints approached the strict monotheism of the Jews; and the new ministers, accepting sex and marriage, resembled the rabbis rather than the Catholic priests. Critics of the Reformers accused them of "Judaizing," [and] called them *semi-Judaei*, "half-Jews."[22]

For some Protestant extremists, however, to be half-Jewish was not enough. No less a Protestant extremist than Lord George Gordon, England's Protestant champion during the second-half of the 18th century, converted to Judaism.[23] In 1848, the American Protestant enthusiast, Warder Cresson, America's first commissioned consul to Jerusalem, also converted to Judaism.[24] Some extreme Protestant sects even claim to be bona fide Jews by virtue of actual descent from Biblical Israel. While these sects have been most popular in the English-speaking world, they have nonetheless crossed all geographic and linguistic frontiers. Thus, for example, in Mexico's last official decennial census (1960), two extreme Protestant sects, the *Casa de Dios* (House of God), and the *Iglesia de Dios* (Church of God) sects, which have branches in the United States as well as in Mexico, registered as *Israelitas* (Jews) because they contended that they were descendants of the Biblical Jacob-Israel.[25] Such sentiments have also been popular among large masses of American Negroes who have been reared and nurtured in this extreme Protestant tradition. Dr. H.M. Brotz points out that:

As early as 1900, Negro preachers were traveling through the Carolinas preaching the doctrine that the so-called Negroes were really the lost sheep of the House of Israel. There is no reason to think, however, that such reflections did not begin much earlier, in fact during slavery itself, when the more imaginative and more daring of the slaves began to wonder about the very human question of who they really were and where they really came from.[26]

To summarize, the Biblical Hebrews and their modern descendants, the Jews, were a group that some American Negroes with their Bible-centered Protestantism could admire and identify with.

2) Jewish Racial Cohesion and Success—Jewish racial cohesion and success in the face of unremitting Christian hostility could not but have made a deep impression on those American Negroes who saw themselves in the same beleaguered position. No less a figure than Booker T. Washington[27] in a famous passage declared:

We have a very bright and striking example in the history of the Jews in this and other countries. There is perhaps no race that has suffered so

much, not as much in America as in some of the countries in Europe.
But these people have clung together. They have a certain amount of
unity, pride, and love of race; and as the years go on, they will be more
and more influential in this country,—a country where they were once
despised, and looked upon with scorn and derision. It is largely because
the Jewish race has had faith in itself. Unless the Negro learns more and
more to imitate the Jew in these matters, to have faith in himself, he cannot expect to have any high degree of success.[28]

One of the early Black Jews told Ruth Landes:

We think the Jews are a great people! They have gone so far in spite of
persecution! They own all the money in the country. Their religion did
that for them, and maybe it will do the same for us. They may help us
to get jobs; Jews should help one another.[29]

Landes added the observation that this man was more honest than the others who
persisted in their claims of inherited Judaism.

In an interview with the *Afro-American* Matthew candidly declared:

The philosophy of the Jews is to acquire wealth and command respect.
It is this religion . . . which impels a Jew to walk several miles from the
Bronx to the Battery to spend a dollar with another Jew. . . . The sooner
the black man is imbued with this philosophy, the sooner will come the
race's forward movement.[30]

3) Political Zionism—In 1917 the British government issued the now-famous
Balfour Declaration pledging British support to the Zionist hope for a Jewish
national home in Palestine. This recognition by one of the world's great powers
of the Jewish People's legitimate national and religious aspirations did not go un-
noticed by America's emerging Black nationalists. Marcus Garvey himself at one
point described his followers as "Zionists."[31] But in comparing Garvey's Black
nationalism with Jewish Zionism, E.D. Cronon notes:

Like their counterparts, most American Negroes would watch with eager
interest the building of a free Zionist state in Africa. . . . But only a very
few would be ready to undertake the hard and thankless pioneer work
needed to create a Black Israel in the African jungle. . . .[32]
However similar the aims and origin of the two movements, Zionism
proved to be by far the stronger and more successful, perhaps because
it managed to secure heavy financial and intellectual support from the
Jews of the world.[33]

In a word, Black "Zionism" was a failure whereas Jewish Zionism was a success.
To those American Negroes who were religio-nationalistically oriented these events
made a deep impression.[34]

ETHIOPIA AND THE FALASHAS

From Ford, too, Matthew learned of the romantic story of the Falashas, the exotic Black Jews of Ethiopia.[35] This discovery of an authentic Black Jewish group in Ethiopia proved to be of incalculable psychological significance to Matthew. Ethiopia too, it may be noted, holds a very special place in the hearts of American Negroes because it is "the wonderful Ethiopia of the Bible." In Matthew's thought, then, it became imperative to find some sort of nexus between himself, Ethiopia, and the Falashas. Italy's invasion of Ethiopia in 1935, which brought that country and its monarch, Haile Selassie, to the attention of the world, provided Matthew with the link that he had been seeking. In 1936 he declared himself to be "official representative of the Falasian order of African Jews, with full authority to practice all rites of the Falasian faith,"[36] and as "Chief Rabbi with credentials from Haile Selassie."[37]

THE COMMANDMENT KEEPERS

Matthew holds services Friday evenings, Saturday mornings, Sunday evenings, and all major Jewish holidays. All the congregants, men, women, and children alike, are neatly dressed, well-behaved, and courteous to visitors. Despite the fact that an Orthodox Hebrew Prayer Book is used, no one, including Matthew, can read Hebrew correctly. When the high point of the service is reached all the male members file up to Matthew and recite publicly their Hebrew names, and the Tribe which Matthew has "assigned" to them upon "examination of their bodies for critical birthmarks."[38] As the Torah is taken out of the Ark, they all line up behind Rabbi Matthew as he leads them around the synagogue singing "Round the Walls of Jerico," or "Marching to Zion." At this time emotions are given free play.[39] But as Brotz shows:

> The ritual, the worship service, and even their basic theological conceptions have never departed very far from that which was familiar to these people from their childhood religious experience. These are the spontaneous sermon, the hymns (Protestant hymns with Old Testament references), the frequent collections of money, testimonials, the enthusiasm . . . the explicit concern with love and friendship, the prayers for authorities (from president to sheriff), and the scaling down of demands in gratitude to God for mere existence or the continued use of one's limbs. . . .[40]

Many of the Commandment Keepers are, like Matthew himself, West Indian in origin. This, perhaps, accounts for the Commandment Keeper's high educational and social aspirations. Living in all of New York's Black ghettoes, yet not part of them, the Black Jews are almost miraculously immune to all the social maladies that ravage the Black ghettoes—crime, drunkenness, juvenile delinquency,[41] sexual license, unemployment.[42] There can be no doubt but that Matthew's fine leadership qualities have contributed significantly to the Black Jews' high level of life. All gainfully employed Commandment Keepers, regardless of age or sex, voluntarily contribute 10% of their salaries to Matthew. Matthew himself lives quite modestly at the Harlem synagogue and uses the moneys collected for the advancement of Commandment Keeper activities. It is no wonder then that Matthew is greatly admired, not only by his own congregants, but by all of New York's Black Jewish congregations who consider him to be their unofficial "Chief Rabbi" to the outside world. This feeling is acknowledged by Matthew and makes him feel both popular and confident. Matthew now sees himself as the herald of a new age of Black Judaism in America. In his interview with the *Afro-American* Matthew declared:

> My mission here is to develop the Hebrew language among my people.
> . . . The colored man was the original Jew. . . . It is my duty to induce
> him to accept his real religion anew. The colored man was a great man
> as long as he could hold on to his true religion. When he lost it, he de-
> veloped an inferiority complex and became the slave of the white man.[43]

In Matthew's eyes, then, the lessons of history are clear. Only Judaism has the spiritual power, once and for all, to put an end to the Black man's spiritual suffering and restore him to what he once was, a free and noble human being.[44]

In 1929, when the Commandment Keepers were first reported on in the press, the membership totaled 100.[45] By 1949, the *Sunday News* reported that there are 3,000 Black Jews in New York City, and that 800 are members of the Commandment Keepers.[46] The most recent estimates place the total number of Black Jews in New York City at 16,000,[47] with 3,000 associated with the Commandment Keepers.[48] Matthew is now ordaining new "Rabbis" to accommodate the ever-increasing growth of the Commandment Keepers.[49] When the time does arrive when America's Black Jews, both genuine and would-be, receive their proper attention from the White Jewish community,[50] it is to be hoped that the proper facilities will be made available to these people for a knowledgeable choice of participation in the worldwide and racially-rich Faith of Israel.

NOTES

1. E. Wolf, "Negro 'Jews': A Social Study," *Jewish Social Service Quarterly* (June, 1933), p. 318.

2. R. Landes, "Negro Jews in Harlem," *Jewish Journal of Sociology* (December, 1967), p. 176.

3. The best biography of Garvey is E.D. Cronon's *Black Moses* (Madison, 1962).

4. The best portrait of Ford has been sketched by Ruth Landes in her excellent study quoted in n. 2 above, from which I have freely drawn. For further details, see S.S. Kobre's "Rabbi Ford," *Reflex* (January, 1929), pp. 25-29.

5. Despite all his disclaimers to the contrary, Garvey was an anti-Semite. See his "The Jews in Palestine," *Black Man* (July-August, 1936), p. 3.

6. Because of increasing rivalry between Ford and Garvey, Garvey had Ford expelled from the U.N.I.A. in 1923.

7. "Head of Black Jewish Cult Dies of Burns," *Afro-American* (August 1, 1936).

8. "New Horrors Bared Among Black Jews," *Chicago Defender* (July 17, 1926).

9. "Founder of Jewish Cult Has Promised to Rise in 60 Days," *Amsterdam News* (July 1, 1931).

10. For a scholarly assessment of Jewish influence on Africa, see J.J. Williams, *Hebrewisms of West Africa* (New York, 1930).

11. That there may be a kernel of truth in this pronunciation is curiously supported by the distinguished American singer Marion Anderson. In her auto biography, *My Lord, What a Morning* (New York, 1956), p. 16, Miss Anderson writes: "Grandfather's religion was of tremendous importance to him. He was not a member of the Baptist Church. In his religion he observed Saturday as his Sabbath, spent the whole day as the Temple, and referred to himself as a Black Jew. The words 'Passover' and 'unleavened bread' I heard first from his lips."

12. H. Brotz, *The Black Jews of Harlem: Negro Nationalism and the Dilemmas of Negro Leadership* (New York, 1964), p. 12.

13. C.E. Lincoln, *The Black Muslims in America* (Boston, 1961), p. 11; E.U. Essien-Udom, *Black Nationalsim: A Search for an Identity in America* (Chicago, 1962), pp. 4-6.

14. H. Waitzkin, "Black Judaism in New York," *Harvard Journal of Negro Affairs*, Vol. 1, No. 3 (1967), pp. 17-18.

15. Landes, p. 186.

16. There are at least 10 Black Jewish congregations in New York City at the present time. See. A. Dobrin, *A History of the Negro Jews in America* (New York, 1965), pp. 50-51.

17. "Black Israel: Harlem Jews Keep the Fast of Yom Kippur," *News-Week* (September 29, 1934), p. 25.

18. L.A. McKethan, "Another Great Moses," *Malach* (March, 1966), p. 1.

19. *News-Week, op. cit.*

20. C. Helm, "Negro Sect in Harlem Mixes Jewish and Christian Religions," *New York Sun* January 29, 1929.

21. H.M. Brotz, "Negro 'Jews' in the United States," *Phylon* (December, 1952), p. 326.

22. W. Durant, *The Story of Civilization*, Vol. VI (New York, 1957), p. 726.

23. G. Lipkind, "Lord George Gordon," *Jewish Encyclpoedia*, Vol. VI (New York, 1904), p. 47.

24. H. Friedenwald, "Warder Cresson," *Jewish Encyclopedia*, Vol. IV (New York, 1903), pp. 354-55.

25. S. B. Liebman, "Mexico," *American Jewish Year Book: 1965* (New York and Philadelphia, 1965), pp. 352-53.

26. H.M. Brotz, *The Black Jews of Harlem*, p. 1.

27. Washington exercised the dominant influence on all shades of Black thought in America during the first three decades of the 20th century. Even the ultra right-wing nationalist Marcus Garvey claimed to have drawn all his inspiration from Washington. See Cronon, p. 16.

28. B.T. Washington, *The Future of the American Negro* (Boston, 1900), pp. 182-83.

29. Landes, p. 186.

30. "Harlem Leader of Black Jews Says Race Deserted Its Faith," *Afro-American* (February 8, 1936).

31. Cronon, p. 199.

32. Cronon, p. 128.

33. Cronon, pp. 199-200.

34. Interestingly enough, a few years after the issuance of the Balfour Declaration, one of the early Black "Rabbis," Mordecai Herman, issued the following declaration of his own: "It is my present belief that Palestine will be free. . . . Our Jewish brothers in America and Europe cannot uphold and protect Palestine; but our black Jewish brothers in India, China, and Abyssinia have a little bit more skill in war and manly heroism that the usual Jewish man. Fast work is being done by the Moorish Zionists to bring together all the black Israelites in one place in Palestine for military reasons and for that purpose funds are being gathered. . . ." See Dobrin, p. 40.

35. For an up-to-date survey of Falasha history and literature, see Prof. Wolf Leslau's excellent *Falasha Anthology* (New Haven, 1951). For the impact of the State of Israel on the

Falashas, see H. Gilroy, "Falasha Jews from Ethiopia Studying in Israel," *New York Times* (March 4, 1955); "Black Jews in Israel," *Our World* (November, 1955), pp. 27-31; "Ethiopia: The Black Jews," *Newsweek* (May 9, 1966), p. 50.

36. *Afro-American, op. cit.*

37. Brotz, *Phylon*, p. 355. Sherry Abel's assertion in her article "Negro Jews," *Universal Jewish Encyclopedia*, Vol. 8 (New York, 1942), p. 145, that Matthew was "ordained by the chief rabbi of the Ethiopian Falashas as well as by the Ethiopian National Church," is pure fiction.

38. Brotz, *Phylon*, p. 330. Matthew has shown this writer the spot where his sixth finger was cut off at birth indicating that he was of the Tribe of Reuben!

39. "Although enthusiasm exists in their worship service, it is far less than the practices prevailing in the Holiness Churches. The Black Jews abstain from possessions, swooning, speaking in tongues, and excessive screaming, all of which Matthew regards as 'niggeritions.' " See Brotz, *Phylon*, p. 336.

40. Brotz, *Phylon*, pp. 329-30.

41. "A notable thing about our sect is that none of our children has ever been arrested for theft or vagrancy." See J. H. Hogans, "Ethiopian Jews to Mark Advent of the New Year," *New York Age* (September 29, 1951).

42. "God and business is one of the principles of our teachings; God first, business next, law and order is the general password." See J.A. Diaz, "Black Jews in U.S.A.—Synagogue Increasing," *Social Whirl* (April 25, 1955), pp. 18-19.

43. *Afro-American, op. cit.*

44. There seems to be some evidence that views curiously akin to Matthew's are being taken up by others within the larger Negro community. On the popular Negro radio program, *Night Call,* the Rev. Albert B. Cleage, a radical Black minister from Detroit discussed the possibility "of whether it might not be more practical for Blacks to identify with Judaism." He said that Black people, in taking Christianity back to its original roots in Judaism and taking from it the distortions the Apostle Paul tried to put in when he tried to take Judaism to the White Gentiles, would be well advised to incorporate into Black churches many of the basic elements of Judaism. He stated that in the coming year he planned to experiment in his church with Jewish holidays that are meaningful to Blacks, such as Israel's escape from Bondage. See "Night Call," *Impact* (January, 1969), p. 17.

45. Helm, *op. cit.*

46. "Brothers Under the Skin," *Sunday News* (August 7, 1949).

47. B.G. Reid, "New York's Black Jews Estimated at 16,000," *New York Courier* (August 9, 1969).

48. G. Simor, "Black Jews of Harlem," *Sepia* (April, 1968), p. 29.

49. Thus, for example, Matthew ordained Matthew E. Stephen as a "Rabbi" in an impressive ceremony on October 8, 1955. See J.H. Hogans, "Ethiopian Hebrews Mark End of Holiday Season," *New York Age Defender* (October 22, 1955).

50. Good work in this direction is already under way with the Falashas of Ethiopia. See n. 35. Unlike the Falashas, however, most of America's Black Jews have no previous Jewish history and cannot, therefore, enter Judaism without formal conversion; a step which most Black Jews vigorously oppose claiming that they are Jews already. A small group, however, has accepted formal conversion. Interestingly enough, some of these bona fide converts are now Lubavitcher Hasidim! See "Black Jews Helped to Integrate," *Jewish Chronicle* (July 18, 1969). See also the pertinent remarks of Abraham Abramson. Chaim Bibbins, and Robert Coleman, three recent Black converts to Orthodox Judaism—"A Reader Speaks Out About Black Jews," *Jewish Press* (July 3, 1970); "Black Jew Says Israel Should Reject 'Other' Black Jews," *Jewish Press* (July 10, 1970); "Why There Are No Orthodox Black Rabbis," *Jewish Press* (July 24, 1970).

A BLACK RABBI
LOOKS TO ISRAEL

FRANK ROSS

Eleven years after he formed a congregation from a group of black families he claims to have converted to Judaism in Philadelphia and led them to the peace of the South Jersey pine country, Abel Respes is fighting to hold his flock together.

He no longer harbors the illusion that he can lead them to Israel from the neat white synagogue and cluster of cottages they built in this Atlantic County community. But he says he has not changed his conviction that blacks eventually will be welcomed there as Jews.

He concentrates instead, he says, on trying to win more acceptance among white Jews of nearby communities—there are few in this rural area—in the hope that some may help him to organize an interracial congregation.

He sees in interracial worship the ultimate answer to the problem of racial tension, but he has a more immediate and practical goal, the salvation of the congregation, which now consists of about 50 men, women and children.

It is difficult to recruit more black converts, he says, because "my people simply don't appear to be ready for conversion, although I believe they would be more inclined if some white Jews would accept the interracial idea."

A VISIT TO ISRAEL

About four years ago, Rabbi Respes and key members of his congregation visited Israel to explore the possibility of returning later with the entire congregation, and with enough money so that they would not become burdens on the new nation.

Rabbi Respes says that as a member of the Synagogue Council of America's

Committee on Black Jews in America, he is hoping to promote his plan for an interracial congregation in the shore communities of Atlantic County, and other nearby
communities such as Hammonton in Atlantic County and Vineland in Cumber-
land County.

He was raised in North Philadelphia, and although his parents were practicing
Jews, he shunned worship and was involved in what he called "a fair share of drinking and gambling and the like" after he dropped out of Central High School.

A tall man who moves with the grace of an athlete and who is the father of 14
children, he says a "miraculous escape from death" and a vivid dream led him to
not only adopt his ancestral religion, but to decide to become a leader.

"I know it sounds like something out of fiction, but I was engulfed by flames
when a bolt of lightning struck the ground near me and was not at all burned, and
it got me to wondering."

"I HEARD A VOICE"

It was not long after that, still marveling over his escape, when he said he dreamed
that a black Bible had been placed in his hands, "and I heard a voice, imploring me
to seek God."

For years after that, he prayed and fasted and spent hours studying Hebrew and
the sacred Torah.

In 1951, he began to assemble the families who had heeded his call in the ghetto
to form a congregation and escape the urban despair. One of the bitter experiences
then was the anti-Semitism among blacks directed at his converts, he recalls.

He recalls that they were encouraged to believe they would be welcomed "in
the mainstream of life in Israel, even to marriage," principally because of the cordial
reception they experienced.

But a later migration to Israel by a group of professed black Jews from Chicago
created tensions that still exist, and Rabbi Respes can see no signs of encouragement.

The 53-year-old rabbi, who says he was born a Jew, is descended from the
Sephardics of Spain and Portugal who were driven to Africa in the 15th century.
He says he "bears no resentment to Israel because I understand the situation."

Israel, he asserts, "is still in its infancy and liberalism must come from within
the ruling Orthodox Jews, to the point where Israel will make room for all Jews
and all forms of Judaic worship."

Rabbi Respes, who is self-taught, is fluent in Hebrew and a busy lecturer throughout the East on black Judaism for the United States Jewish Welfare Board. But like
all black Jews, he says, he cannot "prove my Jewishness" because he cannot produce
a certificate of circumcision from a "mohel," the man who performs the operation.

This is coupled, he points out, with the problem of the black Jews' inability to
produce a history of their Jewishness.

Rabbi Stanley Math, spiritual leader of the Chelsea Congregation in Atlantic City and president of the South Jersey Board of Rabbis, says Rabbi Respes "is not considered a fully ordained rabbi in the sense of training that all of us have had in the divinity school."

But Rabbi Math says rabbis of the area are sympathetic with Rabbi Respes's problems and are impressed by his driving will and sincerity.

"He has an excellent knowledge of Judaism and he has done a good job with his congregation," he says.

It was not until 11 years later when the group of 15 families, their resources pooled, moved to Elwood where they found jobs as clerks, factory workers and farmhands. They financed and built their cottages and synagogue as a single community effort and Rabbi Respes conducted services and taught in their Bible school too.

Some have since left the area, but a tight core remains, devoted to the tall man they have come to regard as a black Moses.

"I realize now that I have been somewhat aloof from the blacks to whom I once tried to preach," he says candidly, "even though I did not want to be. It is just that what I advocate does not attract many of them."

BLACKS AND CONVERSION TO JUDAISM

HAROLD GOLDFARB

There are circles in the Jewish community which claim that the Board of Rabbis has flatly refused to accept blacks who assert that they are Jews as authentic Jews. This charge not only distorts the facts, but implies the existence of racism and prejudice on the part of rabbis.

It is Jewish law, *Halachah*, which determines Jewish status. It is not the personal view of any rabbi or layman that determines it. And the truth is that there *are* black whom the rabbis recognize as authentic Jews, because they fulfill the Halachic requirements of authenticity.

But where there is reason to question an individual's status as a Jew, he must submit proof of his Jewish legitmacy or, if such proof is lacking, undergo the conversion procedure required by *Halachah*, if he wishes to be recognized as a Jew. This is the law for everyone, whether he be black or white, yellow or red. There is no race test in Judaism.

Every convert enjoys the prerogatives and, of course, the responsibilities of Judaism in the same was as a Jew who can trace his biological ancestry to Abraham. In fact, as is well known, the convert always is referred to as so-and-so ben Abraham. Judaism makes it very clear that a convert is an authentic Jew in the same way that Abraham's son, Isaac, was an authentic Jew.

An important legal principle of Jewish law, as it is of every system of law, is the doctrine of "presumption." The historical Jewish community since time immemorial has consisted of whites. This is fact. This creates the presumption, therefore, that a white who claims to be Jewish is, in fact, a Jew unless there is reason to doubt his assertion. In such a situation, being white does not exempt him from submitting proof of his Jewishness and, if required, of undergoing conversion, should he wish to regularize his status.

In the case of blacks, there is no such general presumption. This, too, is a fact of history; it is not discrimination or racism. It is also a fact of history that no Chinese is presumed to be Jewish; neither is an American Indian nor a Polynesian. Even though some Japanese have converted to Judaism, a Japanese claiming to be Jewish cannot be presumed to be one.

As a matter of fact, there is indeed one community of black Jews which is presumed to be legitimately Jewish. This is the B'nai Yisrael community of Cochin-China. Their long and well-documented history led the rabbinate of Israel to accept them as Jews, the only exceptions being some instances resulting from irregularities in divorce procedure which required special Halachic attention.

On the other hand, the Falashas of Ethiopia, as well as other tribes in that country, are not presumed to be Jewish. Although there is historical evidence that more than 2000 years ago, the Falashas were in contact with the main body of Jews, their practices and beliefs are very different from those which developed among the Jews in later Talmudic times. Thus their claim to being Jewish and to being included automatically in the family of Jewry is disallowed. The Karaites and Samaritans, sizable white communities in Israel today and related historically to the Jewish people, also are not accepted as Jews. But anyone within all the above groups, of course, can be converted to Judaism.

On occasion, a group, a congregation or a combination of groups, whether white or black, seeks mass recognition as Jews. Such was the case with an Italian group in Israel some years ago. Another instance recently came to world attention when a group of blacks from Chicago went to Liberia, then to Israel, and desired mass recognition of its entire membership. In both situations the rabbinate of Israel required each individual to submit proof or undergo conversion.

History records one instance of mass conversion to Judaism—the Idumaeans, a tribe descended from the Edomites. It happened in the Second Century BCE when John Hyrcanus, the Hasmonean King of Judea, imposed it. The rabbis of the Mishnah viewed this event as the source of later misfortune for the Jewish people, for from this group came the wicked King Herod, who brought untold misery to Judea just before the beginning of the Christian era. Ever since, mass conversion has been banned by the *Halachah.*

Jews who criticize rabbinic refusal to change the rules are not doing a service either to the blacks who sincerely desire to be included in the household of Israel, or to the Jewish people as a whole. Whether we like it or not, we are a transnational people with responsibilities to all people, not solely to Jews in our own community or in the United States. We have responsibilities to Jews who dwell in countries of oppression, to the Jews in Israel, to Jews of differing religious leanings, even to Jews claiming no religion.

It is wise and prudent that in this troubled and changing era, the age-old rules for establishing Jewish authenticity be retained. This is especially so today, because by observing the rules we prevent barring any individual from joining the people of Israel, if he is genuinely drawn to it.

Blacks, and their white sympathizers who advocate modifying the rules, do not realize the heartbreaking and tragic consequences of such an action by a local segment of the Jewish community. If the Jewish authenticity of blacks accepted as Jews under such modified standards is to be questioned, whether in Israel, in other parts of the world or in our own community, the shock to these converts could thrust them into a state of psychological, spiritual and social insecurity as to be disastrous to the individual blacks and their children.

This also could be shattering to the unity and well-being of the Jewish community as a whole. What may now seem to be a galling (in some cases) procedure that is time-consuming, rigorous and even unnecessary, ultimately will prove to be the very strength by which blacks can assume their full and authentic Jewish identity which rabbis wish them to possess.

The rabbinate is well aware that there are many blacks who, for whatever reason are close to Judaism spiritually and religiously and who feel part of the Jewish people even though their formal status as Jews has not been established according to the requirements of Jewish law. If such blacks are sincere, they will not carp when the religious leaders of Judaism, desiring to maintain the character of the Jewish people and its tradition, require of them the same religious procedure which is applied to *all* would-be Jews, namely, proof of being a Jew or undergoing religious conversion.

We know, to be realistic, that there are many organized groups of black people who maintain that they are Jews. The rabbinate believes that the Jewish community should establish lines of communication with them and assist them in their educational efforts. Therefore, the Board of Rabbis supports the Federation of Jewish Agencies and its granting of aid, financial and otherwise, to these groups which wish to undertake programs of religious activity and education as well as of cultural expression and social service in the spirit of Jewish tradition.

Such aid and communication is not to be taken as recognition of the Jewish authenticity of these groups, but as an act of friendship in the expectation that with closer communication and association with the historical Jewish community, the blacks who love Judaism will be absorbed gradually into the Jewish group by Halachic means.

To achieve this goal, the members of black synagogues, groups and clubs eventually should submit to one of the two criteria which Jewish tradition demands: either proof of being Jewish or accepting the traditional rite of conversion.

That will impose hardships and responsibilities and touch deep sensibilities, but it is the price exacted by life for the privilege of being a Jew and bearing witness to God. To all such genuine devotees of our faith, the rabbinate will extend a heart and cordial welcome.

BLACK AND JEWISH-
AND UNACCEPTED

ROBERT T. COLEMAN

For more than sixty years there have been organized groups of blacks who call themselves Jews. These groups, which represent the largest number of those identified as black Jews, for the most part have synagogues and a sense of Jewish history quite different from that of the larger Jewish community. While not all of these groups stem from the same origins, and while they vary in their degree of both Jewish knowledge and practice, all have the following in common: the belief that the patriarchs Abraham, Isaac and Jacob were black, that black Jews are their descendants, and that white Jews came to Judaism through conversion after the blacks were dispersed from the Holy Land.

The rigidity of this position on the part of black Jews is the basic reason for their rejection of any suggestion that *halakhah* does not recognize them as Jews. They claim that *halakhah*, in its present form, was transmitted by white Jews to their descendants; and could not possibly have included blacks, since no black Jews were involved in the process of developing the present "code of Jewish law." Most of these black Jewish groups see *halakhah* as a device used to exclude them from their "rightful heritage" by whites.

This belief has caused great anguish for those Rabbis who, while wishing to strengthen ties with black Jews have an unalterable fidelity to the *halakhah*. There are, however, those Jews who feel that, while the Jewish status of these groups may be "doubtful," they should nevertheless be given the benefit of the social and educational services which exist in the Jewish community. A very small number of black Jews from this "doubtful" category, who have been exposed to such services have abandoned their claim of being descendants of the "original Jews"—and have undergone conversions and joined white synagogues.

EXPERIENCING REJECTION AFTER CONVERSION

Most black converts, however, come from Christian backgrounds; or background where a father or grandfather was Jewish. In the main, these converts do not join black synagogues and have little or no interaction with those black Jews who have not been formally converted. Though the largest number of black Jewish converts (perhaps some 300-500 nationally) tend to undergo conversions performed by Orthodox Rabbis, there is evidence that in recent years some blacks have undergone Conservative and Reform conversions, and, in some instances, there have bee those who have been converted by Orthodox Rabbis, and later chose Reform or Conservative synagogue affiliation.

Those converts who are married prior to their conversions, and whose spouses and children also undergo the conversion process, experience little difficulty with becoming integrated into the synagogue life of white synagogues. For the unmarried convert seeking to find his or her way, life can be much more difficult, as the is a great deal of resistance on the part of white Jewish families to "mixed" dating and marriage.

When white Jewish youngsters reject the prejudices of their parents in this area and stress the "Jewishness" of the black as being the most important aspect in determining whether or not they would date or marry such a person, life can be mad equally miserable for them. An example that comes to mind is that of an observan black Jewish medical student who married an observant white Jewess against the wishes of the white parents. As a result, the white partner has been cut off from the parents and the parents have refused to recognize the two grandchildren which resulted from the marriage as their own.

On occasion I have been asked by Rabbis to interview prospective black conver as some Rabbis feel that the candidate may raise questions with me as a black Jew which they may not feel comfortable discussing with the Rabbis themselves. I inform all of the candidates of the potential problems that may arise, including that of prejudice. Most find it impossible to believe that Jews would still reject them o the basis of skin color, after conversion. Not a few have called or written me after conversion to inform me of problems ranging from a broken engagement because parents of the white partner objected, to whispers from some of their co-religionis in schule about their being a *"swartza."*

EXPOSING THE RACISM OF CO-RELIGIONISTS

There are also those who call to say that while they wished to be converted, they could not "afford the conversion fee." One black family of three paid $500. in order to be converted. (It must be pointed out here that I cannot attribute the charging of fees to skin color as it may well be that white converts have similar ex periences—I merely raise the issue because it presents still another problem for the sincere black who may not be "financially able" to undertake conversion.) I must also hasten to add that while the charging of fees is a common problem for blacks, I have, during the past three years, worked with Rabbis who never accepted any fees for the services rendered, including a number of pre-conversion interviews and several hours of instruction.

There is also the problem of the attitude of some *Jewish agencies* in dealing with Black Jews. Only a few weeks ago a black Jew, who went to Federation Employment and Guidance for assistance in obtaining employment, was told by the interviewer that it was "too bad he didn't know Sammy Davis, Jr." because "Sammy might be able to get him a job."

Another more recent situation is that of four black Jewish youngsters being placed in black Christian foster homes by the Jewish Child Care Association. When I phoned the agency to inquire as to the reasons these black children (whose Jewish status could not possibly be questioned, since a rather well-known Rabbi had performed the conversions and issued "certificates" to that effect) were placed in non-Jewish foster homes, I was told by a supervisor that children are placed on the basis of skin color and that in the absence of the availability of black-Jewish homes, non-Jewish black homes were sought. When I asked why white Jewish homes were not sought, I was told it would be "psychologically bad for the children."

These are the kinds of situations that make it difficult for one to argue with that group of black Jews who reject conversion and shout "racism" when they are not accepted by the Jewish community, for they readily point out that even those who have complied with Jewish law are experiencing the worst kind of racism at the hands of their white co-religionists.

THE PRICE OF MISINFORMATION

A few Jewish agencies have tried from time to time to deal with the question of black Jews, with little or no success, for numerous reasons. First, there is the problem of the lack of knowledge of the philosophical and historical perspectives of that group which represents the largest number of black Jews—those who reject conversion. This has led such agencies to formulate policies, which leave large segments of the Jewish community open to charges of racism where race may not be a factor.

An example of this was seen repeatedly during the existence of a N.Y. based organization of "multi-racial" Jews which "vouched" for the Jewishness of black Jewish youngsters applying for admission to *Yeshivot*. When the *Yeshivah* investigated their backgrounds, they often found that the youngsters did not meet the *halakhic* standards required by the *Yeshivah* to classify them as Jews. When the children were not admitted, or the parents were told the children in question would have to undergo conversions, the *Yeshivah* administrators were charged with racism.

Another problem has been the tendency on the part of Jewish agencies to lump the *Gerim*, and those groups whose historical and philosophical approach to Juda-

ism is quite different, into one group. This serves to emphasize that skin color and
not Jewish religious status is the prime consideration when dealing with blacks.
Many black *Gerim* complain that this is discriminatory and reflects poorly on both
their Jewish status and outlook, which is the same as that of their white co-religioni.

A CALL FOR GUIDANCE

Of course, there are no easy answers to any of the problems raised—though the
have been serious attempts to resolve such issues. The recent Consultation with
Black Jewish Leaders, sponsored by the Synagogue Council of America, was one
such effort. It brought together for the first time black Jewish leaders of varying
religious and historical perspectives together with the representatives of a national
religious body. The fact that they came together at all is in itself an accomplish-
ment. The Consultation served to provide a forum for discussing differences as wel
as emphasizing areas of agreement between the various groups represented.

It is always a source of bewilderment to me that we have been provided with
guidelines by Rabbinic authorities as to the status of the Falashas in Ethiopia and
the Black Jews of India, but except for a few statements here and there, nothing
definitive has been written by Rabbinic authorities on America's more than 8,000
blacks who call themselves Jews. Perhaps that guidance is what is sorely needed by
white Jews, black converts and those blacks who reject any idea that conversion
is necessary.

A rabbinic statement on what the Jewish tradition says about racism would
also be in order.

6

JEWISH WOMEN

A number of articles have described the Jewish woman's role in family affairs, especially the differences between her previous role and her current role. Liberman, for instance, noted these differences and referred to the former role as the "Yiddishe Mamme" and the current role as the "Jewish mother."[1] Blau's ever-popular "In Defense of the Jewish Mother."[2] was published in 1967, but according to Liberman's terminology, was more accurately defending the Yiddishe Mamme than the Jewish mother. Timberg's 1971 article, "Are Jewish Women Oppressed?", presented both sides of the question she posed.[3]

Despite the traditional importance played by Jewish women in economic areas, there has been "no serious analysis of the contributions of women."[4] Baum's article, which presented some data, is one of the few contributions in this area. Tonner's recent book presents case histories of individual Jewish women who have succeeded in the professional area.[5]

A number of articles have appeared discussing the current religious status of Jewish women, among them, Lipman's "Women's Lib and Jewish Tradition" (1971-1972)[6] and Hyman's "The Other Half: Women in the Jewish Tradition" (1972).[7] In addition comments and articles on the status of Jewish women have appeared in *The Jewish Spectator*.[8] There have also appeared articles in *Sh'ma*, usually in the form of ongoing debates.[9] *Hadassah Magazine* has had several articles, including "Women of Valor" by Dworkin in 1973, "Equality in Judaism" by Greenberg and Greenberg in 1973, and "Feminism: Is It Good for the Jews?" by Greenberg in 1976.[10] The Greenbergs conclude that a halakhic solution is available to the Jewish woman's situation and that "the failure to use this halakhic solution clearly shows that there are political rather than religious obstacles to women's rights involved and that pressures for change are needed."[11] Sigal, in a 1974 article, also concluded that halakhah allows women to be counted in a minyan.[12] Singer, in one of the best statements to date, also agrees with this position and concludes, "In view of ⌊the⌋ abundance of citations supportive of woman's status, rights and protection in the literature and traditions of our people, it is all the more disappointing that the halakhah has not yet fully translated these fine epousals and aspirations into law."[13]

Recent changes in the status of women in Judaism have been discussed in an article in *Network*[14] as well as in Dworkin's article.[15] "Young Women Challenging Their '2d-Class Status' in Judaism"[16] noted that people who are committed to Orthodoxy are increasingly challenging the Orthodox position toward women from within rather than leaving Orthodoxy and is illustrative of a growing number of reports concerning all branches of Judaism. In addition to a growing number of articles, recent years have seen a growing number of journals devoting entire special issues to Jewish women. In 1973, for instance, *Response*[17] devoted an issue to the Jewish woman. More generally oriented publications such as *Women's League Outlook* (a publication of the Women's League for Conservative Judaism)[18] and *Keeping Posted* (a publication of the Union of American Hebrew Congregations, a Reform organization)[19] have also devoted much space to articles on Jewish women. Popularly oriented magazines such as *Ms.* have also had articles specifically on Jewish women.[20] Books have also begun to appear on Jewish women, including *The Jewish Woman in America*,[21] *Judaism and the New Woman*, and *The Jewish Woman: New Perspectives*.[22]

In addition to some of the articles mentioned above that have reported on the progress of liberation for Jewish women, a number of others have also reported on specific issues that have affected the position of women in Judaism in recent years —the ordination by the Reform movement of the first female rabbi in the United States, the change by the Conservative movement to allow women to be counted in a minyan, and the opposition by the Orthodox movement to both of these events, as well as their opposition to the equal rights amendment. The training and ordination of Sally Priesand as the first female rabbi in the United States has been discussed in several articles.[23] Several of these articles have observed the Reconstructionist movement's ordination of a female rabbi [Sandy E. Sasso] in its graduating class of 1974,[24] as well as noting that "inspired by their [Priesand and Sasso examples, other young women are studying to become rabbis."[25] Several articles have discussed the nine to four vote of the Committee on Jewish Law of the Rabbinical Assembly (the Conservative rabbinical body) that "men and women are to be equally included in the count of a required quorum for Jewish public worship."[26] However, it has also been noted that the vote was not binding on all Conservative congregations but rather left the decision to the individual rabbi.[27] In a 1973 article, Spiegel noted that many Orthodox rabbis responded to the Conservative movement's minyan action as "a move of desperation to attract new worshippers" and asserted that there was "no justification for the continued existence of the Conservative movement."[28] Orthodox leaders have opposed the proposed constitutional amendment guaranteeing equal rights to women as a threat to the Orthodox practice of segregating males and females in synagogues and parochial schools and as a threat to morality in the United States.[29] Blau has noted the negative reactions of the Reform and Conservative movements to Orthodoxy's opposition to the constitutional amendment, particularly the implication by Orthodoxy that "those of us who permit mixed seating are catering to 'immorality.' "[30] A few articles have also appeared by "modern" Orthodox who suggest the need for a reexamination of Orthodoxy's position regarding women. Rabbi Saul Berman, a major example, has stated that "relegating the excited voices to a minority does not mean that we can safely, or ought morally and religiously, simply ignore them. Minorities of one generation have a strange way of becoming the majorities of the next. Fingers pointing out manifest injustices seem often to become transformed into fists banging through walls of resistance to rectification."[31] Of all the groups discussed in this book, Jewish women are undoubtedly receiving the most attention today—even though there still is a dearth of empirical research— and any list of articles is bound to be outdated by the time it is published.

The selections in this section describe Jewish women. First is Lipman's article, which suggests that the Jewish religious tradition provides "many foundation-stones of the movement for women's equality."[32] Following is an article by Brin, which, while questioning how far this equality has been realized, notes the potential for this equalization.[33] Because of the date of its publication (1968), it also illustrates the changes that have occurred since that time. Lavender's article presents empirical data on the prospects for Jewish women in cultural as well as religious areas.[34] The final article by Greenberg indicates the future of the Jewish women's liberation movement and questions its effects on the Jewish community.[35]

NOTES

1. Judith A. Liberman, "Demise of the 'Jewish Mother,' " *Jewish Life* 39 (April 1972): 34-37.

2. Zena Smith Blau, "In Defense of the Jewish Mother," *Midstream* 13 (February 1967): pp. 42-49.

3. Judy Timberg, "Are Jewish Women Oppressed?" *The Jewish Radical* (Spring 1971).

4. Charlotte Baum, "What Made Yetta Work: The Economic Role of Eastern European

Jewish Women in the Family," *Response* 18 (Summer 1973): 32-38. Also see Maxine S. Seller, "Beyond the Stereotype: A New Look at the Immigrant Woman, 1880-1924," *Journal of Ethn Studies* 3 (Spring 1975): 59-70.

5. Leslie Tonner, *Nothing But the Best* (New York: Coward, McCann & Geoghegan, 1975 Also see two articles by Tonner: "What Makes Her So Super Successful," *New Woman* (September-October 1975): 33-36, 40; and "The Truth About Being a Jewish Princess," *Cosmopolitan* (September 1976): 212, 226-227, 233.

6. Eugene J. Lipman, "Women's Lib and Jewish Tradition," *Jewish Heritage* 13 (Winter 1971-1972): 21-23.

7. Paula E. Hyman, "The Other Half: Women in the Jewish Tradition," *Conservative Judaism* 26 (Summer 1972): 14-21. Also see articles by Judith Hauptman and David M. Feldman in this issue.

8. See, for example, the following articles by Trude Weiss-Rosmarin, all in *The Jewish Spectator:* "The Unfreedom of Jewish Women" (October 1970); "Women's Liberation" (March 1973); "Female Consciousness-Raising" (September 1973); and "Women in Conservative Synagogues" (October 1973).

9. The articles in *Sh'ma,* a journal that emphasizes issues and controversies in the Jewish community, have been numerous and controversial. See, for example, Phillip Sigal, "Women in a Minyan: But Law Says Yes," and David M. Feldman, "Women in a Minyan: No Is Still No," both in number 4/67 (February 8, 1974); and Phillip Sigal, "Jewish Law Changes with Jewish Life," number 4/70 (March 22, 1974): 78-80. Also see articles entitled "Being Female, Jewish, and Observant," "Childbirth, A Covenantal Experience," "When a Jewish Woman Comes of Age," and "Birth Rituals and Jewish Daughters," all of which appeared in number 6/111 (April 2, 1976).

10. Susan Dworkin, "Women of Valor," *Hadassah Magazine* 54 (April 1973): 14-15, 37; Blu Greenberg and Irving Greenberg, "Equality in Judaism," *Hadassah Magazine* 56 (December 1973): 14-15, 36-38; and Blu Greenberg, "Feminism: Is It Good for the Jews?" *Hadassah Magazine* 57 (April 1976): 10-11, 30-34. Also see Elaine Starkman, "Woman in the Pulpit," *Hadassah Magazine* 56 (December 1973): 15, 39. This latter article discusses Rabbi Sally Priesand, Rabbi Sandy Eisenberg Sasso, and the scheduled ordination in 1975 of Michal Seserman as the third American female rabbi.

11. Greenberg and Greenberg, "Equality in Judaism."

12. Phillip Sigal, "Women in a Prayer Quorum," *Judaism* 23 (Spring 1974): 174-182.

13. Sholom Singer, "The Jewish Woman and Her Heritage," *Reconstructionist* 40 (October 1974): 17.

14. "450 Women Attend National Jewish Women's Conference," *Network,* March 7, 1973, pp. 2-3.

15. Dworkin, "Women of Valor."

16. Enid Nemy, "Young Women Challenging Their '2d-Class Status' in Judaism," *New Yor Times*, June 12, 1973, p. 43.

17. *Response*, no. 18 (Summer 1973), Box 1496, Waltham, Massachusetts 02154.

18. *Outlook* 46 (Winter 1975). This issue includes Lynne E. Heller's "A Memoir of the Founding Mothers" and Sylvia G.L. Dannett's "The 'Brilliant Jewess.'" It is published by the Women's League for Conservative Judaism, 48 East 74th Street, New York, N.Y. 10021.

19. *Keeping Posted* 17 (April 1972). This entire issue is devoted to Jewish women and can be obtained from Keeping Posted, 838 Fifth Avenue, New York, N.Y. 10021.

20. Paula Hyman, "Jewish Theology: What's in It for—and Against—Us"; Audrey Gellis, "The View from the Back of the Shul"; and Bracha Sacks, "Why I Choose Orthodoxy" are all found under the general title of "Is It Kosher to Be Feminist?" in *Ms.* 8 (July 1974): 76-83 104-110.

21. Charlotte Baum, Paula Hyman and Sonya Michel, *The Jewish Woman* (New York: Dial Press, 1976).

22. Rabbi Sally Priesand, *Judaism and the New Woman* (New York: Behrman House, 1975); and Elizabeth Koltun, ed., *The Jewish Woman: New Perspectives* (New York: Schocken, 1976).

23. See, for example, Starkman, "Woman in the Pulpit"; Terence Shea, "Two Seek End to Age-Old Sex Barriers in Ministry," *National Observer,* March 30, 1970, p. 9; Edward B. Fiske, "Ordain Them But with Heads Covered," *New York Times*, April 23, 1972, p. 16; and Eleanor Blau, "1st Woman Rabbi in U.S. Ordained," *New York Times*, June 4, 1972, p. 76.

24. See, for example, Starkman, "Woman in the Pulpit," and George Dugan, "Female Rabbinical Student Asks Increased 'Femininity' in Judaism," *New York Times,* May 7, 1972, p. 37.

25. Starkman, "Woman in the Pulpit," p. 15.

26. Irving Spiegel, "Conservative Jews Vote for Women in Minyan," *New York Times*, September 11, 1973, p. 1.

27. Irving Spiegel, "Orthodox Rabbis Call Easing of Minyan Rules 'Desperation,' " *New York Times*, September 12, 1973, p. 50; and Eleanor Blau, "The 10th Man Can Be a She," *New York Times*, September 16, 1973, p. E7. Spiegel quotes the executive vice-president of the conservative Rabbinical Council that most rabbis would voluntarily follow the liberalized rules.

28. Spiegel, "Orthodox Rabbis," p. 50.

29. Eleanor Blau, "Rabbis See Women's Rights Measure as Threatening Orthodox Practices," *New York Times*, April 4, 1972, p. 12.

30. Eleanor Blau, "Rabbis Assail Orthodox Stand Against Equal-Rights Measure," *New York Times*, April 4, 1972, p. 39.

31. Saul Berman, "The Status of Women in Halakhic Judaism," *Tradition: A Journal of Orthodox Thought* 14 (Fall 1973): 5-28.

32. Lipman, "Women's Lib and Jewish Tradition."

33. Ruth F. Brin, "Can a Woman Be a Jew?" *Reconstructionist* 34 (October 1968): 7-14.

34. Abraham D. Lavender, "Jewish College Females: Future Leaders of the Jewish Community?" *The Journal of Ethnic Studies* 5 (Summer 1977): 81-90.

35. Greenberg, "Feminism: Is It Good for the Jews?," pp. 10-11, 30-34. For further discussion of work being done to change the status of Jewish women (as well as an extensive bibliography of articles), see Richard Siegel, Michael Strassfeld, and Sharon Strassfeld, *The Jewish Catalog* (Philadelphia: Jewish Publication Society of America, 1973), pp. 252-260. Although now outdated, their "A Guide to Jewish Women's Activities" is still beneficial.

WOMEN'S LIB AND
JEWISH TRADITION

EUGENE J. LIPMAN

A new and rapidly-expanding feminist movement is upon us. Women are organizing in a wide variety of institutions to demand full equality with men in our society. This movement addresses itself to men as the deliberate maintainers of an unequal and oppressive legal, social, sexual and economic system; and to women as the too-passive victims and accomplices in that system.

A broad spectrum of demands is being expressed and worked at, ranging from free abortions for women desiring them to abolition of all laws (still extant in some jurisdictions) giving a husband rights over property owned by his wife.

What it regards as the sexual exploitation of women in everything from comic books to *Playboy* magazine is being attacked by the women's liberation movement. The addition of gender as a criterion in all civil rights, civil liberties, and equality legislation is demanded of the Congress and state legislatures. A serious new feminist movement is on the rise, and response is growing among women of all ages, from teenagers to grandmothers.

The status and role of women have been a concern of Halakhah (Jewish law) since the Biblical era. Though both Torah law and rabbinic law were written by men to regulate a society dominated by men, there are many surprisingly egalitarian concepts and statutes in Halakah.

Take, for example, the daughters of Zelophehad (Numbers 27). Their father died in the wilderness; they had no brother. They demanded a full family parcel in the allocation of the to-be-conquered Land of Israel. Moses "consulted the Lord," and the answer was clear: "You shall give them a hereditary holding among their father's kinsmen; transfer their father's share to them. . . . If a man dies without leaving a son, you shall transfer his property to his daughter" (27:7-8).

Additional evidence of early attempts within Jewish law to make women the equal of men appears in The Mishnah. Here are a few examples, together with the appropriate commentaries.[1]

The Mishnah is of course the first part of the Talmud. It is a compilation of statutes and decisions reached by Jewish scholars between the third century B.C.E. and the end of the second century of the Common Era. It is divided topically into six sections or Orders (*Sedarim*), the third of which is devoted to *Nashim* (women).

Jewish law concentrated on the status and role of married women. The reason is simple: marriage was considered to be the natural state for both men and women. The single adult was virtually unknown. Responsibility for seeing to it that young people were enabled to marry was vested in the community if parents were dead or unable to function. There can be no doubt about the fact that the head of the family, according to Halakhah, was the man. What is remarkable is the degree to which women had rights in such a patriarchal system.

The marriage contract (*Ketuvah*) was taken seriously. It specified whether or not the bride was a virgin. In Mishnah *Ketuvot*, we find the following:

> A man married a woman and "found not in her the signs of virginity."
> (Deuteronomy 22:14) She said: "After you did betrothe me, I was raped
> and your field was laid waste."[1] He said: "Not so, but it happened be-
> fore I betrothed you and my arrangement was made in error."[2] Rabban
> Gamaliel and R. Eliezer said: She may be believed. But R. Joshua said:
> We may not rely on her words. She must be presumed to have had inter-
> course before she was betrothed and to have deceived her husband unless
> she can bring proof for her words.[3]
>
> [1] As by a rainstorm or other "act of God." This means that
> though her virginity is no longer intact, her husband has no legal
> recourse and cannot change her *Ketuvah*, written before the be-
> trothal.
>
> [2] And, consequently, the *Ketuvah* is entirely void.
>
> [3] The view of Rabban Gamaliel and R. Eliezer was accepted as
> law. Why destroy a potentially good marriage when so much doubt
> exists about the bride's condition, and R. Joshua's requirement of
> proof is impossible to fulfill.

The Mishnah expands on the written Torah's law granting women the right to own property. We read (*Ketuvot* 11:2):

"A widow, whether her husband died after betrothal or after marriage, may sell property from her husband's estate without the consent of the court." This statement is disputed by one sage in part, but Halakhah followed the original intent of the Mishnah.

Even though the Mishnah uses primitive language in ruling about the "acquisition" of a woman by her husband, she was never chattel in Jewish law. Important she could not be betrothed or married without her explicit consent. No form of duress was permitted to her parents and certainly not to the community at large. There is even disagreement among the sages about the right of her husband to force her to perform household duties, if she brought servants to the marriage as part of her dowry or if they were an affluent family.

In all probability, the most fascinating single concept of Mishnaic law about women is found in the following (*Ketuvot* 5:6):

If a man takes a vow not to have intercourse with his wife, the School of Shammai say: She may consent for two weeks.[1] The School of Hillel say: for one week only.[2] Students may remain away for thirty days without the permission of their wives while they study Torah; laborers, for one week.[3] "The marital duty" (Exodus 21:10) required in the Torah is: every day for the unoccupied; twice a week for laborers, once a week for donkey-drivers;[4] once every thirty days for camel-drivers, and once every six months for sailors.[5]

[1] One of the most progressive principles of Halakhah has been that women, as well as men, have sexual rights. See Exodus 21:10, which, the Rabbis ruled, referred not only to a servant but to all women. Even today, the idea that women need and enjoy sex relationships as much as men is not generally recognized.

[2] The two-week and one-week suggestions are derived from the inplications of the length of time intercourse was prohibited after the birth of a daughter and after the menstrual period. In both cases, the commentators wisely pointed out, a man can have feelings of anger against his wife; for bearing a girl if he wanted a boy, and for menstruating instead of having conceived, if he was anxious for a child. Certainly, they went on, any man who takes a vow against intercourse must be angry with his wife. If he takes a vow for more than two weeks, however, the court could force him to divorce his wife and return her dowry to her. This was how Halakhah protected women's sex rights.

[3] The Hebrew word here, each time a week is mentioned, is Shabbat, both because it meant the end of a week and because intercourse is a mitzvah on Friday night in order to make the Sabbath joy complete.

[4] The driver went out to villages to cart grain and came home only twice a week.

[5] It is interesting to note that if a man wished to change his work to one which brought him home less frequently, his wife could prevent him from doing so—unless he elected to become a scholar.

Jewish women were never expected to limit their lives to *Kinder, Kirche, Kuche* —children, church, kitchen. In many communities over the centuries, women had full economic responsibility, sometimes in partnership with their husbands, sometimes alone if the man was a student and concentrated on his studies all day. Wome were active in communal matters. Within a system structured for male dominance, the Jewish woman was far ahead of her time in the amount of freedom and equality she enjoyed. Her status over the centuries, and within Halakhah and the synagogue today, cannot satisfy the women who champion full equality for their sisters and themselves. But the Jewish community has provided and continues to provide many foundation-stones of the movement for women's equality.

NOTE

1. Quoted from *The Mishnah: Oral Teachings of Judaism* edited by Eugene J. Lipman. B'nai B'rith Jewish Heritage Classic. Norton. 1970.

CAN A
WOMAN BE A JEW?

RUTH F. BRIN

An engraved invitation to my husband to attend a reception for a visiting rabbinical dignitary was followed the next day by a blurred mimeographed postcard indicating that wives, too, might accompany their husbands. This slip on the part of my congregation is typical of the way Jewish women are frequently ignored by the Jewish establishment. In a period when our survival as a people is at stake, I think it is time for our leaders to be honest enough to look at the many subtle ways women are excluded from meaningful participation in Jewish life. If it's hard for a man to be a Jew, let him consider how much harder it is for a woman.

Men may behave and feel as Jews in a variety of ways: through their families, their synagogues, their communities, their education, their vocation, their personal friendships. In the United States today, two major Jewish purposes are usually served through community organization. These are identification with and support of Israel and world Jewry; and, secondly, carrying out the ethical imperatives of Judaism, its demands for social justice. Jewish education is usually offered through the synagogue or community, but may be pursued independently. Religion is expressed privately and in the family, but principally through the synagogue. It is my contention that most of these routes to Jewish identity are, at best, only partially open to women.

VICARIOUS JEWS

Traditionally women were vicarious Jews, "shepping nachis" when a son became *bar mitzvah*, or beaming proudly when a husband was commended for his learning or his charity. At home the Jewish woman set the table and prepared the kosher food, but it was her husband who "made kiddush," led the discussion of Torah, or sang the *birkat ha-mazon*. However in Western secular society today, and that includes Israel, women are frequently offered direct participation and direct, rather than vicarious, satisfactions. Sometimes, of course, the offer is made and then withdrawn. Thus our society encourages women to go to college and prepare for careers, but then tells them they must raise their children before they can enter the job market.

Jewish society behaves in similar contradictory ways. In our local Talmud Torah, girls quite consistently outnumber boys among the graduates of high school and *bet hamidrash* departments. We say to these girls: study to be a good Jew. Then we add: of course you may not be a rabbi, a cantor, a Jewish scholar, a Jewish community leader, the administrator of a Jewish school or community agency, and, with the exception of a few Reconstructionist synagogues, you may not be counted in the *minyan* or be called to the Torah. Shrugging our shoulders, we add, if you are really serious about this, go marry a rabbi.

IN RELIGION

Discrimination against women is probably greatest in the religious establishment. It is true that mixed seating is common in many liberal congregations in the United States and that girls may take part in confirmation or *bat mitzvah* ceremonies. It is also true that women have only recently been accepted as Jewish teachers, but they are nearly always supervised by men. Women are not only excluded from the rabbinate, but the vast majority of congregations are controlled by boards made up of men, or a majority of men. The daily *minyan* often resembles and functions as a men's club. A woman is made to feel embarrassed if she attends services without her husband (or father) and is usually regarded as rather odd if she shows much interest in Jewish scholarship or religion.

There are many reasons why Jewish men prefer women to stay in the synagogue kitchens and to express their ideas at sisterhood meetings on Tuesday afternoons. Not many of the reasons are pleasant. In the matter of ritual law, women are traditionally excused from almost everything except lighting the Sabbath candles and keeping a kosher kitchen. Apologists have said that this was done out of deference to women's role as wife and mother, but I feel that it was a way of excluding women from religious life.

During the middle ages, Christian women probably had even fewer rights than Jewish women when property, marriage and divorce laws are considered. Yet religious ritual demands were made of them, and roles were established for them both in the convent and in works of charity, nursing, and teaching as lay workers for the church. The traditional place of the Christian woman was expressed in the phrase "Kirche, Küche, und Kinder," meaning church, kitchen, and children. The Jewish woman was also assigned to kitchen and children, but she was excluded from the synagogue, except to sit in a balcony where she couldn't be seen or heard and often couldn't see or hear enough to participate in services. The Jewish woman more often entered the world of work, the market place, than did her Christian counterpart.

Why Jewish Women Are Excluded

Jewish culture, or tradition, unfortunately contains two strong, though paradoxical, bases for excluding women from the synagogue and house of study. The first is the feeling that woman is demonic, a source of evil, and has a power for evil that must be controlled. Gershom Scholem, in his classic work in Jewish mysticism, comments that there were no women among Jewish mystics at any period, although there are women mystics among almost every other known religious group. He attributed this exclusive masculinity "to an inherent tendency to lay stress on the demonic nature of women and the feminine elements in the cosmos." While Scholem doesn't elaborate on what he means by the demonic nature of women, Joshua Trachenberg, in describing Jewish folk religion, has retold many of the legends about Lilith and other female demons and witches. Many of the tales of Isaac Bashevis Singer reflect Jewish fear of the powers of witches and wicked women to lead men into sin.

Paradixocally opposed to this idea of the magic power of woman is the notion that women are intellectually and spiritually inferior to men. Again, it is interesting to compare medieval Christian attitudes. Although they considered women inferior in intelligence, they never doubted that women could have spiritual experience and religious vocation. Women can be saints; but was there ever a female zaddik? Among the Jews, where study was an essential part of religion, notions of the intellectual inferiority of women merely added to the idea that woman was inferior spiritually as well. She received little or no religious education and her best hope was to be her husband's footstool in the world to come. A woman without a husband was certainly the most despised and forlorn object of all.

Further Obstacles to Jewish Women

Apologists have often pointed out that women were important in the biblical period; there was a judge, Deborah, and a prophetess, Huldah, although they hardly seem to outweigh the functioning of Eve as a temptress, nor the rather ambiguous pictures of women like Dinah, Tamar, and the Matriarchs as well. Rabbis point to the verses from Proverbs customarily recited on the Sabbath by good Jewish husbands as evidence of the high esteem in which women were held. I would ask them to take a more analytical look at those verses. "A good wife, who can find? She is far more precious than rubies . . . she is like a merchant-ship . . . she considers a field and buys it . . . she plants a vineyard . . . has strong arms . . . rises early and works late . . . spins and weaves . . . makes linen garments and sells them . . . and eats not of the bread of idleness." Meanwhile her husband is "Known in the gates when he sits among the elders of the land." The Jewish woman was not invited to "sit in the gates," nor was she valued for her wisdom, moral or spiritual strength, but she was valued quite simply for her economic utility to her husband.

There were no women priests in ancient Israel, but we do know that women came to the Temple to make sacrifice. After the year 70, when study replaced sacrifice, women were quite effectively prohibited from this activity. This may have been because of ideas about their low intelligence, laws about their ritual uncleanliness during what amounted to more than half of their adult lives, or because of the hostility of Jewish men toward them.

Rabbinic Hostility to Women

Richard Rubenstein, in *The Religious Imagination*, points out that rabbinic legend displays a great deal of hostility toward women, some of which he believes arose because the Jews were a conquered people and females were regarded as spoils of war, not only by the Romans but by all other peoples, up to and including modern nations. Rubenstein also notes that the Rabbis, in observing the pain of pregnancy and childbirth and the rule of men over women, concluded that, since women lived a more punitive life than men, God must be punishing them. They therefore concluded that women were more wicked than men, and accordingly thanked God daily that He created them men and not women or slaves.

Anthropoligists have found exclusive male societies with secret initiation rites in almost every culture, including that of the United States today. What is unfortunate for Jews is that our formal religious practice was for many centuries exclusively male, so that for some men, the synagogue meets the need for a male society. That this need may represent immaturity or an incomplete working out of the Oedipal situation may give us an insight into why some Jewish men find satisfaction in the daily *minyan*. Most of them, I would like to believe, come to pray.

Israel Today

In Israel the all-male religious establishment seems completely unchallenged. I don't think American women can find any helpful clues to a deeper religious life there. When I visited Israel last fall, I was appalled to be turned away from the Western Wall by an Israeli armed guard. Women are only permitted to approach the wall far to one side of the traditionally known site of the "Wailing Wall," and are fenced off so completely that they cannot see or be seen by the men who occupy the many square yards in front of the site. In British mandate times, there was no such separation of men and women in this outdoor area. It is ironical to me that young Israeli women who fought in the army are forbidden access to the sacred and symbolic place they helped recapture. Yet when I spoke with a few Israeli women about this, they didn't share my sense of shock. Most of them were quite indifferent to the Wall, and indeed, to all religious ceremony and symbol.

One of them commented archly. "Let the men play their little games. It does no harm." In other words, she felt that the Jewish religion was a game for Jewish men to play, a male secret society.

A New Place for Women

The question that I feel must be raised now, for those who have a mature conception of Judaism and a deep concern for strengthening the Jewish people, is one of finding or creating a role for those Jewish women who do have deep religious cravings and spiritual strengths. Why should American women be expected to sublimate their desires for religious expression to raising money for Jewish causes or cooking for some synagogue function?

In modern times the comparison to Christian attitudes remains pertinent. Among the Protestants, a woman like Mary Baker Eddy may be taken seriously as a religious leader. Jewish women like Henrietta Szold, Hannah Solomon and Golda Meir have certainly exhibited tremendous capacity, but none of them dared to assert any religious leadership. There are ordained women ministers among the Protestants. A single woman who devotes herself to teaching, church work, nursing or social work, whether in the cloister or outside of it, enjoys high status and the respect of both men and women among the Christians. We Jews still tend to treat our single women as objects of pity (or scorn) and are unwilling to ascribe religious motivations to them even if they choose jobs intended to help others. We usually are willing to accept married women's working, but seldom credit them with any but material motivations.

Why Not Women As Rabbis?

If we are going to give honest consideration to the religious needs and capacities of adult Jewish women, then the *ethical and ritual mitzvot should apply equally to women and women should be given an equal opportunity to fulfill them.* While I realize that this is highly unlikely for the Orthodox, the Conservative, Reconstructionist and Reform congregations could go a long way toward this goal. Many new approaches could be tried. For a small start, a congregation might try scheduling some daily services for the convenience of women rather than men.

For a larger start, I think women should be admitted to rabbinical studies so they can be accepted as qualified religious leaders. The responsibilities of a congregational rabbi today include not only conducting services but also personal counseling, community organization, synagogue administration, and education of young and old. If women were permitted to complete rabbinical studies they could function in some of these specific areas in large congregations. Such women rabbis need not lead services, nor conduct weddings or funerals unless the families involved wished it. They could visit the ill and bereaved, give personal and marriage counseling, serve as synagogue administrators and principals of religious schools or institutions of adult education. In addition, women with rabbinical and academic educations could help fill the demands from universities and colleges for professors of Jewish studies.

IN COMMUNITY ACTIVITIES

Women have somewhat better opportunities in Jewish community organization than they do in the synagogue. Nevertheless, the practice of forming women's auxiliary organizations, such as synagogue sisterhoods, federation of welfare fund women's divisions, women's branches of Jewish Centers, B'nai B'rith and other groups, tend to segregate women and render them incapable of influencing the parent group.

There are women's groups which are not appendages to men's groups. Unlike the male secret society which is nearly universal, women's clubs seem to be a phenomenon of the middle class modern Western culture. Such groups as League of Women Voters and Women's International League for Peace and Freedom grew out of the women's suffrage movement in the United States and England. Others developed to perpetuate a social elite (D.A.R., Junior League, et al.) and still others for a variety of purposes. Outstanding Jewish women's groups begun within the last century are Council of Jewish Women and Hadassah. Hadassah seems far more active and viable than any men's Zionist group in this country; Council had played a unique role in pioneering new forms of social service to both Jews and non-Jews. Thus Jewish women have created for themselves a way to express their concern for Israel and to carry out some of the *mitzvot* of social justice.

Community Not Ready for Women as Professionals

But there are two negative aspects to be considered: first, women's talents and energies have been kept away from general community organization; second, as professionalism increases in all forms of fund-raising, social work and group work, there is less of a role for the volunteer and more desire on the part of women to work as professionals when their family responsibilities permit it. Volunteering is increasingly an activity of women with small children. More and more those whose children are of school age prefer to return to work; yet top Jewish professional jobs are not open to women.

A summary of a study by Dr. Bernard Lazerwitz of Brandeis University was published by the Jewish Welfare Board in April 1968. One of its conclusions read:

"Women scored highest in acceptance of traditional Jewish beliefs but were found to have had less Jewish education than the men in the study. The women among the highly identified group also reported a higher degree of Jewish organizational activity than did the men. The findings indicated that *women are becoming the most active members of the Jewish community but the Jewish community is not changing rapidly enough to give official recognition to this new role of women.*" (italics mine)

IN THE FAMILY

Jewish women and children are cherished and protected, perhaps more than the children and women of other groups. Jews are justifiably proud of their strong family ties, the warmth of home religious ceremonies like the Seder, and their healthy attitudes toward sex (discussed in a May 31, 1968 article in the *Reconstructionist* by Louis A. Berman). Producing a Jewish home is the joint effort of both man and wife and can result only if both are dedicated to the effort. Neither can bring this about alone.

Jewish marriage and divorce law, however, contains provisions which are unjust to women and particularly penalize the woman who lives outside of Israel but wants to remain loyal to Jewish tradition. Biblical restrictions of the rights of women to inherit property from their husbands have been removed through Talmudic decisions and later acceptance of civil law in this area. Jewish laws of divorce remain unfair.

Divorce was an accepted practice in biblical times; a man could give a writ of divorce (*get*) to his wife on any grounds. He was not required to provide for her or her children, and she could not divorce him unless she could persuade him to give her a *get*. During the Talmudic and medieval periods, safeguards grew up to protect women to some degree from masculine whimsy. Drawing up a *get* became so technical that a rabbinical court had to be consulted to do it properly. The court then might intercede to reconcile the partners, or it might threaten excommunication (*herem*) to the man who failed to support his former wife and children. If the wife wanted a divorce and the court found in her favor, it could force a husband to grant her a divorce.

Situations Unjust to Women

While there was a ban on polygamy it was never totally forbidden. Thus if a wife were insane and couldn't understand a *get*, a man might be permitted to take a second wife, while remaining married to the first. Of course this did not work in reverse. If a man were insane and could not sign a *get*, his wife must remain married to him and could not marry anyone else. These provisions hold in Jewish law today.

Other unjust situations arise in the case of the *agunah* or "chained" wife, a woman who is deserted but not divorced by her husband. If she can't find him or prove him dead through reliable witnesses, she can never remarry. After the Hitler period, rabbis wrote responsa indicating they would not require witnesses to the deaths of men presumed sent to concentration camps, but this has not been applied to other deserted wives. In Jewish law a man cannot be presumed dead simply because of his absence, no matter for how many years.

A childless widow is required by biblical law to marry her brother-in-law unless he releases her by going through the ceremony of *halitzah*. If he is a minor, she must wait until he is of age before he can give her the release. Some men have extorted large sums of money from their sisters-in-law in return for *halitzah*. Other men have required payment from their wives before granting a *get*.

In Israel Today

All Jewish marriage and divorce is handled by the Israeli Rabbinate, while Moslem and Christian family law is administered through their respective clergy. The rabbinical courts can enforce their rulings through the police or prisons. There is a way to force a man to give his wife a *get* or pay her support money, should the court so rule. On the other hand, there is no civil marriage and all rabbinical law is scrupulously followed. There is no way, for example, for a "Cohen" to marry a divorced woman or even a woman who was once engaged to be married. *Halitzah* is still required and the *agunah* may not remarry.

The Israeli Rabbinate has questioned the validity of the marriage customs of the B'nai Yisrael, a group of Jews from India, as not conforming strictly to Talmudic law. They have refused to let other Jews marry B'nai Yisrael, unless the latter undergo conversion. This group claims loyalty to Judaism before the Talmud was ever written, and deeply resents this treatment. Recently, the Rabbinate threatened to refuse to perform a marriage ceremony for the granddaughter of David Ben Gurion, because they questioned whether her mother had undergone a proper conversion ceremony when becoming Jewish. It seems clear that the children of Reform Jews might not be considered legitimate Jews by the Israeli Rabbinate, since Reform Judaism follows civil law in matters of divorce. Reform Jewry also accepts converts, permitting them to marry Jews, and very possibly the Israeli Rabbinate would question these conversions. Although the Israeli government wants migration from the West, it has not given consideration to the possibility of the problems that could arise if children of Reform Jews want to marry Israelis in Israel.

In the United States

In all of the countries outside of Israel the double problem of civil and religious divorce is a serious one. Rabbinical courts cannot enforce their rulings in the United States or any other country except Israel, so there is no way to force a man to grant his wife a *get*. But even with a civil divorce, no Orthodox rabbi and very few Conservative rabbis would officiate at a new marriage for a woman unless she also has a Jewish divorce. Thus the woman who wants to follow Jewish law suffers, while the less observant woman may proceed with a civil marriage. The Conservative Rabbinical Assembly has suggested a new paragraph in the marriage contract to indicate that, in the case of civil divorce, the husband promises to grant a Jewish divorce, but the validity of this clause has not been tested in the courts. Orthodox rabbis do not use it.

Jewish law, even Biblical law, is not immutable. Hillel drastically altered the laws of the Sabbatical year through the institution of the *prozbul*. In his book on the Pharisees, Finkelstein interprets this as a gesture to protect the proletariat whom, he says, the Pharisees represented. I am sure that marriage and divorce law could be changed through careful study and reinterpretation as well as through building up a series of precedent-establishing responsa. If there is a conscious desire to make divorce law more equitable for women, it can be done. Particularly if rabbis understand that current practices specifically alienate the very woman who is most loyal to Judaism, they ought to give immediate attention to this problem. Of course rabbis are men, not members of the sex which has borne the injustices of these laws for so long. Finkelstein thought that the Rabbis changed some laws because the Pharisees were members of the proletariat class. Will we have to wait to have women rabbis to remedy Jewish divorce law, or do we now have some leaders with truly broader vision?

WOMEN COULD BE EVEN BETTER JEWS

Can a woman be a Jew? I think women are Jews, and could be much better Jews if they were given equal opportunity with men. I have often wished that Simone Weil could have survived the Second World War. She was a French Jewess, a professor of philosophy, whose brilliant notebooks show a most remarkable spiritual sensitivity. Partly because her family were quite assimilated and she knew little of her heritage, and more because Jewish women have so little access to traditional Jewish learning on their own, she was teetering toward conversion to Catholicism at the time of her death. Yet she died because, in England, suffering from tuberculosis, she refused to eat any more than the diet of the Jews in the concentration camps. How many Jewish women of such intellectual and spiritual capacity have already been lost to us? Do we expect or deserve to survive as a religious civilization if we continue practices in our synagogues, our communities, and our family law, which exclude, discriminate against, or degrade the feminine half of the Jewish people?

JEWISH
COLLEGE FEMALES:
Future Leaders
of the Jewish Community?

ABRAHAM D. LAVENDER

Most writers have concluded that Jewish women have traditionally had more equality relative to Jewish men than non-Jewish women have had relative to non-Jewish men. The historical dimension is discussed by Adler (1973: 81) who notes that, despite many restrictions, Jewish women had many rights centuries before non-Jewish women obtained these rights. That this "closer-to-equality" situation was characteristic both inside and outside the home is illustrated by I. Epstein (1973: 30) who shows that Jewish women were not forced into a subordinate position in the home but rather played a significant role in communal, social, and economic affairs. Although the actual situation has differed greatly at times, this general conclusion on the status of Jewish women had applied to Jews in both of the two dominant cultures—Christian and Islamic—in which Jews have lived in the diaspora. Patai (1971: 179), for example, notes that Jewish women in the Middle East were on the whole better off than Moslem women, and Chouraqui (1968: 206) indicates the same conclusion for the Jewish women in North Africa. Zuckoff (1973: 51) concludes that in the shtetl culture of Eastern Europe, from which the vast migration of American Jews came, women were valued as managers of homes and businesses and not as sex objects. Zborowski and Herzog (1962: 131) observe that it was not uncommon for the Jewish woman to earn the livelihood.

It is generally concluded today that Jewish women have more equality and more opportunity for educational and occupational fulfillment than non-Jewish women.[1] Goldstein and Goldscheider (1968: 65), for example, found that the median education for Jewish women in their study was 12.7 years whereas the median education for their total sample of women was 10.1 years. They also found that, of

Jewish women who were employed, 30.6 percent were employed as professionals, managers, or proprietors, whereas the comparable figure for their total sample of women was 12.9 percent.

Compared to their own past situation, however, it is also generally concluded that the position of Jewish women relative to Jewish men has decreased in the United States in recent decades (see, for example, Zuckoff, p. 52). As Jewish men in the United States rose in the economic sphere and no longer needed Jewish women as economic partners, Jewish women were increasingly relegated to a passive and dependent role as mother, housewife, and "walking example of conspicuous consumption for the husband."

Despite the cultural status of Jewish women, their religious status as women has been characterized by a number of restrictions—at least equaling, and sometimes exceeding, those found in Christianity but much less than those found in Islam—which prohibit them from participating fully in the religious aspects of the Jewish community. Not only have they been prohibited from becoming rabbis, but they have been prohibited from being counted in a minyan (quorum of ten required for a religious service), have been prohibited from performing some rituals such as being called to read the Torah, and have sat in a segregated section of the synagogue.

Recent decades have seen changes in some of these practices in the United States. The Reform movement and most Conservative congregations no longer require segregated seating. The Reform movement has long counted women in a minyan, and the Conservative movement voted in 1973 to allow each Conservative congregation to decide whether women are to be counted in the minyan. The Reform movement ordained its first female rabbi in 1972, with the Reconstructionist movement—which has practiced equality of women since its founding in the United States in the 1920s—following shortly behind. The Orthodox movement, however, has made basically no changes in the position of women. Nevertheless, despite improvement in some segments of the Jewish religious structure, the overall religious position of Jewish women remains unequal. In the Jewish institutional structure, women fill few top positions.

Thus, culturally and socially the American Jewish woman today is more likely than the non-Jewish woman to have an opportunity for equality even though her position is not as good as it was previously, and religiously her position is improving even though it is not yet anywhere near equality. Two questions are raised by these conclusions, however:

1. Are Jewish women obtaining college degrees because of the status conferred and in preparation for continuation of the roles of mother, housewife, and "walking example of conspicuous consumption," illustrated by Parent's (1972) pathetic Sheila Levine or the "spoiled rich bitch" of *Goodbye Columbus* (Gross, 1975); or are Jewish women also planning separate careers outside the home, illustrated by Tonner's (1975) self-confident "Jewish Princess" or the "committed, bright, idealist fighter" of *The Way We Were* (Gross, 1975)?

2. As Jewish women gain higher educational and occupational positions, will they lose their level of Jewish identity, which is currently higher than that of Jewish men (Goldstein and Goldscheider, 1968: 200; Sklare and Greenblum, 1967: 255), or will they maintain this higher level of Jewish identity?

In the sections that follow, I will examine these two questions and provide additional comparative data on the levels of identity of Jewish women and Jewish men.

THE DATA

The sample for this study consisted of 488 Jewish undergraduate students at the University of Maryland. The data were collected in May and June 1971 by means of a mail questionnaire. There were 264 females and 224 males in the sample

Two overall measures of Jewish identity were utilized in this study: a Religious Observance Index (ROI) and an Ethnic Identity Index (EII). The ROI was a weighted index based on observance of selected Jewish holidays (Passover, Rosh Hashanah, Yom Kippur, and Hanukkah), observance of Kashruth, and frequency of synagogue attendance. The EII was a weighted index on membership in Jewish organizations, protests for Jewish issues, frequency of dates being Jewish, attitudes

Table 1

Educational Goals for Females and Males[a]

Degree Planned	Females	N	Males	N	gamma	p
None/two-year	4.5	(264)	4.0	(224)	0.064	0.334
Bachelor's	26.1	(264)	20.1	(224)	0.169	0.009
Master's	56.5	(264)	19.2	(224)	0.690	<0.001
Doctorate/ professional	12.5	(264)	55.4	(224)	0.793	<0.001
Not ascertained	0.4	(264)	1.3	(224)	—	—
Combined master's, doctorate/ professional	68.9	(264)	74.6	(224)	0.137	0.020

[a]In effect, each of these listings is the result of a 2x2 table, with female/male being the independent variable and yes/no to whether the individual plans to obtain that degree as the highest degree being the dependent variable. Rather than present six separate 2x2 tables, the "yes" replies only are presented for the sake of brevity. This procedure is followed in all of the tables here.

toward intermarriage, and number of five closest friends who were Jewish. For purposes of this study, subjects were classified as high or low on each of these measures of identity. In addition to the items necessary to construct these indexes, information was also obtained separately from these items as well as from a number of additional ones.[2]

THE FINDINGS

"What are the future plans of Jewish women who are obtaining degrees in higher education?"

At the University of Maryland, 59 percent of the Jewish students are females whereas only 47 percent of the non-Jewish students are females. The extent to which this indicates the greater likelihood of Jewish females to attend college, or the extent to which it indicates the particular opportunities for females at this particular university, cannot be determined from these data. However, regardless of these factors, an indication of the future career plans of this sample can be obtained from these data. As shown in table 1, Jewish females are similar to Jewish males in their plans to obtain graduate degrees.[3] When master's degrees, doctoral degrees, and professional degrees are combined, the percentages are 68.9 for females and 74.6 for males. While planning to continue one's higher education beyond a bachelor's degree does not necessarily prove commitment to a career, it is suggestive of one. At the least, it suggests a combination of the mother-housewife role with that of a separate career. This interpretation is further suggested by the findings shown in table 2. To the question of what their occupational goals were, nearly all females indicated career plans. While it is unknown whether this refers to a

Table 2

Occupational Goals for Females and Males

Occupation Planned	Females	N	Males	N	gamma	p
Professional, technical	87.5	(264)	75.5	(224)	0.400	<0.001
Manager, official, proprietor	1.1	(264)	4.4	(224)	0.605	<0.001
Sales	0	(264)	1.3	(224)		
Other	0.8	(264)	0.5	(224)		
Not ascertained	10.6	(264)	18.3	(224)	0.307	<0.001

full-time career to the exclusion of the mother-housewife role, it again indicates at the least a combination of roles.

The findings shown in table 3 indicate that Jewish males and Jewish females do differ in their choices of majors. While large numbers of both females and males are in the social sciences and liberal arts (even though males are significantly more represented here), females are significantly more likely to choose education and, to a lesser extent, the fine arts and home economics, while males are significantly more likely to choose business and the hard sciences. While these findings may indicate a continuation of traditional occupational patterns, they hardly justify the continued nonparticipation of females in the Jewish institutional structure. In fact, to the extent that educational background matters, one could argue that a background in social sciences, liberal arts, or education is more likely to prepare one for leadership in the Jewish institutional structure, especially in areas such as inculcating Jewish identity in Jewish youth, educating Jewish youth, serving the needs of the Jewish elderly and the Jewish poor, and counseling individuals of all age

Thus, these data indicate that an increasing number of Jewish women not only have the educational preparation for, but also plan to have, careers outside the home—careers that will bring them more into the orbit of Jewish institutional leadership.

Table 3

Academic Majors for Females and Males

Academic Major	Females	N	Males	N	gamma	p
Business	2.3	(264)	21.9	(224)	0.846	<0.001
Engineering, natural sciences	3.0	(264)	15.6	(224)	0.711	<0.001
Education	47.0	(264)	3.1	(224)	0.929	<0.001
Liberal arts, social sciences	30.3	(264)	47.3	(224)	0.347	<0.001
Fine arts, home economics	10.2	(264)	2.2	(224)	0.666	<0.001
Other	7.2	(264)	8.0	(224)	0.059	0.300
Not ascertained	0	(264)	1.9	(224)		

"Will Jewish women lose their higher level of Jewish identity as they obtain higher educations?"

As shown in table 4, females who plan to obtain graduate degrees, like females who plan to obtain bachelor degrees only, have a higher degree of religious identity than do their corresponding males. The female-male difference for those planning for bachelor degrees only is similar to the female-male difference for those planning for graduate degrees.

For ethnic identity, females and males who plan to obtain bachelor degrees only have similar levels of identity, but females who plan to obtain graduate degrees have a level of identity slightly higher than that of their corresponding males.

Thus, planning to obtain a graduate degree has a positive relationship with higher religious identity and a negative relationship with ethnic identity. The important point for this essay, however, is that females and males exhibit a similar pattern, with females continuing to have a higher level of identity (particularly religious identity) than males.

Table 4

Percentage of Subjects with High Religious Identity and High Ethnic Identity by Educational Goals, for Females and Males

DEGREE PLANNED	FEMALES	N	MALES	N	GAMMA	p
Percentage with High Religious Identity						
None/two-year	66.7	(12)	33.3	(9)	0.600	0.013
Bachelor's	65.2	(69)	51.1	(45)	0.284	0.012
Master's	73.2	(149)	60.5	(43)	0.281	0.008
Doctorate/ professional	72.7	(33)	57.3	(124)	0.331	0.007
Combined master's, doctorate/ professional	73.1	(182)	58.1	(167)	0.324	<0.001
Percentage with High Ethnic Identity						
None/two year	41.7	(12)	77.8	(9)	0.661	0.008
Bachelor's	58.0	(69)	55.6	(45)	0.049	0.352
Master's	53.0	(149)	44.2	(43)	0.175	0.063
Doctorate/ professional	48.5	(33)	46.8	(124)	0.034	0.396
Combined master's, doctorate/ professional	52.2	(182)	46.1	(167)	0.121	0.044

SOME MORE DETAILED FEMALE-MALE
DIFFERENCES IN IDENTITY

To the finding that females have a higher religious identity than do males, regardless of educational goals, it can be suggested that the higher religious identity
of females is limited to home-oriented observances rather than extending also to
synagogue-oriented observances. As the findings in table 5 indicate, this is not the
case. Indeed, observing kashruth—primarily a home-oriented observance—is the
only measure of observance on which females do not have a significantly higher
level of observance. The differences between females and males on the synagogue-
oriented measures of synagogue attendance, observance of Rosh Hashanah, and
observance of Yom Kippur are similar to the female-male differences for the other
two (in addition to observing kashruth) home-oriented measures of observing Passover and observing Hanukkah.

Having indicated previously that higher ethnic identity is also more likely to be
found among females, the findings in table 6 indicate that this higher level of identity is also not limited to sexually stereotyped areas of behavior. Females are more
likely to belong to Hillel, but males are more likely to belong to fraternities. Few
students belong to either the Associated Students for Israel or the Jewish Defense
League, but females are more likely to belong to the former whereas males are
more likely to belong to the latter. Females are more likely to "usually or always"

Table 5

**Percentage Observing Measures of Religious
Identity for Females and Males**

Measure of Identity	Females	N	Males	N	gamma	p
Frequent synagogue attendance (at least High Holy Days)	71.6	(264)	59.8	(224)	0.257	<0.001
Observance of kashruth	25.1	(263)	27.7	(224)	0.066	0.166
Observance of Passover	94.7	(264)	83.0	(222)	0.551	<0.001
Observance of Rosh Hashanah	85.8	(261)	72.6	(223)	0.390	<0.001
Observance of Yom Kippur	83.3	(263)	71.4	(220)	0.332	<0.001
Observance of Hanukkah	90.5	(262)	72.5	(218)	0.565	<0.001

date only Jews and to be opposed to intermarriage, but females and males do not differ greatly on the extent to which most of their five closest friends are Jewish. Females are more likely to be active in protesting for Jewish causes (primarily the treatment of Soviet Jews) and are more favorable than males in their attitudes toward Israel.

Table 6

Percentage Observing Measures of Ethnic Identity for Females and Males

Measure of Identity	Females	N	Males	N	gamma	p
Membership in campus Hillel Foundation	18.9	(264)	12.7	(220)	0.231	0.002
Membership in Jewish fraternity/ sorority	21.7	(263)	33.6	(217)	0.293	<0.001
Membership in Associated Students for Israel	4.5	(264)	0.9	(220)	0.676	<0.001
Membership in Jewish Defense League	0.4	(264)	1.8	(220)	0.659	0.009
Dates are "usually or always" Jewish	66.7	(264)	54.9	(224)	0.243	<0.001
Will not intermarry	37.5	(264)	26.8	(224)	0.242	<0.001
Most (at least four of five) closest friends are Jewish	52.7	(264)	48.2	(224)	0.088	0.071
Have protested for Jewish cause	31.1	(264)	26.3	(224)	0.115	0.042
Very favorable or favorable toward Israel	75.3	(263)	67.1	(216)	0.197	<0.001

In fact, on all three of the issues that are of most contemporary concern to the American Jewish community—intermarriage, Israel, and the treatment of Soviet Jews—females have a higher level of Jewish identity than do males.

That females have a higher level of both religious and ethnic identity than males have is even more noticeable when the religious backgrounds of females and males are compared (table 7). Females are more likely to have received Sunday school educations, whereas males are more likely to have received the more intensive Hebrew School and day school educations. However, males have a lower level of identity despite the more intensive education. While this essay is not concerned with the complex question of the consequences of Jewish education, it is noted again that Jewish females are more likely to have training in formal educational philosophy. It is also noted that the females in this study are more likely than the males to continue their Jewish education on the college level.[4]

Table 7

Religious Education Background for Females and Males

Type of Education	Females	N	Males	N	gamma	p
Sunday school (6+ years)	46.5	(258)	26.5	(223)	0.414	<0.001
Hebrew school (6+ years)	15.1	(259)	23.2	(220)	0.259	<0.001
Day school (6+ years)	3.1	(262)	4.5	(222)	0.199	0.104

CONCLUSIONS

To the extent that the factors which have been discussed in this essay are important in qualifying one for leadership positions in the Jewish community, it is unequivocally concluded from these data that the American Jewish community deprives itself of much needed talent to the extent that it does not encourage all individuals, regardless of sex, to participate in its leadership positions. This is a pragmatic conclusion based on the practical consequences for the American Jewish community. The morality of the situation for both individuals and the community is another situation, for even if Jewish women should be content to limit themselve to noncareer roles and even if they should lose their higher level of identity, that does not decrease the argument that all individuals should be allowed to participate in the community structure to the extent of their desires and abilities. In this case, of course, the loss is the American Jewish community and Jewish women, but the conclusions can be applied to other communities and other women.

NOTES

1. In a recent article, C. Epstein (1973: 912) stated, "To be Jewish, black, foreign born, or a woman have all been bases for exclusion [from a number of occupations]." She explains

how the two negatives of blackness and femaleness have combined to have a positive effect for some black women, but concludes that for black women in general "the status set which includes being black and being a woman has been one of the most cumulatively limiting." This essay suggests that the positive effect of the multiple negative is found more often when the multiple negatives are Jewishness and femaleness. Part of this difference, of course, is due to the different socioeconomic status of blacks and Jews. Even more of a reason, however, may be the fact that some ethnic groups brought their differing values to America and never did accept American values. Seller (1975: 64), for instance, notes that Jewish female immigrants from Eastern Europe brought with them their "intellectual, aggressive, and self-sufficient" life-styles, that same life-style Zuckoff described as characteristic of Jewish women in Eastern Europe. This is an area for further study, but it is not debatable to many members of ethnic groups that mainstream sociology has long overlooked the extent to which some ethnic groups have maintained their own values in regard to women as well as in regard to many other issues. In some cases, these values have been less modern than those of America, but in other cases they have been more modern.

2. For a comprehensive justification of the representativeness of this sample and for a detailed explanation of the choice of measures of identity utilized, see Lavender (1972: 65-82).

3. Rather than report an arbitrary cutoff point of statistical significance, this study reports the levels of probability. Following rationale explained by Hunt and Hunt (1975: 599), gamma is utilized as the statistical measure, with statistical significances being based on a two-tailed test of a Z score derived from Kendall's tau-b.

4. This statement is based on enrollments in Jewish studies courses. Comparison of Jewish Studies enrollments with the other data in this study is not exactly accurate because the data for this study were collected in 1971 when there was not a large offering of Jewish studies courses. The enrollment data utilized are more recent—that of spring 1974—by which time the number enrolled in Jewish studies courses was almost 500. Females outnumbered males approximately two to one (331 to 161) even though they comprised only 54 percent of the 1971 sample. Assuming that these two sets of figures can be compared, the indication is that Jewish females are more interested in advanced Jewish courses than are Jewish males. This general conclusion has also been made by other observers of Jewish studies programs, for example Levenson (1974: 69). Having taught sociology of the American Jewish community and sociology of world Jewish communities twelve times over a period of five years, this author's experience has been the same.

REFERENCES

Adler, Rachel. 1973. "The Jew Who Wasn't There: Halacha and the Jewish Woman." *Response* 18 (Summer): 77-82.

Chouraqui, André N. 1973. *Between East and West: A History of the Jews of North Africa.* New York: Atheneum.

Dworkin, Susan. 1973. "Women of Valor." *Hadassah Magazine* 54 (April): 14-15, 37.

Ebstein, Shoshona. 1974. Review of "The Jewish Woman: An Anthology." *Jewish Frontier* 41 (May): 39-41.

Epstein, Cynthia Fuchs. 1973. "Positive Effects of the Multiple Negative: Explaining the Success of Black Professional Women." *American Journal of Sociology* 78 (January): 912-935.

* Partial support for this research was made possible by a grant from the Computer Science Center, University of Maryland. This is a revised version of a paper originally presented at the 1975 Annual Regional Research Institute of the District of Columbia Sociological Society, March 1975.

Epstein, I. 1973. "The Jewish Woman in the Responsa." *Response* 18 (Summer): 23-31.

Fenig, Ethel C. 1974. "National Conference on Jewish Women and Men: A Report." *Pioneer Woman* 19 (June): 7-8, 12.

Goldstein, Sidney, and Geldscheider, Calvin. 1968. *Jewish Americans: Three Generations in a Jewish Community*. Englewood Cliffs, N.J.: Prentice-Hall.

Gross, Barry. 1975. "No Victim, She: Barbra Streisand and the Movie Jew." *Journal of Ethnic Studies* 3 (Spring): 28-40.

Hunt, Larry L., and Hunt, Janet G. 1975. "A Religious Factor in Secular Achievement Among Blacks: The Case of Catholicism." *Social Forces* 53 (June): 595-605.

Klutznick, Philip M. 1967. Foreword to Maurice Bisgyer, *Challenge and Encounter*. New York: Crown Publishers.

Lavender, Abraham D. 1972. "Dimensions of Pluralism: An Examination of the Generational Hypothesis." Ph.D. dissertation, University of Maryland.

Levenson, Edward R. 1974. "Women and Jewish Studies." *Jewish Spectator* 39 (Summer): 69.

Matzkin, Rose E. 1974. "Half the Population." *Hadassah Magazine* 55 (June): 2.

Parent, Gail. 1972. *Sheila Levine Is Dead and Living in New York*. New York: Bantam.

Patai, Raphael. 1971. *Tents of Jacob: The Diaspora—Yesterday and Today*. Englewood Cliffs, N.J.: Prentice-Hall.

Seller, Maxine S. 1975. "Beyond the Stereotype: A New Look at the Immigrant Woman, 1880-1924." *Journal of Ethnic Studies* 3 (Spring): 59-70.

Sklare, Marshall, and Greenblum, Joseph. 1967. *Jewish Identity on the Suburban Frontier: A Study of Group Survival in the Open Society*. New York: Basic Books.

Tonner, Leslie. 1975. *Nothing But the Best: The Luck of the Jewish Princess*. New York: Coward, McCann & Geoghegan.

Zborowski, Mark, and Herzog, Elizabeth. 1962. *Life Is with People: The Culture of the Shtetl*. New York: Schocken.

Zuckoff, Aviva Canter. 1973. "The Oppression of the Jewish Woman." *Response* 18 (Summer): 47-54.

FEMINISM:
Is It Good for the Jews?

BLU GREENBERG

There is much we can learn from the Women's Movement in terms of our own growth as Jews. There is much that feminism can gain from the perspective of traditional Jewish values. Yet, at this point, the possibility of a positive relationship between the two seems improbable, if not impossible.

Traditional Judaism has written off feminism as a temporary cultural fad, if not an extremist movement. Feminists have vilified the rabbis as woman-haters, male chauvinists or, at best, men with ancient hang-ups. A religion and an ideology which could interact and nurture each other have instead squared off. Why?

The aims, achievements, and even processes of feminism have been revolutionary. Increasingly, public philosophy, policy, and prescription assume that women are full human beings with a potential capacity for achievement in all spheres in which men function. Our secular legal, social, and educational systems are under constant pressure to include women as equals. Our religious systems and institutions, however, lag far behind in the process of recognition.

If, throughout the centuries, Judaism was capable of generating revolutionary ethical teachings, why should it not incorporate the lessons of feminism easily? Equality in various spheres is a fundamental idea in Judaism—equality before the law, equal ownership of property, equality of all men. Logically and theologically, therefore, should not feminist goals be understood as a means to achieving the equality of women and men in the eyes of God and of community?

Oddly enough, the Jewish community, in which many pioneer feminists were nurtured, is one of the last groups to grapple with the challenges of feminism. True, Reform Judaism has taken many steps, beginning with the Breslau Conference's call in 1846 for full equality of men and women in all areas of religion. However, this equalization was largely formal; little substance or leadership was given to women. (Moreover, Reform made fewer religious demands upon both men and women, and the changes it made tended to flow from adoption of liberal, modern values, not from Jewish considerations.)

Basically, the response of most Jews, both male and female, can be characterized in this way: the more traditionally Jewish they were—or the more Jewish their orientation, including elements with Reform—the more they tended to resist the challenges that flowed from feminist ideology.

There are many reasons for this reaction. First, Jewish women, on the whole, have been well treated by Jewish men, who have been imbued with strong cultural values sanctioning or demanding good treatment. So Jewish women have been quite content to live with the traditional roles, both religious and social, assigned them. They agreed with the argument that freedom from communal religious responsibilities, such as synagogue prayer, enabled them to better fulfill the familial role which Jewish society had ordained for them.

Second, halakhic Judaism is currently resistant to change, and halakha includes in its all-encompassing rubric the religious institutionalization of social status. What was a sociological truth about women in previous generations—that they were the "second sex"—was codified in many minute ways into the halakha as religio-ethical concepts binding upon future generations as well.

What is often overlooked today is that, over the ages, Jewish tradition by and large upgraded the status of women, often in response to changes in society at large. One of the virtues of the halakhic system is that it has tried to maintain the dialectical relationship of needs between community and individual, Jew and non-Jew, authority and freedom, religion and society. However, in this century the halakhic authorities have been resistant to such change.

Third, although it is not openly articulated, there is a widespread fear that feminist ideology poses a threat to Jewish survival, similar to the threat that modernism in general has posed. Subconsciously or consciously, Jewish leaders fear that they would open a Pandora's box in exposing Jewish attitudes toward women to the claims of Women's Liberation. This fear is not completely invalid, nor is it restricted to the Orthodox. But feminism will not disappear simply because we ignore it or reject it as a danger. Rather, the dangers posed by feminism should be identified and guarded against in the context of a positive incorporation of feminist virtues into Jewish life.

Today, secular society has opened a great new range of roles and psychological expectations to women, while, at the same time, the halakhic status and religious life of Jewish women remain circumscribed. The situation is comparable to sitting in a stationary vehicle alongside a moving one. The net effect upon one is a sense of moving backwards; upon the other, a sense of pulling away, of losing connection of leaving others behind.

When confronted with harsh but often valid criticism, religious resistance takes the form of apologetics and defensiveness. Some Jewish women cling to traditional prescriptions; others abandon not only observance, but all traditional religious values as well. Since there is no currently sanctioned universe of discourse between feminism and Judaism regarding the religious status of women, the feminist movement has often attacked and rejected the basic structures and values which Judaism has contributed to human society.

What is sorely needed today is the creation of a dialectical tension between Jewish values and the mores of modern society in light of the far-reaching implications of Women's Liberation. One crucial part of the dialectic would be to measure the *halakhic* and religious status of Jewish women by the feminist notion of equality. But there must be a two-way relationship of communication and influence instead of withdrawal and widening of the gap.

An authentic Jewish women's movement would seek to find new approaches within *halakha* to respond to and express women's concerns. Simultaneously, it would seek to imbue women's concerns with Jewish values.

There are four areas in Jewish religious life where the goals of feminism can be applied in a dialectical fashion. This means interaction, not mere aping or assimilation. Though the truth is painful to those of us who live by and love *halakha*, as I do, honesty bids us acknowledge that Jewish women face inequality in these four areas: in the synagogue, in Jewish education, in the religious courts, and in communal leadership. These areas have been examined in depth in the literature of the Jewish women's movement. Here I will touch upon some possible *halakhic* changes.

The time is long overdue for a serious reanalysis of the principle of exemption from time-bound *mitzvot* in light of Rabbi Saul Berman's pioneering analysis of the basis of this exemption. Conceivably, the *halakha* could obligate women to observe time-bound *mitzvot* equally with adult men, yet allow for exemptions during those years when there are massive familial demands made upon their time and energies. This exemption might be operative until a woman's youngest child is 7, 10, or 13.

The model to follow here would be *haosek bamitzva patoor min hamitzva.* (One who is occupied in doing one *mitzva* is excused from the performance of another *mitzva* at the same time.) A further positive implication of this change would be that once women are attuned to prayer, they might continue to pray even during those times when they are exempt.

Sensitive *halakhists* must recognize that the general effect of the prayer exemption conditions women to a negative attitude toward prayer. Women hardly ever pray at home; thus prayer becomes a function of intermittent synagogue attendance alone—hardly an incentive to serious prayer. Although the Law Committee of the Conservative Rabbinical Assembly recently allowed the inclusion of women in the *minyan,* it did not take the necessary further step of equating women and men in prayer responsibilities.

In Orthodox synagogues, where the *mehitza* has been used to further the inequality of the sexes rather than to allow separate but equal *tefilla,* women's *minyanim* might be formed as a way of encouraging the involvement of women in prayer. This means women actually leading prayer, being called to and reading the Torah, and so on.

Prayer should not be a vicarious act, but rather one of personal participation. At present, men generally perform for women even those liturgical roles which are binding upon women, such as *kiddush* and *megilla* reading. The woman thus practices them by proxy, and finds herself helpless if the male in her life is absent.

Even if the proxy situation were to continue to give satisfaction to Jewish women —which is unlikely as their feminist consciousness changes—it operates only within the family context. Single women, divorcees and widows cannot enjoy rituals by family proxy and therefore are consigned to very tangential roles in communities centered around a synagogue.

Furthermore, traditional life-cycle ceremonies for women are either nonexistent or less significant than those of men. Ritual responses to biological events which are uniquely female (such as childbirth and the onset of menstruation) are conspicuously absent in Jewish tradition. Little by little, and with the help and encouragement of some men, women are beginning to develop religious forms to tie into the tradition and the community the emotions and experiences which currently find no communal *halakhic* expression. A lot more is needed.

Halakhic education is the most important area for the final equalization of women in the Jewish community. A great deal of leeway for personal judgment is given to *poskim* (*halakhic* decision-makers). Characteristic of the *halakhic* system is the tendency to find positive solutions to problems which arouse the greatest sympathy of the *poskim.*

Women *poskim* are more likely than men to find sympathetic solutions for women's problems, for they share and experience them in the most intense and personal way. Considering how far the *halakha* will have to stretch to meet women's needs and overcome their disabilities, women *poskim* are essential. Until now, men have studied and understood *halakha,* and they alone have made all the decisions.

With few exceptions, women have been kept ignorant of the sources and process of the Law, although they knew the details which applied to them.

Today, women must return to the sources and apply themselves seriously to Jewish scholarship. There must be institutes of higher Jewish education where women can study uninterruptedly with some degree of financial security. Women must be trained to make legal decisions not only for women, but for the entire Jewish community. And the notion of women rabbis must be accepted in all branches of Judaism, for women *can* make a contribution to the spiritual growth of the Jewish community.

The third area where great pressure must be applied is in overcoming the legal disabilities which deny the dignity of women or cause outright injustice and unjustified suffering. Jewish divorce law (where a woman is dependent on the will of her husband to grant a writ of divorce) has led to frequent discrimination, extortion, and innocent suffering.

Similarly, the problem of the *aguna* (the abandoned wife) must be reevaluated *halakhically*. In every generation, rabbis have worked prodigiously to circumvent the harshness of this law. In this generation, however, divorce has become much more prevalent, and the vast scale of modern warfare has made wife-desertion easier.

A new solution to the problem of a wife's dependence on her husband is needed, the kind of solution offered by Eliezer Berkovits in his work on the use of *tnaim* (conditions) in marriage and divorce. His proposal has not been treated with due respect by *halakhic* leaders here or in Israel.

Religious courts must change to accept women's testimony. A law which once protected women by preventing them from being subpoenaed into the public sector must now be rethought in terms of equality of men and women. All these changes can be wrought by using the principle of change for the better, which obtains in the history of *halakha*, especially in the area of treatment of women.

In the communal arena, there are still strong obstacles to women's assuming leadership roles in many educational, philanthropic and political institutions. Aside from the question of sexual discrimination, the Jewish community can ill afford to reject out of hand one half of the potential pool of capable leaders.

Many aspects of feminism are relevant to us as Jews and to the total Jewish community. Changes can be made within the framework of *halakha*. *Halakha* need not be asked to conform to every passing fad. On the other hand, Jewish leadership must not be allowed to hide behind slogans of immutability that are dishonest caricatures of *halakha*. Fidelity to *halakha* demands openness to new realities which will upgrade and enhance our own ethical and religious system.

Torah un derekh eretz means integrating the best values of the society in which we live with our own tradition—especially where they illuminate or coincide with the tradition's own ultimate goals, in this case the dignity of man and woman as images of God.

However, if we move only in the direction of integrating new (albeit good) values into the tradition, we would not be an authentically Jewish movement. To be Jewish means not only to learn from the societies in which we live, but also to serve as corrective influences within those societies. This dialectical relationship is part of the cosmic mission of the Jewish people throughout history.

Since we are Jews, we need not buy the whole package of feminism. Rather, we must infuse a changing society with our own values and check the excesses to which all revolutionary movements fall prey.

We shall have to walk a very fine line—continually monitering even those parts of the new which we have integrated into our lives to see whether they adequately meet the test of Jewish authenticity. This means readiness to reject those aspects of new movements which are antithetical to Jewish values in their very essence.

Feminism, for all its worth in upgrading the status of Jewish women, does not bode well in its entirety for Jewish survival. Some of its directions may be wrong or even destructive when judged from a Jewish perspective.

One of the by-products of the feminist striving for equality has been a strong attack on the family as the locus of abuse of women in all previous generations. Thus, Women's Liberation has escalated the crushing assault mounted on the famil by contemporary society. The Jewish family, the most stable of all, is also beginni to crumble. We see signs of this erosion everywhere—increasing divorce rate, lack of communication between parents and children, and poor models of family life for the next generation to learn from.

Many young Jewish women today state outright their objections to marriage and having children—in striking contrast to the previous generation, whose primary goals were marriage and childrearing. Today, we must recognize that not every women can find happiness in marriage alone. But feminist influence is so strong that we risk the danger of having the other option—a traditional marriage and famil relationships—being rejected altogether from consideration.

This particularly threatens Judaism, where the family is so central to educationa and religious life. Much of our religious life takes place within a family context, an the Jewish family has been the primary source of strength and support in coping with the often hostile and dangerous world Jews have lived in for two thousand years.

The very centrality of the family means that feminists who take Judaism serious will explore every possible way to strengthen the family and correct its evils before dismissing it. (This includes a willingness to suffer some disabilities, if necessary, an at times to live with frustration for the sake of the greater goal of Jewish survival and stability.)

We need to reintroduce into the women's movement, into women's conscious-ness, a sense of the perspective of a total life, a sense that there is a time and place for everything. This might help many women who regard as a sign of their libera-tion the freedom to raise families when they want to.

Respect for family is important not merely for old time's sake. Despite contem-porary desire to believe otherwise, the family remains the most important determi-nant of educational achievement and religious values and commitment.

The modern tendency to let school and synagogue do the family's job of trans-mitting Jewish values is mistaken. So central is the family, and so effective, that I would reverse the modish argument that *havurot* and peer groups are the education wave of the future; I believe the *havura* can best be understood as growing out of the search of many isolated singles (and couples) for a family contect in which to express their Jewishness.

George Gilder, in *Sexual Suicide*, places the responsibility for the decay in socie on the breakdown of the traditional family unit. Certainly, the family survived for so many thousands of years as an institution, even with its imperfections, because it was—and is—the most ethical and viable of relationships.

Although the family was the context in which women functioned as the second sex throughout history, and the role of enabler was the only one open to them, neither of these conditions is axiomatic to a woman's choice of the wife-mother role today. The family was also a source of security, honor, merit, and satisfaction for the majority of women in the past and for most women today who consider their freedom to serve exclusively as wives and mothers during one part of their lives a sign of their own liberation.

We should not denigrate the traditional roles, nor those who choose them. Just as women resented the restrictive mold which confined them in the past, so we must not coerce all women into a new restrictive mold—that which excludes enablers. We must check the negative tone which abounds in references to childrearing. More than that, to counteract the current negative stereotype of wife-mother, we must educate others to the excitement, fun and sweetness of being married and raising children.

True, we must bring the husband into a central role in the family, not just as provider, but as childraiser, as involved husband. We should aim for the liberation of men and children as well as women. Support of career women, single women, and women involved in political change need not imply denigration of the family.

One of the subtle indications of the prejudices of the feminist movement has been its ordering of priorities. The movement campaigns for equal jobs and equal pay for full-time careers, while neglecting discrimination in salaries and benefits for part-time jobs, most of which are filled by mothers. Nor has the feminist movement seriously dealt with the adjustments necessary to help reintegrate women who have been out of the labor market while raising children and now want to go back to work.

One current trend that should be confronted by Jewish feminists is the "new morality." Although this code of sexual license was on the scene well before Women's Liberation, feminism has spread its message to the female population, thereby legitimizing it for all. Extra-marital affairs, formerly "a man's thing" and oppressive to women, are now a symbol of the equality of women, undermining family stability and contributing to the soaring divorce rate.

Jews, concentrated in urban, higher-income areas, are among the most exposed to these new values and their dangers. In previous generations, Jews lived by a moral code which may have been based in part on principles coercive to women. Today's shift in mores is a grim warning of the destructive potential in many well-intentioned feminist clichés—particularly sexual freedom.

Judaism nurtured healthy sexual outlets within marriage, and even recognized them before marriage, yet put very strict curbs on extra-marital sexuality. One need not identify with male privilege or the double standard suggested in traditional Jewish definitions of adultery to agree with the main goal of the prohibitions involved. As Jews, we have learned that freedom comes only within an ethical structure. Given human limitations, ethics of interpersonal relationships necessarily involve restraint and frustration.

Although Judaism always understood divorce as a necessary, if regrettable, way to end an unsatisfactory marriage, the parameters of the marital relationship, while it was being lived, were, at the least, sexual fidelity and mutual respect. Feminists, who claim that now women should have full sexual freedom, define freedom as allowing the ex-slave to have the same right to abuse that previously only the master had. Jewish feminists should rather challenge and censure these values in male society; we should press for equal morality, not equal amorality.

A good example of the dialectical relationship between Judaism and feminism is our attitude toward abortion. In an era when six million Jews were killed—and one and a half million of them were children—we have to state both sides of the abortion issue. From our perspective, we must talk about the preciousness of life, not just the right to life. Stressing a woman's right to control her own body, and the legitimacy of considering the quality of life that she and her child will have, should go hand in hand with emphasis on the sanctity of life and on the risk of devaluating it in unthinking or easy medical solutions. We must ensure that abortion does not become a preferred method of birth control.

Orthodox rabbis currently oppose abortion on demand. As Jews we must demonstrate that abortion need not eliminate reverence for life and joy in creating life. On the one hand, this would lead to new *halakhic* attitudes toward abortion. On the other, *halakha* could help curb facile and nonchalant attitudes toward abortion and the abuses which have grown out of abortion reform. The protection of the quality of life (which is the ethical basis of abortion) could be offset or destroyed by a loss of reverence for life.

A further application of this principle would be the establishment of adoptive agencies for pregnant Jewish women who cannot, or do not want to, keep their own babies. The scarcity of Jewish babies for adoption, due to the growing resort to abortion, causes serious problems for Jewish couples who want to adopt a child.

The feminist movement has accepted another unfortunate attitude of modern society—its materialist orientation. People are judged by what and how much they produce, the kind of jobs they hold, the titles they have, and the salaries they get —not by personal values or character. This has consistently led to dehumanization, worship of success, and contempt for "failures," including the poor. As Jews, we must reject these standards and declare that each human being is valuable in his or her very being.

As part of the revolt against exclusion of women from high-paying jobs, feminism has scorned and undercut women's voluntary philanthropic activities. As Jews we affirm that there is value and validity in serving and giving to others—in volunteer action and professional work, in being good family members and friends, in doing good works. The traditional role of enabling is still a valid one, as long as it is not limited to women or women limited to it. We must attempt to infuse these values into the society we seek to create, rather than simply copy the errors of today's male-dominated society. The truly revolutionary (and admittedly more difficult) task is to change these social values and judgments, to overcome the production-value standard and liberate men and women for more humane living.

Many interpret Women's Liberation as liberation to fulfill their own personal needs, narrowly defined. This leads to an emphasis on self-fulfillment, to the exclusion of any concern for other people's needs and a denial that there can be fulfillment in giving to others. Good family situations have been exploded by unreal expectations and demands for immediate and unlimited personal gratification. The capacity to live with frustration has been dangerously weakened. The skyrocketing divorce rate can be explained, in part, by the influence of the extremists in the women's movement who attempt to deny the undeniable: that successful marriages and parent-child relationships take time, energy, a measure of sacrifice and generosity of soul—all the very opposites of instant gratification.

Similarly, charity and giving of oneself to others are being undercut in the fight for self-actualization. Volunteerism is under heavy attack by die-hard feminists, and Jewish charitable organizations, which rely on voulteer work, are suffering as a result. The feminist slogans—"self-esteem comes from a paying job," or "if it isn't paid for it's not taken seriously"—are half-truths. Not everyone wants to or can afford to work without pay—but volunteerism, *tzedaka*, certainly should remain a respected option. Those who find satisfaction in giving of themselves to others should be praised, not scorned.

We must check the excesses of those feminists who are hostile to men. Jewish women do not need to hate men to liberate themselves. Nor should Jewish men be seen as crude oppressors of women throughout history. For most of our history, Jewish men and women suffered equally from outside persecution and hostility, and their mutual solidarity carried them through. Instead of polarizing, we must try to liberate men so that they will not continue to be slaves to the rat-race, but will strive for a sense of dignity and self-worth. "Making it in a man's world" isn't all that easy for men either. We must also liberate men Jewishly so that they too can come to understand and grow in our tradition.

Finally, we must reject the notion that equality means identity. From the perspective of Judaism, there can be separate clear-cut roles in which men and women function as equals without losing their separate identities. Male and female are, admittedly, difficult concepts to define, but we must be aware in every instance whether we are dealing with the dignity of equality, which is an essential value in Judaism, or the identicalness of male and female, which is not.

Those Jewish women who have identified with many of the feminist goals have an added measure of responsibility, for we are in a better position to be heard by both sides and to influence them. It is no mean task to walk the fine line between old and new, status quo and avant garde, God's commandments and the emerging needs of society. But one reason Judaism has survived against all odds, and managed to contribute greatly to world civilization, is that in each era it managed to do exactly that.

To keep the fine tension and balance between these opposing forces is probably harder now—the forces are stronger, tension is higher, and society is more open. But our faith in Judaism and the Jewish people gives us the strength to demand, and expect, the same achievement in our time. It is a task worth the effort.

7

SEPHARDIC JEWS

Little empirical knowledge is available on the Sephardim in the United States. Albert Adatto's *Sephardim and the Seattle Sephardic Community* appeared in 1949 as a master's thesis, but did not receive wide attention.[1] Two books on Sephardic culture—*The Sephardic Heritage* by Barnett[2] and *The Sephardic Tradition* by Lazar[3]—have been published recently, but neither was a study of Sephardim in the United States. In addition, Lazar's book was criticized for presenting an inaccurate overall coverage of Sephardim.[4] Birmingham's *The Grandees* discusses the remnants of the colonial Sephardic community[5] but has been criticized for this limited focus as well as for presenting an inaccurate picture of "the Sephardic Jews of the Levantine diaspora, with whom it deals in passing."[6] *Hispanic Culture and Character of the Sephardic Jews* by Benardete, published in 1952, has a chapter on Sephardic Jews in the United States that remains one of the best sources.[7] Empirical studies are limited, however; Sanua's 1967 article,[8] a 1968 article by Zenner,[9] which discussed Syrian Jews in New York City, and Cohen's 1971 article on marriage patterns of United States Sephardim[10] have helped to correct this lack of empirical information. Nevertheless in 1973 Sanua stated that "literature on the Sephardi Jews in the United States, apart from journalistic reports, tends to be scarce."[11] Sanua's 1973 paper and Angel's exploratory study, also published in 1973,[12] have given wider recognition to the available information as well as the need for more research.

The most comprehensive description of the Sephardic community in the United States today is Angel's 1973 article, "The Sephardim of the United States: An Exploratory Study."[13] Published by the *American Jewish Yearbook* in 1973, its appearance perhaps indicates an increasing awareness of the Sephardic culture in the United States. *The American Sephardi*,[14] *The Sephardic Scholar*,[15] *The Sephardic World*,[16] *The Sephardic Voice*,[17] and *Yeshiva University's Sephardic Bulletin*[18] are also helping focus attention on Sephardim. The inauguration of a Sephardic studies program at Yeshiva University and the formation of several organizations, including the umbrella American Sephardi Federation, also point to increasing concern with—and knowledge of—Sephardim.[19]

Several articles explaining the "distinctive spirit and culture of Sephardic culture" have also appeared. Angel has been a major contributor in this area with, for example, "Sephardic Culture,"[20] "The Sephardic Theater of Seattle,"[21] and "Ruminations About Sephardic Identity."[22] Lasry, as well as Angel, has answered the criticism that Sephardic Jews are stressing points of difference with the larger Jewish community. Lasry has noted that "we [Sephardim and Ashkenazim] are all first and foremost Jews,"[23] and Angel has noted that "unity is not uniformity" and that "the more a person knows of the cultural forces which produce him, the more he will know himself."[24] The religious outlook of the Sephardim has also been discussed by Angel, who points out that "the Sephardic approach to halakhah stressed the idea that the law is a practical guide to human behavior" whereas the Ashkenazim "developed a tendency to deal with law in an abstract, pilpulistic way."[25] Jose Faur has contributed several scholarly articles including "Introducing the Materials of Sephardic Culture to Contemporary Jewish Studies" and "Early Zionist Ideals Among Sephardim in the Nineteenth Century."[26] In addition to these publications, several observational or impressionistic studies have appeared—such as Schulter's article on the Moroccan Jewish community in Washington, D.C.[27]

The selections in this section describe Sephardic Jews. The first selection by Angel describes the general situation of United States Sephardim today.[28] The article by Sanua provides information on several Sephardic communities and gives a review of current research,[29] while the following article by Schulter describes one segment—the Moroccan—of the Sephardic community in Washington, D.C.[30] The article by Liebman on the Cuban Jewish community in Miami is not specifically a study of a Sephardic community but illustrates the interaction between non-Sephardim and Sephardim (largely from a Turkish background) in one particular community in which the Sephardim comprise about one-fourth of the specific (Cuban) Jewish community but a much smaller part of the larger (Miami) Jewish community.[31] The last selection by Lavender discusses the current "revival" of Sephardic culture in the United States and the future of Sephardism in the United States.[32]

NOTES

1. Albert Adatto, *Sephardim and the Seattle Sephardic Community*, unpublished master's theses, University of Washington, 1939 (approved 1949).

2. Richard Barnett, ed., *The Sephardic Heritage* (New York: Ktav Publishing House, 1971).

3. Moshe Lazar, ed., *The Sephardic Tradition: Ladino and Spanish Jewish Literature* (New York: W.W. Norton, 1972).

4. Marc. D. Angel, "Ruminations About Sephardic Identity," *Midstream* 18 (March 1972): 66.

5. Stephen Birmingham, *The Grandees* (New York: Harper & Row, 1971).

6. Angel, "Ruminations About Sephardic Identity," p. 66.

7. Mair José Benardete, *Hispanic Culture and Character of the Sephardic Jews* (New York: Hispanic Institute in the United States, 1952).

8. Victor D. Sanua, "A Study of the Adjustment of Sephardi Jews in the New York Metropolitan Area," *Jewish Journal of Sociology* 9 (June 1967): 25-33.

9. Walter P. Zenner, "Syrian Jews in Three Social Settings," *Jewish Journal of Sociology* 10 (June 1968): 101-120.

10. Hayyim Cohen, "Sephardi Jews in the United States: Marriage with Ashkenazim and Non-Jews," *Dispersion and Unity* 13/14 (1971): 151-160.

11. Victor D. Sanua, "Contemporary Studies of Sephardi Jews in the United States" (Paper presented at the Sixth World Congress of Jewish Studies, Jerusalem, Israel, August 1973).

12. Marc D. Angel, "The Sephardim of the United States: An Exploratory Study," in Morris Fine and Milton Himmelfarb, eds., *American Jewish Yearbook* (New York: American Jewish Committee, 1973).

13. Ibid.

14. *The American Sephardi* is published by the Sephardic Studies Program of Yeshiva University in association with the Community Service Division.

15. *The Sephardic Scholar* is published by the American Society of Sephardic Studies.

16. *The Sephardic World* is published by the World Institute of Sephardic Studies.

17. *The Sephardic Voice* is published by the American Sephardi Federation.

18. The *Yeshiva University's Sephardic Bulletin* reports activities of the Sephardic Studies Program and the Sephardic Community Activities Program and is published by the Community Service Division of Yeshiva University.

19. For a more complete discussion of publications and activities, see Abraham D. Lavender, "The Sephardic Revival in the United States: A Case of Ethnic Revival in a Minority-within-a-Minority," *Journal of Ethnic Studies* 3 (Fall 1975): 21-31.

20. Marc D. Angel, "Sephardic Culture," *Jewish Spectator* 37 (December 1972): 23-24.

21. Marc D. Angel, "The Sephardic Theater of Seattle," *American Jewish Archives* 25 (November 1973): 156-160.

22. Angel, "Ruminations About Sephardic Identity."

23. George Lasry, "Editorial," *The Sephardic World* 1 (Summer 1972): 3.

24. Angel, "Ruminations About Sephardic Identity," p. 67.

25. Marc D. Angel, "A Sephardic Approach to Halakhah," *Midstream* 21 (August-September 1975): 66-69.

26. Jose Faur, "Introducing the Materials of Sephardic Culture to Contemporary Jewish Studies," *American Jewish Historical Quarterly* 63 (June 1974): 340-349; "Early Zionist Ideals

Among Sephardim in the Nineteenth Century," *Judaism* 25 (Winter 1976): 54-64. Also see Faur's "Sephardim in the Nineteenth Century: New Directions and Old Values," proceedings of the American Academy for Jewish Research, vol. 44, 1977. This latter article, along with Marc Angel's "A Sephardic Approach to Halakhah" (*Midstream*, vol. 21, August-September 1975, pp. 66-69) is outstanding for giving a "feel" for Sephardic outlook.

27. John Shulter, "Washington's Moroccan Jews—A Community of Artisans," *Washington Post Potomac Magazine*, July 26, 1970.

28. Marc D. Angel, "Sephardic Culture in America," *Jewish Life* 38 (March-April 1971): 7-11

29. Sanua, "Contemporary Studies of Sephardi Jews in the United States."

30. Schulter, "Washington's Moroccan Jews."

31. Seymour B. Liebman, "Cuban Jewish Community in South Florida," in Morris Fine and Milton Himmelfarb, eds., *American Jewish Yearbook* (New York: American Jewish Committee, 1969), pp. 238-246.

32. Lavender, "The Sephardic Revival in the United States."

SEPHARDIC CULTURE IN AMERICA

MARC D. ANGEL

When the first Sephardic Jews to settle in Seattle, Washington arrived there in the early 1900's, the local Ashkenazim had difficulty accepting them as Jews. The Sephardim spoke Judeo-Spanish rather than Yiddish. Their names—Alhadeff, Calvo, Policar, etc.—did not sound "Jewish." Even when the newcomers from the Levant showed their Tephillin, the Ashkenazim were not absolutely convinced of their Jewishness.

This episode is indicative of the cultural gap that divides Sephardim and Ashkenazim. Products of different historical forces, it is not surprising to find the two groups varying in their attitudes and life-styles. Indeed, the Jewishness of the two groups, though ultimately based on the same beliefs and religious sources, manifests itself in quite different ways. Thus, it is possible for members of one group to misunderstand the Jewishness of the other group.

Certainly most Ashkenazic Jews have little or no understanding of Sephardic Jews. They either know nothing of Sephardic existence, or they foster false ideas based on incomplete knowledge. The result of this phenomenon is that the Sephardim have not been fully integrated into the American Jewish community, and have not been able to make the cultural contributions of which they are capable.

Since the Ashkenazim form the vast majority of American Jews, their brand of Jewishness has been accepted by the general public as the standard. Jewish stereotypes are inevitably drawn from Ashkenazic prototypes. When national women's magazines give recipes for Jewish cooking, they describe Ashkenazic foods like gefilte fish and tzimmes. When politicians want to attract Jewish voters, they drop Yiddish phrases into their campaign speeches—even when their audiences are Sephardic. What effect has the equating of Jewishness with Ashkenazic standards had on Sephardim? How can a legitimate minority within Jewry maintain its identity when its very existence is misunderstood or ignored?

Before we can answer that question, we must first give a general definition of
who the Sephardim in America are and what their culture is. The old American
Sephardic families are, of course, the most widely known. Their association with
the Spanish and Portuguese congregations of New York, Philadelphia, and Newport
has been the subject of many works. Most recently, Steven Birmingham has written
a book about them significantly entitled, *The Grandees: America's Sephardic Elite.*
But these old families represent a minute percentage of the American Sephardim.
The largest number came to the United States during the twentieth century, mostly
from the Balkan countries. Concerning these Levantine Sephardim, little has been
written. It is precisely among them that the identity crisis is most crucial.

The Sephardi immigrants from the Levant, descendants of the Jews expelled
from Spain in 1492, had several major obstacles to overcome in order to adapt to
American society. They were separated from the non-Jews not only by religion,
but by language (Spanish) and culture (Oriental). The last two factors also divided
them from their Ashkenazic coreligionists. Notwithstanding these problems, the
Sephardim made a significant adjustment to their new environment, and achieved
economic security. They established large communities in New York, Los Angeles,
and Seattle, and smaller ones in such places as Atlanta, Cincinnati, Indianapolis,
Miami Beach, Montgomery (Alabama), Highland Park (New Jersey), and Portland
(Oregon). All of these communities have become quite Americanized within several
generations.

The culture of the Levantine Sephardim has been profoundly influenced by its
Spanish sources. The Sephardic mother tongue, until recently, has been Judeo-
Spanish. At all family and communal gatherings, Sephardim would sing Judeo-
Spanish ballads and folk-songs, developing in the course of centuries a rich folklore. Sephardic culture has been able to blend religion and life into a harmony;
thus, Sephardic folklore contains sensitive poems of nature and passionate love-
songs as well as religiously oriented poems. The religion-secularism clash that so
much bothers orthodox Ashkenazim is irrelevant for the Sephardic mind.

Another characteristic of Separdic culture is *joie de vivre.* Religion is not austere
and meticulously strict for the Sephardim. Rather, it is the spirit that subtly per-
vades their daily activities and celebrations. The Sephardim are optimistic. Their
positive view of life manifests itself in their many parties and gatherings, in their love
for music, in their enthusiastic communal synagogue singing.

Sephardic culture also imbues the individual with a strong sense of personal
pride. Sephardim do not look at themselves as lowly, humiliated people, but as
worthy and dignified citizens. They face man and God with self-respect. Rich and
poor, learned and ignorant, all have a feeling of self-worth and dignity.

Aside from the features already mentioned, other components which make up
Sephardic culture include: Sephardic liturgy, hazzanuth, and pronunciation in the syn-
agogue; Sephardic minhagim; Sephardic cuisine. All of these factors, differing from
Ashkenazic modes in so many ways, go into the making of Sephardic Jewishness.

Due to the initial lack of communication between the Sephardic and Ashkenazic groups, the Sephardim were compelled to maintain their culture in isolation.

This was feasible in the first generation because the Sephardim were saturated with their Sephardic character. They spoke Spanish to one another, they lived in the same neighborhoods, they enjoyed a closely knit community. These factors served to help them preserve their Sephardic identity. However, the second and third generation Sephardim do not have the same forces working for them. They are no longer tied to their heritage by the Spanish language or the Sephardic neighborhood. Hence the identity crisis of the young Sephardic Jew. He may try to delve into his own history and culture, renewing himself as a Sephardi. He may assimilate into the Ashkenazic community. He may, tragically, find no tie to Judaism at all, seeing that his notions of Judaism are inextricably tied to his Sephardic roots and that these roots have now become weakened.

The forces of Americanization have nearly destroyed Judeo-Spanish among the new generations. Therefore, the language which bound Levantine Sephardim together as Jews for nearly five centuries no longer unites young American Sephardim. With the language, much of the folklore has fallen into obscurity. Celebrations and religious observances have tended to assume an American rather than Oriental or Spanish air. The secularism of American civilization has also lessened general religious observance among Sephardim.

Americanization and secularization, though, are problems all Jews must face. The particular difficulty the Sephardim have in preserving their culture, however, stems from the fact that Jewishness in America is set by an Ashkenazic standard. The Sephardi's customs and attitudes, his history and people, are ignored. Sephardim are expected to be Ashkenazim if they want to be recognized as Jews, especially as orthodox Jews. Several years ago, Dr. Alan Corre delivered a paper for the American Society of Sephardic Studies called "The Importance of Being Ashkenazi." Dr. Corre argued that Sephardic culture in America cannot survive on its own, but will assimilate into the Ashkenazic mainstream. He suggested areas where Sephardim might influence the Ashkenazim. Even when addressing Sephardic scholars, Dr. Corre contended that Sephardim must, in effect, become Ashkenazim.

The Ashkenazication process is clearly evident, for example, in the day schools and yeshivoth. Sephardic students quickly learn to use Yiddish words, to dress and think like the other students. Sephardic history and culture are seldom if ever taught. Most Sephardi students, let alone Ashkenazi students, know practically nothing of post-1492 Sephardic history. The yeshivoth hardly ever mention the names and works of the great Levantine Sephardic rabbis. Thus, Sephardic students who want advanced Jewish education in America run the risk of losing their own culture in the process.

Another example of the Ashkenazication of Sephardim may be drawn from some Ashkenazic rabbis who occupy pulpits of Sephardic synagogues. Although several such rabbis have made sincere attempts at fostering Sephardic culture, most have not. They lead congregations without knowing the first thing about their congregants' heritage. They casually introduce Ashkenazic melodies into the Sephardic synagogue service. They teach their congregants to call the synagogue "shool" instead of "kahal." They preach sermons and give lectures without ever drawing on the classic works of the Levantine Sephardim. They do not realize that Sephardim are not Ashkenazim.

The main problem in the preservation of Sephardic culture, though, is the Sephardim themselves. Not having built day schools and yeshivoth of their own, they have necessitated their children's attendance at Ashkenazic schools. Not having trained enough of their own rabbis, they have been required to turn to non-Sephardim for leadership. Moreover, the inability of the older generations to transmit the Sephardic heritage to their children has been detrimental. They showed their children the external features of Sephardic culture, but did not convey the history and philosophy of Sephardim well enough. Thus, unsatisfied with a seemingly superficial culture, many educated young Sephardim have become disenchanted with Judaism and have drifted away. Whatever ties they have with Judaism, though, are inextricably linked with their Sephardic backgrounds. To increase their involvement with orthodox Judaism, we must first teach them their Sephardic roots. We must explain Judaism to them in terms of their own Sephardic heritage. It is an error to try to attract them to Orthodoxy by asking them to follow Ashkenazic patterns.

People are the products of their culture. In each individual's mind are the latent voices, dreams, and visions of generations of his ancestors. Sometimes when he least expects it, a voice from his past will emerge. He may see something, or hear something, or do something that will give him a profound sense of nostalgia, that will let him penetrate into his past. Without this dimension in human experience, he is deprived of something sacred. To carelessly ignore or suppress Sephardic culture is to deracinate the Sephardim. As their Sephardic roots are weakened, so ultimately will their Jewish roots wither.

The challenge to American Jewish Orthodoxy is significant. The Sephardim, whose rich heritage goes back to the golden age of Spanish Jewry, have historically been traditional in their Jewish practices. If we seize the day, we may stimulate a renaissance of Sephardic culture and a consequent return to orthodox Judaism. The key to the solution rests in the acknowledgment that Sephardim have a right to exist as Sephardim. They have a right to have a Sephardic Jewishness.

Day schools and yeshivoth could establish Sephardic studies programs. Teachers could help their Sephardic students to appreciate their heritage. Ashkenazic rabbis and leaders could make serious attempts at understanding the Sephardim and their past. The Ashkenazic laity could encourage the existence and development of Sephardic culture and not doubt Sephardic Jewishness because Sephardim do not necessarily eat gefilte fish, wear kippoth in public, or have the same liturgy as the Ashkenazim.

The main hope is, of course, that the Sephardim themselves will be able to impart their own culture. There are indications that they are beginning to do just that. The time is ripe for an upsurge in Sephardic culture.

It is not easy for a Sephardic Jew to maintain his identity. Being a Jew, he is a minority among Americans. Being a Sephardi, he is a minority among Jews. But the Sephardic Jew must maintain his Sephardic identity—or ultimately lose his Jewish identity.

CONTEMPORARY STUDIES OF SEPHARDI JEWS IN THE UNITED STATES

VICTOR D. SANUA

It has been estimated that the total Jewish population of the United States is approximately 5.5 million. No one knows the number of Sephardi Jews among them. The rough estimates that have been offered in the literature range between 60,000 and 200,000. Probably the actual figure may be between these two extremes. A large percentage reside in the New York metropolitan area.

The earliest Jewish settlers who came to the New World about three hundred years ago were of Spanish-Portugese descent. However, in time they lost their traditional Sephardi characteristics, and this group has been completely assimilated. The late Judge Cardozo of the Supreme Court of the United States, in a letter sent to Professor José Benardete in 1952, indicated that as far as his family was concerned, it had no cultural traditions with reference to the survival of Spanish Jewish traits.

In addition to the great immigration from Poland and Russia, small groups of Sephardi Jews came to the United States in the early years of the twentieth century. Because of political upheavals and rising nationalism in the Ottoman Empire, Ladino-speaking Jews from the Balkans, and later, Arabic-speaking Jews, primarily from Syria, immigrated to the United States, impelled by a desire for security and to better themselves economically. Before 1908 only a trickle came to the United States, but the majority came between 1908 and 1924.

Following the Israel-Arab wars, other Jews from the Mediterranean reached the United States, particularly Egyptian Jews following the 1956 war and Lebanese Jews after the 1967 war. Individual families of Morroccan and Iraqi Jews have also immigrated to the United States.

Literature on the Sephardi Jews in the United States, apart from journalistic reports, tends to be scarce. One of the earliest attempts at a sociological study of Sephardi Jews in New York was undertaken by Hacker (1926).[1] Right at the start Sephardi Jews established themselves on the Lower East Side of New York City and opened typical coffeehouses as a place for recreation. The author remembers visiting one of the last remaining coffeehouses when he came to the United States after World War II. He saw a group of elderly men playing backgammon, some smoking the narguileh, and others drinking the thick Turkish coffee. However, all that has disappeared, and the new generation of educated Sephardi Jews has acculturated to American Jewish life. The social activities of the Ladino-speaking Sephardi Jews center around fund raising for the maintenance of an old-age home. They often meet at fund-raising functions at catered dinner-dances or resort facilities in the Catskills, where the language of communication is virtually entirely English, except that some of the old-timers may still converse in Ladino. The vestiges are to be found in their fondness for Mediterranean foods and Greek and Turkish group dances. At many of these functions they also arrange for belly dancers to entertain, and some Sephardi women take private lessons. It is to be noted that presently there is a trend among Ashkenazim to include Greek group dancing at bar mitzvahs and weddings.

More than forty years after Hacker's pioneering study, another sociological study of a Sephardi group was undertaken in New York—particularly of Egyptian Jews and Jews from Aleppo and Damascus in Syria. This was conducted by the author with the assistance of a French-speaking student.[2] I shall now summarize a number of reports and studies on Sephardi Jews in various communities in the United States.

SEATTLE, WASHINGTON

The Spanish Sephardi community in Seattle, which has been estimated to number 3,000, is of special interest, particularly because it is far from the mainstreams of Judaism, which are mostly found in the East. The relative isolation of this community has permitted it to hold more staunchly to its way of life than in other communities, such as New York City. Podet and Chasen write the following in connection with the discovery of Sephardim by the Reform Jews in Seattle:

> Calvo and Policar were delighted to learn that Seattle had a Jewish community, but the two Reform Jews were skeptical about the authenticity of Calvo and Policar. The new arrivals were swarthy men who spoke Greek and absolutely no Yiddish; they seemed to be Greek fishermen doing a bad job of impersonating Jews. After a while, though, Calvo and Policar dug into their sea bags and pulled out their ritual phylacteries and Hebrew prayer books, which they began reading aloud in strangely accented Hebrew. At last the two Reform Jews were convinced that Calvo and Policar were for real, and in due course introduced them to the Jewish community.[3]

The most adventuresome members of this Seattle community were the Marmaralis who have lived on the small island of Marmara near the Bosphorus in Turkey. Some of their Greek friends had already gone ahead of them. In time, the Seattle community grew large enough to afford the luxury of two synagogues. The community grouped itself into a congregation of Rhodeslies, who came from the island of Rhodes, and a congregation of Tekirdolis, who came primarily from other parts of Turkey.

The Sephardi Jews in Seattle were able to maintain their isolation until the advent of World War II, which helped break down the barriers between Ashkenazim and Sephardi Jews. Marriage between them, once unthinkable, became commonplace. Sephardi boys, while in the army, and later in college under the G.I. bill, and Sephardi girls dating non-Sephardi Jewish soldiers, drew the community out of its isolation. As the younger generation lacked attachment to the old culture, and many became professionals, they joined more prestigious non-Sephardi synagogues. The Ladino language is hardly ever spoken among the third generation. While the first arrivals worked in small shops, shoe stands, and grocery stores, and some worked as longshoremen, tailors, barbers, and butchers, now the Sephardi community of Seattle is well represented in the fields of law, science, medicine, engineering, and education.

NEW YORK CITY

Two groups studied by the author include the Syrian Jews in Brooklyn and the Jews recently arrived from Egypt, who are primarily of Sephardi origin and reside in Brooklyn and Queens.[4] The data collected on these two groups were obtained through interviews and mailed questionnaires.

Syrian Jews

With the Syrian Jews, we selected 150 names out of a total of 1,500 from a list maintained by a senior employee of the mother congregation, Magen David, in Brooklyn, and kept up to date in 1965. The Syrian Jews in Brooklyn are possibly the last remaining homogeneous Sephardi religious group in the United States. Approximately 15,000 to 20,000 of them live in the Ocean Parkway section of Brooklyn. Not only do they tend to live in the same area, but they spend their summer vacations in the same resorts—Bradley Beach and Deal, New Jersey—where they have built synagogues for summer use. On Shabbat the synagogue overflows with congregants. A number of Syrian Jewish families have opened businesses in other cities, where they are integrated into the majority Ashkenazi community. When their children are of marriageable age, many return to New York or rent homes for the summer at the beach resorts mentioned to ensure that their children marry within the group.

While the impact of acculturation has been very strong in other Sephardi communities, it seems that Syrian Jews have maintained their stability. From Bensonhurst, they moved out to better neighborhoods in Ocean Parkway where they have built $4 million synagogues. On Shabbat and holidays they overflow with men, women, and young adults, and the streets are cordoned off. They intermingle very little with non-Syrian Jews and with Gentiles. The largest congregation is Shaare

Zion, mostly attended by Jews originating from Aleppo. The Syrian Jews from Damascus attend the Ahi Ezer congregation, a newly constructed building on Ocean Parkway. In addition, two new congregations, B'nei Magen David and Congregation Beth Torah, composed mainly of the younger generation, have recently emerged. Yet another congregation is currently being organized on Bedford Avenue in the Midwood section of Brooklyn. The community supports two yeshiva day schools that have a full enrollment. Approximately 90 percent of Syrian Jewish youth attend yeshivoth, either under Syrian-Jewish or Ashkenazi auspices.

The modern trend in Judaism has hardly had an effect on Syrian Jews. Rabbi Jacob Kassin, the chief rabbi of the community, indicated in examining the questionnaire that it would be superfluous to include the question inquiring about the denomination to which the respondent belonged. He was quite right, since only one Syrian Jew checked the item "Conservative" while all the others checked "Orthodox." In contrast, the Jews from Egypt, where there was no other denomination except Orthodox, consider themselves as follows: 30 percent Orthodox, 36 percent Conservative, 6 percent Reform, and 28 percent Jewish secular. Thus, wh many Jews worry about assimilation and intermarriage, the danger for such trends among the Syrian Jews is still quite remote. It is to be noted that during the High Holidays both young and old attend services, and during certain periods of the day hundreds of young people stroll around the synagogues.

Economically, the Syrian Jews are relatively well off. About 60 percent of the respondents operate their own business. A large percentage of them own retail stores or are in the dry goods import and export business. Some are wealthy enough to own manufacturing plants abroad. In 1965, the average age of the household head was forty-three years, with more than 20 percent having had some college education and graduate degrees. Only 10 percent indicated that they have any regular contacts with non-Jews.

Approximately 50 percent of the household heads attend religious services weekly or daily; 50 percent of the families light candles on Friday night regularly and 25 percent occasionally; all buy kosher meat, and with one exception, all respondents use separate dishes, while 60 percent never eat nonkosher food outside the home; 95 percent light Chanukah candles; and all of them contribute to Jewish philanthropies and participate in the usual Jewish fund raising. When we asked where most of their relatives live, 85 percent indicated that they live in the same neighborhood, which reflects the high concentration in one single area. Only 13 percent of the wives of Syrian Jews are Ashkenazim.

In general, we have here an extremely cohesive group of Jews. We believe it will remain homogenous for a long period to come. There was not a single case of divorce in the sample, although there were known instances of divorce.

Egyptian Jews

While we call this particular group Egyptian, their education is primarily French. Twenty-five percent came with an Egyptian passport, while the rest had either a

European passport or were stateless at the time they left Egypt. A list of Egyptian Jews, which was not readily available, was arranged through the "pyramiding effect." Fifteen Egyptian Jews were requested to list the names and addresses of their relatives and friends, and in turn, these were asked to send similar forms to their friends and relatives. By eliminating duplicate names, we were able to establish a list of 450 families, and random samples were selected from them. Thirty-six Egyptian families were interviewed, and they were compared with the fifty-six families who responded to the questionnaire, representing a 35 percent response on the mailing.

We found that there were no significant differences between the two groups from the economic point of view. Like the Syrian Jews, Egyptian Jews belong predominantly to the middle and upper socioeconomic classes. Fifty percent of them spoke English fluently before their arrival in the United States and had a high level of formal education. About 50 percent of the total had a partial college education, with 20 percent holding graduate degrees. They lived mostly in rented apartments, with only 12 percent owning their homes. Twenty-five percent indicated that at one time they had lived outside New York City. Twenty-five percent were self-employed; 30 percent of the wives held full-time jobs. Sixty-two percent indicated that they had regular contacts with non-Sephardi Jews, and 36 percent had contacts with Gentiles. It would seem that the Egyptian Jews in New York City have more contacts with non-Jews that the Syrian Jews, despite the latter group's older settlement in the United States. Egyptian Jews are much less observant than Syrian Jews. Only 50 percent of them buy kosher meat; 32 percent use separate dishes; 60 percent eat nonkosher food outside their home. Egyptian Jews tend to reside in Brooklyn and in the Rego Park section of Queens, where they have been able to establish a synagogue, together with other Sephardi groups.

In general, compared with their Syrian Jewish brethren, the Egyptian Jews have not been able to maintain a serious degree of cohesiveness and do not exist as a community. Since they are spread out in New York City, they have no leadership or synagogue that they can call their own. We feel that, in time, they will be absorbed into the regular mainstream of Judaism. It is to be noted that Egyptian Jews are approximately divided into three groups: those of Spanish origin, Ladino-speaking; those whose families emigrated from Syria early in the century and are Arabic-speaking; and other Sephardi groups. The lingua franca is French among all.

SPANISH JEWS IN BROOKLYN

This study of Spanish Jews in Brooklyn was carried out in the Brighton Beach area by David Cohen, a student at City College,[5] whose grandfather was the rabbi of Torah Israel, which was founded in 1920. This particular congregation never became affluent. By the time they were able to build a synagogue, their children had passed the age of going to Talmud Torah. As the children marry, they move away from the Brighton Beach area. The study is based on a sample of twenty-five families of a total of 125 families who belong to the congregation. In general, Cohen found that the Syrian Jews are more prolific—3.7 children per family as compared to 2.9 children in the Spanish Jewish group. More of the Syrian Jews are native born, 58 percent and 40 percent, respectively. There was a high incidence of marriage with non-Sephardim among the Spanish Jews. Sixty-four percent have regular contacts with non-Sephardi Jews compared with 30 percent of the Syrian Jews.

Cohen found that the incidence of intermarriage with non-Jews was 24 percent for this Spanish group, which is relatively high. A correct incidence of intermarriage among Jews in New York City is not available at this time, but in such states as Indiana and Iowa, it was found that the intermarriage rate for Jews is 50 percetn. One might possibly draw the conclusion that the greater interaction of Spanish Jews with non-Jews has led to the increase of intermarriage. As to religious identification, 64 percent of the Spanish Jews consider themselves Conservative. It should be noted that this category was not appropriate for Syrian Jews. Sixty percent of the Spanish Jews buy kosher meat, and 20 percent use separate dishes.

Thus, it appears that the Spanish Jew in Brighton Beach is more typical of the American Ashkenazi Jew in his religious practice in that he attends services for the important holidays and keeps the traditions of Passover and Chanukah but does not observe kashrut as intensively. Spanish Jews of this congregation have less Jewish education. None have sent their children to yeshivas or day schools. Of the respondents who reported on married children, 80 percent indicated no Sephardi daughter or son-in-law. It is thus very unlikely that Torah Israel will remain a Sephardi congregation in the years to come.

OTHER SEPHARDI GROUPS

During the past twenty years, two new groups of Sephardi Jews have been arriving in the United States. Because of fear of persecution in Morocco, about 100 families emigrated and settled in New York. They live mostly in the Queens area of New York City and are making efforts to organize themselves as a group. According to one respondent we interviewed regarding the status of this particular group, most of them are French-educated through the Alliance Israelite, but they have little knowledge of Judaism. It would seem that the Alliance Israelite was more interested in making Frenchmen of Moroccan Jews rather than Jews.

Dr. Jean-Claude Lasry, research associate at the Institute of Community and Family Psychiatry of the Jewish General Hospital in Montreal, Quebec, has undertaken a survey of Jews from North Africa who arrived in Montreal from 1957 to 1970. Over 600 people were interviewed. In a personal communication Dr. Lasry has indicated that parallel to this study, he did a statistical research on intermarriage over the last ten years (1,565 marriages). Results on intermarriage are staggering: over the last ten years, 67 percent of North Africans intermarried with non-Jews while 31 percent of Sephardi Jews and 21 percent of Ashkenazim did the same.

Following Israel's six-day war in 1967, about 1,500 Jews from Lebanon came to the United States, Canada, and Mexico. Approximately 2,500 went to Israel.

Most of the Lebanese Jews in New York, who are themselves of Syrian origin, have been employed by Syrian Jews in New York. It would seem that Lebanese Jews prefer to be engaged in export-import trade than in retailing. They have blended well within the Syrian Jewish community.

Two other studies pertain to surveys of the Sephardi population at large and not within specific communities. The first was conducted by Dr. Haim Cohen of the Hebrew University, Jerusalem, and the results have been published as "Sephardi Jews in the United States: Marriage with Ashkenazim and non-Jews."[6] He sent out 3,000 questionnaires, some to Sephardis who were members of various congregations across the United States. In New York City he selected Sephardi names from the telephone directory. Dr. Cohen found that the Jews of Spanish origin are scattered in many areas in the United States, while the Syrian Jews are concentrated in one area of Brooklyn. He found that 81 percent of the first generation of Spanish-speaking Sephardi Jews had Sephardi wives; 17 percent were married to Ashkenazi women and 2 percent to non-Jewish women. No differences were found among first-, second-, and third-generation Syrian Jews in their rate of marriage with Ashkenazim. However, with the Spanish Jews, he found the rate to be about 50 percent in the second and third generation. This group also had the highest rate of inter-marriage—12 percent. This high rate of marriage outside the group is reflected by the attitudes of the respondents. While 40 percent of the Syrian Jews would agree to the marriage of their children with non-Sephardis, the rate for the Spanish Jews was approximately 75 percent. According to Dr. Cohen, the Syrian Jews are more observant that other groups, maintain old customs and way of life, and encourage marriage within the community. And, as already mentioned, they like to spend their summer vacation in the same resorts.

A more recent study (which was published in the *American Jewish Yearbook* in 1973) is by Rabbi Marc Angel from Seattle, who is presently assistant rabbi at Shearith Israel Congregation in New York City.[7] His study is being carried out exclusively with Spanish-speaking Jews. It shows that the rate of marriage with non-Sephardis (75 percent) is as high as the rate found by Dr. Cohen. Eleven percent are married to non-Jews, a figure which is also close to that in Dr. Cohen's study.

Other findings of Angel's study further corroborate the disintegration of the Spanish Jewish community. Jewish education among Spanish Jews is found to be very poor. To this day, in contrast to the Syrian Jews, they have no day school anywhere in the United States. The community that has produced the most rabbis is Seattle. A majority do not consider themselves to be Orthodox. Judeo-Spanish as a living language is in its death throes.

Other demographic information provided by Rabbi Angel is that economically the community could be described only as well off. Nearly all Spanish Sephardis of college age are in college or plan to attend college. The birth rate is low, 2.3 per family. It would seem that in two or three generations, this group will be assimilated like those who came 300 years ago.

While there have been many attempts in the past to federate all Sephardi communities in the United States, none has been successful so far. However, in 1973, under the chairmanship of Daniel Elazar, a professor at Temple University, the first national convention of leaders of Sephardi organizations was held at Shearith Israel Congregation in New York City for the purpose of establishing the American Sephardic Federation as part of the World Sephardi Federation. Hopefully, this might represent the beginning of a renaissance of Sephardi life in the United States.

NOTES

1. L.M. Hacker, "The Community Life of Sephardic Jews in New York City," *Jewish Social Service Quarterly* 3 (1926): 32-40.

2. Victor D. Sanua, "A Study of the Adjustment of Sephardi Jews in the New York Metropolitan Area," *Jewish Journal of Sociology* 9 (June 1967): 25-33.

3. A.H. Podet and D. Chasen, "Heirs to a Noble Tradition: Seattle's Storied Sephardim," *Jewish Digest* 8 (September 1968): 130-140.

4. Sanua, "Study of the Adjustment."

5. David Cohen, "A Study of a Sephardic Congregation in Brooklyn" (Unpublished paper, 1972).

6. Hayyim Cohen, "Sephardi Jews in the United States: Marriage with Ashkenazim and non-Jews," *Dispersion et Unite* 13/14 (1971-1972): 151-160.

7. Marc D. Angel "The Sephardim of the United States: An Exploratory Study," in Morris Fine and Milton Himmelfarb, eds., *American Jewish Yearbook* (New York: American Jewish Committee, 1973).

ADDITIONAL BIBLIOGRAPHY

M.J. Benardete. *Hispanic Culture and Character of the Sephardic Jews.* New York: Hispanic Institute, 1952.

B.G. Frank. "Where Mideast Meets in West: See Strong Accord Between Syrian and Lebanese Jews in Brooklyn." *Sentinal*, December 14, 1972.

D. Romey. "The Sephardim of Seattle." *Jewish Life* (May-June 1964): 47-55.

WASHINGTON'S MOROCCAN JEWS-A COMMUNITY OF ARTISANS

JOHN J. SCHULTER

When they talk to each other, it is either in Arabic, French, Spanish or English (in that order); when they dine together, it is more likely to be cous-cous (a kind of semolina with meat and vegetables), harira (a dry vegetable soup heavily flavored with lemon and yeast) or ftyre (a triangular Napoleon filled with meat and spices); when they party together, the men wear conventional dress, but the women wear caftans (a long velvet or silk dress with buttons down the front, usually embroidered in silver and gold); when they sing and dance, it will usually be to a huud (a stringed instrument similar to a guitar), a darbouka (tambourine) or a mandolin; when they pray together, it will be a Sephardic service in Ladino (a mixture of Spanish and Hebrew) and usually at the 16th Street orthodox Ohev Sholom Synagogue, which they rent for the high holidays.

Who are they?

They are Washington's Moroccan Jewish community, which numbers some 250 in about 60 close-knit and often intermarried families. Like other ethnic groups in pluralistic Washington, they are often indistinguishable from the mainstream of the city's population, and yet like many other foreign-born, they cling tenaciously to the customs and habits of their country of origin. For the Sephardic Jews of the Middle East, whether Moroccan, Tunisian, Algerian, Syrian, Egyptian, Lebanese, Greek, or Turkish, these customs date back some 500 years to the Spanish Inquisition when the Jews were expelled from Spain during the reign of Ferdinand and Isabella.

They serve the Washington community in many ways: hair-dressers, barbers, plumbers, electricians, restaurateurs, etc. It is no caprice that many of the leading beauty parlors of Greater Washington (Maison Marcel, Michel et Patrick, Maison

Jacques, Jean Paul et Norbert, Daniel, Val's Hair Stylists, Elysee) are owned and operated by Moroccan Jews, for the dean of the Moroccan Jewish community is Marcel Cadeaux, 68-year-old cosmetologist, wig and toupee maker, who served as chairman of the D.C. Board of Cosmetology for 10 years (1960-70). The owner of one of the largest beauty culture schools in the District is Albert Emsellem, also originally of Morocco.

Cadeaux is usually the first person that an itinerant Moroccan Jew will contact upon arrival in Washington. Even as Cadeaux was being interviewed, a call came that a Moroccan family of seven was arriving that afternoon from Rabat. "They will have dinner at my house tonight," said Cadeaux. "Naturally, I can not ask my wife to prepare dinner for so many people, so she will call other members of our community and they will come, each bringing some dish, and we will have a party. We love Arabic things and we are at home with the food and the music."

Cadeaux has earned his role as mentor, counselor, and the elder statesman to the Moroccan Jewish community for having launched scores of them in business and professions and by virtue of his seniority. He came to this country in 1924 when, he estimates, there were about 50 Moroccan Jewish families in the United States. "It was the Second World War that accelerated the migration of the Moroccan Jewish families," he explains. "American soldiers found our daughters interesting and unique, married them and brought them over. The daughters, in turn, brought over other members of the family, usually the mother or father, and that's how it went."

The subsequent emigrations, though, have been more political and economic than filial, especially since Jews throughout the Middle East are finding it increasingly difficult, since the escalation of Israeli-Arab hostilities, to pursue a profession or earn a living. In the case of the Moroccan Jews, actually only a scattering have come to this country. Most of them have gone to either France or Israel, where their prior knowledge of the language and French citizenship provided easier access into the economic life.

Entering the American mainstream has been for the Moroccan Jew relatively easy, certainly easier than it had been for earlier Jewish arrivals, despite his unfamiliarity with the language. For one, he has come during a period of relative affluence, from 1952 on, and having marketable skills, he has quickly secured employment. Moreover, the tradition of self-help, particularly strong among all Sephardic Jews, served always to provide a bed and a meal and even a financial stake until the migrant was established. Cadeaux estimates, however, that some 10 percent of those arriving are rich men, bringing with them fortunes in excess of $100,000, or more. "You must remember," he says, "that Sephardic Jews have traditionally been some of the world's leading diamond merchants and naturally some of them have settled in this country." This scarcely compares with the first settlement of Sephardic Jews who came to New Amsterdam in 1654 from the Portuguese colony of Brazil, sick with scurvy and dressed in rags.

Washington's Moroccan Jews defy the usual stereotype of an ethnic group that has traditionally followed the mercantile profession of buying and selling. In the main, they are artisans of one kind or another. Since so many of the leading hairdressers in Washington are Moroccan Jews and since so many Moroccan Jews in Washington are hairdressers, this occupational incidence suggests some explanation. Here the trail inevitably leads to Emsellem, owner of the Capitol Beauty Institute at 1012 H St. NW.

For 15 years, he traveled the national and international beauty culture circuit as Albert de Paris, lecturer, instructor, hair stylist. His knowledge of seven languages enabled him to work on three continents. To the Moroccan Jewish community and to the women of Washington who patronized his establishment on Connecticut Avenue for 20 years, he is Albert Emsellem, owner and operator of one of the largest beauty culture schools in the District.

Born in Fez, Morocco, son of a distinguished rabbi and an early pioneer in Zionism, Rabbi Macklouf Emsellem of Fez and Jerusalem, Albert learned the ways of the Sephardic people as he learned to walk. His father was one of Jewry's celebrated experts on the Cabala, a collection of mystic religious writings. His father's 800-page book is now being printed in Hebrew in this country. The son recalls with some pride the visits of Chaim Weizmann, the first president of Israel, to his father's home. "My father, besides being a rabbi, was also a chemist and he and Mr. Weizmann used to discuss chemistry at our home as a kind of relief from their Zionist work." When the elder Emsellem died in Jerusalem, a day of mourning was declared in the city.

Already familiar with English when he came to America in 1928, Emsellem started life here as a Fuller Brush salesman. "I had to find an occupation in which I would not have to work on Saturdays," he explained (the Jewish sabbath is from sundown Friday to sundown Saturday). At night he attended a beauty culture school, which started the career he has followed ever since. He came to Washington in 1941 as the proprietor of the Louey Venn of London, Inc., a cosmetic and beauty shop. The only other Moroccan family in the city at that time was the Cadeaux family.

Unlike other Moroccan Jews, Emsellem joined an Ashkenazi group because, as he says, there were not enough Sephardim in the city to form a congregation. He went on to help organize the orthodox Tiffereth Israel Synagogue, on 16th Street, where he served two terms as its president. Now settling comfortably into late middle age, the former Albert of Paris is still active in his business, but is more content to dabble in real estate, play with his four grandchildren, and arrange for the publication of his father's work.

Emsellem estimates that from 60 to 70 per cent of those hairdressers in Washington who came from Morocco were trained in his beauty culture school. The others either learned their trade in Morocco itself or in Paris, where many of them went when Morocco attained its own sovereignty. Did they make good students? "Very good students," he said. "A good hairstylist must be something of an artist.

He must have a soft, delicate touch and know what he is doing. Otherwise he could create a lot of mischief."

The professions of hairdressing and barbering have historically favored the immigrant all over the world. Compared with other professions or trades, it requires only a minimum of training and communication. Unless the operator is a loud mouth, which is not uncommon, he can learn the essentials in months and get by with no more than a few hundred words. Reading and writing are not necessary. Hence, in most urban areas, these professions are nominally filled by foreign-born. A seeming preference on the part of women for beauty parlors with foreign-sounding names is a further advantage.

Given these favorable factors, the Moroccan coming to Washington found an already built-in, if not institutionalized, setup that allowed him to enter a profession that lent itself to immediate financial return. However, given the high priority that American Jews accord to education and the professions, it is dubious whether the profession of hairdressing will pass on to the second and third generations. Indicative of this upward mobility is the Cadeaux family itself, which now finds one son as consul for the State Department in London; another son a lawyer; and a daughter married to a lawyer.

Heavily interwoven into the lives of all Middle Eastern Jews without exception is the religious and cultural impact of the Sephardic branch of the Hebrew faith. Although they were spared the worst of the excesses of the Hitler period, each recalls, as if by rote, the expulsions from Spain, said now more in pride than in anger.

Washington's Sephardic historian is the 75-year-old, multilingual (Turkish, French, Spanish, Greek, Italian, and Hebrew) Rabbi Solomon Ereza, somewhat immobile as a result of a foot injury, but nevertheless very much alive and sustained by the warmth and personal reminiscences from 40 years of unpaid service to the District's Sephardic community.

Rabbi Ereza, son and brother of distinguished rabbis, was born in Istanbul (then Constantinople), Turkey. He came to this country when he was 16. He learned the religion at his father's knee and he was first sought out in New York, where he conducted his original Sephardic service on Coney Island. After a short sojourn in Atlanta, one of the nation's largest Sephardic centers, Rabbi Ereza came to Washington in 1921. He now resides in semi-retirement at 3801 Connecticut Avenue.

There were no Moroccan Jews in Washington in 1921 and the 45 Sephardim in the city largely came from Turkey, Greece, Egypt, Syria, and Lebanon. As he relates the story, the initial group of Sephardim met in the home of one of the richer members. There was no Shofar (a ram's horn) and no Ark to hold the Torah (the only book). Pained by the inadequacy of such a service, Rabbi Ereza went to see the late Dr. Abram Simon, who, at that time, presided over the Washington Hebrew Congregation, then on 8th Street, between H and I.

Rabbi Simon was surprised and delighted to hear that there were Sephardim in Washington and, taking Rabbi Ereza by the hand, led him into the vestry, saying, "Here. It is all yours. We are all Jews and this will be your home." In 1926 the Sephardim moved to the old Hebrew Home for the Aged, then on Spring Road. There they formed the Congregation Yom Tov ("Good Day" in Hebrew), and there they worshipped for 21 years. The rabbi's daughter, Mrs. Luna Diamond, wife of attorney Norman Diamond, remembers as a little girl seeing the congregation praying on the porch of the Home, always with Rabbi Ereza as their spiritual leader and guide. Although the seven or eight Turkish Jewish families and an occasional Egytian and Syrian family continued to remain as the core of the congregation, it was the subsequent infusion of Moroccan Jews into the congregation that gave it its present numbers, as well as new life and vigor.

"For 500 years we have stayed together—ever since the Inquisition," Rabbi Ereza says pridefully. "We still speak the same Ladino that we brought from Spain and we have carried it intact throughout the Levantine as far as India."

Victor Handeli, 74, of 2200 19th St. NW, is one of the few living Turkish Jews who was a member of the original group. According to him, the group failed to grow in the 1920s due to the then-prevailing immigration laws. "The quota for Turkish citizens at that time was only 200 a year and this number was largely taken up by Turks of Moslem faith. Although we Jews carried Turkish citizenship, we were never considered to be real citizens by the Turkish government." (It should be added that the Turkish rulers of the Inquisition period opened the doors of their country to the Spanish Jews and that some 200,000 settled there.) Like many immigrants who did not know English, but did know how to cook and wash dishes, Handeli went into the restaurant business. He and his partner, Cadeaux, built up Le Petit Paris on Connecticut Avenue. Handeli retired from the business two years ago. Another Turkish Jew of the original group who found economic sanctuary in the restaurant business is the 65-year-old Jack Angel of 3201 Cummings La., Chevy Chase. With his brother, Angel owned the old Angel Restaurant on the present site of the Manger Annapolis and then ran another restaurant at 12th Street and New York Avenue before that site was torn down. Angel came to this country in 1928 from Verria, a small town near Salonika, Turkey. "Those were difficult days for us," he recalls. "We were lucky to be able to find enough men for a 'minion' (service which requires 10 people). Most of the Sephardim who came to this country remained in New York, where by the '20s, there were already from 150,000 to 200,000."

The generation gap between old and young, between those born here and in Morocco, is beginning to assert itself on such fundamental questions as marriage and religious customs. Whether out of wish fulfillment and/or self-deception, the older generation tends to pooh-pooh the idea that a Sephardim from Morocco would want to marry anybody else but a Moroccan Jewess. "The Moroccan male prefers one of his own when it comes to marriage," says Cadeaux. "In that sense we are very Arabic. Our men are spoiled brats. Their mothers wait on them in the Middle Eastern way and they expect their wives to do the same. An American Jewish girl is not going to do that."

This view of Moroccan singularity is disputed not only by Robert Cadeaux,

Cadeaux' son, but also by other young people. The younger Cadeaux is 33 and a member of the law firm of Middleton, Jasen and Cadeaux. "When I marry it will be because of reasons not necessarily religious," he says. The view of the elders is also disputed by Henri Fedida, a hairdresser at Jean Paul et Norbert on L Street. Fedida, age 36, has been in this country four months and is married to a Moroccan Jewish girl. He maintains that, although the younger Moroccans share the religious views of the older generation, they feel no compulsion to worship in a Sephardic synagogue or to marry within the Sephardic branch. He and his family worship at the Ashkenazi Summit Hill Synagogue.

Are the old-world customs sufficiently binding as to enable them to maintain their group identity?

Robert Cadeaux doesn't believe they are. "Only among the older members of the community. Many of the young Moroccan Jews either never lived in Morocco or left Morocco at such a young age that they could not have developed the required ties. Many who left Morocco went to France before coming here and their influence is mostly French."

Do they (the Moroccan Jews) feel a strong sense of identity towards other members of the Jewish community?

Not especially. Ethnically and culturally, Moroccan Jews are Arabs. Their preference in food and entertainment differs radically from that of the European Jews

Family ties among the Moroccan Jews are patently and obviously closer than they are among Jewish families who have been in this country for a longer period. Respect for parental wishes and customs is still a very important consideration and probably would be decisive where marriage is concerned. This may well erode as the older generation dies out and the newer generation becomes more firmly implanted in the American milieu.

Are their views on the Arab-Israeli conflict any different from those of other members of the Jewish community?

Says Robert Cadeaux, "They are very pro-Israel. The Moroccan Jew has strong cultural ties with the Arabs, but always as a subculture within the larger Arab natio The Moroccan Jew has a greater practical awareness of a homeland. The European Jew is more motivated by an ideal."

The history of the Jews in their 5,000 years of dispersion from the Holy Land has long been a subject of intensive study by scholars and historians. As the eminen social anthropologist, Franz Boaz, has documented, the Jews do not constitute a race. Over the centuries they have so intermarried and so intermingled with the populations of their host countries that they have lost many of the characteristics, physical and cultural, that might have distinguished them from other peoples; e.g., Chinese Jews look like other Chinese, Ethiopian Jews are dark skinned, Indian Jews are undistinguishable from other Indians, etc.

The Moroccan Jewish community also reflects the influence of the Spanish and Middle Eastern cultures in both appearance and in family names. Almost uniformly dark complexioned, very much like other Middle Eastern peoples, dark haired with closely set eyes, their noses tend to be straight, coming high from the forehead. They appear to be a relatively small people. The women are equally dark, and generally dressed in the most cosmopolitan attire and makeup. In disposition, they appear to be soft and gentle and more disposed to an Oriental rather than a western aggressive posture. If the latter attribute were not there in the first place, they have acquired it as a consequence of their profession of hair dressing.

Whatever their family names may have been in antiquity, they now carry the flavor of their Spanish and Arabic hosts. The local community consists of such family names as Morena, Atias, Suissa, Kadoch, Colon, Haim, Benisty, Assarass, Soussan, Silvera, Elmaleh, Nahoum, Ben Simon, Coan, Tatiaro, Benjoar, etc. These names are as familiar in the Sephardic community as Goldberg. Weinberg, etc., are in the Ashkenazi branch, denoting strong Germanic origin.

The desire on the part of Washington's Sephardic community to achieve its own autonomy and thereby preserve its own individuality is now attaining full flower in their plans to build the first Sephardic synagogue in Washington. According to Marcel Cadeaux, they have already acquired enough money to purchase the land and the drive is now on to secure enough money to erect the building. According to Cadeaux, every Sephardic family engaged in business will be asked to contribute $1,000 per household. This should ensure the down payment for a modern synagogue.

CUBAN
JEWISH COMMUNITY
IN SOUTH FLORIDA

SEYMOUR B. LIEBMAN

No demographic study had ever been made of the Jews in Cuba. Estimates of their number before 1960 ranged from a low of 11,000 to a high of 16,000. Appraisals of the size of the two principal communities, Ashkenazi and Sephardi, and their respective percentages of the total population, differed widely. Those of the smaller group, the Sephardi, varied between ten·per cent and one-third of the total. Jacob Schatzky in *Yiddische Yischuvim en Latin Amerika* (Buenos Aires, 1952, p. 185), put the number of Ashkenazim at 5,300 and Sephardim at 2,700 in 1925, and the total at 12,000 in 1951.

According to well informed sources, the Jewish population, both citizens and permanent residents, in Cuba before Castro was some 14,500. Of this number, 10,000 were Ashkenazim and 3,500 Sephardim. There was a third group of approximately 1,000 consisting of English-speaking Jews and many unaffiliated. The latter included descendants of Jews living in Cuba before the Spanish-American War in 1898 and who, though not converted to another faith, had little identification with their own. It also included the intermarried who did not adopt the faith of the non-Jewish spouses. Some of these unaffiliated secretly contributed to local Jewish and Israeli philanthropies.

Except for the small Jewish communities in the provinces of Camaguey and Oriente with a total membership of about 1,200, and a few other small settlements, most Jews lived in Santa Suarez, Habana Vieja, or Miramar, three districts of the capital. Miramar, the newer residential area of Havana, attracted the more affluent.

JEWISH SETTLEMENT IN CUBA

Jews have lived in Cuba ever since it was settled by Spain about 1502. Despite the edicts of their Catholic majesties, Ferdinand and Isabella, and their successors that no Jews, Moors, or other heretics, or their fourth-generation descendants, could reside in any part of the Spanish empire in the new world, the Jews were there.

The early Jewish inhabitants were known as Marranos. Their number increased rapidly, and, as the Bishop of Cuba wrote to Spain in 1508, practically every ship docking at Havana was filled with Hebrews and New Christians, as Jews recently converted to Christianity were called.

Inquisition proceedings against the Marranos in Cuba began as early as 1520. In the 17th century large-scale persecutions against the secret Jews were instituted. Among the arrested were some of the wealthiest and most influential people in the country: Antonio Méndez, Luis Rodríguez, Blas Pinto, Luis Gomez Barreto, Manuel Alvarez Prieto. Trials continued almost up to the abolition of the Spanish Inquisition in 1834. Two wealthy merchants, Antonio Santaella and Juan Rodríguez Mexia, were tried in 1783.

Many of the Jews who settled in Cuba during the colonial period, particularly in 1580-1640, were Portuguese or their descendants. In the 17th and 18th centuries Portuguese and Jewish were synonyms in the New World. Twenty-three Jews, who fled Brazil in 1654 when it was retaken from Holland by Portugal, stopped at Cuba en route to New Amsterdam in the Colonies, and established contacts with the Cuban Marranos. Among others, the secret Jews of Cuba arranged for trade between the Thirteen Colonies and the Jews of Jamaica, Barbados, and other Caribbean islands, enabling the Colonies to sell goods as well as to buy military and civilian supplies.

The new Spanish Constitution of 1869 removed all restrictions on the settlement of Jews in Latin America. One writer, in 1898, stated that there were over 500 Spanish Jews engaged in commerce in Cuba at that time and earlier, and that five or six Jewish families were among the wealthiest on the island. Jews were also among the founders of the commercial cane sugar fields and the first sugar refineries. Several important families such as Brandon, Marchena, Machado, and Dovalle had come from Panama, Curacao, and Surinam. The famous Cuban actress and poetess, Dolores de Dios Porta, who died in Paris in 1869, was an observant Jewess.

Many American Jews joined Cubans in their fight for independence as early as 1892 and in their revolution of 1895. Among them were August Bondi, Louis Schlesinger, General Roloff formerly known as Akiba Roland, Captain Kaminsky and Horacio Rubens. Joseph Steinberg, a captain in the army of liberation, and his brothers Max and Edward were personal friends of Cuba's Apostol, José Marti.

The first Jewish cemetary in Cuba was established by the United States Army for the American Jewish soldiers who died during the Spanish-American War in 1898, following demands by American Jewish organizations for separate interment according to Jewish law. The cemetary was sold in 1906 to the United Hebrew Congregation, the first official Cuban Jewish body created primarily by American Jews. Most members of the congregation, later named Temple Beth Israel, were Americans who fought in Cuba or who came from Key West and other parts of Southern Florida immediately after the end of the war.

Many Sephardi Jews were established in Cuba in 1908; they began to come in

1902. Among them were Young Turks who had participated in the earlier abortive revolt against the Sultan of the Ottoman Empire. Others came from Mexico, North Africa and other areas of the Mediterranean. The Sephardim spoke Spanish and were of swarthy complexion, which made them indistinguishable from the great majority of Cubans. This was an important reason for the almost total absence of overt antisemitism in Cuba. There were other factors militating against antisemitism the Cuban non-Jew was the most extrovert of all Latin Americans and had less guile the fight for independence was too recent to be forgotten, and many Cubans remem bered the part some Jews played in it; Catholicism in Cuba was female-oriented and little affected the life of Cubans outside the Church; the Cubans had not forgotten that they too had been a persecuted people. The Sephardim, then, integrated into their new milieu with little difficulty.

In 1914 the American Jews and the Sephardim, who until then had been to gether for religious purposes, parted ways; the latter established Congregation Sheve Achim. The parting was due partly to the differences in ethnic and social back ground. The American Jews maintained a higher standard of living, moved in upper Cuban social and economic circles, and were accepted in the most exclusive clubs. By contrast, the Sephardim were small merchants, artisans, and peddlers, who did not speak English. However, many American Jews were made honorary members of Shevet Achim in recognition of their assistance to the Sephardi community. Late the Ashkenazi Jews, too, expressed appreciation to the American Jews for assisting East European Jews.

Two significant events occurred before the large immigration of Ashkenazim. One was the activity of David Blis, who used the newspaper El Día to agitate for Cuban endorsement of the Balfour Declaration. Blis, a Jew, came from Mexico, and quickly established himself in Cuba as an active Zionist. The other was the first dis play of Jews as an ethnic-religious group in Cuba, when a contingent marched as Jews in the Havana parade on November 11, 1918, celebrating the armistice.

Ashkenazim began to come to Cuba in 1920. They were considered German nationals. Their first shops, whether dry cleaning, grocery, textile, or general mer chandise, bore names such as Bazaar Aleman, Berlin, or Hamburg. Shortly after becoming established, they ceased attending the Sephardi Shevet Achim and built their own synagogue. Since this split, both groups maintained their own complex of institutions. There was little socializing between them, except at large social functions and in the B'nai B'rith lodge. There were friendly relations as well as some intermarriage between individuals of both groups.

The friendlier relations between the Ashkenazi and Sephardi groups in the decad before the Castro revolution may be attributed to the coming of age of a generation of native-born Jews who attended the same parochial elementary schools and secula secondary schools. Spanish became the leading language and began to replace Yid dish and Ladino as the immigrant generation passed away.

The Cuban Ashkenazim have had a twenty-year history of internecine disputes. Personal rivalries and religious and ideological differences were insurmountable obstacles to communal unity. The Jewish Communists were the most intransigent on all issues; some of them remain in Cuba to the present day. They and the Bundists were viciously anti-Zionist. The Communists even attempted to sabotage fundraising campaigns for Israel. However, there was also feuding among the Zionists; Labor Zionists with General Zionists and Mizrachi.

One of the factors contributing to the failure to achieve unity in the Ashkenazi ranks was difference of origin. The earlier wave of immigrants came mainly from Russia and Poland. The immigrants of the 1930s and the post-World War II period came from Austria and Germany. The most notable exception to the divisiveness of Cuban Jews was evinced during the period of virulent antisemitism between 1938 and 1940, which coincided with the worst outrages against the Jews in the Third Reich.

Cuban antisemitism was fostered by the Nazis (Camisas Doradas), Falangists (Spanish merchants and a few clerics), and the Catholic-owned newspapers *Diario de la Marina, Alesta,* and *El Día,* apparently with funds provided by the German embassy in Havana. Responsibility for the tragic incident of the S.S. *St. Louis,* which sailed from Hamburg on May 13, 1939, with 1,000 Jewish refugees, has been laid at the door of some Spanish merchants in Havana who feared business competition from these unfortunates. The passengers were in possession of valid Cuban visas, which had been issued at the direction of Minister of Migration General Manuel Benítz, against a payment of $300 to $500 per visa by Cuban Jews wishing to save their brethren from Hitlerism. The Cuban merchants revealed the details of the transaction, and President Laredo Bru, for reasons best known to himself, voided the visas while the ship was on the high seas, and refused the ship permission to land in Havana. Appeals to the United States to use its good offices to bring about a reversal of this decision brought no action.

Adolfo Kates and his brother Gustave have been acknowledged as principally responsible for the Cuban government's reversal of the antisemitic trend. The former, now residing in Miami, was outstanding among Cubans of all faiths with respect to the number of decorations he received from Cuba, Spain, France, and Belgium for his civic, philanthropic and diplomatic works.

The number of Jews in the various professions were: 20 lawyers, of whom one was a judge; close to 50 doctors and dentists, and about 40 architects, engineers and accountants. There were over 300 Cuban Jews who were pursuing higher studies at universities in Cuba, the United States, and Europe.

The Cuban Jews left five communal structures in Havana, in addition to their cemeteries: The buildings of the Centro Hebreo Sefaradi de Cuba, a religious and communal center resulting from a merger of the Union Hebreo Sefaradi and Congregation Shevet Achim; the Jewish Community House, known as Patronato para la Communidad, of the Ashkenazi; Congregation Adath Israel; the Zionist building on the Prado, and the Autonomous Jewish Circle School. The total cost of these buildings exceeded $2 million.

Fidel Castro assumed power in January 1959, following an armed revolution against the Batista dictatorship. In the summer of 1960 the Jews began a great emigration from Cuba. They looked upon Castro's Communism as a danger to their way of life and to their property interest. It was the fear of expropriation, not anti-semitism, that was the primary motive for their departure. Some also feared that Castro might stifle a Jewish way of life in order to achieve his communal society.

CUBAN JEWS IN SOUTH FLORIDA

South Florida includes the Greater Miami area, also known as Dade County; Hollywood, and Fort Lauderdale in Broward County; Key West and Tampa on the West Coast of Florida. It was not possible to ascertain the exact number of Cuban Jews now residing in this area. While the Cuban Jews have formed two indigenous organizations, not all Cuban Jews were members of them. Many chose to integrate into the American Jewish community. Among these were some Orthodox, many who had socialized with American Jews who permanently lived in Cuba, and former members of the Reform Temple Beth Israel in Havana.

A large number of Cuban Jews had friends and relatives in Florida and had invested money in the Miami area for many years before 1960. Some had spoken mainly English in their homes in Cuba. The statistics of the National Council of Jewish Women and United HIAS Service, the two organizations that have participat in the Cuban refugee program since 1961, were not representative of the total number of Cuban Jews who migrated to the United States. Many had come earlier, and many came via Venezuela, Colombia, Spain, Israel, Puerto Rico, and other places, making definite identification difficult.

Areas of Settlement

The HIAS figure of Cuban Jews registered under the Cuban refugee program, was approximately 4,500. Another 2,500 Cubans probably came to Miami from other countries, and even from other cities in the United States. HIAS resettled over 3,00 from the Southern Florida area in almost 300 cities in thirty-one states, in Puerto Rico and Costa Rica. A partial breakdown of the HIAS resettlement in 1961-67 revealed the following:

Alabama	8	Louisiana	18	New York State	31
Colorado	39	Maryland	42	Ohio	87
Connecticut	58	Massachusetts	76	Pennsylvania	111
Costa Rica	2	Michigan	46	Puerto Rico	53
Delaware & District		Minnesota	7	Rhode Island	39
of Columbia	30	Mississippi	3	Tennessee	4
Georgia	27	Missouri	44	Texas	137
Illinois	111	New Jersey	128	Washington	3
Indiana	10	North Carolina	11	West Virginia	2
Iowa	1	New York City	1,680	Wisconson	3
Los Angeles	176				

Since HIAS did not follow up on the activities of those it resettled, there was no assurance that many of the Cuban refugees did not return to South Florida once they accumulated enough money, or to join friends or relatives. This was particularly likely since, of all states, the climate of Florida most closely resembles that of Cuba.

Extensive investigation produced an estimate of about 3,500 Cuban Jews living in South Florida, many of them, if not most, in Miami Beach. Here they were to be found in the northern part (North Shore area running from 62nd Street to 95th Street) and in the South Beach area, below Lincoln Road.

For many years since World War II, Cubans of all faiths came to Miami Beach during the summer, when hotel and restaurant rates, as well as prices in general, were much lower than in the winter season. This was particularly so before 1959. Local residents of Miami Beach called the summers the "Cuban invasion." Cubans were familiar with the streets, shops, and general area of Miami Beach. This familiarity and the proximity to the ocean contributed to their choice of this city for settlement.

Composition of Community

Cuban Jews in the United States continued to maintain some of their former divisions. There were three distinct groups in South Florida: Sephardim, Ashkenazim, and the youth—under sixteen years of age—of both groups. The youngsters, who associated with other children at school, integrated rapidly and were mixing with all types of Jews. They fail to see any significant distinctions between Sephardim and Ashkenazim.

Ashkenazi adults and children differed little in appearance and religious practice from the general Jewish community. By contrast, the Sephardim, who remained in the minority, stood out because of their olive complexion, their volatility, emotionally and otherwise, and their strong adherence to tradition. They lived within voluntarily prescribed areas, and their pattern of life facilitated the preservation of their customs. However, the movement away from one area, loosening of family ties, and greater exposure to outside influences, soon may break down Sephardi distinctiveness. Also the lack of American-trained Sephardi rabbis may alienate Sephardi youth reared in America.

Commitment to Judaism

Synagogue affiliation to Cuban Jews was comparable to that of American Jews in the various neighborhoods. Still, one of the first things the Cuban Jews wanted to know when they arrived was the location of synagogues and schools where their children could receive a Jewish education. As with most American Jews, their identification with Judaism was much greater than observance of ritual. But their commitment to Jewish education for their children was stronger than that of American

Jews. A strong inducement for many Cubans to settle on the North Shore was that Temple Menorah (Conservative) in the area was the most hospitable of all Greater Miami congregations. It invited the newcomers to share, without charge, its services, including seats for the High Holy Days, and its Talmud Torah for the education of their children. It continued this practice for five years. Most other congregations, including the Sephardi Jewish Center in Miami Beach, requested nominal payment, thus antagonizing the Cuban Sephardim. They now organized the Cuban Sephardi Hebrew congregation, which they named after Shevet Achim in Havana.

The new Shevet Achim had a membership of 150 families, a cuban rabbi, Nissim Mayer, and Sunday School classes. Not all Cuban Sephardi Jews belonged to this congregation. Some attended the original Sephardi Center, also in Miami Beach. It was rather surprising that the Floridian Sephardim did not show more cordiality toward the new arrivals, since many of them, like the Cubans, were of Turkish ancestry. The Sephardi Center, with about 200 member families, also conducted Sunday School classes, but the Cuban congregation had a larger enrollment. The two institutions were only two blocks apart. They had a combined student body of 60. Both considered themselves Orthodox, but many of their members, who were scattered throughout Dade county, had to travel on the Sabbath and Holy Days in order to attend. *Kashrut* was observed by a small percentage. To many, it meant only abstinence from pork and shellfish.

A distinguishing feature between Ashkenazi and Sephardi religious observance was attendance by Sephardim at all synagogue services, morning and evening, and total participation in the recital of all prayers. There was no problem of having a *minyan* (quorum) on weekdays or Saturdays and Sundays.

The Ashkenazim held religious services in the Circulo Cubano Hebreo, with Rabbi Dov Rosenzweig officiating. Also located in South Beach, the Circulo was more than a religious institution; it was the largest social center for all shades of Cuban Jews, with over 700 member families. Its New Year's party was attended by more than 800 people. It also conducted weekday classes for some 20 children with a staff of three teachers.

Religious affiliation of the more affluent Ashkenazim was centered in the North Shore area. A few Orthodox Jews belonged to congregations close to their homes. The American Jews and those who belonged to the Reform Temple in Havana were affiliated with Reform temples in South Florida. However, with the exception of the Conservative Temple Menorah, more Cuban Jewish children attended the Orthodox all-day Hebrew Academy than any other single school. Their parents saw no conflict between the Orthodox education their children were receiving and their much less rigid religious observance at home.

Social Life

As most other Latin Americans, Cuban Jews were family-centered. In the United States, this kind of relationship was breaking up because of resettlement and a high degree of mobility. Cuban Jews still had Christian Cuban friends, but there was a loosening of ties. They also tended to maintain friendships with other Cuban Jews, but new relationships with American Jews were encroaching on them. Working hours in the United States differed from those in Cuba, and the pace was much faster. While in Cuba there was little socialization between Jews and Christians during the evening hours, there was much during the day. They found little time for such day-time activity in South Florida.

Economic Situation

The adjustment of Cuban Jews to American economic life has been phenomenal. Two lawyers were in high posts in the banking field. The main occupations of Cuban Jews were engraving, manufacture of leather goods, and selling insurance. Several Cubans have built multimillion dollar exporting and importing businesses, dealing in sugar and other articles, especially shoes. Many of the retail stores in the Miami downtown business area were now Cuban-owned and-operated. Cuban Jews also were predominant in the sale of textiles and remnants, but they also were engaged in all retail businesses, except food services. Many successful Cuban Jews took their Cuban Jewish friends and members of their families into their businesses, as junior partners. Within the younger generation, the division between Ashkenazim and Sephardim was quickly disappearing in all fields of activity.

Cultural Life

The newcomers have become citizens of the United States and, despite the use of Spanish in some homes, succeeded in their desire to assimilate into American life. Their adherence to Spanish as the language of the home was remarkable. In several homes, where Yiddish had been the main language before emigration, it now was Spanish. Parents wanted their children to speak Spanish. Of course, Spanish was spoken with pride by all who came to South Florida from Latin America. This was quite unlike the reaction to Yiddish by first-generation Americans, who wanted their parents to discard Yiddish.

The Cuban Jew did not seem to have been a great participant in Cuban or Spanish cultural life. His knowledge of Spanish was, and continued to be, confined to its use as a means of communication. The most plausible explanation of their devotion to Spanish in their new home may be found in what immigrants generally considered the most agreeable aspect of life in Cuba, namely their acceptance as equals by Cubans. Having themselves been exposed to persecution or having heard stories of what pogroms in Russia, Poland, and other East European countries and Nazi persecution did to their families, the Jew found Cuban acceptance of him as a citizen a most heart-warming experience. His gratitude to that country was expressed by adherence to its tongue.

FUTURE OF THE COMMUNITY

The Cuban Jews in South Florida had no intention of returning to the island in the event of Castro's downfall. Of the more than 100 interviewed, only three though they would do so. Many said they would go back to try to regain some of the possessions they were forced to leave behind, and then return to the United States. The children, like their parents, have become completely integrated into American life.

Few of the immigrants expressed a desire to settle in Israel. Some explained that for them America was the third home, and the mere thought of having to establish a new life for a fourth time in Israel was too much. However, they were active in pro-Israel causes. In December 1968 they sponsored an Israel Bond dinner with Adolfo Kates as guest of honor. The attendance was over 350 and the drive was a success, not so much in the total amount sold as in the number of sales. However, in the view of this writer, the disintegration of traditional ties among former Cuban Jews precluded many more such annual affairs. As individuals, they were likely to continue attending similar functions, sponsored by their temples, synagogues, Zionist organizations, or fraternal groups.

The 1969 Greater Miami Jewish Federation campaign marked the third year of participation by Cuban Jews as a group. Each year the number of contributors and the amount of their gifts showed marked increases. Sender Kaplan was coordinator of the Federation's annual dinners and drives among the Cuban Jews. He was former editor of *Habaner Leban*, a Yiddish semiweekly and the sole publication of the Cuban Jewish community, which he published for over 20 years.

The Cuban Hebrew Circle was making a valiant effort to maintain the insularity of Cuban Jewish Life. Its leaders sponsored a professionally directed cultural program of lectures and discussions for youths and adults. Since one of the program's aims was to have the new citizens acquire a greater understanding of the American way of life, its long-range effect might be the dissolution of the community of former Cuban Jews.

THE SEPHARDIC REVIVAL IN THE UNITED STATES:
A Case of Ethnic Revival in a Minority-within-a-Minority

ABRAHAM D. LAVENDER

Social scientists have long known of the great diversity among Protestants in the United States, and now there is increasing recognition that not all Catholics are alike—that one "thinks of himself not so much as Catholic, but as Polish Catholic, Irish Catholic, Italian Catholic, French Catholic, thus distinguishing himself not only from Protestants but also from Catholics of other ethnic backgrounds."[1] And yet, there is little recognition of the reality that not all Jews are alike.

It is true that the differences which previously existed in the United States between German or Western European Jews and Russian/Polish or Eastern European Jews have diminished greatly, and that indeed these groups already shared the similarity of an Ashkenazic (European) background.[2] There is still ethnic diversity within the Jewish community in the United States, however. Within the United States Jewish community, which numbers almost six million individuals and comprises slightly less than 3% of the United States population, is a minority-within-a-minority numbering about 180,000 and comprising about 3% of the total United States Jewish community: Sephardic Jews.[3] The New York area has the largest population of Sephardim, followed by Los Angeles, California, Seattle, Washington, and Atlanta, Georgia. Washington, D.C., and Miami, Florida, along with several other cities, also have active Sephardic communities.

Laypersons—both Jewish and Gentile—and social scientists, however, generally neglect the Sephardim when discussing the Jewish community in the United States. Jewishness is often interpreted as synonymous with Yiddish (German-Hebrew), and it is assumed—by Jews probably more than by Gentiles—that all "good" Jews know certain "Jewish" (Yiddish) words, eat certain "Jewish" (German or Eastern European) foods, and have a "Jewish" (German or Eastern European derived) name. As

Angel notes, however, Sephardic Jews have different "Jewish" words and eat different "Jewish" foods. He also notes that Sephardic Jews often have not been readily accepted by Ashkenazic Jews because they (Sephardic Jews) do not have "Jewish" names, and that politicians—when speaking in Jewish neighborhoods—often speak Yiddish even when the Jewish neighborhood is Sephardic.[4] While a few scholars have recognized the "possibility of enduring social differences within the minority community" between Ashkenazim and Sephardim,[5] there are few studies of Ashkenazic-Sephardic differences in the United States. Articles such as Cohen's "Sephardi Jews in the United States: Marriage with Ashkenazim and non-Jews" are noticeable by their rarity.[6]

This neglect of Sephardim is mostly due to the overwhelming predominance of Ashkenazim in the United States, and yet there are several factors which suggest that more attention should be given to this diversity within the Jewish community. First is the basic fact that the Sephardim do exist as a separate group, and hence should receive the attention due any ethnic group. Second is the fact that while Sephardic Jews comprise only 3% of United States Jewry, they comprise about 16% of world Jewry, and about 60% of Israeli Jewry, and hence are consequential to the future of Jewry.[7] Third, as this paper will demonstrate, few groups are as potentially rich in the lessons which can be learned concerning the relations between the dominant society and minority groups.

In an attempt to bring this group more to the attention of social scientists this paper (1) gives a brief background of the group, (2) reviews some recent events which suggest a revival in several areas of concern to Sephardic Jews in the United States, (3) examines some sociological reasons for this revival of ethnic identity, and (4) suggests the importance of this revival to the sociological study of dominant society-minority group relations. Finally, this paper (5) suggests that the total United States Jewish community can gain from an increased recognition and appreciation of Sephardism.

BACKGROUND

Strictly speaking, the term "Sepharad" is Hebrew for Spain, and Sephardic Jews are those whose ancestors lived in Spain or Portugal before being forced out by the Christian Inquisition in the 1400s. In actuality, however, the term has long been used to also mean Jews living in or coming from Islamic countries.[8] Sephardic Jews (mostly descendants of refugees from Spain or Portugal) formed the majority of United States Jewry in the early decades of settlement. Although outnumbered numerically by Ashkenazic Jews (Western European and Eastern European Jews; from the Hebrew word Ashkenas meaning Germany) as early as 1720, Sephardic Jews maintained their cultural predominance within United States Jewry until the beginning of the 1800s.[9] With the sizable migration of German Jews to the United States in the 1800s, followed by the vast migration of Eastern European Jews from 1880 to 1924, Sephardic Jews were to become increasingly even more of a minority-within-a-minority. Approximately 20,000 to 25,000 Sephardic Jews migrated to the United States from the Levant (mainly Turkey, Greece, and Syria) in the period from about 1908 to 1924,[10] and a number of Sephardic Jews came to the United States from Arab countries in North Africa and the Middle East in the 1950s and 1960s.[11] In addition, there was a migration of a few thousand Sephardic Jews (along with a larger number of Ashkenazic Jews) from Cuba in the 1960s.[12]

Despite these migrations, however, the Sephardic community in the United States remains small, and faces problems along with other small minority groups in maintaining and perpetuating group identity. In the most comprehensive recent (1973) article on Sephardic Jews to appear in a major Jewish publication in the United States, a bleak picture was painted for the future of Sephardic culture in the United States "if there is no reversal in the trends" indicated.[13] On the other hand, Lévy has concluded that "After several decades of almost total passiveness, suddenly, Sephardic Judaism has entered into a revival phase, which has been appropriately termed 'The New Renaissance.' In the United States, this renaissance has taken the place of a 'Revolution.' "[14] Lévy's statement may be overly optimistic, but there are indications that the trend feared by Angel has begun to reverse, and that Sephardim in the United States will not only continue as a distinct group within the larger Jewish community, but even increase in self-identity and in influence on the larger Jewish community.

AREAS OF "ETHNIC REVIVAL"

The particular area of concern emphasized by a minority group in its efforts at self-pride depends on several factors such as the stage of identity and cultural development of the group, the amount and type of power available to the group, the values held by the group and the group's relationship with "brothers and sisters" in other geographical areas. Sephardic Jews already identify with a fertile Sephardic culture, and hence are at the stage of perpetuating that culture rather than having to develop a consciousness of culture. Lacking power because of their small numbers, they nevertheless are economically and educationally middle class and upper-middle class and hence have readily been able to utilize education as a force for building identity. Not being economically oppressed, they have been able to focus on non-economic aspects of their lives. Futhermore, concerned with the condition of Sephardic Jews (often close relatives) in Arab lands and in Israel, they have been able to give and have given much of their attention to international relations. While taking much of their time, however, this concern has added to their sense of solidarity.

The Educational and Scholarly Area

With a fertile written and oral literature, and with a high value put on education by Sephardim, a major area of revival has been the educational and scholarly area.

This area of revival was at least partly due to the recognition that time was of an essence, that, as noted by Lévy, scholarly research and preservation had to be done "before both oral and written sources are lost forever."[15] Scholarship is concerned, however, not only with preserving the past contributions of the group, but also ensuring future contributions of the group. A major impetus to revival in this area was the establishment of the Sephardic Studies Program at Yeshiva University in 1964.[16] Today, over 235 students are training to be rabbis, teachers, cantors, and community leaders in the Sephardic community.[17]

The American Society of Sephardic Studies, founded in December 1967, has added to the scholarly knowledge of "Sephardic culture, literature, religious life and mores."[18] This organization published *The American Sephardi* which later became the journal of the Sephardic Studies Program at Yeshiva University.[19] Yeshiva University now also publishes a bulletin, and *The Sephardic Scholar* is the journal of The American Society of Sephardic Studies.[20] The World Institute of Sephardic Studies, established in 1973, publishes *The Sephardic World*, has a program of printing and reprinting Sephardic books of contemporary interest, gives scholarships to Sephardic youth and to scholars doing research on Sephardism, and offers adult education and college level courses.[21] The furtherance of scholarly knowledge of Sephardism is also furthered by the establishment of three Sephardic high schools in the New York area in the last three years.[22] The Foundation for the Advancement of Sephardic Studies and Culture also has added to scholarly contributions to Sephardism.[23]

The Cultural and Social Area

The educational and scholarly overlaps to some extent with the cultural and social area, and some of the same organizations active in the first area are also active in the second area. The World Institute of Sephardic Studies, for example, also has arrangements for religious counseling, and arranges lectures, courses, and festivals of Sephardic interest. The Foundation for the Advancement of Sephardic Studies and Culture, as its name implies, has also made contributions in this area.[24] Yeshiva University sponsors an annual Sephardic Cultural Festival. Begun in 1969, the Festival annually attracts several thousand individuals. A Fiesta Sephardi is also sponsored by the American Sephardic Federation (see below) and other organizations.[25] In addition, a number of synagogues and other organizations now offer an increased number of programs.

The Political and International Relations Area

Israel is now approximately 60% Sephardic—Jews from countries such as Yemen, Morocco, Algeria, and Iraq—and a major concern of United States Sephardim is with helping Israeli Sephardim gain better living standards in such areas as jobs, education, and housing, as well as helping them gain more equal social acceptance.[26]

For example, the Moroccan Jewish Organization, a member of the American Sephardi Federation, "has been raising funds for scholarships for Moroccan Jewish youth in Israel and for a youth center in Dimona."[27] Israel in general is also a concern of the American Separdi Federation which is "working for increased aliyah, more volunteers for work programs, additional contributions, more tourism, and more support for Israel."[28] The living conditions of Jews in Arab lands are also of major importance to United States Sephardim. Organizations such as the American Association of Jewish Refugees from Arab Lands have been founded,[29] and the American Committee for Rescue and Resettlement of Iraqi Jews gives particular attention to Iraqi Jews.[30] The treatment of the approximately 4,500 Jews in Syria has been of particular concern, with organizations such as the Committee for the Rescue of Syrian Jews and the American Sephardi Federation being involved.[31]

An Area of Special Concern: Youth

As with other minority groups, the youth are of special concern to the Sephardic community. This concern is particularly strong in the "revival" because of the previous scarcity of educational opportunities for Sephardic youth and because of the numbers of youth the Sephardic community was losing through intermarriage with Ashkenazim. Again as with other minority groups, the youth have not only benefited from the revival of ethnic interest, but have been in the forefront of the revival.[32] The American Sephardi Federation founded a youth commission at a 1973 convention in Atlanta. A number of events have been sponsored by Sephardic youth, and Sephardic youth have been sent to Israel "for travel and study seminars to prepare them for work among American Sephardim."[33]

ATTEMPTS AT "ETHNIC REVIVAL": A SOCIOLOGICAL APPRAISAL

As interest in Sephardic issues continued to increase, concern was expressed that United States Sephardim might once again fail at efforts to increase group identity because of the proliferation of organizations and issues to the point of infighting, divisiveness, and self-inflicted losses. Largely because of this recognition, the American Sephardi Federation was founded in 1973. It has joined national Jewish groups in order to give Sephardim a voice, and, as we have seen, has been active in many areas in the Sephardic community.[34]

There are indications that United States Sephardim—for the first time since they lost their cultural predominance to the Ashkenazim in the early 1800s—may be beginning to gain more recognition from within the United States Jewish community. In the past these efforts for unity and for recognition from the larger Jewish society failed, partly because of small numbers, partly because of internal divisiveness,[35] and partly because of a lack of issues around which to unify, as well as because of the demands from the larger society—in this case both the United States society and the larger Ashkenazic Jewish community—to assimilate to the ways of the majority.

This paper suggests, however, that there are three major sociological variables which were not present previously, and which can increase the likelihood of a "successful ethnic revival." First, with the migration of Jews from Arab countries beginning in the 1950s, the number of Sephardim in the United States has increased greatly. These numbers now make available facilities and programs not previously feasible. As has happened with other minorities such as American Indians, the numbers are also augmented slightly by individuals who have previously "assimilated" into the dominant society but who begin to come back as they find increased pride in their identity and increased opportunities to realize this identity.[36] Second, a number of issues—e.g., the condition of Sephardic Jews in Israel and the treatment of Sephardic Jews in Arab lands—now have a power of arousal which can overcome the previous apathy.[37] Most of the Sephardic immigrants to the United States in the last few decades, who now comprise a large segment of United States Sephardim, came from North Africa and the Middle East (especially Syria) where they often were in a precarious position between a ruling European elite and an oppressed Arab population. While these Sephardic Jews left these areas largely because of their marginal status and the growth of nationalist movements in which they could not fully participate as Jews, and while they do not usually subscribe to the "Third World Ideology" which has become popular in these areas, it is nevertheless possible that they too have become more conscious of the social and economic status of their fellow Sephardim in Israel because of the emphasis on class consciousness. Third, the resurgence of ethnicity in the United States has also affected United States Jews—and, within this context, has also affected United States Sephardim both as Jews and more specifically as Sephardim. All of these factors, plus the suggested recognition by the Sephardim of their own self-defeating infights in the past, may make a difference in the current period.

SOCIOLOGICAL BENEFITS FROM THE STUDY OF SEPHARDISM

It is increasingly being recognized that much can be learned from the study of minority group values and from minority group-dominant society relations.[38] Sephardim are an especially fertile area of study. For one thing, an increased interest in Sephardism in general can lead to an increase of interest in the study of Ashkenazic-Sephardic and Arabic-Sephardic relations in Israel. Few countries in history provide the model of a "living laboratory" of ethnic group relations provided by Israel, a country with Jewish citizens—60% of whom are Sephardim—from over a hundred countries plus a large Arab minority comprised of both Moslems and Christians, as well as other minorities. Few areas of the world are in as much need of wisdom in solving majority-minority problems as the Middle East, thus adding a practical factor to the study of these relations. In addition, few minority groups have, throughout history, lived in such varied conditions as have the Sephardim—including a "glorious" era in Islamic Spain and an oppressive era in Christian Spain; a mixed (according to time, place, and ruler) and still debated situation in Islamic North Africa and the Islamic Middle East which, whatever the conclusions about the historical past, have changed greatly in the last few decades; a minority-within-a-minority status for most of its residence in the United States; and a numerical majority but socially deprived status within Israel.[39]

A REAPPRAISAL OF "JEWISHNESS" AND OF JEWISH-GENTILE RELATIONS

In addition to scholarly knowledge which can be gained from a study of Sephardism, this paper concludes by suggesting that the United States Jewish community can also gain from an increased recognition and appreciation of Sephardic perspectives and values. Sephardic Judaism is not the same as Ashkenazic Judaism, and Sephardic Jews have not interacted with their non-Jewish neighbors as have Ashkenazic Jews. Sephardic Judaism has a "relaxed and natural" approach to Judaism which "has much to commend to those Ashkenazim who want to be religious Jews but who find certain attitudes and cultural patterns common in many religious Ashkenazic communities hard to take."[40]

The Ashkenazic version of Judaism which predominates in the United States developed in the East European shtetl (Jewish village) and ghetto, in which there were only two alternatives for Jews, cultural assimilation or cultural isolation, in which the Jew had to "either accept the values and key symbols of his society or live in a spiritual ghetto."[41] Formalized and solidified in the shtetls and ghettos of anti-Semitic, Crusade-ridden, pogrom-ridden Christian Europe, perhaps understandably from a sociological perspective Ashkenazic Judaism accepted the belief of the dominant society that Judaism and non-Jewish culture were mutually exclusive.

Sephardic Judaism, in contrast, developed in a pluralistic society of relative tolerances and multi-dimensional values where the Jew could take the best of non-Jewish humanistic cultural values, adapt them to express and strengthen the uniqueness of his Jewishness, and still remain distinctly Jewish.[42] As Elazar has stated, Sephardim "have never had to face religious fanaticism or a militant secularist assault on the unity of their communal life."[43] Although not accepted by all scholars, it is generally agreed that this "relatively better" condition which existed in Islamic Spain, has also held until recent decades in other Islamic and Arabic countries. Rosenbloom, for instance, discusses the situation for Moroccan Jews and reports that "The relation of the Sephardic Jew to the Arab may be compared to that of Isaac to Ishmael: they live together in easy compromise, both parties being rather easygoing, unexcitable, passive, getting by imperfectly, perhaps, but getting by nonetheless. The Ashkenazic Jew, on the other hand, in his relationship with Christians relives the struggle between Jacob and Esau. Here it is either one or the other; they simply cannot exist together, and their struggle and strife are destined to continue; the very existence of Judaism is seen as a threat by Christianity . . . this is not true for Muslims."[44]

Thus far in United States history, the White Anglo-Saxon Protestant model of behavior has been held up as the model toward which all people in the United States should strive. Emphasis on this model—with major emphasis on the White aspect, but also with much emphasis on the Protestant (sometimes broadened to mean Christian) aspect, and even some remaining emphasis on the Anglo-Saxon aspect—has basically given the United States a unidimensional definition of the "good American." In this sense the United States has been closer to the unidimensional nature of eastern and western Christian Europe in which Ashkenazic Jews lived than to the multi-dimensional nature of Spain and other Islamic lands in which Sephardic Jews have lived. Even though the unidimensionality of the United States has not been nearly as strong and violent as that of eastern and western Christian Europe, for many Ashkenazic Jews it has been sufficiently similar to cause a feeling of precariousness.[45] On the other hand, it may be that the unidimensionality of the United States is sufficiently weaker and less violent than that previously known by Ashkenazic Jews allowing one to conclude that the practical situation for the Jew in the United States is closer to that of the Jew in Islamic countries.

Even if this is not accurate thus far, there are suggestions that the United States is beginning to develop a broader (and multi-dimensional) definition of the "good American." As Greenbaum has noted, "The Protestant Anglo-American ideal of assimilation has failed in important ways and cannot continue to guide the policies of our social institutions. . . . Even a conservative United States Supreme Court . . . [has] recognized the tenuousness of the present order and the need to sustain alternative systems."

If it is accurate that "the situation of the Jew in America is closer to [or is becoming closer to] the condition of the Jew in medieval Granada and Toledo than to the Jew in the Eastern European shtetl and ghetto,"[46] then not just United States Sephardim, but all United States Jews as well as some other ethnic minorities, stand to gain by knowledge of this situation.

NOTES

1. Andrew M. Greeley, *The Denominational Society: A Sociological Approach to Religion in America* (1972), p. 125.

2. Marshal Sklare, *America's Jews* (1971), p. 14.

3. This number of 180,000 is given by Jose A. Nessim, "Editorial," *The Sephardic Voice*, Volume 2, February, 1974, p. 3. Estimates vary from 100,000 to 300,000; see, for example, "Sephardic Heritage and Language Feared on Wane," *The New York Times*, August 26, 1974, p. 35.

4. Marc D. Angel, "Sephardic Culture in America," *Jewish Life*, 38 (March-April 1971), 7-11.

5. Sklare, *America's Jews*, p. 13.

6. Hayyim Cohen, "Sephardi Jews in the United States: Marriage with Ashkenazim and non-Jews," *Dispersion and Unity*, Number 13/14, 1971, pp. 151-160. For a bibliography of relevant articles, see Marc D. Angel, "The Sephardim of the United States: An Exploratory Study," in Morris Fine and Milton Himmelfarb, editors, *American Jewish Yearbook*, American Jewish Committee, New York, 1973, pp. 77-138.

7. Geoffrey Wigoder, editor, "Sephardim," *Encyclopedic Dictionary of Judaica*, Leon Amiel Publisher, New York, 1974, p. 542.

8. José Faur, "The Sephardim: Yesterday, Today and Tomorrow," *The Sephardic World*, Volume 1, Summer 1972, p. 6.

9. Sklare, *America's Jews*, p. 6; Angel, "The Sephardim of the United States," p. 82.

10. Angel, "Sephardim of the United States," p. 84.

11. Joseph A. Hasson, "Jews in Arab Countries," *American Sephardi*, Volume 3, September 1969, pp. 94-102.

12. Seymour B. Liebman, "Cuban Jewish Community in South Florida," in Morris Fine and Milton Himmelfarb, editors, *American Jewish Yearbook*, American Jewish Committee, New York, 1969, pp. 238-246.

13. Angel, "The Sephardim of the United States," p. 136.

14. Rene H. Levy, "Youth Sephardim Unite at National Convention," *The Sephardic Voice*, Volume 2, February 1974, p. 12.

15. Isaac Jack Lévy, "Folklore and Reality: The Key to a People," *The Sephardic Scholar*, Series 2, 1972-1973, p. 29.

16. "Sephardic Studies Program," *The American Sephardi*, Volume 4, Autumn 1972, p. 119.

17. Ben G. Frank, "The Sephardic Revival," *Keeping Posted*, Volume 20, November 1974, p. 6. In fairness to critics, it should be noted that there are Sephardim and others who question the appropriateness of the Sephardic Studies Program being headquartered at Yeshiva University, a university which the critics interpret as epitomizing the "shtetlized" and "ghettoized" Eastern European version of traditional Judaism. For a general discussion of this position concerning the effects of Ashkenazic Judaism upon Sephardic learning, see Faur, "The Sephardim: Yesterday, Today and Tomorrow," p. 7.

18. "The American Society of Sephardic Studies," *The American Sephardi*, Volume 2, 1968, p. 13.

19. Ibid., p. 14.

20. The bulletin published is the *Yeshiva University's Sephardic Bulletin*. The reference regarding *The Sephardic Scholar* is found in Isaac Jack Lévy, "Foreword," *The Sephardic Scholar*, Series 2, 1972-1973, p. 5.

21. *New York Times*, "Organization Set Up By Sephardic Jews to Promote Culture," February 26, 1973, p. 22; Raymond Harari, "The Awakening of Sephardic Youth," *Keeping Posted*, Volume 22, November 1974, p. 22.

22. Harari, "The Awakening of Sephardic Youth," p. 22.

23. Frank, "The Sephardic Revival," p. 6.

24. "World Institute for Sephardic Studies: The Founders' Statement," *The Sephardic World*, Volume 1, Summer 1972, p. 16.

25. Frank, "The Sephardic Revival," p. 6.

26. Alan D. Corré, "The 60 Percent Minority," *The Sephardic World*, Volume 1, Winter 1973, pp. 18-20; Frank, "The Sephardic Revival," p. 5.

27. Frank, "The Sephardic Revival," p. 6.

28. Frank, "The Sephardic Revival," p. 6.

29. "Association Formed," *Yeshiva University's Sephardic Bulletin*, Volume 1, December 1973, p. 3.

30. Pamphlet published by the American Committee for Rescue and Resettlement of Iraqi Jews, Inc., New York.

31. Frank, "The Sephardic Revival," p. 6.

32. Harari, "The Awakening of Sephardic Youth," p. 22.

33. Frank, "The Sephardic Revival," p. 6; Harari, "The Awakening of Sephardic Youth," p. 22; Cohen, "Youth Sephardim Unite at National Convention," p. 12.

34. Frank, "The Sephardic Revival," p. 5.

35. Angel, "Sephardim of the United States," pp. 95-100.

36. In a letter to the editor of *The Sephardic World*, Volume 1, Winter 1973, p. 9, for example, a writer says: "As an assimilated Sephardic who lost a beautiful and precious heritage, I have long been searching for a means to regain it. It has been my fate to be separated from Sephardic culture and leadership, and I am unable to recreate it for myself and my children. Ashkenazi thought and culture is so foreign and often times so unattractive to me that I always feel like a stranger among my fellow Jews."

37. Cohen, "Youth Sephardim Unite at National Convention," p. 13.

38. William Greenbaum, "America in Search of a New Ideal: An Essay on the Rise of Pluralism," *Harvard Educational Review*, Volume 44, August 1974, p. 439.

39. For two good discussions of conditions under which Sephardic Jews have lived, see Raphael Patai, *Tents of Jacob*, Prentice-Hall, Englewood Cliffs, N.J., 1971; and André N. Chouraqui, *Between East and West: A History of the Jews of North Africa*, Atheneum, New York, 1973.

40. This particular quote appears in a letter to the editor of *The Sephardic World*, Volume 1, Winter 1973, p. 6.

41. José Faur, "Introducing the Materials of Sephardic Culture to Contemporary Jewish Studies," *American Jewish Historical Quarterly*, Volume 63, June 1974, p. 342.

42. For a classic discussion of Ashkenazic-Sephardic differences, see H.J. Zimmels, *Ashkenazim and Sephardim*, Oxford University Press, London, 1958.

43. Daniel J. Elazar, "Israel's Sephardim: The Myth of Two Cultures," *The Sephardic Voice*, Volume 2, February 1974, p. 17.

44. Joseph R. Rosenbloom, "Moroccan Jewry: A Community in Decline," *Judaism*, Volume 15, Spring 1966, p. 222. There remains much debate on this point. Saul S. Friedman, "The Myth of Arab Toleration," *Midstream*, January 1970, concludes that "Even if one grants Islam a better history in this respect [than Christianity], the fact remains that the notion of great and unadulterated Arab friendship and tolerance of Jews through the centuries is purely a myth" (p. 59). In somewhat contrasting conclusions, as an example, André Chouraqui, *Letter to an Arab Friend*, University of Massachusetts Press, Amherst, 1972, p. 23, points out that "In the Mohammedan Empire, Jews and Christians were equal, both inferior, but both benefitting from an egalitarian legal statute. For the Jews, this situation was without precedent since they had lost their country. For the first time in the course of history of their exile, they were no longer pariahs but had an official status which makes understandable their strong sympathy for the developing Empire. In Palestine, Syria, and Spain, the Jews helped the Arab conquerer and fought in the ranks of the Islamic armies. In Algeria, they took the side of the Mohammedan against the Christian. . . ."

45. As the sociologist W.I. Thomas wrote years ago, "If men define situations as real they are real in their consequences." See W.I. Thomas, *The Child In America*, Knopf, New York, 1928, p. 572. According to this concept, if the individual believes that he has only two alternatives, then he may behave as if he has only two even though there may be more. Thus, one may decide to either maintain traditional definitions of Judaism or reject it altogether, when in actuality there are flexible valid definitions available.

46. Greenbaum, "America in Search of a New Ideal," p. 411 and p. 437.

APPENDIX

This book is about Jewish subcommunities in the United States, and when we refer to American Jews or America's Jews we mean the United States' Jews. This is done not from ethnocentrism but simply for brevity of terminology. In many ways Canadian Jews are similar to United States Jews, and the points made about these seven subcommunities in the United States could apply in many cases to Canada. The same holds true to a lesser extent for much of Latin American Jewry. But one has to limit one's scope in most things, and I have limited myself to the United States.

"Small-town Jews" can refer to Jews who live in small towns or to Jews who live in small Jewish communities in larger towns. This book utilizes both definitions, even though usage is more often limited to the former. In the empirical studies referred to, for example, Rose studied communities having fewer than 10,000 permanent residents and having ten or fewer Jewish families. Schoenfeld studied twelve small towns ranging in population from 4,400 to 16,000, and having from three to twelve Jewish families. On the other hand, Gordon studied a community of 70,000 residents but with only fifty-six identified Jewish households (174 individuals).

"Southern Jews" are those who live in the twelve states of Alabama, Arkansas, Florida, Georgia, Kentucky, Louisiana, Mississippi, North Carolina, South Carolina, Tennessee, Texas, and Virginia. Jews who live in the border states of Maryland, Missouri, and Oklahoma are not included. These states are included in some definitions of the South, but they are not in this book since we are not concerned as much with the "geographical-only" South as with the "geographical-ideological"

South—that is, the South as a compact region with a distinct outlook, including "outposts of deviance" that are "embedded" within the region, but not including fringe areas that serve as transition areas to the non-South. Hence, for instance, Miami, very much nonsouthern in origin and ideology but embedded within and very much affected by the southern ethos is included, but the border states of Maryland, Missouri, and Oklahoma (including, for example, Baltimore, the northern suburbs of Washington, D.C., St. Louis, and Kansas City) are not.

The official definition of poverty or "poor" varies with time and place. Since the purpose of this book is to describe and bring attention to the situation facing the Jewish poor, including the controversy surrounding the estimate of numbers involved, a varied definition of poor is reflected in the discussions in this book. It is noted that Wolfe utilized under $3,000 income a year per household as her cut-off point but that the comments on her article suggest modifications of this definition. The other selections also utilize different cut-off points, but it is evident that the life-styles accompanying the different levels of income are similar.

Hasidic Jews form a clearly distinct community, strongly oriented to keeping itself separate from the larger society. Hence, no major problems of definition arise. There is some ambiguity at times concerning community membership of specific individuals, but the community criteria of who is a Hasid nevertheless remain firm. This book presents selections on Hasidic communities, not individuals, and hence the term "Hasidic Jews" refers to those Jews who are identified with such a community.

Similar to the controversy over which Jews are "poor Jews" is the controversy over which blacks are "black Jews." The selections in this book describe groups of blacks who claim to be Jews, as well as bringing attention to the controversy surrounding this claim, since the purpose of this book is to describe and bring attention to the situation rather than to solve or unilaterally decide the controversy over definitions. The selections are concerned primarily with black congregations and groups rather than with individual blacks, but this is not meant to decrease concern for those individual black Jews who may still face problems of acceptance.

The only comment necessary concerning Jewish women is to note that the term is utilized to refer to all Jewish women as a group, including (as with the other "subcommunities") some individuals who may not consciously perceive of themselves as such. From the group perspective utilized, this definition of "Jewish women" is appropriate.

Sepharad is the Hebrew word for Spain, but "Sephardic Jews" refers in a broader sense to those Jews (and their descendants) who lived in Spain and Portugal in the Middle Ages. After being forced out of the Iberian Peninsula by the Inquisition, they settled in France, Holland, England, Italy, Greece, Turkey, Israel, North Africa, the Americas, and a few other localities. "Sephardic Jews" in this book also refers to those Jews (and their descendants) who have lived in countries of the Middle East and North Africa since the ancient expulsions from Israel. While they have not lived in Spain, they follow a ritual that is similar to that of the Spanish-Portuguese Jews and have lived in and been influenced by an Arabic and/or Islamic culture as have many of the Jews of Spanish-Portuguese background who migrated to the Ottoman Empire after the Inquisition. Hence, despite attempts by some scholars to argue that these groups cannot be treated as one group, this book follows the equally scholarly argument that they can be grouped together as one. Ashkenas is the Hebrew word for Germany, but in actual usage "Ashkenazic Jews" refers to those Jews (and their descendants) who have lived in either Western or Eastern Europe (except some Sephardic communities within this area). "Ashkenazic Jews" is also often used interchangeably with "Yiddish-oriented" Jews. As utilized in this book, Ashkenazim and Sephardim are the two major divisions of Jews in the world and in the United States.

INDEX

About the Author

Abraham D. Lavender was born in 1940 in the rural community of New Zion, S. C. He received A.B. and M.A. degrees in psychology from the University of South Carolina where he was president of the Hillel Foundation, a member of Phi Epsilon Pi-Zeta Beta Tau fraternity, and a member of Phi Beta Kappa. While an officer in the United States Air Force, he was liaison representative for the military Jewish community in Izmir, Turkey. He received a doctorate in sociology from the University of Maryland in 1972 with a dissertation on Jewish identity and has since taught at St. Mary's College of Maryland and the University of Maryland, specializing in sociology of the American Jewish community and sociology of world Jewish communities. He is the author of approximately fifteen articles in scholarly journals, and is currently on the faculty of the Department of Sociology of the University of Miami, Coral Gables, Fl. He is associated with the Magen David Sephardic Congregation of Washington, D. C.